The New Climate Policies of the

Internal Legislation and Clima

Sebastian Oberthür and Marc Pallemaerts (eds.)
with Claire Roche Kelly

The New Climate Policies of
the European Union

Internal Legislation and Climate Diplomacy

VUBPRESS

Brussels University Press

Institute for European Studies – publication series, nr. 15

The Institute for European Studies is a Jean Monnet Centre of Excellence. It promulgates European Studies in general, and studies of European and Comparative Law, Environment, Media, Migration and Regional (European) Integration specifically. The IES is an education and research centre, carrying out research on various European issues relating to the EU in international affairs, and responsible for the Masters of European Integration and Development, and for the internationally renowned LL.M of International and European Law (formerly PILC programme).

Institute for European Studies (IES)
Vrije Universiteit Brussel
Pleinlaan 2
B-1050 Brussels
ies@vub.ac.be
http://www.ies.be

Cover design: Koloriet, Leefdaal
Book design: Style, Hulshout
Print: Silhouet, Maldegem

© 2010 VUBPRESS Brussels University Press
VUBPRESS is an imprint of ASP nv (Academic and Scientific Publishers nv)
Ravensteingalerij 28
B-1000 Brussels
Tel. ++ 32 2 289 26 50
Fax ++ 32 2 289 26 59
E-mail info@vubpress.be
www.vubpress.be

ISBN 978 90 5487 607 6
NUR 740 / 828
Legal Deposit D/2010/11.161/001

Table of Contents

Abbreviations

ACEA	Association des Constructeurs Européens d'Automobiles
ASEAN	Association of Southeast Asian Nations
CARS21	Competitive Automotive Regulatory System for the 21st Century
CCS	Carbon capture and storage
CDM	Clean Development Mechanism
CEEC	Central and Eastern European Country
CFSP	Common Foreign and Security Policy
CO_2	Carbon dioxide
DG	Directorate General
EC	European Community
ECCP	European Climate Change Programme
EEA	European Economic Area
	European Environment Agency
EEAS	European External Action Service
EIA	Environmental impact assessment
ENGO	Environmental non-governmental organisation
EP	European Parliament
ETS	Emissions Trading System
EU	European Union
EU-15	Austria, Belgium, Denmark, Finland, France, Germany, Greece, Ireland, Italy, Luxembourg, the Netherlands, Portugal, Spain, Sweden and the United Kingdom
EU-27	EU-15 plus Bulgaria, Cyprus, Czech Republic, Estonia, Hungary, Latvia, Lithuania, Malta, Poland, Romania, Slovakia and Slovenia
FAO	Food and Agriculture Organisation of the United Nations
g CO_2/km	Gram of CO_2 emitted per kilometre
G8	Group of Eight
GDP	Gross Domestic Product

GEEREF	Global Energy Efficiency and Renewable Energy Fund
GEF	Global Environment Facility
GHG	Greenhouse gas
Gt	Gigatonne
HR/VP	High Representative of the European Union and Vice-President of the European Commission
ICAO	International Civil Aviation Organisation
IEA	International Energy Agency
IMF	International Monetary Fund
IPCC	Intergovernmental Panel on Climate Change
IPPC	Integrated Pollution Prevention and Control
JAMA	Japanese Automobile Manufacturers Association
JI	Joint Implementation
KAMA	Korean Automobile Manufacturers Association
LDC	Least developed country
LDCF	Least Developed Countries Fund
MEDT	Ministry of Economic Development and Trade of the Russian Federation
MEP	Member of European Parliament
MIT	Massachusetts Institute of Technology
Mt	Megatonne
MWh	Megawatt hour
NAP	National Allocation Plan
NAPA	National Adaptation Programme of Action
NGO	Non-governmental organisation
ODA	Official Development Assistance
OECD	Organisation for Economic Co-operation and Development
PV	Photovoltaics
REACH	Registration, Evaluation, Authorisation and Restriction of Chemicals
REDD	Reducing Emissions from Deforestation and Forest Degradation in Developing Countries
REEEP	Renewable Energy and Energy Efficiency Partnership
REIO	Regional Economic Integration Organisation
RREC	Russian Regional Environmental Centre
SCCF	Special Climate Change Fund

SET-Plan	European Strategic Energy Technology Plan
SIDS	Small Island Developing States
SRU	German Advisory Council on the Environment
T&E	Transport and the Environment
UN	United Nations
UNDP	United Nations Development Programme
UNECE	United Nations Economic Commission for Europe
UNEP	United Nations Environment Programme
UNFCCC	United Nations Framework Convention on Climate Change
WHO	World Health Organisation
WMO	World Meteorological Organisation
WPIEI	Working Party on International Environmental Issues
WSSD	World Summit on Sustainable Development
WTO	World Trade Organisation
WWF	World Wide Fund for Nature

Introduction

Claire Roche Kelly, Sebastian Oberthür and Marc Pallemaerts

Climate change has come to be acknowledged as one of the most serious challenges facing human kind in the twenty-first century. The fourth assessment report of the Intergovernmental Panel on Climate Change (IPCC), released in 2007, found that the warming of the global climate was "unequivocal", and that the increased concentrations of greenhouse gases (GHGs) in the atmosphere, the greatest cause of climate change, is the result of human activities.[1] While implying a mix of mitigation and adaptation responses to climate change, the report suggests that global GHG emissions have to fall by more than 50 per cent by 2050 compared to 2000 levels to secure a reasonable chance to avoid an average global temperature increase of more than two degrees Celsius.[2] Overall, the IPCC report confirmed that climate change is one of the most serious threats to both international security and human security, i.e. the health, livelihood and well-being of billions of individuals of present and future generations. The Stern Review on the economics of climate change, published in 2007, examined the costs of action and inaction on climate change. It concluded that it is cheaper to act, and that the earlier action is taken, the lower the costs will be. The review estimated the overall costs from the impacts and risks of climate change at 5-20 per cent of global gross domestic product (GDP). In contrast, the investment costs that would need to be incurred in order to reduce GHG emissions and prevent dangerous climate change can be limited to about one per cent of global GDP.[3]

Climate change has also become part of the security agenda. It was discussed at a special meeting of the UN Security Council in April 2007 (although on that occasion, several developing countries, in particular, expressed that they were unconvinced about the appropriateness of the Security Council as the forum for addressing this issue). At the European level, the EU High Representative for Common Foreign and Security Policy, in a paper he presented to the European Council in 2008 together

---

1. IPCC 2007, 30 and 37.
2. IPCC 2007, 67.
3. Stern 2007, vi.

with the European Commission, argued that investment in mitigation and adaptation measures should go hand-in-hand with addressing the security threats caused by climate change.[4]

It is not therefore surprising that climate change has increasingly taken centre stage in international affairs and has become an issue of "high politics". Since 2005, it has been a top priority at most G8 Summits, and the UN General Assembly has systematically placed it high on its agenda. Overall, there is hardly any high-level international political encounter in which the issue is not discussed.[5] In the run up to the Copenhagen climate conference in December 2009, the issue featured high on the agenda of nearly every single high-level international meeting. This included the July 2009 G8 summit in L'Aquila, Italy, and the G20 meetings in London in April and in Pittsburgh in September 2009. The Major Economies Forum on Energy and Climate, originally launched by the US, held meetings in July 2009 in La Maddalena, Italy, with a follow-up meeting in London in October.[6] A special Summit on Climate Change was convened by UN Secretary-General Ban Ki-moon in conjunction with the opening of the UN General Assembly in September 2009. Nearly 100 heads of state and government were in attendance. This summit – the third of its kind at UN headquarters in New York – aimed to mobilise political will ahead of the Copenhagen conference and to highlight the urgency of taking action on climate change. The importance given to the climate change issue, and its newfound status as a high politics issue, is further confirmed by the commitment of many heads of state or government to personally attend the climate conference in Copenhagen in December.

At the European level, climate change has been established as a major agenda item regularly discussed by the European Council of EU heads of state and government. It has become a central and constant item for debate on the European agenda, with the impetus often coming from the highest political level. Since 2005 especially, the European Council has become a driving force for furthering action on climate change within the EU, and for promoting action on climate change internationally.[7] It was the European Council that, in March 2007, established that the EU would implement a 20 per cent reduction in GHG emissions from 1990 levels by 2020 as well as a target of 20 per cent for the share of renewable energies

4. Commission 2008.
5. See, for example, Ott et al. 2008.
6. The 17 "major economies" include: Australia, Brazil, Canada, China, the European Union, France, Germany, India, Indonesia, Italy, Japan, Korea, Mexico, Russia, South Africa, the United Kingdom, and the United States.
7. Oberthür and Dupont 2010.

in EU energy supply.[8] It was then also the European Council that secured agreement on the set of legislative acts, known as the "climate and energy package" and designed to achieve the aforementioned 2020 targets, in December 2008, along with the European Parliament, thus firmly establishing climate change as an issue for deliberation by EU heads of state and government. In addition, *Eurobarometer* surveys since the turn of the century have shown increasing levels of concern about climate change among European citizens, who give their support for action at the European level. Although economic concerns gained ground in the financial crisis in 2008 and 2009, 50 per cent of European citizens still viewed climate change as a major global challenge in 2009.[9]

Since the early 1990s, the EU has established itself as the most prominent leader in international climate policy by pushing for stringent international commitments. In general, it has been one of the most fervent supporters of the United Nations Framework Convention on Climate Change (UNFCCC) and its Kyoto Protocol, striving to sustain its leadership in the efforts to reach a new global agreement post-2012. In the international negotiations on the UNFCCC in 1991 and 1992, the EU called for a binding obligation of industrialised countries to stabilise their CO_2 emissions at 1990 levels by 2000. In the negotiations on the Kyoto Protocol in 1997, the EU proposed the deepest emission cuts and accepted the highest reduction target among the major industrialised countries (minus eight per cent). Subsequently, it has also championed calls for ensuring the "environmental integrity" of the Protocol by demanding priority for domestic action and limits on the use of forests and other carbon sinks.[10] Over the years, the EU has been able to improve its leadership record significantly, not only in its external action, but also, most importantly, in its internal policies. First of all, the Union has enhanced the organisation and coordination of its external climate policy. At the same time, progress in the development and implementation of internal climate policies has helped to reduce a long-lasting credibility gap between international promises and domestic action. Most prominently, the Union introduced a GHG emissions trading system (ETS) in 2005.[11]

The EU has striven to sustain its international leadership position in the crucial debates on the future of international cooperation on climate

8.   European Council 2007, 12.
9.   Commission 2009; see also the chapter by Adelle and Withana in this volume.
10. Oberthür and Ott 1999; Damro 2006; Bretherton and Vogler 2006.
11. Oberthür and Roche Kelly 2008; see also the chapter by Oberthür and Pallemaerts in this volume.

change post-2012, following the expiry of the first commitment period of the Kyoto Protocol. With the initiation and adoption of the aforementioned EU climate and energy package, the period 2007-2008 saw a major overhaul and leap forward in the development of the new domestic climate policies of the EU, as further explored in this volume. The new legislation on climate and energy policies, politically agreed in December 2008 but officially adopted in April 2009, is designed to enhance the effectiveness of EU climate policy. In announcing the independent commitment to reduce GHG emissions in the EU by 20 per cent by 2020, the European Council furthermore offered to strengthen this commitment by moving to 30 per cent in the context of an acceptable international agreement. Finally, the EU made efforts also to develop forward-looking positions on adaptation, technology development and transfer and financing, indicating that it would be prepared to contribute its fair share of any financing arrangement agreed in Copenhagen.[12]

In this context, three factors that have supported the EU's motivation for continued international leadership on climate change deserve particular highlighting. First, climate policy is an important driver of European integration in general. After the failure of the Treaty Establishing a Constitution for Europe in 2005, the European institutions were looking for opportunities to reinforce their legitimacy and reinvigorate the European integration process. The urgency and importance of the issue of climate change was increasing with the IPCC Fourth Assessment Report and public opinion polls showed high support for European-level action in this field.[13] The European institutions grasped the window of opportunity to enhance their legitimacy by moving climate change into the centre of the European integration process and advancing both internal and external EU climate policy.

Second, intensifying discussions on the security of future energy supplies to Europe have lent strong support to the development of stringent climate policies. Since 2005, soaring oil and gas prices have highlighted the EU's dependence on energy imports which, without targeted counter-measures, is projected to increase from 50 per cent in 2005 to about 70 per cent by 2030.[14] At the same time as oil and gas prices have increased, political

12. European Council 2009; Council 2009; see also the chapter by Oberthür and Pallemaerts in this volume.
13. Eurobarometer Special Public Opinion polls (1972-2009): http://ec.europa.eu/public_opinion/archives/eb_special_en.htm, and "Tomorrow's Europe" poll (2007): http://www.tomorrowseurope.eu/IMG/pdf/Final_results_summary_Oct_22.pdf (Accessed: 13 November 2009). See also IPCC 2007.
14. Commission 2006.

developments in regions with major reserves, including the Middle East and Russia, have fuelled concern about the security of Europe's energy supplies. The resulting energy security agenda has significantly reinforced the climate agenda, especially regarding the promotion of energy efficiency and the use of alternative sources of energy.

Third, the position of the EU in the international system and its established strong support for multilateralism also reinforce EU leadership on climate change. The EU has for some time pursued the objective of enhancing its role as a global actor and has been one of the most fervent supporters of multilateralism and international law as the backbone of global govern-ance.[15] Under these circumstances, climate change is an area particularly well-suited to the EU's pursuit of international leadership. Climate change and the Kyoto Protocol enjoy a high international profile, and leadership in this area is proven and can build upon the EU's soft power resources.

Against this backdrop, the Institute for European Studies (IES) at the Vrije Universiteit Brussel (VUB) and the Institute for European Environmental Policy (IEEP) co-organised a lecture series on "The European Union and the Fight against Climate Change" during the autumn/winter term 2008. The 13 lecture evenings aimed to provide a comprehensive overview of the most relevant European and international regulatory frameworks and policies – and the interconnections between them. What are the prospects for the EU keeping its international leadership and brokering a new global deal on climate change? How do international and domestic climate policies of the EU interact, and are they mutually supportive? Are domestic climate policies sufficient to meet the environmental, economic and political challenge posed by global climate change? These were among the core guiding questions addressed in the lecture series.[16]

This volume springs from the lecture series of 2008. While the lecture series took place at the time of the negotiations on the climate and energy package, the book was completed following the adoption of the package. It thus provides a timely overview and assessment of the new EU climate policies in force since mid-2009. The analysis of the various elements of the climate and energy package is complemented by a focused look at the climate diplomacy of the EU, its international policy on adaptation to the impacts of climate change, in particular in developing countries, as well as

---

15. Commission 2003; Commission 2004.
16. The full lecture series programme, including the slide presentations of the speakers and podcasts of their talks, remain available on the IES website: http://www.ies.be/ climatelectures.

by perspectives on two other major players: Russia and the US. Overall, the contributions to this volume analyse whether the new EU climate policies are sufficient to meet the environmental, economic and political challenge posed by climate change and to retain the EU's leading role in international climate policy. In so doing, the volume aims to enhance understanding and contribute to further discussions on the current and potential role of the EU in the fight against climate change.

Organisation of the book

The book's following eleven chapters are organised in three sets. As an introduction to the subject of the volume, the next chapter gives a general historical overview of the development of EU internal and external climate policies. The subsequent six chapters address the main elements of the new EU climate policies elaborated in 2008, including the reformed EU emissions trading system (ETS), Member States' targets for reducing GHG emissions in the non-ETS sectors, the new Renewable Energy Directive, carbon capture and storage (CCS), and CO_2 and passenger cars. While these chapters also shed light on the external repercussions of the EU legislation they review, the four remaining chapters explicitly take a look beyond EU-internal policies by discussing the EU's model for climate diplomacy, EU assistance for adaptation to climate change in developing countries, the role of Russia in the international cooperation on climate change, and EU and US public perceptions on climate and energy issues.

The next chapter provides a historical overview of the EU's internal and external climate policies. Sebastian Oberthür and Marc Pallemaerts trace the development of the tools and instruments used by the EU in the fight against climate change, both internationally and domestically, since the late 1980s. The authors demonstrate that EU climate policy has developed in interaction with the multilateral regime-building process. In this process, the EU has attempted to profile itself as an international leader on climate change from the beginning, in the early 1990s. Oberthür and Pallemaerts establish that little, if any, serious efforts to mitigate GHG emissions in the EU were visible in the 1990s. International EU leadership gained credibility in the 2000s when EU regulation on the matter increased and an EU-wide emissions trading system became operational, not least in an attempt to implement the Kyoto Protocol. Whereas the new EU climate policies agreed in 2008 continue this progress, they also amount to a major overhaul of the climate policy framework of the EU. The authors argue that EU climate policy has made important progress in the first decade of the twenty-first century, although it may nevertheless fall short of the EU's declared ambition of keeping global average temperature increase below two degrees Celsius of pre-industrial levels.

Jon Birger Skjærseth and Jørgen Wettestad deal with the EU ETS, as the cornerstone of the climate and energy package of 2008. Their chapter traces the historical background of the ETS and its development from the first phase (2005-2007) through to the third phase (2013-2020) that was established as a result of the significant revisions of the ETS Directive agreed as part of the 2008 package. The authors ascertain that the significance of the 2008 reforms lies in particular in the centralisation of the ETS through the establishment of an EU-wide cap of GHG emissions for the ETS sectors, and in auctioning replacing free distribution of emission allowances as the standard method of allocation. They use three "explanatory lenses" to explore the move to a more centralised system in the third phase, with more auctioning than free allocation of emission allowances, and less control in the hands of the Member States. Firstly, a liberal intergovernmentalist approach is used to shed light on how Member State governments that are constrained by domestic interests shaped decision-making on the revisions of the EU ETS. Secondly, a multi-level governance approach leads the authors to focus on the role of EU institutions and non-state actors in the decision-making process. Finally, the impact of the international climate regime is taken into account to explain the developments of the EU ETS. The authors pinpoint the respective contributions that these explanatory lenses, in particular liberal intergovernmentalism and multilevel governance, can make to explaining the significant 2008 revisions of the EU ETS. While highlighting the continual development of the ETS, they cautiously expect a strengthened and more effective ETS to be in operation in the third (post-2012) phase.

The subsequent chapter by Nuno Lacasta, Sebastian Oberthür, Eduardo Santos and Pedro Barata takes in view the "Effort-Sharing Decision". The Effort-Sharing Decision complements the post-2012 set-up of the EU ETS by setting annual GHG emission reduction or limitation targets for the non-ETS sectors of each EU Member State for the period 2013-2020. The authors highlight the differences between the preceding burden-sharing agreement of EU Member States under the Kyoto Protocol and the new effort sharing. Most importantly, the old burden sharing applied to all sectors of the economy while the new effort sharing only addresses the non-ETS sectors. Agreement on the Effort-Sharing Decision was not least supported by it being part of the overall climate and energy package. Side payments to the new EU Member States in the ETS part of the package facilitated acceptance of the emission targets proposed by the Commission.

At the same time, negotiations on the Decision itself focused on ensuring higher degrees of flexibility for Member States in implementing their commitments than originally foreseen by the Commission, including the use of international offsets. Only with respect to the introduction of a specific compliance mechanism, which draws inspiration from the compliance system under the Kyoto Protocol, was the Commission proposal significantly strengthened in the negotiations. While cutting out the non-ETS sectors seems to reinforce respect for Member State competence in this area, the authors argue that the Effort-Sharing Decision may well set the stage for a further Europeanisation of EU climate policy also for the emission sources it covers.

In the next chapter, Tom Howes focuses on the EU's new Renewable Energy Directive. He points out that promoting renewable energy is a key element of the EU's climate strategy. Since renewable energy replaces the consumption of fossil fuel-based energy sources, it contributes directly to the reduction of GHG emissions. In addition, it improves the diversity of the EU's energy sources and the security of energy supplies, and promoting renewable energy drives technology innovation and creates net economic benefits in the EU. These advantages provide for further motivations for the development of renewable energy within the EU. Against this backdrop, Howes looks at the development of renewable energy policy in the EU (as distinct from climate policy). The EU's renewable energy policy has developed several tools and instruments over time, including the Green Electricity Directive (Directive 2001/77/EC) and subsidy mechanisms, such as feed-in tariffs, implemented by Member States. It is a policy area that also has strong external dimensions, as it not only decreases EU reliance on foreign energy sources, but also heightens the EU's leadership role in the international climate change regime. The author goes on to discuss the new Renewable Energy Directive in detail, outlining the national targets agreed, the pathways for Member States to reach their target, and the various mechanisms in place to assist in this aim. Howes argues that the new Renewable Energy Directive makes important progress on the previously "patchy" and inadequate development of renewable energy within the EU. The demanding targets set in the Directive provide a much-strengthened basis for consistent growth in renewable energy production in the EU, ensuring less GHG emissions, improving energy security and creating new and innovative jobs.

The chapter by Joana Chiavari on the legal framework for carbon capture and storage (CCS) in the EU outlines the policy context leading to the adoption in the EU of Directive 2009/31/EC on the geological storage of CO_2. CCS refers to a system of technologies that integrates CO_2 capture, transport and geological storage and is regarded as an innovative element in the fight against climate change. Chiavari highlights that it can bridge the gap between increasing demand for fossil fuel use and the need to reduce CO_2 emissions. While providing an overview of the main arguments in favour of and against CCS technology, she argues that CCS will be required to achieve the necessary reductions in GHG emissions. Against this backdrop, she outlines the negotiation process leading to the adoption of Directive 2009/31/EC as well as the main provisions of the Directive, the world's first example of dedicated CCS legislation. The Directive focuses primarily on the regulation of geological storage of CO_2 and on the removal of unintended barriers in existing EU legislation to CCS. A central step to secure financing for the first commercial CCS demonstration projects (the allocation of emission allowances from the ETS new entrants' reserve) was made as part of another element of the climate and energy package, namely the ETS reform. While Chiavari appreciates the risk management framework of the Directive and recognises the CCS Directive as a significant step towards a low-carbon economy, she also points to the lack of clarity on how to finance the development of the first CCS projects. She argues in particular that the ETS is not sufficient to get CCS off the ground in the EU, and that additional efforts are required for the crucial successful demonstration of the first CCS projects within the next decade.

The new Regulation to mitigate CO_2 emissions from passenger cars in the EU is the focus of the following chapter by Patrick ten Brink. As transport is one of the fastest growing sources of CO_2 emissions in the EU, the Regulation provides the legal framework for reducing emissions from a central element of this sector. With more people in the EU driving cars greater distances, policy developments focused on energy efficiency and emission reductions of cars are critical. Ten Brink traces the history of the Regulation and analyses its content. He demonstrates how the imminent failure of the voluntary agreements with car manufacturers, concluded in the 1990s, prepared the ground for the preparations for a legislative proposal and the final agreement on the Regulation. The discussion outlines the many compromises and difficult negotiations relating to targets, instruments, and competition fears on the way to the adoption of the Regulation. In his analysis, ten Brink highlights the emphasis placed on costs to manufacturers and to consumers, as well as the struggle for a solution that would provide an appropriate balance between manufacturers of smaller and bigger vehicles. Even though the final agreement enshrined in the Regulation was weakened significantly from the original proposal of the European Commission and will thus delay much needed emission reductions in the sector, it represents a quantum shift away from the preceding voluntary approach towards binding emission targets. To realise the vision of a large-scale decarbonisation of the transport sector by 2050, ten Brink argues forcefully that a suite of further measures, including measures that address the demand for vehicles and for mobility services, will be required in addition to a significant strengthening of the reduction targets for specific average emissions of passenger cars contained in the Regulation.

The chapter by Christian Hey continues the discussion on the Regulation on the CO_2 emissions from cars with a focus on Germany. He highlights the apparent paradoxical position of Germany as an environmental leader within the EU, and yet as one of the main opponents to stringent targets in the Regulation. In providing an overview of the development of German and EU climate policies, he emphasises that Germany has historically supported far-reaching climate commitments at the EU level. Hey contrasts this German support for effective EU climate policies with Germany's laggard role in the development of the Regulation on CO_2 emissions from passenger cars. In this process, the German government consistently defended what Hey calls "conservative industry interests" that argued for a "competition-neutral solution" that would not disadvantage the high fuel-consuming German market segment of premium cars. The author outlines several factors to explain the paradoxical German position. Firstly, the development of the German car industry remains in the realm of premium cars, highlighting a contradiction between Germany's climate policy aims and the aims of industry. Secondly, there are several policies in place that benefit the car industry and not the environment, such as providing tax relief for buying large company cars. Thirdly, the political influence of the car industry is traditionally and historically very great, both at a federal and at a regional level. Hey highlights the unstable power balance between German environmental aspirations and the traditional industrial lobby. He argues that Germany may, in fact, suffer more by protecting the current premium car industry than by pushing the industry to become more innovative.

The following chapter by Jessica Ayers, Saleemul Huq and Achala Chandani takes a Southern perspective in addressing the issue of EU adaptation assistance for developing countries. The impacts of climate change are already being experienced in all parts of the world, yet the most vulnerable developing countries are suffering the greatest impacts and facing the urgent need to adapt. As the authors point out, adaptation describes "the process of adjustment in natural or human systems in response to actual or expected climatic stimuli or their effects, to moderate harm or exploit beneficial opportunities". The authors provide an overview and analysis of the EU's response to the adaptation challenge. They discuss several instruments developed and/or supported by the EU to assist third countries to adapt, including the EU Action Plan on Climate Change and Development and the Global Climate Change Alliance, among others. The authors examine the policy documents of the European Commission on adaptation, including the 2007 Green Paper and the 2009 White Paper. They also analyse the European Commission's communication on a Copenhagen climate agreement from the adaptation perspective. The analysis leads to several conclusions. Firstly, the authors highlight the significant progress made by the EU in supporting adaptation to climate change in developing countries. However, they argue that many of the achievements remain at the level of policy discourse and are not adequately translated into concrete action. Secondly, the authors highlight the continuous failure of the EU to agree on firm financial assistance for adaptation. Finally, the authors claim that, although the EU is to be commended on its progress, too much emphasis remains on mitigating GHG emissions, and too little commitment is put forward on adaptation needs.

Louise van Schaik focuses in her analysis on the performance of the EU in the international climate negotiations and the world of climate diplomacy more broadly. The success of the EU's climate diplomacy is related to the EU's ability to act as a united bloc. Van Schaik discusses the EU's performance historically and analyses the prospects for continued success into the future, in the context of even more complex negotiations. First, the chapter provides a discussion on the EU as a global actor. In this context, the author highlights several leading factors in the external representation of the EU, including EU external unity, institutional features of the EU, division of competencies, the preference for a common EU view, and the influence of informal norms on EU unity. Second, van Schaik focuses on the EU external representation in the international climate negotiations in particular, and how the EU position is coordinated. While conceding that the EU has been relatively successful in the negotiations, she outlines some shortcomings. In particular, the need for consensus and a common EU view leads to time-consuming coordination and a relatively inflexible negotiating mandate, and the rotating Presidency can create coordination difficulties and damage continuity within the negotiations. Van Schaik presents two alternative models for EU climate diplomacy, namely a take-over of the negotiations by either the European Commission or the High Representative of the Union for Foreign and Security Policy under the Lisbon Treaty, which both could increase consistency and continuity within the negotiations. However, Member States' objections to such options would be likely due to their desire to retain control over external climate policy. In conclusion, the author argues that the current model of EU climate diplomacy has, despite several shortcomings, operated relatively successfully. Although the alternative models suggested may have further potential, there is no guarantee that they would be any more successful than the current model.

In the subsequent chapter, Wybe Douma, Michael Kozeltsev and Julia Dobrolyubova focus on the role of Russia in the international fight against climate change. Russia is the third largest GHG emitter of all countries. It was Russia's ratification of the Kyoto Protocol that finally brought the instrument into force. Therefore, the authors argue, a credible international agreement requires the participation and active engagement of Russia. However, such engagement is not guaranteed. The authors provide a historical overview of Russian involvement in the international climate change regime, with a view to assessing the likelihood of continued and intensified Russian engagement into the future. Firstly, the chapter provides an analysis of both the positive and the negative impacts of climate change on the various regions of the vast Russian territory. Furthermore, the authors discuss and analyse Russia's activities in implementing the UNFCCC and the Kyoto Protocol (including Joint Implementation projects). Subsequently, the chapter identifies possible barriers to further engagement by Russia in the international climate change regime, including a lack of concern for climate change domestically and the lack of priority given to the issue within the government. Furthermore, the authors highlight the cumbersome domestic decision-making process and the lack of urgent concern about energy security issues (as Russia holds the world's largest natural gas reserves) as further barriers to action. The expected difficulties of keeping Russia engaged in the international climate change regime are further illustrated by the "bumpy road" to the ratification of the Kyoto Protocol, and by Russia's negotiating position for a future climate change regime. The authors suggest that the level of engagement by Russia in the international efforts may largely depend on the commitments made by other large GHG emitters (e.g. USA and China). However, even with comparable commitments, ensuring the continued involvement and participation by Russia will remain a major challenge.

The final chapter of the volume discusses and compares the public perception of climate and energy issues in the EU and in the USA. Camille Adelle and Sirini Withana examine public opinion surveys in both the EU and the US and explore how the perceptions have changed over time. They examine the level of concern of EU citizens and US citizens towards climate and energy issues, and also the understanding they have of the issues involved. They also analyse public opinion in both jurisdictions of various climate technologies and of policy options proposed to combat climate change. On the basis of this review of available survey data in the US and the EU, Adelle and Withana discuss their implications for the internal and external dimensions of US and EU climate policies. In this respect, they note important limitations of such an interpretation of the available public opinion data, including the varying designs of the US and EU surveys examined and difficulties in linking public attitudes to specific policy choices. Keeping in mind these limitations, the authors nevertheless come to the interesting conclusion that public perceptions in the EU and the US of climate and energy issues have much in common. For example, concern about climate change has increased in both jurisdictions and support for action to tackle climate change at the federal level in the US and at the EU level in Europe is high. Despite these commonalities, government action in both places has varied significantly in the past. Whereas the Bush administration likely underestimated the degree of public concern about climate change in the US, policy-making in the EU may even be leading public opinion on the issue. Importantly in this context, the authors acknowledge that the relationship between public attitudes and policy-making is subtle and complex, and public attitudes, while important, are but one of many factors that shape public policy.

Acknowledgements

This book is the result of a collaborative effort of the Institute for European Studies (IES) at the Vrije Universiteit Brussels (VUB) and the Institute for European Environmental Policy (IEEP), an independent, non-profit policy research institute with offices in London and Brussels. This collaborative effort involved the organisation of a lecture series entitled "The European Union and the Fight against Global Climate Change" in the autumn/winter term of the academic year 2008-2009 and the production of this volume that builds on the lecture series.[17]

We are particularly grateful for the financial support received under the European Commission's Jean Monnet Programme (Lifelong Learning) for both the organisation of the lecture series and the publication of this book.

17. More information on the lecture series is available at http://www.ies.be/climatelectures.

We would furthermore like to thank the various staff members of the IES who contributed to the smooth organisation of the lecture series, which turned out to be very timely and attracted wide public attention. The contributors to this volume deserve our gratitude for their very constructive collaboration and timely responses to our requests and comments. Last but not least, particular thanks go to Daniel-Sebastian Mühlbach for his tireless and diligent assistance in preparing the manuscript.

References

Bretherton, Charlotte and John Vogler. 2006. *The European Union as a Global Actor*. London: Routledge.

Commission (EC). 2003. The European Union and the United Nations: The Choice of Multilateralism. COM (2003) 526 final. Brussels: European Commission.

Commission (EC). 2004. The Enlarging European Union at the United Nations: Making Multilateralism Matter. Brussels: European Commission.

Commission (EC). 2006. Green Paper: A European Strategy for Sustainable, Competitive and Secure Energy. COM (2006) 105 final. Brussels: European Commission.

Commission (EC). 2008. Climate Change and International Security. Paper from the High Representative and the European Commission to the European Council. S113/08. Brussels: European Commission.

Commission (EC). 2009. European Attitudes Towards Climate Change. Special Eurobarometer 313 Wave 71.1. Brussels: European Commission.

Council of the European Union (Environment). 2009. Council Conclusions. 21 October 2009. 14361/09 (Presse). Brussels: Council of the European Union.

Damro, Chad. 2006. EU-UN Environmental Relations: Shared Competence and Effective Multilateralism. In *The European Union at the United Nations: Intersecting Multilateralisms*. Edited by Katie V. Laatikainen and Karen E. Smith. 175-192. Basingstoke: Palgrave MacMillan.

European Council. 2007. Presidency Conclusions. 9 March 2007. 7224/1/07 REV 1. Brussels: Council of the European Union.

European Council. 2009. Presidency Conclusions. 30 October 2009. 15264/09. Brussels: Council of the European Union.

IPCC (Intergovernmental Panel on Climate Change). 2007. Climate Change 2007. Fourth Assessment Report: Synthesis Report. Geneva: IPCC.

Oberthür, Sebastian and Hermann E. Ott. 1999. *The Kyoto Protocol: International Climate Policy for the 21st Century.* Berlin: Springer.

Oberthür, Sebastian and Claire Roche Kelly. 2008. EU Leadership in International Climate Policy: Achievements and Challenges. *The International Spectator* 43(3): 35-50.

Oberthür, Sebastian and Claire Dupont. 2010. Council and European Council in Internal and External EU Policy-Making on Climate Change. In *The European Union in International Climate Change Politics* (provisional title). Edited by Rudiger Würzel and James Connelly. London: Routledge (forthcoming).

Ott, Hermann E., Wolfgang Sterk and Rie Watanabe. 2008. The Bali Roadmap: New Horizons for Global Climate Change? In *Climate Policy* 8(1): 91-5.

Stern, Nicholas. 2007. *The Economics of Climate Change. The Stern Review.* Cambridge: Cambridge University Press.

The EU's Internal and External Climate Policies: an Historical Overview

Sebastian Oberthür and Marc Pallemaerts

1. Introduction

Throughout their two decades of history, international and European climate policy have evolved in tandem and have fed back on each other. As the international regime on climate change – based upon the United Nations Framework Convention on Climate Change (UNFCCC) and its Kyoto Protocol – emerged and matured in the 1990s and early 2000s, an EU climate policy has gradually taken shape and moved from the stage of development to implementation. At the same time, the EU has been a major actor and leader in international climate policy.

This chapter attempts to provide an overview of the inter-related development of international and European climate policy and law since the late 1980s and the beginning of the 1990s, including the role of the EU in the development of the international regime on climate change. We couch this development in analogy to the revolving "policy cycle" encompassing agenda setting, policy formulation, policy adoption/selection, policy implementation and policy evaluation leading to policy-reformulation.[1]

The first half of the 1990s can thus be characterised as the agenda-setting phase during which climate change was firmly put on both the international and European policy agendas, including through the UNFCCC (section 2). The period 1995-2001 saw international policy formulation and adoption, through the negotiation and adoption of the 1997 Kyoto Protocol as well the subsequent implementing rules contained in the so-called "Marrakesh Accords" of 2001, and a delayed response at EU level (section 3). In the 2000s, the Kyoto Protocol entered its

---

1.   While the policy cycle is usually used with regard to individual policies, we use the concept here as a heuristic tool to structure the discussion of the development of overall EU climate policy. On the policy cycle, see, for example, Howlett and Ramesh 2003.

implementation stage and triggered substantial implementing legislation at the EU level, with the EU Emissions Trading System (ETS) becoming operational in 2005 (section 4). While implementation is ongoing, international and European climate policy entered a phase of evaluation and policy reformulation to prepare for the post-2012 era, after the end of the Kyoto Protocol's first commitment period and the EU ETS' second phase (section 5). The evolution is summarised in the concluding section 6.

In analysing the evolution of international and European climate policy, we argue that the EU has gradually reduced the gap between its external and internal policy and law. Whereas EU climate policy and law were lagging behind international policy development until the early 2000s, they have moved ahead of the international framework since then. In particular, the climate and energy legislation elaborated and adopted in 2008 and 2009 implement further greenhouse gas (GHG) emission reductions by 2020 prior to agreement on international climate policy for the time after 2012.[2] As a result, the long-standing, self-proclaimed leadership role of the EU has grown increasingly credible – even though EU climate policy may still be considered insufficient for effectively responding to the environmental challenge.[3]

2.   Agenda setting: the emergence of international and European climate policy (late 1980s and early 1990s)

2.1   EU external and international climate policy

The agenda of international and European climate policy was firmly established with the negotiation, adoption and entry into force of the UNFCCC in the first half of the 1990s. The EU, then consisting of twelve Member States, pushed international policy development, but made only very modest progress towards developing a European policy framework. Progress on limiting GHG emissions in the EU also remained slow.

The late 1980s saw a number of policy initiatives that set the stage for the negotiations of the UNFCCC. In 1988 the Intergovernmental Panel on Climate Change (IPCC) was established under the joint auspices of the

---

2.   See also the other contributions to this volume.
3.   On international EU leadership on climate change see, for example, Gupta and Grubb 2000; Groenleer and van Schaik 2007; Schreurs and Tiberghien 2007; Oberthür and Roche Kelly 2008.

United Nations Environment Programme (UNEP) and the World Meteorological Organisation (WMO).[4] Its purpose was to develop international consensus on the science of climate change, its causes, repercussions and possible response strategies. In March 1989, over 20 heads of state and government from North and South called for "a new approach" at the Hague summit on the protection of the atmosphere.[5] Organised by the Dutch government in November 1989, the Noordwijk Ministerial Conference was the first high-level intergovernmental meeting specifically devoted to climate change, with 66 countries formally represented. In November 1990, the Second World Climate Conference, organised by the WMO, discussed the policy conclusions of the IPCC's first summary report published in August 1990. It prepared the stage for the UN General Assembly resolution that launched the intergovernmental negotiations on the UNFCCC in December 1990.[6]

In response to these developments, the European Commission and EU Member States developed a common EU position for the international negotiations. In June 1990, climate change was on the agenda of the European Council for the first time, with EU leaders calling for "targets and strategies" to be agreed for limiting GHG emissions.[7] On the eve of the Second World Climate Conference, a joint meeting of the Community's energy and environment ministers concluded on 29 October 1990 that, assuming similar commitments from other countries, the EC would be prepared to take measures to stabilise CO_2 emissions at their 1990 levels by the year 2000 in the Community as a whole. However, the Council failed to specify how this target would be achieved; neither did it elaborate any distribution of the common target to individual Member States ("burden sharing") nor implement measures at EU level. Only some Member States had announced national emission limitation or reduction targets. The Council conclusions thus presented a progressive position to the outside world, while postponing the difficult decisions about its actual implementation.[8]

Still, the EU, on the basis of the mentioned agreement in the joint Energy/Environment Council, pushed for a binding commitment for all industrialised countries to stabilise their CO_2 emissions at the 1990 level by the year 2000 in the international negotiations leading to the adoption of the

4. The IPCC was formally established by Resolution 4 (EC-XL) of the Executive Council of the WMO, pursuant to preliminary discussions at the 10th World Meteorological Congress and the 14th session of the UNEP Governing Council.
5. Hague Declaration 1989.
6. UNGA 1990.
7. European Council 1990.
8. Council 1990; Oberthür 1993, 108; Wettestad 2000, 27.

UNFCCC in 1992. However, this demand met with very little enthusiasm from other OECD countries, notably the US. Even though the then future Vice-President Al Gore accused then US President Bush senior of "the single worst abdication of leadership ever", the US successfully resisted EU pressure.[9]

As a result, the UNFCCC, adopted in New York in May 1992 and opened for signature at the United Nations Conference on Environment and Development in Rio de Janeiro in June 1992, primarily provides a framework for the development of future climate policy and law. It determines the overall objective of the regime that is "the stabilisation of greenhouse gas concentrations in the atmosphere at a level that would prevent dangerous anthropogenic interference with the climate system" (Article 2). Its further principles and rules (including the principle of common but differentiated responsibilities and respective capabilities) are of a general nature and provide, together with a system of reporting on GHG emissions and relevant policies, the foundation for international cooperation on climate change. However, the UNFCCC does not lay down any specific measures or quantified objectives to achieve the mentioned goal.[10]

The EC and its Member States signed the Convention in Rio as a "mixed agreement", implying that its implementation would fall partly within the competence of the Community, and partly within that of the Member States. Formal participation rules for the EC follow the practice established under other multilateral agreements. Article 22 of the UNFCCC enables the participation of "regional economic integration organizations". It requires the EU and its Member States to decide on their respective responsibilities for fulfilling their obligations, and determines that the EC shall declare the extent of its competence in relevant matters in its instrument of ratification. Given the evolutionary character of the division of competence, the EC and its Member States, when ratifying the UNFCCC in 1993,[11] declared in general and non-committal terms that "the commitment to limit anthropogenic CO_2 emissions set out in Article 4(2) of the Convention will be fulfilled in the Community as a whole through action by the Community and its Member States, within the respective competence of each".[12]

---

9.   Oberthür 1993, 142; on the negotiations on the UNFCCC, see Bodansky 1993; Oberthür 1993.
10. On the UNFCCC, see Bodansky 1993; Yamin and Depledge 2004; Pallemaerts and Williams 2006.
11. Decision 94/69/EC.
12. Decision 94/69/EC, Annex C.

2.2   EU internal climate policy

At the same time, substantial disagreement persisted on the need and content of common measures to implement the Community's emission stabilisation commitment at the European level. This disagreement became particularly apparent with respect to the proposal for a directive introducing a tax on CO_2 emissions and energy, which the Commission submitted to the Council on the eve of the Rio Conference[13] and which would have enabled significant emission reductions. Under Article 130s of the EC Treaty, as it then stood, the adoption of this proposal for a fiscal measure required unanimous agreement of the Member States. A small but vocal minority of Member States, led by the UK, were adamantly opposed to such a measure. As a result, the proposed CO_2/energy tax was never adopted.[14]

Without the implementation of this flagship proposal, the development of the Community's climate policy framework made little progress and effectively left it up to the Member States to elaborate national emission reduction programmes. Harmonised energy efficiency standards for consumer products were laid down under Article 100a (now Article 95) of the EC Treaty for hot-water boilers in 1992,[15] and later for household refrigerators and freezers in 1996,[16] and for fluorescent lighting ballasts in 2000.[17] These binding minimum requirements were complemented by a harmonised labelling system designed to inform consumers of the energy consumption of household appliances.[18] Despite rapid technological progress and rising concern about energy efficiency, no efforts were made to revise these efficiency standards and labelling requirements until the adoption, in 2005, of a new Directive on eco-design requirements for energy-using products (Directive 2005/32/EC, see below).

As a complement to these early energy efficiency measures, Directive 93/76/EEC ("SAVE") required Member States to establish "programmes" to limit CO_2 emissions through improvements in energy efficiency, particularly in areas such as energy certification and thermal insulation of buildings, regular inspection of boilers, and energy audits of undertakings with high energy consumption. However, no quantitative objectives were

13.   Commission 1992.
14.   Skjaerseth 1994; Collier 1996; Haigh 1996; Wettestad 2000.
15.   Directive 92/42/EEC.
16.   Directive 96/57/EC.
17.   Directive 2000/55/EC.
18.   Directive 92/75/EEC.

set, and the content of these programmes was left to the Member States' discretion. At the same time as the SAVE Directive, the Council adopted the "Altener" programme, a Community financial instrument for the promotion of renewable energy sources.[19] Both policy initiatives were considerably weakened by the Council of Ministers during the legislative process.[20]

In addition, the Council addressed Decision 93/389/EEC to the Member States, establishing a "monitoring mechanism" for CO_2 and other GHG emissions. Under this Decision, the Member States had to establish, and communicate to the Commission, "national programmes" for limiting their CO_2 emissions. They were also bound to communicate information on the levels of the GHG emissions to the Commission. On the basis of the information received, the Commission was mandated to assess progress towards the fulfilment of the Community's international obligations. Significantly, the decision provided the basis for furthering and assessing compliance by the Community as a whole, but did not contain commitments of individual Member States.

Figure 1 – GHG emissions of the EU-15 and EU-27 1990-2008

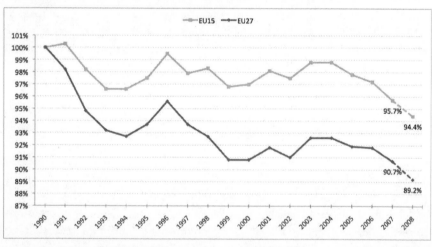

Source: EEA 2009a; 2009b; 2008 data are provisional estimates.

Under the circumstances, GHG emission reductions achieved in the EU during the first half of the 1990s (Figure 1) were hardly the result of the

19. Decision 93/500/EEC.
20. On the early stages of EU climate policy in the 1990s, see Skjærseth 1994; Collier 1996; Haigh 1996; Wettestad 2000.

implementation of effective climate policies. While a detailed evaluation of the climate policies implemented in the Member States is beyond the scope of this chapter, it is clear that the GHG emission reductions of the early 1990s were mainly a result of two developments unrelated to climate policy: German reunification, and the dash from coal to gas in the UK. The insufficient progress in the implementation of mitigation policies at both the EU and the Member State level became more apparent when GHG emissions in the EU-15 rose again after 1994 (Figure 1).

3.   Delayed EU response to international policy formulation and adoption (1995-2001)

3.1   EU external and international climate policy

The EU remained in a leadership position at the international level during the negotiations on the Kyoto Protocol, which was adopted in December 1997. Negotiations on a "protocol or another legal instrument" were launched at the first Conference of the Parties to the UNFCCC in Berlin in March 1995. As a first significant step in June 1996, the EU Council of Environment Ministers established the objective that "global average temperatures should not exceed 2 degrees above pre-industrial level".[21] Since, then, this objective has continuously guided EU (external) climate policy (see below).

More importantly for the negotiations on the Kyoto Protocol, the EU again advocated binding international commitments by industrialised countries to reduce their GHG emissions. After intense internal discussions – which caused a group of more progressive Member States to break ranks and present their own proposal in March 1996[22] – the EU finally agreed on a common proposal for the level of emission reductions in March 1997. Specifically, it proposed that industrialised countries reduce their emissions of the three main GHGs (CO_2, CH_4, N_2O) by 15 per cent by 2010. In June 1997, it complemented this proposal with an interim target of 7.5 per cent by 2005. This position was far more ambitious than the proposals of other industrialised countries that suggested little more than a stabilisation of GHG emissions by 2010.[23]

---

21.   Council 1996.
22.   Oberthür and Ott 1999, 52.
23.   Oberthür and Ott 1999, 54-58.

The common EU proposal was enabled and underpinned by an internal "burden-sharing agreement". In order to establish credibility for its negotiating position, the Council agreed, in its Conclusions of 3 March 1997, on a provisional table setting out the emission limitation and reduction targets for each of the now 15 Member States, and a menu of various possible "common and coordinated policies and measures". Limiting the credibility of the EU's negotiating position, the agreed targets for the individual Member States covered a wide range and only amounted to a reduction of 9.2 per cent, with the gap to the proposed reduction of 15 per cent to be filled after an international agreement (see Table 1).

Table 1 – The EU Burden-Sharing Agreements of 1997 and 1998/2002

Member State	March 1997: Emission Reduction by 2010	June 1998: Emission Reduction by 2008-12
Austria	-25.0 %	-13.0 %
Belgium	-10.0 %	-7.5 %
Denmark	-25.0 %	-21.0 %
Finland	0.0 %	0.0 %
France	0.0 %	0.0 %
Germany	-25.0 %	-21.0 %
Greece	+30.0 %	+25.0 %
Ireland	+15.0 %	+13.0 %
Italy	-7.0 %	-6.5 %
Luxembourg	-30.0 %	-28.0 %
Netherlands	-10.0 %	-6.0 %
Portugal	+40.0 %	+27.0 %
Spain	+17.0%	+15.0 %
Sweden	+5.0 %	+4.0 %
United Kingdom	-10.0 %	-12.5 %
EU-Total	**-9.2 %**	**-8.0 %**

Source: Council 1997; Decision 2002/358/EC.

The Kyoto Protocol in 1997 established a first set of targets for industrialised countries to limit and reduce their emissions of a basket of six (groups of) GHGs during the commitment period 2008-2012 compared with 1990. The EU took the highest reduction target of eight per cent among the major industrialised countries. In addition, the Protocol is particularly known for creating a number of market-based mechanisms for the implementation of these targets, including international emissions trading, the clean development mechanism (CDM) and joint implementation (JI). Both the CDM and JI allow investors to gain emission credits from emission-reduction projects financed in developing countries (CDM) and Eastern European countries with "economies in transition" (JI). The Kyoto Protocol also contains important provisions on how to account for emissions and removals of GHGs from forests and other sinks, as well as on reporting and reviewing emission data and other information submitted by parties. Article 18 of the Protocol also mandated the elaboration of "appropriate and effective procedures and mechanisms to determine and to address cases of non-compliance". Importantly, the Kyoto Protocol itself represented "unfinished business",[24] since many of the mentioned provisions required further elaboration before they could be properly implemented.[25]

The Kyoto Protocol necessitated a re-negotiation of the 1997 burden-sharing agreement. The 1997 agreement was in need of adaptation in light of the EU's joint emission reduction target of eight per cent under the Kyoto Protocol and other elements of the agreed Protocol (commitment period, basket of gases). A revised burden-sharing agreement was negotiated under the UK Presidency during the first half of 1998 and politically agreed by the Council on 16 June 1998. It resulted in reduction targets for individual Member States ranging from minus 28 per cent for Luxemburg to plus 27 per cent for Portugal (Table 1) and was codified into EU law four years later in Decision 2002/358/EC of 25 April 2002 on the conclusion of the Kyoto Protocol.

The EU strove to keep its international leadership position during the negotiations on the implementing rules of the Kyoto Protocol that were eventually adopted as the "Marrakesh Accords" in 2001. During the elaboration of the Marrakesh Accords, the EU championed calls for ensuring the "environmental integrity" of the Protocol in particular by demanding priority for domestic action (rather than the use of international offsets) and limits on the use of forests and other carbon sinks. After President Bush announced, in March 2001, that the United States would not ratify the agreement which had been signed by his predecessor, the EU launched a major diplomatic campaign to save the Kyoto Protocol and helped pave the way to agreement on the Marrakesh Accords in November 2001.[26]

---

24.   Ott 1998.
25.   On the Kyoto Protocol, see Oberthür and Ott 1999; Yamin and Depledge 2004.
26.   Vrolijk 2002; Ott 2002; Grubb et al. 2003.

While this agreement represented a major victory for the EU and its partners, it also led to some difficult compromises regarding environmental integrity. In response to the US withdrawal from the Kyoto process, the Union vowed to stick to its Kyoto commitment and pushed for an agreement on the Protocol's implementation without US participation. The Bonn Agreement reached in July 2001 and the subsequent Marrakesh Accords of November 2001, which enabled the entry into force of the Kyoto Protocol, proved the ability of other countries, including the EU, to act jointly even without the only remaining superpower. However, the EU had to temper its demands for environmental integrity to secure agreement of other industrialised countries, in particular Japan, Canada and Russia, whose cooperation now became even more crucial. As a result, the rules on accounting forest sinks, especially, turned out weaker than many had hoped for from an environmental perspective.[27]

3.2   EU internal climate policy

Whereas the EU continued and even reinforced its environmental leadership at the international level, the credibility gap regarding its own domestic action remained and even widened in the course of the 1990s. No further significant Community legislation to reduce GHG emissions was adopted during the 1990s. In 1998 and 1999, voluntary agreements were concluded between the Commission, with the backing of the Council, and European, Japanese and Korean car manufacturers, under which the latter undertook to reduce the average CO_2 emission levels of new passenger car models placed on the EU market to 140g/km by 2008/2009, in exchange for a commitment by the Commission not to propose any legislation in this field.[28] Soon, it became clear that this commitment would not be met, and in 2007, the Commission eventually decided to propose legislation.[29] In addition, the Landfill Directive 1999/31/EC had a clear positive impact on the emissions of methane from landfills. However, these emissions reductions came as a side-effect of waste policy rather than as the result of targeted climate policy.

In April 1999, the Council further decided to amend Decision 93/389/EEC in order to strengthen the monitoring mechanism of Community GHG emissions and the exchange of information on national emission reduction programmes. The resulting Decision 1999/296/EC increased the range of

---

27.   Vrolijk 2002; Ott 2002.
28.   Pallemaerts 1999.
29.   See the chapter by ten Brink in this volume.

information to be provided by the Member States, and envisaged an annual evaluation by the Commission of progress achieved.

It was only at the beginning of the 2000s, and thus with a considerable delay after the adoption of the Kyoto Protocol in 1997, that the EU accelerated its legislative activities to curb GHG emissions in order to back up its bid for global leadership in the struggle against climate change. In particular, the Commission stepped up its efforts to develop EU-wide measures. In March 2000, it launched the "European Climate Change Programme" (ECCP), a multi-stakeholder process to prepare, in collaboration with Member State experts, business and non-governmental organisations, common and coordinated policies and measures against climate change,[30] as the Council had repeatedly demanded since 1997. Working groups were set up to evaluate the potential of various possible measures, and their recommendations were subsequently used by the Commission as a basis for drawing up legislative proposals for submission to the Council and the European Parliament. As one of the priority areas, work focused immediately on the elaboration of an EU-wide ETS (see further below).

Elaborated outside the ECCP, a first significant measure to reduce GHG emissions from the power sector and integrate environmental considerations in energy policy was adopted in September 2001: Directive 2001/77/EC on the promotion of electricity produced from renewable energy sources. Building on a 1997 Commission White Paper on renewables, this directive requires Member States to take measures to promote the growth of electricity produced from renewable sources in order to reach, by 2010, *indicative* (i.e. non-binding) national objectives spelled out in an annex to the directive. Though this measure was taken in the context of energy market liberalisation, it was based on Article 175(1) EC Treaty and prompted primarily by the EU's emerging climate policy, recognising that "increased use of electricity produced from renewable energy sources constitutes an important part of the package of measures needed to comply with the Kyoto Protocol".[31]

GHG emissions and projections confirm that there was insufficient progress in the implementation of EU climate policies in the 1990s. After the reduction of GHG emissions in the EU-15 during the first half of the 1990s, progress in reducing emissions stagnated, and emissions even increased slightly after 1994. Furthermore, projections at the turn of the

30.   Commission 2000.
31.   Directive 2001/77/EC, preamble; see also the chapter by Howes in this volume.

century showed that with existing measures only, GHG emissions in the EU would increase to one per cent above base year levels (1990) by 2010.[32] Nevertheless, the EU-15 achieved its goal of keeping GHG emissions below 1990 levels by the year 2000 (Figure 1).

4. International and European implementation of the Kyoto Protocol (2002-2009)

4.1 EU external and international climate policy

With the adoption of the Marrakesh Accords in November 2001, the implementing rules of the Kyoto Protocol had been sufficiently elaborated for industrialised countries to initiate the ratification process. Consequently, efforts moved from elaborating the international regulatory framework to securing the entry into force of the Kyoto Protocol. Article 25 of the Protocol provides that the Protocol would enter into force once 55 Parties to the UNFCCC, incorporating industrialised countries which accounted for at least 55 per cent of the total CO_2 emissions for these countries, ratified it. The emission figures to be used in the calculation were defined as those reported to the UNFCCC prior to the adoption of the Protocol. Given the withdrawal of the US which accounted for 36.1 per cent of 1990 CO_2 emissions, nearly universal support from other industrialised countries was required. In particular, Russia held a potential veto position with a share of 17.4 per cent.

In an effort to use the momentum of the Johannesburg World Summit on Sustainable Development (WSSD) to achieve entry into force, the EU Council of Ministers adopted Council Decision 2002/358/EC on the ratification of the Kyoto Protocol in April 2002. As mentioned above, the Decision also served to codify the 1998 burden-sharing agreement (see Table 1). When the EC and its Member States submitted their ratification on 31 May 2002, they also announced the burden-sharing agreement in accordance with Article 4 of the Kyoto Protocol. Accordingly, compliance with the EU's Kyoto target of minus eight per cent will be assessed for the EU as a whole. In the case of non-compliance, each Member State individually, and together with the EC acting in accordance with the declared division of competence between the EC and its Member States, will be responsible for its target under the burden-sharing agreement (joint-and-several liability). As in the case of the Convention, the EC made

32. Commission 2001.

a rather general declaration on the division of competence when ratifying the Protocol (as required by its Article 24). Accordingly, it declared that it will implement its target "through action by the Community and its Member States within the respective competence of each" and that it "will on a regular basis provide information on relevant Community legal instruments" in the context of fulfilling its normal reporting obligations.[33]

Soon, Russia became the country on which the fate of the Kyoto Protocol depended. While the EU's campaign for an entry into force of the Protocol in 2002 turned out to be unrealistic, the great majority of industrialised countries ratified the Protocol before the end of 2002 – with the notable exception of Russia. Diplomatic efforts to achieve Russian ratification intensified over the coming years. Central to these efforts was the Russian demand for the EU to support its claim for membership in the World Trade Organisation (WTO). After a number of contradictory declarations and developments arising from the internal Russian debate, Russia eventually ratified the Kyoto Protocol on 18 November 2004 so that the Protocol entered into force on 16 February 2005. Achieving Russian ratification is widely considered a major success of EU climate diplomacy.[34]

Before and after the entry into force, the implementation of the Kyoto Protocol proceeded smoothly at the international level. Parties to the Protocol further developed and advanced the implementation of the marked-based mechanisms (most importantly the CDM) as well as the Protocol's compliance mechanism. This included some important decisions, for example, on the eligibility of sink projects under the CDM. Overall, the machinery for the international implementation of the Protocol was successfully established and sustained. The EU, as the main industrialised player in the framework of the Kyoto Protocol, also made a major contribution to this end, both in terms of decision-making and (financial) support.[35]

4.2   EU external climate policy coordination and representation

The change of mode of international climate policy – moving from rule establishment to implementation – also lay behind a significant reform of the organisation of EU external policy-making on climate change,

---

33.   Decision 2002/358/EC, Annex III.
34.   Damro 2006; Groenleer and van Schaik 2007; see also the chapters by Douma et al. and by van Schaik in this volume.
35.   However, see the chapter by Ayers et al. in this volume. For the decisions taken under the UNFCCC and the Kyoto Protocol, see www.unfccc.int.

implemented in 2004. At the core of the reform lay a redefinition of the role of the EU Presidency and a strengthening of the role of the working/expert level in both the elaboration of EU positions and in their international representation.

External EU climate policy has traditionally been coordinated in the framework of the Council of Ministers. The Council Conclusions adopted by EU environment ministers contain the major negotiating guidelines for EU negotiators at the international level. In the second half of the 1990s, a Council working party attended by senior Member State officials, usually from environment ministries, was established not only to prepare the Council Conclusions but also to discuss more detailed position papers and background papers on the international negotiations. A number of "expert groups", consisting of representatives from Member States' ministries, were established to support the work of the working party and prepare position papers and background papers. This apparatus did not only operate in Brussels in between international meetings, but also at the international meetings in order to be able to respond to new developments. It was the duty of the Presidency to chair and provide direction to the Council, the Council working party and all expert groups – a heavy burden, not only for small member states.

The prominent role of the Presidency in external representation at the international negotiations further added to this burden. The Presidency had come to speak exclusively on behalf of the EU and its Member States internationally, in formal as well as informal settings. Only in informal bilateral contacts was the Presidency supported by other members of the so-called "troika", which since the Amsterdam Treaty consists of the current and next Presidency as well as the Commission (before: the previous, the current and the subsequent Presidency). Given the increasing number of international negotiating groups under the UNFCCC and the Kyoto Protocol, this arrangement meant that each Presidency had to supply a negotiating team of up to 20 negotiators – who would have to become familiar with the situation quickly before the next team would take over.

The core of the reform implemented under the Irish Presidency during the first half of 2004 consisted of the delegation of authority from the Council working party and the Presidency to the expert level, especially through the establishment of a system of "issue leaders" and "lead negotiators".[36] Instead of the Presidency leading negotiations itself, the Presidency thus

36. See also Oberthür and Roche Kelly 2008, 38.

now determined a suitable lead negotiator for each item on the international agenda. In support of the lead negotiator and a streamlined/ more efficient elaboration of negotiating positions, the Presidency usually mandated up to three experts to become "issue leaders". These issue leaders spearheaded the development of position and background papers as well as submissions to the international process within the responsible expert group and provided the link between the lead negotiator and the expert group at large by supporting the lead negotiator at the international negotiations and serving as his/her backup. The Presidency, as a general rule, continued to provide the chairpersons of the expert groups themselves. This new system generalised an occasional practice applied until then in which individual Presidencies, for reasons of lack of resources or negotiating efficiency, had drawn on experts from other countries (frequently from the former Presidency) or the Commission to lead on particular issues.[37]

The reform responded to increasing demand and was enabled by a particular window of opportunity. On the demand side, the more specialised expert discussions in subgroups under the international regime became, the more the lack of continuity and accompanying expertise and experience on the side of EU negotiators who changed every few months was felt. Furthermore, the expanding international negotiating agenda, combined with the enlargement of the EU, from 15 to first 25 and then 27 Member States, increasingly overloaded the internal coordination agenda. Overall, the EU had become increasingly known for its failure to deploy capable and experienced negotiators with institutional memory as well as for its navel gazing and bunker mentality resulting in a lack of outreach activities to others.[38] On the opportunity side, the relaxing international process in the wake of the conclusion of the Marrakesh Accords in 2001 allowed for an increased focus on the internal organisation of work.

The reforms resulted in a significant increase in the negotiating capacity of the EU in the 2000s. The Presidencies, building on the bottom-up advice of individual expert groups, have largely determined lead negotiators on the basis of expertise, qualification and merit. The specialised issue leaders have significantly enhanced the support structure for lead negotiators. Since lead negotiators under the new scheme were not subject to the rotation of the Presidencies and have stayed in their positions for longer periods of time, the reforms enhanced the continuity of EU representation and the EU's "institutional memory" at the expert level. Finally, with the

37. Van Schaik and Egenhofer 2005, 8.
38. Yamin 2000; van Schaik and Egenhofer 2005; Lacasta et al. 2007.

time required for EU internal coordination at international negotiating sessions decreasing, the outreach to international partners has markedly improved. The establishment of a Green Diplomacy Network, in 2003, to coordinate environmental foreign-policy initiatives, including on climate change, across EU foreign services further contributed to an improved outreach beyond the formal negotiating sessions.[39]

4.3   EU internal climate policy

At the same time, EU policy-making on climate change accelerated significantly after the Bonn/Marrakesh accords in 2001, and especially after the entry into force of the Kyoto Protocol in 2005. The initial strong reluctance of Member States to contemplate common measures to cut GHG emissions was gradually overcome, and climate policy in the EU has been increasingly based on such measures. As a result, the gap between the international leadership position of the EU and the lagging domestic implementation has significantly narrowed.

As the centrepiece of the EU's new climate policy, the EU Emissions Trading Directive (2003/87/EC) was adopted in 2003. The ETS set limits for the CO_2 emissions of large installations accounting for about 40 per cent of the EU's CO_2 emissions. In 2004, the Emissions Trading Directive was complemented with Directive 2004/101/EC linking the ETS to the Kyoto Protocol project mechanisms, namely the CDM and JI. An apparent over-allocation of emission allowances for the ETS pilot phase 2005-2007 led to more stringent review arrangements for national allocations for 2008-2012.[40]

As a consequence of the ratification of the Kyoto Protocol by the EC, the Council also completely revised the GHG emissions monitoring mechanism set up by Decision 93/389/EEC and first revised in 1999. Decision 280/2004/EC established a "mechanism" that is intended not only to monitor GHG emissions, but also to implement the Kyoto Protocol. To an extent, it formalises the existence of the European Climate Change Programme (ECCP). Any measures elaborated by the Commission within the framework of that programme will need to be adopted in the normal EU legislative process in order to take effect.

39.   Birkel 2009; Oberthür 2009; see also chapter by van Schaik in this volume.
40.   Delbeke 2006; Skjærseth and Wettestad 2008; see also the chapter by Skjærseth and Wettestad in this volume.

Two EU measures in the energy efficiency field taken after the entry into force of the Kyoto Protocol include Directive 2005/32/EC establishing a framework for the setting of eco-design requirements for energy-using products, and Directive 2006/32/EC on national programmes for energy end-use efficiency and energy services. The former provides a legal framework for the adoption of minimum energy efficiency standards for a wide range of products such as computers, fridges and light bulbs "where market forces fail to evolve in the right direction or at an acceptable speed", and effectively re-launched EU standard-setting efforts, which had stagnated in the 1990s. The latter, which replaces and repeals the above-mentioned 1993 SAVE Directive, requires Member States to draw up national action plans showing how they intend to reach an indicative energy savings target of nine per cent by 2016.

Other important pieces of EU legislation on climate change adopted in the 2000s to implement the Kyoto Protocol include:
- Directive 2002/91/EC on the energy performance of buildings;
- Directive 2003/30/EC on the promotion of the use of biofuels in transport;
- Directive 2004/8/EC on the promotion of combined heat and power production; and
- Regulation EC 842/2006 and Directive 2006/40/EC on reducing the emission of fluorinated GHGs.

The combined effect of these measures on EU GHG emissions, together with supplementary measures taken by Member States individually, brought the EU-15 closer to its Kyoto target of minus eight per cent, while also reducing emissions in the new member states. The effect of the measures could only be seen with some delay in actual emission figures. Also, the combined actual effect of the measures did not exploit their full emission reduction potential because of ubiquitous implementation deficits so that some doubts about the ability of the EU-15 to comply with their Kyoto targets still remained until at least 2007. However, the world-wide economic and financial crisis of 2008-2009 has greatly improved the chances that the EU will be able to achieve the necessary emission cuts (Figure 1), especially when taking into account the use of the market-based mechanisms CDM and JI as well as accounting of sinks.[41]

---

41. EEA 2009a and b.

5. Policy evaluation and review: preparing climate policy for post-2012 (2005-2009)

5.1 EU external and international climate policy

With the entry into force of the Kyoto Protocol secured, and its implementation well on track, international and European discussions increasingly turned towards evaluating and reviewing the achievements so far in order to prepare for the post-2012 period, when the first commitment period of the Kyoto Protocol will have expired. Article 3(9) of the Kyoto Protocol requires the parties to start considering commitments of industrialised countries for after 2012 in 2005. Consequently, parties to the Kyoto Protocol initiated this consideration when they first met at the end of 2005 in Montreal. At the same time, the non-participation of the US in the Protocol and the rising share of GHG emissions of major developing countries provided a strong rationale for discussion on action beyond industrialised Kyoto parties. To this end, the Montreal conference established a dialogue on long-term cooperative action under the Convention.[42]

The dialogue on long-term cooperative action paved the way for the next step, the launch of real negotiations, two years later at the climate conference in Bali in December 2007. With the US administration of President Bush junior nearing the end of its term, parties to the UNFCCC agreed "to launch a comprehensive process to enable the full, effective and sustained implementation of the Convention through long-term cooperative action, now, up to and beyond 2012, in order to reach an agreed outcome and adopt a decision" at the end of 2009.[43] This Bali Action Plan entailed several building blocks, including mitigation by both industrialised and developing countries, adaptation to the negative impacts of climate change, technology development and transfer, and provision of financial resources and investment. It also covered the issue of reducing emissions from deforestation and forest degradation in developing countries (REDD). The second track of discussions on emission mitigation targets of industrialised country parties to the Kyoto Protocol continued in parallel, with the relationship between the Convention track and the Protocol track remaining unclear.

---

42. IISD 2005.
43. Decision 1/CP.13 in UNFCCC 2008, 3.

The EU retained its leadership role in these discussions about the future international policy framework. The major foundation for its international leadership in the multilateral negotiations on a post-2012 global climate regime was laid when the Spring European Council under the German Presidency in March 2007 agreed on what has subsequently been called the 20-20-20 by 2020 package. In particular, EU heads of state and government:

- made a "firm independent commitment to achieve at least a 20 per cent reduction" of GHG emissions in the EU from the 1990 level by 2020;
- agreed to increase the share of renewable energy sources in the EU energy supply to 20 per cent in 2020, including a binding minimum target of 10 per cent for the share of biofuels in transport by 2020; and
- approved the objective of saving 20 per cent on the EU's projected energy consumption for 2020.

Particularly important for the international leadership role of the EU were two further elements of the Presidency Conclusions of the European Council. First, EU heads of state and government offered to commit to a 30 per cent reduction in the context of a comprehensive global agreement with comparable commitments by other industrialised countries and adequate contributions by advanced developing countries. Second, the Commission was invited to prepare by 2008 a new package of internal measures, most of them in the field of energy policy, to implement the announced targets, including a review of the EU ETS, a new comprehensive directive on renewable energy sources, strengthened energy efficiency measures, and a Strategic Energy Technology Plan to support the accelerated development and deployment of energy efficient and low-carbon technologies, including carbon capture and storage and second-generation biofuels.[44]

The EU's position for the Copenhagen climate summit in December 2009 was subsequently further elaborated by the European Council and the Council of Environment Ministers, with some input from the Council of Finance Ministers. Accordingly, the EU supported that global GHG emissions should start falling from 2020 and be reduced by at least 50 per cent as compared with 1990 levels by 2050. Developed countries should thus collectively reduce their emissions by 25-40 per cent by 2020 and by 80-95 per cent by 2050. Developing countries should achieve a substantial relative emission reduction in the order of 15-30 per cent from the currently predicted emission growth rate ("business-as-usual"). The emissions of international aviation and maritime transport should be

---

44.   European Council 2007; Council 2007; Commission 2009.

reduced by 10 per cent and 20 per cent, respectively, below 2005 levels by 2020. Gross tropical deforestation should be reduced by at least 50 per cent by 2020 and global forest cover loss be halted by 2030. Estimating the demand for international public support for the implementation of ambitious mitigation and adaptation strategies in developing countries to lie in the range of 22-50 billion Euro per year by 2020, the EU declared its readiness to take on its fair share of total international public finance. It suggested that emission levels and GDP should serve as criteria for determining the fair share of all countries contributing, excluding least developed countries, with a considerable weight on emission levels.[45]

Several driving forces of the review and revision of international and European climate policy after 2005 deserve mentioning. First of all, the IPCC Fourth Assessment Report published in 2007 emphasised the urgent need for action.[46] The IPCC analysis was supplemented, and its message reinforced, by the so-called Stern Report on the economics of climate change, which highlighted the net benefits to be reaped from climate protection.[47] In addition, soaring oil and gas prices, together with political developments in regions with major reserves (including the Middle East and Russia) helped to advance the energy security agenda worldwide and provided further support for action to reduce dependence on fossil fuels. In Europe, progressive climate policies received additional support because they could serve to re-legitimise European integration more broadly and provided a suitable arena to strengthen the EU's role on the world scene and demonstrate its commitment to multilateralism.[48]

5.2   EU internal climate policy: the climate and energy package

The development of EU climate policy in the second half of the 2000s goes a long way to closing the gap between international words and domestic deeds that has characterised EU climate policy for a long time. Most importantly, the Council and Parliament agreed a set of legislative proposals, widely known as the "climate and energy package", in order to implement the European Council's decisions of March 2007. After the Commission presented its proposals on 23 January 2008, they progressed through the legislative process with record speed, with a political

---

45.   Council 2009; European Council 2009.
46.   IPCC 2007.
47.   Stern 2007.
48.   See also van Schaik and van Hecke 2008; Oberthür and Roche Kelly 2008; the chapter by van Schaik in this volume.

agreement reached in the European Council on 11-12 December 2008 and a first reading agreement adopted by the European Parliament on 17 December 2008. The Council formally adopted the package on 9 April 2009 and it was signed into law two weeks later. The climate and energy package was complemented with a number of other legislative agreements reached in 2008, including a Regulation on CO_2 emissions of new passenger cars and a Directive including aviation in the EU ETS. In the following, we focus on the four legislative acts forming the climate and energy package.

The speed at which the package progressed through the legislative procedure – only eleven months from proposal by the Commission to political agreement in December 2008 – reflects the high level of political resolve on the part of EU leaders as well as the increased political profile of the combined energy and climate policy fields. The climate and energy package was declared a key priority by the French Presidency, which invested substantial political effort in achieving agreement within the EU a few days before the end of the UNFCCC conference in Poznan in order to preserve European leadership ahead of the crucial Copenhagen conference in December 2009. However, this political objective was achieved at the expense of a significant watering down of the Commission's initial proposals.

Marking the start of an important new stage in the development of EU climate and energy policy, the climate and energy package consists of four pieces of legislation: a revision of the 2003 Emissions Trading Directive, a Decision on sharing the effort of GHG emissions reductions in the non-ETS sectors among Member States, a new and comprehensive Renewable Energy Directive, and a Directive on carbon capture and storage (CCS). Amended guidelines on state aid for environmental measures formed the fifth element of the package and were adopted by the Commission itself pursuant to its Treaty powers to regulate state aid.[49]

The individual elements of the climate and energy package together regulate the whole of the EU's GHG emissions, determine the division of the reduction efforts between ETS and non-ETS sectors and set the framework for how best to create synergy in achieving the objectives set by the European Council for 2020. The revised Emissions Trading Directive and the Effort-Sharing Decision together regulate the whole of the EU's GHG emissions so as to reduce them by 14 per cent from 2005 levels by 2020 (equivalent to the 20 per cent reduction from 1990 levels). Following

---

49.   Commission 2008.

cost-effectiveness considerations, the ETS sectors were accorded the lion's share and have to reduce their emissions by 21 per cent from 2005 levels. The diffuse sources of the non-ETS sectors regulated under the Effort-Sharing Decision need to reduce their emissions by 10 per cent from 2005 levels to achieve the overall objective. The Renewable Energy Directive's target of 20 per cent renewable energy in total final energy consumption in 2020 influenced this distribution and set certain parameters for implementing the GHG emission reduction target. In contrast, the CCS Directive primarily set a framework for developing CCS technology whose major potential for influencing EU GHG emissions lies beyond 2020. Figure 2 illustrates the relationship between the revised ETS Directive, the Effort-Sharing Decision and the new Renewable Energy Directive.

Directive 2009/29/EC on an improved and extended EU ETS significantly amends the ETS Directive 2003/87/EC. In particular, a single EU-wide cap is defined, replacing the existing system of 27 national allocation plans. Installations covered by the ETS will collectively be required to reduce emissions by 21 per cent compared to their aggregate 2005 emissions levels by 2020. The cap is reduced stepwise from 2013 to 2020 to achieve this goal, following a linear trajectory. Instead of granting most of the emission allowances free of charge, as is the case under the current system running until 2012, auctioning will become the principle and free allocation the exception, starting with power plants in 2013. However, contrary to the Commission's original proposal, a transitional and gradually decreasing possibility for the free allocation of allowances will apply to certain power plants in new Member States during the period 2013-2020. In the manufacturing sector, auctioning will be phased in gradually throughout the EU, "with a view to" reaching full auctioning by 2027. However, a broad exception was inserted for industrial sectors at risk of "carbon leakage", which are to be identified through a comitology procedure. While the European Parliament's Environment Committee had sought to earmark all auction revenues for the purpose of funding climate-related measures and research and development, the final compromise agreement only contains a legally unenforceable recommendation stating that "at least 50 per cent" of the proceeds "should" be used for climate related adaptation and mitigation purposes.[50]

50. See also the chapter by Skjærseth and Wettestad in this volume.

Figure 2 – The revised ETS Directive, the Effort-Sharing Decision and the new Renewable Energy Directive

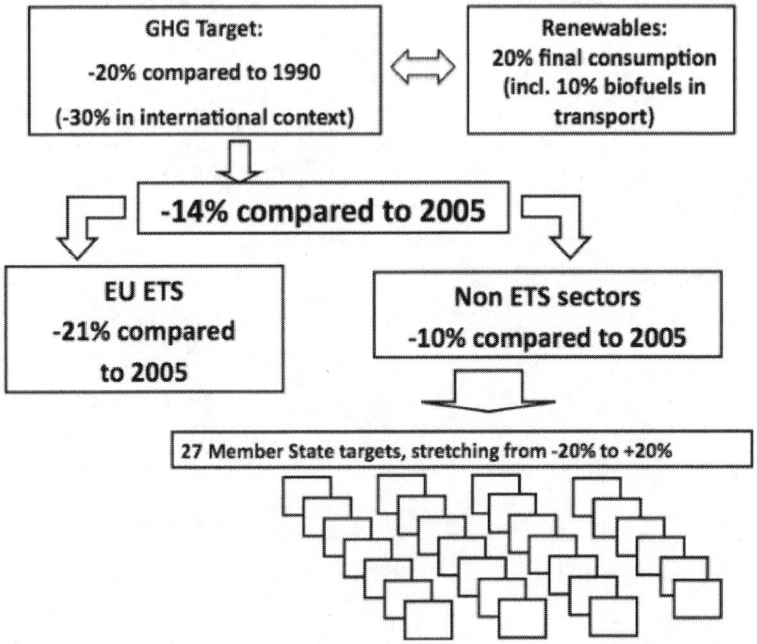

Source: adapted from European Commission.

Decision 406/2009/EC – now entitled "effort-sharing" in contrast to its predecessor Decision 2002/358/EC informally known as the "burden-sharing" decision – lays down national reduction targets in the non-ETS sectors (i.e. households, buildings, transport, services, agriculture and smaller industrial installations) in order to contribute the remaining share of the 20 per cent overall reduction objective by 2020. The national reduction targets for the period 2013-2020 are formulated differently from those for the current 2008-2012 period. In particular, the reference year is 2005 instead of 1990 and the effort has been divided among Member States taking into account their per-capita GDP, in order to grant more leeway to the new Member States who are not included in the EU "bubble" for the first Kyoto commitment period. The Decision also allows Member States to transfer part of their assigned GHG emission allocation to subsequent years and to other Member States, as well as to acquire credits resulting from CDM and JI projects in developing countries and Eastern European countries, respectively, up to an annual limit which may not exceed three per cent of their respective GHG emissions in the baseline year 2005.[51]

The Commission's initial proposal would have provided for an automatic proportional adjustment of both the effort-sharing targets and the overall reduction under the ETS in the context of an international agreement on climate change under which the EU would commit itself to a higher 30 per cent reduction target, as indicated by the European Council in March 2007. However, those provisions were deleted from the agreed texts and replaced by a simple invitation to the Commission to put forward proposals to amend the Effort-Sharing Decision and the Emissions Trading Directive for consideration by the European Parliament and the Council through the regular co-decision procedure in the event of such a global agreement.

The new Renewable Energy Directive 2009/28/EC lays down mandatory national targets for Member States' use of renewables (electricity, heating and cooling, and transport sectors) adding up to 20 per cent of the EU's total energy consumption by 2020. These targets were determined on the basis of two main criteria: first, all Member States are to increase the share of renewable energy by 5.5 per cent; second, further mandatory increases were apportioned on the basis of GDP, with an adjustment to reward early movers. The Directive allows Member States to cooperate in order to achieve their renewable targets jointly, e.g. by running joint projects or transferring renewable energy "statistically" between them. It also provides that by 2020 renewable energy – biofuels, electricity and hydrogen produced from renewable sources – shall account for at least 10 per cent of each Member State's total fuel consumption in all forms of transport. This measure replaces the 2003 biofuels Directive 2003/30/EC which set lower, non-mandatory targets for biofuels only. The 2009 Directive furthermore establishes binding criteria to ensure that biofuel production is sustainable. In particular, it requires a minimum of 35 per cent GHG emission reduction compared to fossil fuels from 2013, increasing to 50 per cent from 2017 onwards.[52]

Finally, Directive 2009/31/EC on the geological storage of CO_2 establishes a legal framework for the permanent containment of CO_2, designed to ensure that CCS technology is deployed safely and responsibly. The provisions of this Directive, therefore, mainly concern the regulation of

---

51. In addition to this three per cent, certain Member States with stricter targets will be able to use additional credits from projects in least developed countries and small island developing states amounting to up to one per cent of their 2005 emissions. See the chapter by Lacasta et al. in this volume for more detail.
52. See the chapter by Howes in this volume for more detail.

CO_2 storage and the removal of unintended barriers in existing legislation to such storage. It ensures that CO_2 capture is subject to permitting procedures under Directive 2008/1/EC on integrated pollution prevention and control (IPPC) for certain industrial activities, and that both the capture and pipeline transport of CO_2 are activities for which an environmental impact assessment (EIA) is mandatory in accordance with the requirements of the EIA Directive (Directive 85/337/EEC). Criteria for site selection are set out to ensure that only sites with a minimal risk of leakage are chosen. While it will be up to Member States to determine the areas to be made available for CCS operations and the conditions for site use, the new Directive provides for a review of draft permit decisions by the Commission, assisted by an independent scientific panel. The main financial incentive for the deployment of CCS technology will be provided by the EU ETS, under which the CO_2 captured and safely stored according to the provisions of the CCS Directive will be considered as not emitted. In addition, up to 300 million allowances will be made available from the ETS new entrants' reserve until the end of 2015 to subsidise the construction of up to twelve CCS demonstration plants. The actual value of this support mechanism will ultimately depend on the price of emission allowances at the relevant time.[53]

Three other legislative measures relating to the EU's climate change mitigation policy were proposed by the Commission prior to January 2008 and adopted by Parliament and Council in 2008-2009. Directive 2008/101/EC amending the Emissions Trading Directive 2003/87/EC with a view to including aviation activities in the EU ETS from 2012 was adopted in November 2008, prior to the more far-reaching overhaul of the ETS by Directive 2009/29/EC. Directive 2009/30/EC sets new harmonised specifications for liquid fuels aimed at curbing emissions not only of CO_2, but also of other air pollutants such as sulphur and nitrogen oxides. Finally, Regulation 443/2009/EC sets CO_2 emission performance standards for cars.[54] The latter two were effectively added to the climate and energy package by the European Parliament, which decided to vote on these proposals at the same plenary session as the other four Commission proposals.

While the climate and energy package and the related legislative acts primarily aimed at the post-2012 period (and up until 2020), the new climate policies of the EU are also relevant for the implementation of the EU's Kyoto targets. Several of the agreed policies are set to lead to a

---

53. See the chapter by Chiavara in this volume for more detail.
54. See the chapter by ten Brink in this volume for more detail.

reorientation of Member State policies that may deliver first results even before 2012. Most importantly, agreement on the ETS framework until 2020 has had an immediate stabilising effect on prices on the emissions trading market because emission allowances issued prior to 2012 can be transferred to the third phase of the ETS. In this sense, 2009 prices reflect expectations of supply and demand not only until 2012, but up to 2020.

Overall, the package amounts to a major overhaul of EU climate policy and constitutes a significant step for both EU climate policy and EU integration more broadly, even though ambitions are still far from compatible with the EU objective to limit global temperature increase to two degrees Celsius. The new EU climate policies support international EU leadership by implementing a significant GHG emission reduction by 2020 ahead of international agreement. They are also significant for European integration more broadly because they result in a considerable harmonisation and communitarisation of this important policy area, which can be interpreted as a partial renunciation of the EU's "better regulation" agenda.[55] On the negative side, the new climate policies require little more than half of the emission reductions to be achieved in the EU itself. Perhaps more importantly, even a 30 per cent reduction – the proposed EU target in the case of a satisfactory international agreement – is at the lower end of the range of 25-40 per cent of emission reductions expected from industrialised countries as a whole by 2020. Arguably, more ambition may be expected from an actor aspiring to lead other international actors in the fight against climate change.

6.   Conclusion

EU climate policy and the multilateral regime on climate change within the framework of the United Nations have developed in parallel and in close interaction. Since the late 1980s, both have gone through a full cycle of policy development. Climate change was established on the international and European policy agendas in the late 1980s and early 1990s in the context of negotiations on the UNFCCC. The first substantive policies were subsequently formulated and adopted in the context of the elaboration of the 1997 Kyoto Protocol and its implementing rules, the Marrakesh Accords. The Kyoto Protocol was then implemented, internationally and in the EU, in the 2000s. In the second half of the first decade of the 2000s, both European and international policy processes

---

55. Hey forthcoming.

turned to the evaluation and to the elaboration, in particular, of a new set of (reformed) policies. In the EU, this resulted in the elaboration of the climate and energy package of legislative acts in 2008 and their adoption in 2009. At the international level, discussions focused on the policy framework for after the year 2012, in which the first commitment period of the Kyoto Protocol expires.

During the inter-related development of international and EU climate policies over the past two decades, the interaction between the policy-making at both levels has changed significantly. During the 1990s, internal EU climate policy was mostly driven by international policy development. The lack of clear mitigation commitments in the UNFCCC resulted in the failure to establish effective GHG mitigation policies at the EU level, although it did result in the establishment of an EU GHG monitoring mechanism. Later on, the Kyoto Protocol triggered efforts to enhance EU climate policies, which led to the development of a more effective and encompassing policy framework, with the EU Emissions Trading System as its core.

In the 2000s, EU climate policy-making gradually moved ahead of international policy development. With the climate and energy package of 2008/2009, the EU established an internal climate policy framework for the time after 2012 and until 2020, ahead of international agreement on a post-2012 policy framework. Given their significant external implications, the "new" climate policies of the EU may also be expected to have an important impact on the evolving structures of the international regime (still uncertain at the time of writing). Overall, domestic EU climate policy has moved from a "taker" to a "maker" of international climate policy.

As a result, the character of EU leadership on climate change at the international level has also changed. Throughout the history of international climate policy, the EU has been the major pusher, by regularly proposing the most stringent climate protection measures and commitments, by moving from a stabilisation of industrialised countries' CO_2 emissions by 2000 in the negotiations on the UNFCCC, to a 15-per cent reduction of their GHG emissions by 2010 in the Kyoto negotiations, to an emission reduction in the order of 30 per cent by 2020 in discussions on the post-2012 policy framework. While the EU regularly put forward ever more ambitious negotiating positions on the international scene, its rhetoric was not matched by equally ambitious domestic policies. The lack of such policies created a considerable credibility gap in the 1990s – a gap that has gradually been closed in the 2000s, in particular as a result of the adoption of the climate and energy package.

The advances of its domestic climate policies have produced the first noticeable impacts on the EU's emission trajectory. While GHG emissions in the EU fell during the early 1990s due to developments unrelated to climate policy (German reunification and the transition from coal to gas in the UK), little progress was made in reducing emissions until 2005. Since then, EU GHG emissions appear to have taken a downward trend that is expected to continue (Figure 1). As a result, the EU as a whole is expected to achieve, and even overshoot, its Kyoto target of reducing GHG emissions by eight per cent from 1990 levels by 2008-2012. The climate and energy package also sets the EU on a path towards achieving a 20-per cent emission reduction by 2020.

Despite the important progress made, EU climate policy faces significant challenges. The new climate policies of the EU arguably still fall far short of what would be required to initiate and advance the structural changes in the European energy systems so as to limit global temperature increase to an average of two degrees Celsius above pre-industrial levels. Since the climate and energy package requires little more than half of the emission reductions to be achieved in the EU itself, it gives an insufficient political signal for a full-scale transformation of the EU's energy systems. This weak signal is further dampened by the financial and economic crisis that led to additional emission reductions, at the same time reducing the effort required to achieve the established mitigation goals. Living up to the environmental challenge would require the EU to move beyond even its current plans for a 30-per cent reduction target by 2020 in the context of an international agreement (the realisation of which remains uncertain at the time of writing). A 30-per cent target may be considered minimalist and insufficient given the scientifically recommended range of 25-40 per cent for industrialised countries as a whole and the aspiration of the EU to show leadership on climate change. As importantly, the climate and energy package anchors considerable spoilers in the implementation of such a strengthened international commitment (sinks, international offsets) that again contradict the strong signal needed to sustain a transition to a European low-carbon economy and society.

Overall, the prospect for continued EU leadership on climate change may be good, while doubts persist about whether it will be sufficient in light of the environmental challenge. The shape of the international policy framework and the extent to which it will reflect EU priorities remains uncertain at the time of writing. Also, the re-engagement of the US and the rise of China as a pivotal actor in international climate policy constitute challenges for the EU's international role. However, despite their shortcomings, the new EU climate policies ensure that the EU remains at the forefront of the development and implementation of concrete climate policies. They provide the EU with a strong basis and starting position in the unfolding international regulatory competition for the economic and technological opportunities of low-carbon development. Maintaining its competitive edge in this field means that the EU cannot rest on its laurels, but must strengthen and reinforce its efforts.

References

Birkel, Kathrin. 2009. *We, Europe and the Rest: EU Discourse(s) at Work in Environmental Politics*. PhD Thesis, July 2009. Nijmegen: Radboud University.

Bodansky, Daniel. 1993. The United Nations Framework Convention on Climate Change: A Commentary. *Yale Journal of International Law* 18(2): 451-558.

Collier, Ute. 1996. The European Union's Climate Change Policy: Limiting Emissions or Limiting Powers? *Journal of European Public Policy* 3(1): 122-138.

Commission (EC). 1992. Proposal for a Council Directive Introducing a Tax on Carbon Dioxide Emissions and Energy. COM (92) 226 final. Brussels: European Commission.

Commission (EC). 2000. Communication from the Commission to the Council and the European Parliament on EU Policies and Measures to Reduce Greenhouse Gas Emissions: Towards a European Climate Change Programme (ECCP). COM (2000) 88 final. Brussels: European Commission.

Commission (EC). 2001. Third National Communication from the European Community under the UN Framework Convention on Climate Change. Brussels: European Commission.

Commission (EC). 2008. Notices from European Union Institutions and Bodies. Community Guidelines on State Aid for Environmental Protection. *Official Journal of the European Union*, 1 April, C 82/1.

Commission (EC). 2009. Communication from the Commission to the European Parliament, the Council, the European Economic and Social Committee and the Committee of the Regions Investing in the Development of Low Carbon Technologies (SET-Plan). COM (2009) 519 final. Brussels: European Commission.

Council of the European Union (Energy and Environment). 1990. Press Release. 1436th Joint Council Meeting: Energy/Environment. 29 October 1990. 9482/90. Luxembourg: Council of the European Communities.

Council of the European Union (Environment). 1996. Press Release. 1956th Council Meeting: Environment. 15 October 1996. 10458/96. Brussels: Council of the European Union.

Council of the European Union (Environment). 2007. Press Release. 2785th Council Meeting: Environment. 20 February 2007. 6272/07. Brussels: Council of the European Union.

Council of the European Union (Environment). 2009. Press Release. 2968th Council Meeting: Environment. 21 October 2009. 14361/09. Brussels: Council of the European Union.

Council Directive 85/337/EEC of 27 June 1985 on the Assessment of the Effects of Certain Public and Private Projects on the Environment. *Official Journal of the European Union*, 5 July, L 175/40.

Damro, Chad. 2006. EU-UN Environmental Relations: Shared Competence and Effective Multilateralism. In *The European Union at the United Nations: Intersecting Multilateralisms*, edited by Katie V. Laatikainen and Karen E. Smith. 175-192. Basingstoke: Palgrave Macmillan.

Decision 93/389/EEC of the Council of the European Union of 24 June 1993 Establishing a Monitoring Mechanism of Community CO_2 and Other Greenhouse Gas Emissions. *Official Journal of the European Union*, 9 September, L 167/31.

Decision 93/500/EEC of the Council of the European Union of 13 September 1993 Concerning the Promotion of Renewable Energy Sources in the Community (Altener Programme). *Official Journal of the European Union*, 18 September, L 235/41.

Decision 94/69/EC of the Council of the European Union of 15 December 1993 Concerning the Conclusion of the United Nations Framework Convention on Climate Change. *Official Journal of the European Union*, 7 February, L 33/11.

Decision 1999/296/EC of the Council of the European Union of 26 April 1999 Amending Decision 93/389/EEC for a Monitoring Mechanism of Community CO_2 and Other Greenhouse Gas Emissions. *Official Journal of the European Union*, 5 May, L 117/35.

Decision 2002/358/EC of the Council of the European Union of 25 April 2002 Concerning the Approval, on Behalf of the European Community, of the Kyoto Protocol to the United Nations Framework Convention on Climate Change and the Joint Fulfilment of Commitments Thereunder. *Official Journal of the European Union*, 15 May, L 130/1.

Decision 280/2004/EC of the European Parliament and of the Council of 11 February 2004 Concerning a Mechanism for Monitoring Community Greenhouse Gas Emissions and for Implementing the Kyoto Protocol. *Official Journal of the European Union*, 19 February, L 49/1.

Decision 406/2009/EC of the European Parliament and of the Council of 23 April 2009 on the Effort of Member States to Reduce their Greenhouse Gas Emissions to Meet the Community's Greenhouse Gas Emission Reduction Commitments up to 2020. *Official Journal of the European Union*, 5 June, L 140/136.

Delbeke, Jos (ed.). 2006. *EU Environmental Law: The EU Greenhouse Gas Emissions Trading Scheme. EU Energy Law, Volume IV*. Leuven: Claeys & Casteels.

Directive 92/42/EEC of the Council of the European Communities of 21 May 1992 on Efficiency Requirements for New Hot Water Boilers Fired with Liquid or Gaseous Fuels. *Official Journal of the European Union*, 22 June, L 167.

Directive 92/75/EEC of the Council of the European Union of 22 September 1992 on the Indication by Labeling and Standard Product Information of the Consumption of Energy and other Resources by Household Appliances. *Official Journal of the European Union*, 13 October, L 297/16.

Directive 93/76/EEC of the Council of the European Union of 13 September 1993, to Limit Carbon Dioxide Emissions by Improving Energy Efficiency (SAVE). *Official Journal of the European Union*, 22 September, L 237/28.

Directive 96/57/EC of the European Parliament and of the Council of 3 September 1996 on Energy Efficiency Requirements for Household Electric Refrigerators, Freezers and Combinations Thereof. *Official Journal of the European Union*, 18 September, L 236/36.

Directive 1999/31/EC of the Council of the European Union of 26 April 1999 on the Landfill of Waste. *Official Journal of the European Union*, 16 July, L 182/1.

Directive 2000/55/EC of the European Parliament and of the Council of 18 September 2000 on Energy Efficiency Requirements for Ballasts for

Fluorescent Lighting. *Official Journal of the European Union*, 1 November, L 279/33.

Directive 2001/77/EC of the European Parliament and of the Council of 27 September 2001 on the Promotion of Electricity Produced from Renewable Energy Sources in the Internal Electricity Market. *Official Journal of the European Union*, 27 October, L 283/33.

Directive 2002/91/EC of the European Parliament and of the Council of 16 December 2002 on the Energy Performance of Buildings. *Official Journal of the European Union*, 4 January, L 001/65.

Directive 2003/30/EC of the European Parliament and of the Council of 8 May 2003 on the Promotion of the use of Biofuels or Other Renewable Fuels for Transport. *Official Journal of the European Union*, 17 May, L 123/42.

Directive 2003/87/EC of the European Parliament and of the Council of 13 October 2003 Establishing a Scheme for Greenhouse Gas Emission Allowance Trading within the Community and Amending Council Directive 96/61/EC. *Official Journal of the European Union*, 25 October, L 275/32.

Directive 2004/8/EC of the European Parliament and of the Council of 11 February 2004 on the Promotion of Cogeneration Based on a Useful Heat Demand in the Internal Energy Market and Amending Directive 92/42/EEC. *Official Journal of the European Union*, 21 February, L 52/50.

Directive 2004/101/EC of the European Parliament and of the Council of 27 October 2004 Amending Directive 2003/87/EC Establishing a Scheme for Greenhouse Gas Emission Allowance Trading within the Community, in Respect of the Kyoto Protocol's Project Mechanisms. *Official Journal of the European Union*, 13 November, L 338/18.

Directive 2005/32/EC of the European Parliament and of the Council of 6 July 2005 Establishing a Framework for the Setting of Ecodesign Requirements for Energy-Using Products and Amending Council Directive 92/42/EEC and Directives 96/57/EC and 2000/55/EC of the European Parliament and of the Council. *Official Journal of the European Union*, 22 July, L 191/29.

Directive 2006/32/EC of the European Parliament and of the Council of 5 April 2006 on Energy End-Use Efficiency and Energy Services and Repealing Council Directive 93/76/EEC. *Official Journal of the European Union*, 27 April, L 114/64.

Directive 2006/40/EC of the European Parliament and of the Council of 17 May 2006 Relating to Emissions From Air-Conditioning Systems in Motor Vehicles and Amending Council Directive 70/156/EEC. *Official Journal of the European Union*, 14 June, L 161/12.

Directive 2008/1/EC of the European Parliament and of the Council of 15 January 2008 Concerning Integrated Pollution Prevention and Control (Codified version). *Official Journal of the European Union*, 29 January, L 24/8.

Directive 2008/101/EC of the European Parliament and of the Council of 19 November 2008 Amending Directive 2003/87/EC so as to Include Aviation Activities in the Scheme for Greenhouse Gas Emission Allowance Trading within the Community. *Official Journal of the European Union*, 13 January, L 8/3.

Directive 2009/28/EC of the European Parliament and of the Council of 23 April 2009 on the Promotion of the Use of Energy from Renewable Sources and Amending and Subsequently Repealing Directives 2001/77/EC and 2003/30/EC. *Official Journal of the European Union*, 5 June, L 140/16.

Directive 2009/29/EC of the European Parliament and of the Council of 23 April 2009 Amending Directive 2003/87/EC so as to Improve and Extend the Greenhouse Gas Emission Allowance Trading Scheme of the Community. *Official Journal of the European Union*, 5 June, L 140/63.

Directive 2009/30/EC of the European Parliament and of the Council of 23 April 2009 Amending Directive 98/70/EC as Regards the Specification of Petrol, Diesel and Gas-Oil and Introducing a Mechanism to Monitor and Reduce Greenhouse Gas Emissions and Amending Council Directive 1999/32/EC as Regards the Specification of Fuel Used by Inland Waterway Vessels and Repealing Directive 93/12/EEC. *Official Journal of the European Union*, 5 June, L 140/88.

Directive 2009/31/EC of the European Parliament and of the Council of 23 April 2009 on the Geological Storage of Carbon Dioxide and Amending Council Directive 85/337/EEC, European Parliament and Council Directives 2000/60/EC, 2001/80/EC, 2004/35/EC, 2006/12/EC, 2008/1/EC and Regulation (EC) No 1013/2006. *Official Journal of the European Union*, 5 June, L 140/114.

EEA (European Environment Agency). 2009a. Annual European Community Greenhouse Gas Inventory 1990-2007 and Inventory Report 2009. Submission to the UNFCCC Secretariat. EEA Technical Report, No. 4/2009. Copenhagen: EEA.

EEA (European Environment Agency). 2009b. Greenhouse Gas Emission Trends and Projections in Europe 2009. EEA Report No 9/2009. Copenhagen: EEA.

European Council. 1990. 25/26 June 1990, Dublin. *Presidency Conclusions.* Annex II: The Environmental Imperative. http://www.europarl.europa.eu/ summits/dublin/du2_en.pdf. Accessed: 26 November 2009.

European Council. 2007. Brussels European Council 8/9 March. *Presidency Conclusions.* 7224/1/07. Brussels: Council of the European Union.

European Council. 2009. Brussels European Council 29/30 October. *Presidency Conclusions.* 15265/09. Brussels: Council of the European Union.

Groenleer, Martijn L. P. and Louise G. van Schaik. 2007. United We Stand? The European Union's International Actorness in the Cases of the International Criminal Court and the Kyoto Protocol. *Journal of Common Market Studies* 45(5): 969-98.

Grubb, Michael, Tom Brewer, Benito Müller, John Drexhage, Kirsty Hamilton, Taishi Sugiyama and Takao Aiba. 2003. *A Strategic Assessment of the Kyoto-Marrakech System.* The Royal Institute of International Affairs, Sustainable Development Programme, Briefing Paper, No.6.

Gupta, Joyeeta and Michael Grubb (eds.). 2000. *Climate Change and European Leadership.* Dordrecht: Kluwer Academic Publishers.

Hague Declaration. 1989. Hague Declaration on the Environment. 11 March 1989. UN Doc. A/44/340. *International Legal Materials* 28: 1808.

Haigh, Nigel. 1996. Climate Change Policies and Politics in the European Community. In *Politics of Climate Change: a European Perspective,* edited by Tim O'Riordan and Jill Jäger. 155-185. London: Routledge.

Harris, Paul G. (ed.). 2007. *Europe and Global Climate Change. Politics, Foreign Policy and Regional Cooperation.* Cheltenham: Edward Elgar.

Hey, Christian. Forthcoming. Rediscovery of Hierarchy: The New EU Climate Policies. In *EU Environmental Policies and Governance: Climate Change and Beyond,* edited by Annette Bongardt and Francisco Torres, Cheltenham: Edward Elgar.

Howlett, Michael and M. Ramesh. 2003. *Studying Public Policy. Policy Cycles and Policy Subsystems.* 2nd Edition. Oxford: Oxford University Press.

IISD (International Institute for Sustainable Development). 2005. Summary of the Eleventh Conference of the Parties to the UN Framework Convention on Climate Change and First Conference of the Parties Serving as the Meeting of the Parties to the Kyoto Protocol. *Earth Negotiations Bulletin* 12(291).

IPCC (Intergovernmental Panel on Climate Change). 2007. Climate Change 2007. Synthesis Report. Contribution of Working Groups I, II and III to the Fourth Assessment Report of the Intergovernmental Panel on Climate Change [Core Writing Team, Pachauri, R.K and Reisinger, A.(eds.)]. Geneva: IPCC.

Lacasta, Nuno S., Suraje Dessai, Eva Kracht and Katharine Vincent. 2007. Articulating a Consensus: The EU's Position on Climate Change. In *Europe and Global Climate Change – Politics, Foreign Policy and Regional Cooperation*, edited by Paul G. Harris. 211-231. Cheltenham: Edward Elgar.

Oberthür, Sebastian. 1993. *Politik im Treibhaus: Die Entstehung des internationalen Klimaschutzregimes.* Berlin: Edition Sigma.

Oberthür, Sebastian. 2009. The Negotiating Capacity of the EU in International Institutions: The Case of Climate Change. Paper presented at 5th ECPR General Conference Potsdam, 10-12 September 2009.

Oberthür, Sebastian and Hermann E. Ott. 1999. *The Kyoto Protocol. International Climate Policy for the 21st Century.* Berlin: Springer.

Oberthür, Sebastian and Claire Roche Kelly. 2008. EU Leadership in International Climate Policy: Achievements and Challenges. *International Spectator* 43(3): 35-50.

Ott, Hermann E. 1998. The Kyoto Protocol. Unfinished Business. *Environment* 40(6): 16-20 and 41-45.

Ott, Hermann E. 2002. Global Climate. *Yearbook of International Environmental Law* 12 (2001): 211-221.

Pallemaerts, Marc. 1999. The Decline of Law as an Instrument of Community Environmental Policy. *Law & European Affairs* 9(1999): 338-354.

Pallemaerts, Marc and Rhiannon Williams. 2006. Climate Change: the International and European Policy Framework. In *EU Climate Change Policy: the Challenge of New Regulatory Initiatives,* edited by Marjan Peeters and Kurt Deketelaere. 22-50. Cheltenham: Edward Elgar.

Regulation (EC) No 842/2006 of the European Parliament and of the Council of 17 May 2006 on Certain Fluorinated Greenhouse Gases. *Official Journal of the European Union*, 14 June, L 161/1.

Regulation (EC) No 443/2009 of the European Parliament and of the Council of 23 April 2009 Setting Emission Performance Standards for New Passenger Cars as Part of the Community's Integrated Approach to Reduce CO_2 Emissions from Light-Duty Vehicles. *Official Journal of the European Union*, 5 June, L 140/2.

Schreurs, Miranda A. and Yves Tiberghien. 2007. Multi-Level Reinforcement: Explaining European Union Leadership in Climate Change Mitigation. *Global Environmental Politics* 7(4): 19-46.

Skjærseth, Jon Birger. 1994. The Climate Policy of the EC: Too Hot to Handle? *Journal of Common Market Studies* 32(1): 25-45.

Skjærseth, Jon B. and Jørgen Wettestad. 2008. *EU Emissions Trading: Initiation, Decision-Making and Implementation*. Aldershot: Ashgate.

Stern, Nicholas. 2007. *The Economics of Climate Change. The Stern Review*. Cambridge: Cambridge University Press.

UNFCCC (United Nations Framework Convention on Climate Change). 2008. Report of the Conference of the Parties on its Thirteeth Session, Held in Bali from 3 to 15 December 2007, Addendum. Part Two: Action Taken by the Conference of the Parties at its Thirteenth Session. FCCC/CP/2007/6/Add.1. 14 March 2008. Geneva: UNFCCC.

UNGA (United Nations General Assembly). 1990. UNGA Resolution 45/212 of 21 December 1990. Protection of the Global Climate for Present and Future Generations of Mankind. UN Doc. A/RES/45/212.

Vrolijk, Christiaan. 2002. A New Interpretation of the Kyoto Protocol: Outcomes from The Hague, Bonn and Marrakesh. Briefing Paper No. 1 (April 2002). London: The Royal Institute of International Affairs.

Yamin, Farhana. 2000. The Role of the EU in Climate Negotiations. In *Climate Change and European Leadership: A Sustainable Role for Europe?*, edited by Joyeeta Gupta and Michael Grubb. 47-66. Dordrecht: Kluwer Academic Publishers.

Yamin, Farhana, and Joanna Depledge. 2004. *The International Climate Change Regime. A Guide to Rules, Institutions and Procedures*. Cambridge: Cambridge University Press.

Van Schaik, Louise G. and Christian Egenhofer. 2005. Improving the Climate. Will the New Constitution Strengthen the EU's Performance in International Climate Negotiations? *CEPS Policy Brief,* No. 63, February 2005. Brussels: CEPS.

Van Schaik, Louise G. and Karel Van Hecke. 2008. Skating on Thin Ice: Europe's Internal Climate Policy and its Position in the World. Working Paper Egmont Institute, December.

Wettestad, Jørgen. 2000. The Complicated Development of EU Climate Policy. In *Climate Change and European Leadership: A Sustainable Role for Europe?*, edited by Joyeeta Gupta and Michael Grubb. 25-45. Dordrecht: Kluwer Academic Publishers.

The EU Emissions Trading System Revised (Directive 2009/29/EC)

Jon Birger Skjærseth and Jørgen Wettestad[1]

1.   Introduction

In December 2008, the Heads of States or Government of the European Union and the European Parliament agreed a new climate and energy policy for Europe. The policy consisted of a package of binding measures to deliver on the EU's unilateral target to reduce greenhouse gas (GHG) emissions by 20 per cent by 2020 (or by 30 per cent with an "adequate" international agreement), and put the EU on track towards a low carbon energy economy based on renewable energy sources, energy efficiency and technological innovation.[2] The declared cornerstone of the new package is a reformed EU Emissions Trading System (ETS).

The ETS is the first large-scale international emissions trading system in the field of the environment, covering about half of the CO_2 emissions in the EU. The ETS is a cap-and-trade system; there are limits set to the overall level of national emissions, but companies are allowed to buy and sell allowances for their GHG emissions within those limits.[3] The first ETS Directive was adopted in mid-2003 and established a three-year pilot phase (2005–2007) to precede the main commitment period of the Kyoto Protocol (2008–2012).[4]

The ETS was initially established as a "decentralised" system, as is further elaborated in section 2 of this chapter.[5] Key decisions about the amount

---

1.   Many thanks to Sebastian Oberthür for helpful comments on earlier drafts of this manuscript. Thanks to Maryanne Rygg for editing assistance. Research for this chapter benefited from several interviews with stakeholders in Brussels in 2008 and 2009.
2.   See the chapter by Oberthür and Pallemaerts in this volume.
3.   Allowances are denominated in metric tonnes of carbon dioxide equivalent (CO_2 eq.). One tonne CO_2 eq. is a unit of measurement reflecting the potency of GHGs.
4.   Directive 2003/87/EC.
5.   Skjærseth and Wettestad 2008.

and allocation of allowances were in the hands of the Member States, who drew up National Allocation Plans (NAPs). The overall cap on emissions then became the aggregate of national caps. Allowances were mainly handed out free of charge, and the scope of the system was rather narrow with regard to which sectors and the emission of which GHGs were covered. It targeted the power sector and some selected industries, as well as CO_2 emissions. The system also allowed credits to be imported from third countries through the Kyoto Protocol flexible mechanisms, mainly the Clean Development Mechanism (CDM). The pilot phase proved that emissions trading between 27 countries, by placing a price on carbon, could certainly work in practice. However, the initial ETS did not function very well and the carbon price fluctuated significantly between 2005 and 2008.

In January 2008, the European Commission (hereafter: the Commission) put forward a proposal for a revised ETS post-2012 as part of the climate and energy package.[6] This was a proposal signalling a significant change to the system established in 2003: a much more centralised ETS by excluding NAPs completely; auctioning allowances as the general principle; and more restrictive rules on importing credits from third countries. After a speedy decision-making process, the European Council and the Parliament finally agreed a modified version of the Commission's proposal for a revised ETS Directive in December 2008, together with the rest of the EU climate and energy package.

In this chapter, the following section will document this fascinating process of change: "from the old ETS to the new ETS". In the third section, we will discuss three main explanations for the significant changes which have been adopted, focusing on the role and importance of the Member States, the EU institutions as actors and arenas, the positions of non-state actors and the international climate regime. The fourth and final section will sum up the main findings and discuss the prospects ahead. The changes in the ETS will have significant consequences for the division of power between the EU and the Member States and is likely to enhance companies' incentives to invest in climate-friendly technology.

6. Commission 2008.

2.   Developing the "new" ETS

2.1   The old ETS (2005-2007, 2008-2012): decentralisation, free allowances, and start-up problems

In the process leading up to the 1997 Kyoto Protocol, the EU was a leading sceptic of the US-flavoured idea of using flexibility mechanisms such as emissions trading to attain international climate policy goals.[7] The EU was concerned that such mechanisms would be a strategy for main emitters to avoid domestic action, and had previously favoured and utilised other policy instruments, such as technology standards. But flexibility mechanisms did become an integral part of the Kyoto Protocol, and from mid-1998 onwards, the Commission initiated a turn-about in the EU position. The EU decided to develop its own internal emissions trading system and become an international frontrunner in the field.

As an important step in the process of designing such a system, a Green Paper was put forward in 2000.[8] This paper was based on reports from European and US consultants, among others.[9] Although the paper was a discussion paper, it was already evident that the Commission favoured a design with similarities to the quite centralised US air-pollutants trading system.[10] Such a design would also place the Commission in a prominent position. Hence, the paper pleaded for a centralised approach to decide the total amount of allowances (the cap) and the allocation of these allowances. It was noted that a more decentralised approach could lead to national differences and an uneven economic playing field. Furthermore, the system was to have quite a narrow scope. The main focus was on electricity and heat production, with five other less significant industrial sectors also singled out. This would facilitate the administration of the system and the monitoring of emissions. Auctioning was the preferable method of allocating allowances, based on standard economic textbook wisdom.

However, critical responses from key Member States, such as Germany and the UK, and from industry were put forward both in position papers and in consultation meetings. The Commission then advanced a directive

7.   See Grubb et al. 1999; Skjærseth and Wettestad 2008.
8.   Commission 2000.
9.   This was the London-based "Foundation for International Environmental Law and Development" (FIELD) and the US "Center for Clean Air Policy" (CCAP).
10.   The US started a SO_2 trading programme in the mid-1990s. See e.g. Stavins 2003; Kruger and Pizer 2004.

proposal in October 2001 that differed on several important points from the design options positively outlined in the Green Paper. First and foremost, it was proposed to establish initially a system with a fundamentally decentralised approach to setting emission caps. Hence, these caps and the more specific distribution of allowances in each Member State were to be set out in NAPs. The Commission would play the role of watchdog to ensure states adhered to the agreed common allocation criteria. Furthermore, a system based on free allowances was proposed. There was significant scepticism to the prospect of allowance auctioning, both among Member States and industries. In addition, a more specific monitoring and compliance system was proposed, with a pilot phase penalty for non-compliance of 50 Euro (or twice the average market price) per tonne of CO_2 emitted above the allocated quantity; this penalty was to double in the Kyoto Protocol commitment period.

In other respects, however, the 2001 directive proposal was in line with the Green Paper. The system would start with a first pilot phase from 2005-2007, followed by the second, Kyoto commitment phase from 2008-2012. A narrow and limited initial system was proposed, targeting only CO_2 and "energy activities", representing by far the main part of regulatory action. Three other groups of "activities" were also included, covering e.g. steel, cement, glass and pulp and paper industries. The option to bank (i.e. save) allowances from the pilot phase for the Kyoto phase was a decision for each Member State, as such banking did not sit well with the fact that it was in the Kyoto commitment phase that the EU and Member States first had binding international obligations, and the need for regulatory action was most pressing. But banking would be less problematic from the Kyoto phase to subsequent phases; as such banking would take place between phases where the EU most likely had binding international obligations. Links between the ETS and the Kyoto Protocol's flexibility mechanisms, i.e. the Clean Development Mechanism (CDM) and Joint Implementation (JI), were seen as desirable. Due to uncertainty at the time about the final rules of these mechanisms, however, a separate subsequent linking proposal was suggested.

As important concerns and sentiments among the Member States had hence been integrated into the directive proposal, key elements of the proposal were not altered in the decision-making process and became central features of the final 2003 ETS Directive. This goes for decentralisation, free allocation as a ground rule, and the narrow scope. Furthermore, with regard to the included sectors, there were no signals to national decision-makers about a sectoral differentiation in the distribution of allowances.

As to new elements, eleven more specific criteria for producing NAPs were now specified in Annex III of the Directive. It was particularly specified that, prior to 2008, the total quantity of allowances to be allocated should be consistent with a path towards achieving or over-achieving the Kyoto Protocol target.[11] Although the system was basically set up as a mandatory one, there was an opening up for a temporary exemption or opt-out of "certain installations" on specified conditions, and also an opening for unilateral inclusion of additional activities ("opt-in"). The chemicals, aluminium and transport sectors were mentioned as specific candidates for future inclusion in the system, to be further discussed in a 2006 review report. Although free allocation was the ground rule, a limited amount of auctioning was possible, particularly as a nod to inputs from the European Parliament, i.e. maximum five per cent in the pilot phase and ten per cent in the 2008-2012 phase. With regard to the external links to the Kyoto mechanisms, Article 30 also contained a further specification of the nature of the link, by emphasising that the use of the mechanisms should be supplemental to domestic action.

A process to specify the links to the global flexibility mechanisms immediately followed the 2003 Directive. This process was finalised in April 2004. It was then possible to use CDM credits during the ETS pilot phase, and JI credits could be used from 2008.[12] The Linking Directive did not, however, establish a specific ceiling on the use of such external credits.

The ETS was then launched as planned in January 2005. Assessments of the Allocation Plans produced in the course of 2004 indicated that Member States had adopted a cautious approach and allocated generous amounts of allowances to industry.[13] Hence, there were low expectations for a significant scarcity in the market and corresponding high allowance prices. Contrary to these expectations, allowance prices climbed to surprisingly high levels from mid-2005 on, peaking at around 30 Euro in July 2005. This was probably due to the fact that many (small) industries were slow to enter this new market, creating an artificial impression of scarcity. The high allowance price was also accompanied by increasing electricity prices. Some claimed that the latter was caused by the former, and energy-

11. In the 1998 Burden Sharing Agreement, the EU's eight per cent reduction target taken on in the Kyoto Protocol was distributed among the then 15 Member States. See e.g. Ringius 1999 and the chapter by Lacasta et al. in this volume.
12. Directive 2004/101/EC; Hægstad Flåm 2009.
13. E.g. Ecofys 2004; Grubb et al. 2005.

intensive industries complained about power companies making "windfall profits".[14] This discussion continued throughout the pilot phase.

However, ETS dynamics changed dramatically in the spring of 2006, when the verified ETS 2005 emission figures were put on the table and showed that four per cent more allowances had been handed out than were really needed.[15] The suspicion that the whole ETS pilot phase was "over-allocated" was then confirmed and the allowance price immediately halved – and continued to drop to close to zero in 2007. When the second phase of the ETS started in 2008, allowance prices gained some strength again. The second round of allocation of allowances was mainly carried out in 2006 and produced more ambitious and hence less generous NAPs. This was due largely to a tougher watchdog line adopted by the Commission, leading to significant cuts in the NAPs of key ETS countries such as Germany and Poland. Furthermore, a new element in this second phase was that allowances could more easily be banked to subsequent phases, potentially stabilising allowance prices.[16] In January 2008, allowances were sold for around 22 Euro. But at this point in time, the Commission had put forward a proposal for a significantly reformed ETS post-2012.

2.2 Preparing the "new" ETS (2013-2020): centralisation and auctioning

Article 30 of the 2003 Directive stated that, on the basis of experiences and progress achieved, the Commission was to draw up a review report by 30 June 2006, "accompanied by proposals as appropriate". The Commission started working on the review in the autumn of 2005, initiating, among other things, a web survey on the ETS for government officials and non-governmental stakeholders. As a linked development, the process of extending the scope of the ETS to aviation had started, and a first Communication on the subject was put forward.[17] Strong impetus for ETS reform was the Commission's November 2006 Communication on

---

14. Windfall profits for power producers stem from these producers receiving emissions trading allowances for free, and also reaping profits from increases in electricity prices related to the very introduction of emissions trading.
15. E.g. Ellerman and Buchner 2007.
16. Commission 2001, 12. In the Commission's 2001 directive proposal, it was suggested that the right to bank allowances from one trading period to another would be a legally binding requirement from 2008 onwards. This was not explicitly repeated and adopted in the final 2003 Directive however.
17. Commission 2005a.

"Building a Global Carbon Market".[18] A special working group under the second European Climate Change Programme (ECCP II) was to prepare recommendations for a revised ETS in close collaboration with important stakeholders (industry, environmental non-governmental organisations and think-tanks).

At this point in time, climate change had really started to climb the political agenda of Member States and EU institutions. In 2003, 39 per cent of respondents to a Eurobarometer survey listed climate change as their main worry, increasing to 45 per cent in 2005. By 2007, this figure had increased to 57 per cent.[19] Strongly signalling that times were changing with regard to EU climate policy, the Commission proposed a package of climate and energy policies[20] with several new "20 per cent" targets. These so-called 20+20+20 targets were then adopted by EU leaders in March 2007.[21] Most importantly for ETS reform was the EU's overall pledge to cut GHG emissions by 20 per cent from 1990 levels by 2020 (and 30 per cent if the world followed suit). Other targets adopted by the Council include a binding target of 20 per cent share for renewable energy by 2020, matched by a ten per cent target for biofuels, and a 20 per cent target to improve energy efficiency by 2020.[22]

With the backdrop of new targets and a new dynamic in EU climate policy, four stakeholder meetings were held in the working group on the ETS reform under the ECCP II. The first meeting was held in the beginning of March 2007, discussing "the scope of the directive" and the expansion of the ETS to other sectors and gases. A cautious broadening came forward as a natural development. The second meeting took place in April and focused on "robust compliance and enforcement". Although this part of the ETS had worked reasonably well, there was a clear need for further harmonisation of practices. The theme of harmonisation was followed up at the third meeting in late May, discussing "further harmonisation and increased predictability". A strong call for more harmonisation could be noted at this meeting, although not necessarily a centralised EU cap. The participants from the new EU Member States emphasised the need for some continued flexibility also, in order to accommodate differences in economic development and possible impact on economic growth. With regard to the method of allocation, a number of Member States spoke out

18. Commission 2006a.
19. Commission 2008.
20. Commission 2007c.
21. European Council 2007.
22. See the chapters by Howes and by Oberthür and Pallemaerts in this volume.

in favour of auctioning.[23] But there was also considerable opposition and hesitancy within industry towards auctioning, particularly among the energy-intensive industries. The fourth and final ECCP meeting, held in June, discussed "linking with emissions trading schemes of third countries". With regard to the character of the links to CDM/JI, positions were mixed – only some favoured stricter quantitative limits.[24]

After intense lobbying in late 2007 and early 2008, not least from energy-intensive industries, the Commission put forward the ETS reform proposal on 23 January 2008.[25] Significant changes were proposed. First, the Commission proposed to introduce a single, EU-wide cap, and allocate allowances on the basis of fully-harmonised rules for the period 2013–2020. NAPs would therefore simply no longer be needed. The level of the EU-wide ETS cap would be calculated on the basis of the 20 per cent by 2020 at 1990 levels target, which is equivalent to a 14 per cent reduction compared to 2005. The linear reduction consistent with this target amounts to 1.74 per cent per year, arriving at a reduction of ETS emissions of 21 per cent below 2005 emissions in 2020.

The second important change proposed that auctioning would be the main principle for all allocation. However, a key differentiation was proposed between installations "engaged in electricity production" and "industrial installations". With regard to the former, full auctioning was the proposed rule from 2013 onwards, taking into account power producers' ability to pass on the increased costs of CO_2 emissions.[26] For the energy-intensive industry and other sectors covered by the ETS, a transitional system was foreseen, where the amount of free allocations would be gradually reduced from 80 per cent in 2013 to zero in 2020. In the event that other developed countries and other major emitters did not participate in an international agreement, and certain EU industries and sub-sectors subject to international competition could be put at an economic disadvantage, the Community would allocate allowances free of charge up to 100 per cent to sub-sectors meeting relevant criteria. Such sub-sectors ought to be identified by mid-2010, but a re-assessment would be carried out in mid-2011 referring to any new international or sectoral climate agreements that may then be in place.

No new CDM or JI credits were to enter the system (only those banked from the 2008-2012 phase) unless a "satisfactory" new global climate

---

23. Commission 2007a, 19.
24. Commission 2007b.
25. Commission 2008.
26. Commission 2008, 15.

agreement was agreed and a move to the more ambitious 30 per cent EU goal took place. In that case, additional CDM and JI credits would be allowed into the ETS, covering up to half of the additional reduction effort needed. In addition, the Commission proposed a gradual increase in the scope of the system, with regard to sectors (e.g. to include aluminium and some chemicals sectors) and gases (i.e. to include nitrous oxides and perfluorocarbons). Carbon Trust analysed that "the proposals for allocation amount to a revolution in the approach adopted and in the division of powers between the EU and Member States".[27]

Complementing the ETS reform proposal, three other proposals made up the 2008 climate and energy package: a proposal on burden-sharing for emissions reductions in the non-ETS sectors, in the form of differing national targets; a proposal for an increase to 20 per cent of the share of renewable energy of total energy consumption; and a proposed regulatory framework for developing carbon capture and storage (CCS) in the EU. New legislation was also underway for CO_2 emissions from cars and for fuel quality. Hence, in the further decision-making process, there was clearly a potential for horse-trading and linking between the proposals; both of the positive, integrative kind and the negative, complicating kind. It should further be added that the process of including aviation had progressed on the basis of a Commission proposal put forward in December 2006 and was entering its final decision-making stages in 2008.[28]

2.3   The speedy decision-making process

It was clear that the ETS reform needed to be completed before the seminal UNFCCC Copenhagen meeting in 2009, and time was very tight – even tighter than in the process leading up to the 2003 Directive. Hence, discussions of various aspects of ETS reform started in the EU bodies soon after the launching of the Commission's proposal. By summer 2008, the preliminary discussions had outlined some main positions and issues before the decisive ETS reform battle unfolded in autumn. First, the suggested key move towards a centralised approach was, perhaps surprisingly, little debated. Second, several key countries, such as Germany, highlighted the situation of energy-intensive industries and the possibility of global "carbon leakage" if these industries were not guaranteed continued free allowances. Follow-up meetings on this subject

---

27.   Carbon Trust 2008, 17.
28.   See the chapter by Oberthür and Pallemaerts in this volume.

were held within the ECCP. Third, new Member States, such as Poland, voiced fears that the introduction of auctioning would threaten the economic viability of the many coal-fired power stations in these countries. Hence, an East-West dimension had become manifest in the ETS reform process.[29]

As an important decision-making clarification, the French EU Presidency announced in mid-October that ETS reform was going to be decided at a European Council meeting scheduled for December, together with the other elements of the package.[30] This was another sign of the elevation of climate change to the top-level political agenda. As decisions in the European Council are made by unanimity due to its traditional role as the venue for "history-making decisions" in the EU,[31] it had important implications for the whole decision-making dynamic, as will be further discussed in section 3.3.

A key move in the process was the Parliament's Environment Committee debate on ETS reform in early October. The Committee finally gave support to the basic reformed ETS architecture proposed by the Commission, on centralisation, on the move towards more auctioning, and on the rather restrictive line on the use of external credits.[32] Nevertheless, the Committee also called for *all* auctioning revenues to be earmarked for climate-related purposes, and that up to 500 million allowances from the new entrants reserve should be set aside as a funding mechanism for CCS projects. The new entrants reserve is a pool of allowances for companies starting up production in the allocation period. In the end, the proposals were carried by 44 to 20 votes in the Committee (with one abstention).

The parallel process of including aviation in the ETS was brought to its conclusion following the vote in the Environment Committee. Aviation was to be included in the ETS from 2012 onwards.[33] The ETS reform process was now entering its final and decisive decision-making month – against the

---

29. E.g. EU Energy 2008, 5; Point Carbon 2008c; Reuters Planetark 2008.
30. European Council 2008.
31. See e.g. Peterson 1995; McCormick 1999, 116.
32. Looking at this in more detail, the Committee put forward a different formula and procedure than that of the Commission. Analysts in *Point Carbon* indicated afterwards that the EP in fact opened up for a little *more* use of CDM in the ETS than proposed by the Commission (Point Carbon 2008c). The Committee also suggested that only "high-quality" CDM credits should be allowed into the ETS, without defining this element.
33. The 2012 cap was set at 97 per cent of average 2004-2006 airline emissions, and 85 per cent of allowances would be allocated for free. From 2013 onwards, the cap would be set at 95 per cent of average 2004-2006 emissions. See Directive 2008/101/EC.

backdrop of a worsening financial crisis. Most of this phase consisted of so-called trialogue meetings and negotiations between representatives from the Commission, Parliament and Council. The December Council meeting needed not only to decide on ETS reform, but also the final negotiations on the non-ETS effort sharing decision and the CCS Directive. Hence, the stage was set for some frantic final horse-trading and complex compromises.

Let us then sum up the main elements of the final outcome. First, the Council adopted what the Commission proposed in January with regard to the cap. So from 2013 onwards, the ETS will have a single, EU-wide cap; allowances will be allocated on the basis of fully harmonised rules; the level of the EU-wide cap will be calculated on the basis of the target for 20 per cent GHG emission reductions by 2020 compared to 1990 levels, which is equivalent to a 14 per cent reduction compared to 2005; the linear reduction principle of 1.74 per cent per year means arriving at a reduction of ETS emissions of 21 per cent below 2005 levels (and ten per cent for the sectors not covered by the ETS).[34]

Second, significant elements of the outcome on allocation were in line with the Commission proposal. Hence, auctioning was introduced as the main allocation method, based on a differentiated system between the power-producing sector and the power-consuming sector, i.e. various energy-intensive industries. As a general principle, the power sector needs to buy all of its allowances from 2013. Other industries only need to buy at least 20 per cent of their allowances in 2013, increasing to at least 70 per cent by 2020 (with a view to reaching 100 per cent in 2027). Furthermore, within the group of energy-intensive industries, some industrial sectors or sub-sectors particularly exposed to global competition and hence in danger of "carbon leakage" will be guaranteed free allowances in the period 2013-2020, based on state-of-the-art technology benchmarks.[35] Allocation based on benchmarks will, where feasible, replace allocation based on historical

---

34. This path has been calculated by starting at the mid-point of the 2008-2012 period average annual total amount of issued allowances. Also, the linear factor of 1.74 will continue to be applied to trading periods beyond 2020 to achieve necessary reductions by 2050 to limit the global average temperature increase to 2 degrees Celsius above pre-industrial levels. See Article 9 of Directive 2009/29/EC.
35. The Commission will assess whether the direct and indirect additional production costs induced by the implementation of the ETS Directive as a proportion of gross value added exceed five per cent *and* whether the total value of its exports and imports divided by the total value of its turnover and imports exceeds ten per cent. If the result for either of these criteria exceeds 30 per cent, the sector would be considered to be exposed to a significant risk of carbon leakage. See Article 10(a) of Directive 2009/29/EC.

emissions. Such benchmarks better reward operators that have taken early action, give stronger incentives to reduce emissions and conform more fully to the polluter pays principle. The discussion and determination of the sectors and installations in danger of carbon leakage has commenced and the Commission's list will be published by 31 December 2009.[36] Hence, the clarification timetable here has been stepped up compared to the Commission proposal.

More new elements were added to the outcome on the allocation of allowances. For instance, a differentiation was introduced within the power sector. Installations poorly integrated into the European electricity grid or that individually provide more than 30 per cent of national electricity in countries with relatively low GDP (such as Poland and other Eastern European countries) can opt for free allocation up to a maximum total of 70 per cent of all allowances in 2013, declining gradually to zero by 2020.[37] With regard to auctioning revenues, 80 per cent of such revenues will be distributed among the Member States according to their ETS emissions in 2005 (or average of 2005–2007). Ten per cent of these revenues are to be redistributed from Member States with high per capita incomes to those with low incomes, in order to strengthen the capacity of the latter to invest in climate-friendly technologies. An additional two per cent is to be distributed to countries whose GHG emissions in 2005 were at least 20 per cent below their Kyoto base-year emissions. As emphasised by the Parliament, 300 million allowances from the new entrants reserve will be set aside to support up to twelve CCS demonstration projects and projects demonstrating renewable energy technologies. In addition, as a piece of non-binding guidance, the Member States are *recommended* to use 50 per cent of the revenues on measures to fight and adapt to climate change mainly within the EU, but also in developing countries.[38]

Third, with regard to external links to the Kyoto flexibility mechanisms, a cap has been introduced on the use of imported credits.[39] In the second

---

36. The situation and risk of carbon leakage will also be reviewed by the Commission in the wake of the Copenhagen 2009 meeting by 30 June 2010. See Article 10(b) of Directive 2009/29/EC.
37. Other conditions are: 1) no country can allocate more than 70 per cent free allowances to the power sector in 2013, with this share declining; 2) free allowances can only be given to installations operational or under construction no later than end 2008. See Article 10(c) of Directive 2009/29/EC.
38. See particularly Article 10(3)(c) of Directive 2009/29/EC.
39. Compared to a 2003/2004 baseline, this is a clear change. However, such a cap was first introduced in 2006, in connection with the process of producing allocation plans for the 2008-2012 period.

trading period (2008-2012), the Member States allowed participating companies to use significant quantities of credits to cover part of their emissions. The revised Directive extends these rights for the third trading period (2013 onwards) and allows an additional quantity up to 50 per cent of the EU-wide reductions for the 2008-2020 period. There are no binding quality criteria for projects in third countries, but buyers must report on their quality. If a satisfactory new international climate agreement is adopted in Copenhagen at the end of 2009, and the EU's overall reduction target is increased to 30 per cent, then half of the extra effort required by ETS installations may be covered by such external credits.

3. Explaining the significant reform

3.1 Three explanatory lenses

The focus for explanation is the *change* from the old to the new ETS. The following analysis concentrates on explaining three main developments and changes of the ETS, related to cap-setting and harmonisation; allocation method; and links to the Kyoto Protocol's flexible mechanisms. As elaborated in far more detail elsewhere,[40] we find it useful to apply three main complementary explanatory perspectives. These perspectives should here be seen as heuristic devices emphasising changes in different actors and institutions at different levels over time.

First, the *liberal intergovernmentalist* approach regards EU policy-making and integration mainly as a result of interstate bargaining, so that the interests and preferences of the EU Member States are the key to understanding the ETS reform. The core claim is that EU policy-making is determined primarily by national governments that are constrained by domestic political interests.[41] The *changes* of the EU ETS are thus compatible with a liberal intergovernmentalist approach to the extent that the Member States changed their positions or gained more influence.[42]

Second, *multi-level governance* is an alternative to state-centred intergovernmentalist approaches of European policy-making.[43] There are

40. Skjærseth and Wettestad 2008; 2009.
41. E.g. Moravcsik 1998.
42. The main reasons for changes in position can be new knowledge based on experience with the old system, new material interests, and new ideas and norms concerning emissions trading as a policy instrument.
43. E.g. Hooghe and Marks 2001; Fairbrass and Jordan 2004.

many different variants of multi-level governance approaches, but all share the same assumption that European integration has weakened the state. This approach would explain the EU ETS by pointing to the complexity of actors and institutions involved at different levels of decision-making. Key assumptions are, first, that institutions (such as the Commission and Parliament) are supranational actors and have acquired an independent influence on policy-making that exceeds their role as agents for national governments. Moreover, institutions are arenas[44] that determine who deals with what, how, when and where, which can affect actors' incentives to adopt changes.[45] Second, non-state actors influence policy-making, not only through the formation of national preferences but also directly at EU-level, and form an important part of the integration process. The changes in the EU ETS are in line with multi-level governance to the extent that non-state actors, and particularly supranational EU institutions "as actors", changed their positions, or the EU institutions "as arenas" changed and affected the ETS changes.

Common to both liberal intergovernmentalism and multi-level governance is the emphasis on EU internal factors and processes to explain EU policy-making. However, factors external to the EU can also affect EU policies.[46] Our point of departure here is the impact of international regimes. The most relevant regime in this specific context is the climate regime including the 1992 UN Framework Convention on Climate Change (UNFCCC), its 1997 Kyoto Protocol and the negotiation on a possible new UN-based climate treaty in 2009. The changes in the EU ETS are in line with an international-regime approach to the extent that the EU institutions and actors reformed the EU ETS in response to changes in the international climate regime, particularly pertaining to the link between the EU ETS and the Kyoto Protocol's flexible project mechanisms CDM and JI.

3.2 Member States

The baseline positions of the Member States were already mentioned in section 2: a majority of the EU-15 preferred a decentralised system with

---

44. Institutions as arenas are compatible with liberal intergovernmentalist approaches to the extent that they serve as an arena for interaction between states. In this paper, we will use the term more broadly in a multi-level governance context to depict relationships between states, non-state and organisational actors at different levels and sectors of society.
45. Underdal 2002, 24.
46. E.g. Weale et al. 2000; Skjærseth and Wettestad 2002.

regard to the cap, free allocation of allowances based on historic emissions (grandfathering) and full access to external credits.[47]

The positions of the Member States changed on most of these key design elements in the process leading up the Commission's proposal for a revised ETS in January 2008. First, the emerging changes in positions on harmonisation surfaced in the Climate Change Committee in the autumn of 2006 and in the consultation process within the European Climate Change Programme (ECCP) framework in 2007.[48] As noted, there was now a strong call for more harmonisation, but not necessarily a centralised EU cap. This change, along with a preference for more auctioning, was indicated in the mentioned web survey as early as 2005.[49] But the new Eastern European Member States emphasised the need for some continued flexibility in order to accommodate possible impacts on economic growth.

With regard to the allocation method, the more positive view on the use of auctioning indicated in the 2005 survey was now further confirmed.[50] As to auctioning revenues, the dominant mood among Member States emphasised national control, but with a certain openness to the idea of earmarking some of these revenues for environmental purposes.[51] The Member States' experiences of the pilot phase, including cumbersome NAP processes, suspicions of "free riders", and debates about "windfall profits", encouraged the turn to centralisation and more auctioning.

Did the decision-making process in 2008 show some other significant changes in Member States' positions? One interesting aspect of the decision-making process is the very limited attention given to the undoubtedly important turn towards a cap-setting process at EU level. Brussels' insiders refer to the cap as the "firewall" in the ETS.[52] It is likely that lack of attention reflects the strong call for more harmonisation and the already settled overall 20 per cent target. If Member States really had questioned this part of the reform, they would likely have faced demands for further emission reductions from non-ETS sectors instead.

The Member States instead fought other battles. One such battle was the use of auctioning revenues. Quite soon after the Commission launched its proposal, Member States (read: finance ministries) came out strongly

47. Skjærseth and Wettestad 2008.
48. Wettestad 2009.
49. Commission 2006b.
50. See Commission 2007a, 19.
51. Commission 2007a, 20.
52. Interviews in Brussels, May 2009.

against the Commission's earmarking proposal.[53] This position was basically retained throughout the decision-making process. The final outcome, providing mainly non-binding recommendations on the use of revenues, was a clear victory for the Member States' common position.

As to the more general question of auctioning, the noted East-West split only grew stronger in the course of the negotiation process, fuelled by the global economic crisis unfolding in autumn 2008. Poland in particular, but also other Eastern European Member States, increasingly emphasised the need to protect their coal-fired power stations from 100 per cent auctioning from 2013 onwards. In this, they largely succeeded, with derogations all the way to 2020.[54] However, probably the liveliest debate was regarding the treatment of energy-intensive industries and the identification of the sectors most vulnerable to global competition. Member States were more impatient to identify these sectors than the timetable suggested by the Commission, and they managed to move their identification from mid-2010 to December 2009. Germany, in particular, stood out as a staunch proponent for securing free allowances to energy-intensive industries.

With regard to access to external credits, Member States also fought a rather united battle against the Commission's and the Parliament's suggested tightening, albeit less intense than on auctioning revenues. Particularly countries such as Spain and the Netherlands, with quite extensive CDM portfolios, argued for a more liberal access to such credits.[55] The final outcome must be counted as a partial success for these countries: more liberal rules than those proposed by the Commission, but still a cap on the quantity of credits.

The impression is that the positions of the Member States changed and contributed significantly to the outcome of the ETS reform process. However, the outcomes appear more far-reaching and ambitious than the positions of the least enthusiastic states and coalitions, particularly in light of the requirement for unanimity in the European Council. For example, the Eastern European Member States did not favour a stringent EU wide-cap and auctioning as the main principle.

---

53. ENDS Europe Daily 2008.
54. However, the derogations only represent possibilities and options. As revenues are tempting for finance ministries, it remains to be seen to what extent they are used in practice.
55. ENDS Report October 2008, 46.

3.3   EU institutions and non-state actors

As in the "old ETS", the Commission and the Parliament clearly favoured a centralised, harmonised ETS, with limits on import of credits and auctioning of allowances as the main principle. Although the preferences of these bodies changed little, these positions could now be put forward on the basis of practical experiences. As indicated, experiences from the pilot phase (2005-2007) highlighted the problematic "decentralised anarchy" and windfall profits related to the handing out of free allowances. Recognition that these problems needed resolving was widely shared within the EU, including among non-state stakeholders.

Parts of industry and environmental organisations (ENGOs) supported the Commission's quest for a reformed and more effective ETS. While ENGOs were previously only lukewarm supporters of the emissions trading idea, they now came forward as more enthusiastic supporters of the proposed changes. Within industry, the most decisive change was the support of cap-setting at EU-level to ensure a level playing field. Power-producing industries also accepted the turn towards more auctioning. For the Commission, the fact that the industry itself, to a significant extent, called for change was seen as a "watershed development".[56] However, energy-intensive industry strongly opposed auctioning and all industries have argued for full access to external credits. Parts of the energy-intensive industry lobbied ferociously, and the European Parliament had registered over 160 groups lobbying mainly for free allowances in October 2008.[57]

The broader institutional arena and political context also changed significantly from the old to the new system. Of prime importance in this regard is the broader climate and energy policy drive that started in the EU in autumn 2005. In addition to the initiation of the more specific climate and energy package described in section two, the Commission presented a broader energy policy "vision" in the January 2007 Communication "An Energy Policy for Europe".[58] The wording was certainly radical, speaking of "catalysing a new industrial revolution".[59] A strategic energy plan was put forward, seeing the goals of mitigating climate change, security of supply, and provision of competitive energy as mutually reinforcing

---

56.   Interviews in Brussels, May 2009.
57.   Interviews in Brussels, May 2009.
58.   Commission 2007c. See also the chapter by Howes in this volume.
59.   Commission 2007c, 5.

objectives in line with the 2000 Lisbon Strategy.[60] When the Council adopted the 20 per cent targets and the energy plan in March 2007, it invited the Commission to "review the EU Emissions Trading Scheme in good time with a view to increase transparency and strengthening and broadening the scope of the scheme".[61] This means that the strengthening of the ETS had the backing of the highest political level in all of the EU countries well before the Commission's proposal in January 2008. Underlying this broad drive was the general increase in climate policy saliency in the EU from 2006, influencing both Member States and EU institutions.

There were also more specific changes to the process of how decisions are made. Three other Directives were initially negotiated at the same time as the reform of the ETS. This package approach allowed more bargaining between rich and poor Member States, compared to negotiating emissions trading in isolation from other policies. A guiding principle for the package is that no Member State should make investments which diverge too far from 0.5 per cent average of GDP. This was ensured by the reform of the ETS and the links to other parts of the package in at least three ways: first, by setting differentiated national targets in the non-ETS sectors; second, by setting differentiated national targets for the share of EU energy consumption to be achieved by renewable energy; and, finally, by using auctioning revenues to compensate lower-income Member States.[62]

Direct links were established between the process of negotiating a Directive on carbon capture and storage (CCS) and the use of ETS allowances from the new entrants reserve to fund CCS demonstration projects.[63] The fact that the Parliament was able to get a larger share of allowances to finance CCS projects than proposed by the Commission made it easier for the Parliament to accept the increase of free allowances for energy-intensive industries particularly, which was a main element of the European Council outcome. With regard to the effort-sharing decision covering emissions of the non-ETS sectors,[64] additional flexibility with regard to importing CDM credits probably made it easier for the Commission and Parliament to withstand an even further watering down of ETS reform. The new

60. The European Council in Lisbon in March 2000 adopted the target of making the EU the most dynamic and competitive knowledge-based economy in the world, capable of sustainable economic growth, with more and better jobs, greater social cohesion, and respect for the environment by 2010.
61. European Council 2007, 12.
62. See the chapters by Howes and by Lacasta et al. in this volume.
63. See the chapter by Chiavari in this volume.
64. See the chapter by Lacasta et al. in this volume.

legislation on cars and fuel quality, which was initially kept outside the package, also became part of the negotiations in autumn 2008.[65] Italy got more lenient emissions rules for small cars in exchange for supporting the package, and Germany got its way on free allocation for energy-intensive industry in exchange for accepting more stringent rules on car emissions than originally preferred.[66]

In addition to ETS reform being negotiated side-by-side with various other Directives, the French Presidency's push to decide everything at the December 2008 European Council was an important (and for many, surprising) move.[67] It meant that the legislative proposal did not go through the full co-decision procedure, including a common position in the Council, two rounds ("Readings") in the Parliament, and sometimes even a final round in a conciliation committee. Instead, trialogue talks between the Commission, Parliament and the Council were to sort out the main disagreements in a much more rapid, *single* round. The most unusual element here was the involvement of the European Council in hammering out a final deal in December 2008. As the action-packed European Council meeting took place *prior* to the first reading in the Parliament, the basic possibilities for the Parliament were narrowed down to two choices: accept or reject. It accepted. Still, the Parliament did not demand radical changes, so the alleged "sidelining of the Parliament" was perhaps mainly a matter of injured pride.[68] The European Parliament endorsed the deal on 17 December 2008.

To tentatively sum up, acknowledging EU institutions as both arenas and actors, at least three main changes occurred, which contribute to under-standing the significant changes of the ETS. First, although the Commis-sion's and Parliament's preferences for centralisation and auctioning did not change, these preferences could now be put forward in a much more convincing manner, based on actual experience with the ETS. Second, the preferences for a much more streamlined and effective system also played well with changes in how decisions are made. As a response to the increased saliency of climate change among EU citizens, the EU started developing a vitalised and much more integrated climate and energy

65. See the chapters by ten Brink and by Hey in this volume.
66. Interviews in Brussels, May 2009.
67. This was a Directive put forward under the co-decision procedure, to be adopted by the Council and Parliament under the formal rule of qualified majority voting.
68. Still, the Parliament's Rapporteur Avril Doyle stated that she was satisfied with the outcome. The Parliament did achieve something with regard to the number of ETS allowances set aside for CCS, an issue that very much originated from the Parliament (Interviews in Brussels, May 2009).

policy. More ambitious targets were matched by a package of new policies, where energy policy and climate policy were linked in a new way. Third, as the European Council's unanimity requirement made it necessary to placate laggards and water down the final outcome, the package approach also made it possible to let those reluctant to have more of their way in other processes (such as non-ETS effort-sharing and car emissions) and hence withstand a further watering down of ETS reform. This may, of course, also have worked the other way around, i.e. that some ETS compromises may have countered a further watering down of other policies. This is a matter for further research.

3.4   The international climate regime

Under the Kyoto Protocol, the EU made a commitment to reduce emissions by eight per cent in the period 2008–2012. Furthermore, the Protocol established three flexible mechanisms, i.e. international emissions trading; the CDM; and JI. This development of the climate regime made it an important "source institution" for the main phases in the development of the EU ETS.[69]

When the EU and other actors met for further deliberations on a successor to the Kyoto Protocol in Bali at the end of 2007, "slow progress" was the message to the world. However, the adoption of the Bali Action Plan, aiming for the adoption of a post-2012 global agreement in Copenhagen in 2009, was a comforting element. When the Commission put forward its ETS reform proposal in January 2008, it was, in several ways, placed within a global context. First, echoing earlier ambitions for the EU to exert global leadership,[70] the very package was cast as a means and source to achieve an ambitious and comprehensive agreement in Copenhagen. Hence, the global regime had become mainly a target institution for the EU. The 20 per cent commitment was meant to demonstrate that the EU was serious, and the possibility of increasing the ambition to 30 per cent if the world followed suit was meant to sweeten any global deal.

Second, with regard to the CDM/JI link, the Commission sought to balance several concerns. Due to the uncertainty about the real inflow of external credits into the ETS in the 2008-2012 phase, the related fears of downward pressure on carbon prices and reduced EU-internal abatement, as well as the uncertainties about the effects of banked emission credits on the post-

---

69.   Oberthür and Gehring 2006; Skjærseth and Wettestad 2008.
70.   On EU climate leadership, see for example Gupta and Grubb 2000; Oberthür and Roche Kelly 2008.

2012 market, the Commission put forward a quite restrictive proposal for CDM/JI inflow post-2012. Mainly banked credits were to be used. On the other hand, as a further global negotiation sweetener and a comforting nod to the CDM institution, if a "satisfactory" global deal *was* reached and the EU moved to the more ambitious 30 per cent ambition, half of the extra reduction efforts then required of ETS participants could be covered by external credits.[71]

Third, as the discussion of possible global carbon leakage had increasingly dominated the 2007 discussions about the treatment of energy-intensive industries, the Commission's proposal on this treatment was deliberately ambiguous and open. Again, seen against the backdrop of considerable uncertainty of what would come out of Copenhagen, the Commission suggested carrying out a clarification of the most vulnerable sectors after Copenhagen. Hence, by leaving the degree of EU "protectionist" measures somewhat open, this was another attempt to influence the international negotiations.

4.   Conclusions

This chapter has documented the significant change from the "old ETS" (i.e. the first pilot phase 2005-2007 and the second Kyoto commitment phase 2008-2012) to the "new ETS", meant to govern the system from 2013 to 2020. The old ETS was "decentralised", with no common EU cap on emissions and the total amount and distribution of allowances was mainly decided by Member States. Furthermore, allowances were mainly handed out for free. The initial link to the global CDM/JI mechanisms was loose, although a temporary cap on the use of such credits was introduced.

Compared to this, the new ETS from 2013 will be governed in a much more centralised way. There will be a common and tighter ETS cap, based on the ETS' contribution to achieving the overall ambition of a 20 per cent cut of GHG emissions by 2020. Further allocation specifications mean that the considerable flexibility enjoyed by Member States in the old ETS will almost completely wither away. Furthermore, many more allowances will be auctioned. Sectors will also be treated differently. Most of the power sector's allowances will be auctioned, although only a small part of the energy-intensive   industries'   allowances   will   initially   be   auctioned

---

71. The CDM's Executive Board Chairman stated that the Commission's suggested tightening in the 2008 proposal would be "a pity for the CDM". See Point Carbon 2008a.

(increasing over time). Industries identified as particularly vulnerable to global competition and hence "carbon leakage" will be guaranteed free allowances all the way to 2020. Preliminary findings presented by the Commission in May 2009 indicate that as many as half of the relevant industries may qualify for such free allowances.[72] With regard to external links to the Kyoto flexibility mechanisms, the ad-hoc cap has now been strengthened and written into the formal ETS constitution.

In order to understand these significant changes, we outlined three compatible explanatory perspectives as heuristic devices, focusing on the role of the Member States; the EU institutions as arenas and actors, the role of non-state actors; and the international climate regime. The main conclusion is that all perspectives contribute to understanding the changes, but their relative explanatory power varies. First, the expectation that the Member States changed their positions and requested the reform is to a significant extent supported by our observations. This is in line with a liberal intergovernmentalist understanding of the changes. A likely central background factor is unsatisfactory experiences with the "old ETS". However, another noteworthy observation is that changes in the positions of the Member States are insufficient to explain the scope and the magnitude of the reform, given the decision rule applied.

The second conclusion is that drawing upon a multi-level governance perspective is in several ways important for understanding the significant change of the ETS. First, the very ideas of a centralised and harmonised ETS based on auctioning of allowances were initially launched and favoured by both the Commission and the Parliament (and supported by ENGOs). In addition, the EU institutions, as arenas for initiating and negotiating the reform, changed and affected the outcomes. The reform of the EU ETS was linked to new mandatory targets, EU energy policy and a package of binding climate instruments in a way that would reduce costs and ensure a fairer distribution of costs within the EU.

The third conclusion is that the proposition derived from the international regime approach gained least support. The reform was not a response to changes in the international climate regime, but partly an effort to affect the international climate negotiations. In a way, the reform was to some extent the result of a desire for international change. The international regime context is thus relevant to understand the outcomes, but in a different way than may be anticipated.

72. ENDS Europe Daily 2009.

Is the stage then firmly set for a strengthened and more effective ETS? The answer is, most likely, a "qualified yes". Interviews with a string of Brussels' insiders in the spring of 2009, however, indicate that the December 2008 outcome should possibly be seen more as a very important milestone rather than the final word on the ETS post-2012. If the EU increased its target to a 30 per cent reduction, then the stage could be set for some new and complicated rounds of ETS negotiations. For instance, if global sectoral agreements were reached and the risk of carbon leakage was significantly reduced, what would be left of the so far effective arguments of energy-intensive industries for special treatment and free allowances?

References

Carbon Trust. 2008. *Cutting Carbon in Europe – The 2020 Plans and the Future of the EU ETS*. London: Carbon Trust.

Commission (EC). 2000. Green Paper on Greenhouse Gas Emissions Trading within the European Union. COM (2000) 87 final. Brussels: European Commission.

Commission (EC). 2001. Proposal for a Directive of the European Parliament and of the Council Establishing a Framework for Greenhouse Gas Emissions Trading Within the European Community and Amending Council Directive 96/61/EC. COM (2001) 581. Brussels: European Commission.

Commission (EC). 2005. Winning the Battle Against Global Climate Change. *Communication from the Commission to the Council, the European Parliament, the European Economic and Social Committee and the Committee of the Regions*. SEC (2005) 180. Brussels: European Commission.

Commission (EC). 2006a. Building a Global Carbon Market – Report Pursuant to Article 30 of Directive 2003/87/EC. *Communication from the Commission to the Council, the European Parliament, the European Economic and Social Committee and the Committee of the Regions*. COM (2006) 676. Brussels: European Commission.

Commission (EC). 2006b. EU ETS Review – Report on International Competitiveness. *Report by McKinsey and Ecofys for the European Commission*. Brussels: European Commission.

Commission (EC). 2007a. Further Harmonisation and Increased Predictability. *Final Report of the 3rd Meeting of the ECCP Working Group on Emissions Trading on the Review of the EU ETS.* Brussels: European Commission.

Commission (EC). 2007b. Linking with Emissions Trading Schemes of Third Countries. *Final Report of the 4th Meeting of the ECCP Working Group on Emissions Trading on the Review of the EU ETS.* Brussels: European Commission.

Commission (EC). 2007c. An Energy Policy for Europe. *Communication from the Commission to the European Council and the European Parliament.* SEC (2007) 12. Brussels: European Commission.

Commission (EC). 2008. Attitudes of European Citizens Towards the Environment. *Special Eurobarometer Report.* Brussels: European Commission.

Directive 2003/87/EC of the European Parliament and of the Council of 13 October 2003 Establishing a Scheme for Greenhouse Gas Emission Allowance Trading Within the Community and Amending Council Directive 96/61/EU. *Official Journal of the European Union,* 25 October 2003, L 275.

Directive 2004/101/EC of the European Parliament and of the Council of 27 October 2004 Amending Directive 2003/87/EC Establishing a Scheme for Greenhouse Gas Emission Allowance Trading Within the Community, in Respect of the Kyoto Protocol's Project Mechanisms. *Official Journal of the European Union,* 13 November 2004, L 338/18.

Directive 2008/101/EC of the European Parliament and of the Council of 19 November 2008 Amending Directive 2003/87/EC so as to Include Aviation Activities in the Scheme for Greenhouse Gas Emission Allowance Trading Within the Community. *Official Journal of the European Union,* 13 January 2009, L 8/3.

Directive 2009/29/EC of the European Parliament and of the Council of 23 April 2009 Amending Directive 2003/87/EC so as to Improve and Extend the Greenhouse Gas Emission Allowance Trading Scheme of the Community. *Official Journal of the European Union,* 5 June 2009, L 140/63.

Ecofys. 2004. *Analysis of the National Allocation Plans for the EU Emissions Trading Scheme.* Utrecht: Ecofys.

Ellerman, Denny and Barbara Buchner. 2007. The European Union Emissions Trading Scheme: Origins, Allocation, and Early Results. *Review of Environmental Economics and Policy* 1(1): 66-87.

ENDS Europe Daily. 2008. Ministers Reject Carbon Cash Ring-Fencing. *ENDS Europe Daily*. 12 February 2008, Issue 2482. London: Environmental Data Services.

ENDS Europe Daily. 2009. Huge Array of Sectors to Get Free ETS Allowances. *ENDS Europe Daily*. 8 May 2009, Issue 2538. London: Environmental Data Services.

EU Energy March 2008. Poland Rejects Plans for 100 Per Cent ETS CO_2 Permit Auctions. *EU Energie*, March 21 Issue 179: 5.

European Council. 2007. Brussels European Council 8 and 9 March 2007. *Presidency Conclusions*. 7224/07. Brussels: Council of the European Union.

European Council. 2008. Brussels European Council 15 and 16 October 2008. *Presidency Conclusions*. 14368/08. Brussels: Council of the European Union.

Fairbrass, Jenny and Andrew Jordan. 2004. Multi-level Governance and Environmental Policy. In *Multi-level Governance,* edited by Ian Bache and Matthew Flinders. 147-164. Oxford: Oxford University Press.

Grubb, Michael, Christiaan Vrolijk and Duncan Brack. 1999. *The Kyoto Protocol – A Guide and Assessment*. London: Earthscan.

Grubb, Michael, Christian Azar and Martin Persson. 2005. Allowance Allocation in the European Emissions Trading System: a Commentary. *Climate Policy* 5(1): 127-136.

Gupta, Joyeeta and Michael Grubb, eds. 2000. *Climate Change and European Leadership*. Dordrecht: Kluwer Academic Publishers.

Hooghe, Liesbet and Gary Marks. 2001. *Multi-Level Governance and European Integration*. Oxford: Rowman & Littlefield.

Hægstad Flåm, Karoline. 2009. Restricting the Import of "Emission Credits" in the EU: A Power Struggle between States and Institutions. *International Environmental Agreements: Politics, Law and Economics* 9(1): 23-38.

Kruger, Joseph and William A. Pizer. 2004. *The EU Emissions Trading Directive: Opportunities and Potential Pitfalls*. Washington D.C.: Resources for the Future.

McCormick, John. 1999. *Understanding the European Union – A Concise Introduction*. Houndmills: Palgrave.

Moravcsik, Andrew. 1998. *The Choice for Europe. Social Purpose and State Power from Messina to Maastricht*. London: Routledge/UCL Press.

Oberthür, Sebastian and Thomas Gehring, eds. 2006. *Institutional Interaction in Global Environmental Governance – Synergy and Conflict among International and EU Policies*. Cambridge, Mass.: The MIT Press.

Oberthür, Sebastian and Claire Roche Kelly. 2008. EU Leadership in International Climate Policy: Achievements and Challenges. *The International Spectator* 43(3): 35-50.

Peterson, John. 1995. Decision-Making in the European Union: Towards a Framework for Analysis. *Journal of European Public Policy* 2(1): 69-93.

Point Carbon. 2008a. *Tough EU Limits on the Use of Kyoto Credits Seen as CDM Setback*. January 2008, Oslo.

Point Carbon. 2008b. *Widespread Auctioning of EU Allowances Will Cause Economic Hardship*. 5 June 2008, Poland.

Point Carbon. 2008c. *MEPs Vote to Change EU Carbon Market from 2013*. 7 October 2008.

Ringius, Lasse. 1999. Differentiation, Leaders, and Fairness: Negotiating Climate Commitments in the European Community. *International Negotiation* 4(2): 133-166.

Skjærseth, Jon B. and Jørgen Wettestad. 2002. Understanding the Effectiveness of EU Environmental Policy: How Can Regime Analysis Contribute? *Environmental Politics* 11(3): 99-120.

Skjærseth, Jon B. and Jørgen Wettestad. 2008. *EU Emissions Trading: Initiation, Decision-making and Implementation*. Aldershot: Ashgate.

Skjærseth, Jon B. and Jørgen Wettestad. 2009. Explaining the Significant 2008 Changes of EU Emissions Trading. Paper Presented at the International Studies Association 50th Annual Convention. New York, February 15-18.

Stavins, Robert N. 2003. Experience with Market-Based Environmental Policy Instruments. In *Handbook of Environmental Economics, Vol. 1*, edited by Karl-Goran Maler and Jeffrey Vincent. 355-435. Amsterdam: Elsevier.

Underdal, Arild. 2002. One Question, Two Answers. In *Environmental Regime Effectiveness: Confronting Theory with Evidence*, edited by Edward L. Miles, Arild Underdal, Steinar Andresen, Jørgen Wettestad, Jon Birger Skjærseth and Elaine M. Carlin. 3-46. Cambridge, Mass.: MIT Press.

Weale, Albert, Geoffrey Pridham, Michelle Cini, Dimitrios Konstadakopulos, Martin Porter and Brendan Flynn. 2000. *Environmental Governance in Europe: An Ever Closer Ecological Union?* Oxford: Oxford University Press.

Wettestad, Jørgen. 2009. European Climate Policy: Towards Centralised Governance? *Review of Policy Research* 26(3): 311-328.

From Sharing the Burden to Sharing the Effort: Decision 406/2009/EC on Member State Emission Targets for non-ETS Sectors

Nuno Lacasta, Sebastian Oberthür, Eduardo Santos and Pedro Barata

1.   Introduction

The key to understanding the "Effort-Sharing Decision" (Decision 406/2009/EC) agreed as part of the climate and energy package lies in the overall design of the package, in general, and the centrality of the reform of the EU Emissions Trading System (ETS), in particular. Prior to the package, the only large-scale policy instrument developed under EU climate policy had been the ETS. Given its teething problems, mostly due to a reluctance to harmonise basic rules in the infancy of the system, it is understandable that the first driver of the new policy would be EU ETS harmonisation. That, in turn, meant that a significant portion of overall EU climate policy would follow an autonomous distribution key, more sector-related than nation-based, and established in Brussels.[1] The remainder of the EU emission budget control would then need to be carved out and distributed according to a different key, more in line with the previous exercise in "burden sharing", to implement the EU's emission reduction commitment under the Kyoto Protocol.

Against this backdrop, this article argues that the development from burden sharing in the framework of the Kyoto Protocol, to the 2009 Effort-Sharing Decision reflects several far-reaching changes. Next to the experience gained in the implementation of the EU ETS and the emergence of the ETS as a single, harmonised system, the accession of 12 new Member States with very different economic situations, including energy systems, in 2004 and 2007 left a significant imprint. By enrolling ten countries with circumstances that are very different from those of the previous 15 Member States, and two others that are not part of the industrialised countries listed in Annex I of the United Nations Framework Convention on Climate Change (UNFCCC), the EU has come to encompass a wider variety of national circumstances than before. As a result, the EU faces new

---

1.   See the chapter by Skjærseth and Wettestad in this volume.

challenges, including in the fields of energy and climate change. Nevertheless, with the climate and energy package, including the Effort-Sharing Decision, EU climate policy now reaches into sectors from which the Community had steered away under the banner of subsidiarity. In a political climate in which the trend has moved away from the "communitarisation" of policies, this development may have wider implications for the architecture of the EU.

This chapter analyses the EU's 2009 Effort-Sharing Decision in three steps. The next section first puts the decision in the historical context of what can be considered its predecessor: the "burden sharing" of 2002 as originally agreed in 1997 and 1998, which covered the greenhouse gas (GHG) emissions of the then 15 EU Member States. Subsequently, section 3 puts the Effort-Sharing Decision into the context of the overall climate and energy package and the agreement on ETS reform. Section 4 then analyses the negotiations and their outcome. The chapter ends with a brief conclusion.

2. The 1997-1998 burden-sharing agreement

The issue of burden sharing has, throughout the history of climate policy, had both an external and an internal dimension for the EU and its Member States. Hence, the EU's external political stance, whereby it proposes, with one voice, what it is jointly willing to commit to in the context of an international agreement, is complemented with a consideration of internal burden sharing.[2]

The issue of sharing contributions of EU Member States to an overall EU effort in reducing GHG emissions first emerged in the process leading to the adoption of the UNFCCC in 1992. In October 1990, Environment and Energy Ministers meeting jointly for the first time, agreed to a combined commitment for the EU (formally: the EC) to stabilise CO_2 emissions by the year 2000 at 1990 levels.[3] It was clear that achieving this joint target would require differentiated contributions from the then 12 Member States. However, a formalisation of any burden-sharing agreement was rendered void because the EU was unsuccessful in its attempt to achieve a binding commitment of all developed countries to stabilise their GHG emissions under the UNFCCC. In the end, the UNFCCC contained only aspirational language to this effect.[4]

2.   See also the chapter by Oberthür and Pallemaerts in this volume.
3.   Council (Energy/Environment) 1990; Lyons 1998, 85.
4.   See also the chapter by Oberthür and Pallemaerts in this volume.

The issue of international commitments, and thus the question of how to share a commitment internally, again arose in the run-up to Kyoto. After the Berlin Mandate had launched negotiations on the Kyoto Protocol because the commitments contained in the UNFCCC were considered inadequate, the Intergovernmental Panel on Climate Change (IPCC) underpinned the necessity for further action. In 1996, the IPCC stated in its Second Assessment Report that "the balance of evidence suggests that there is a discernible human influence on global climate, and that global temperatures are projected to rise by between 1 and 3.5 degrees Celsius by the end of the next century, compared with 1990, leading to changes in climate patterns and increases in sea levels with the risk of significant damage and disruption".[5] Subsequently, in March 1997, the environment ministers of the then EU-15 called for a reduction target of 15 per cent for developed countries, individually or jointly, by 2010 compared to 1990 levels. The target covered an average reduction for a basket of three GHGs (CO_2, CH_4 and N_2O) and was complemented by an initial agreement on sharing the internal burden that amounted to an emission reduction of 9.2 per cent by 2010, while remaining silent regarding the distribution of the additional 5.8 per cent which the EU was ready to commit to (see Table 1). Later, in June 1997, Environment Ministers also called for a 7.5 per cent intermediate reduction target by 2005.[6]

The basis for the March 1997 agreement was the so-called "Triptych" approach that provided a transparent and neutral assessment of Member States' potential targets, even though the final agreement was eminently political. The Triptych approach calculated national emission targets bottom-up, based on three different sectors and using a different allocation rule for each: the domestic sector; heavy industry; and the electricity generation sector. Emission allowances were calculated by applying rules, such as limitation of coal use in power production, minimum requirements for renewable energy and minimum energy efficiency improvement rates in industry. For the domestic sectors a per capita emission allowance was used.[7] The approach provided a useful starting point for the negotiations, which led to some horse-trading and changes in national targets of Member States.[8]

---

5.   IPCC 1996.
6.   Commission 1997, 2; Oberthür and Ott 1999; Oberthür and Pallemaerts in this volume.
7.   Phylipsen et al. 1998.
8.   Aidt and Greiner, 2002, 20-21; see also Ringius 1999; Haug and Jordan 2010.

Aidt and Greiner identify three political aspects that had a major influence on the 1997 agreement: external political pressure as negotiations towards Kyoto approached; adoption of national reduction targets by Member States prior to the burden-sharing negotiations; and holding the EU Presidency at the time of negotiations. The latter two are of particular relevance as regards the balance of negotiation power within the EU. Member States that had adopted strong national emission reduction targets left themselves open to taking on a bigger share of the burden than otherwise. This may in particular be apparent when comparing the high targets assigned to Austria, Denmark, Germany and Luxembourg with the more moderate targets of the UK, the Netherlands and Belgium.[9]

Table 1 – The EU Burden-Sharing Agreements of 1997 and 1998/2002

Member State	March 1997: Emission Reduction by 2010	June 1998: Emission Reduction by 2008-12
Austria	-25.0 %	-13.0 %
Belgium	-10.0 %	-7.5 %
Denmark	-25.0 %	-21.0 %
Finland	0.0 %	0.0 %
France	0.0 %	0.0 %
Germany	-25.0 %	-21.0 %
Greece	+30.0 %	+25.0 %
Ireland	+15.0 %	+13.0 %
Italy	-7.0 %	-6.5 %
Luxembourg	-30.0 %	-28.0 %
Netherlands	-10.0 %	-6.0 %
Portugal	+40.0 %	+27.0 %
Spain	+17.0 %	+15.0 %
Sweden	+5.0 %	+4.0 %
United Kingdom	-10.0 %	-12.5 %
EU-Total	-9.2 %	-8.0 %

Source: Council 1997; Decision 2002/358/EC.

In the first half of 1998, the EU internal burden-sharing agreement of 1997 was renegotiated in light of the agreement on the Kyoto Protocol reached in December 1997. In addition to establishing a five-year commitment period (2008-2012) instead of a single target year (2010), the Kyoto

9.   Aidt and Greiner 2002; see also Table 1.

Protocol contained a target of eight per cent for the EU-15 (rather than the 9.2 per cent of the 1997 burden-sharing agreement) and a broader basket of GHGs (including fluorinated GHGs). It also established market-based mechanisms and land-use change and forestry provisions that needed to be taken into account when redistributing the EU's reduction target. The 1998 agreement reached under the UK Presidency is reflected in Table 1.[10]

This agreement was eventually codified in EU law by Council Decision 2002/358/EC on the ratification of the Kyoto Protocol by the EC. On the basis of Article 4 of the Kyoto Protocol that enables the EU Member States to redistribute their joint commitment prior to ratification, the burden-sharing agreement codified in Decision 2002/358/EC forms the basis of the EU's participation in and commitments under the Kyoto Protocol. As its main purpose was the ratification of the Kyoto Protocol, the Decision was adopted on the basis of Article 175(1) *in conjunction with* the first subparagraphs of Article 300(2) and (3) of the EC Treaty. Consequently, the European Parliament was consulted but could not execute the co-decision powers it possesses with regard to standard EU environmental legislation.

While the burden-sharing agreements of 1997 and 1998 reflected principles of both efficiency and equity, political power may have diluted equity to some extent. Efficiency arguments had an influence on the burden sharing since Member States with higher marginal abatement cost curves of GHG emissions were assigned easier targets. Equity was also considered to the extent that Member States with lower standards of living in terms of consumption were assigned easier targets.[11] Nevertheless, the burden-sharing agreement arguably did not fully equalise marginal abatement costs among Member States so that relatively poorer Member States should have been given higher emissions allowances.[12] To this end, the renegotiation of the burden-sharing agreement in 1998 did not help. Perhaps the most outstanding difference between the 1997 and 1998 agreements is that non-cohesion countries were better off while all cohesion country targets were tightened. This can be attributed to a weaker negotiating position of the cohesion countries after the adoption of the Kyoto Protocol, since failing to achieve a burden-sharing agreement among the EU-15 would have bound these countries to an eight per cent reduction commitment (as inscribed in the Kyoto Protocol).[13]

10. On the burden-sharing agreement, see Ringius 1999.
11. Marklund and Samakovlis 2004.
12. Eyckmans et al. 2002.
13. Aidt and Greiner 2002.

3. The 2009 Effort-Sharing Decision in the context of the climate and energy package

Like the burden-sharing arrangements of the 1990s, the 2009 effort sharing also has both internal and external dimensions. Not least, the 2009 attempts to distribute the effort of implementing abatement measures again flew from an international commitment. In March 2007, the European Council of Heads of State or Government made an independent commitment to reduce GHG emissions by 20 per cent from 1990 levels by 2020 and to move this target to 30 per cent once an international agreement is in place. European leaders also committed to increasing the share of renewable energies in total EU energy consumption to 20 per cent by 2020. At the same time, they invited the European Commission to come forward with appropriate legislative proposals.[14]

In January 2008, the Commission put forward its proposals for a package of implementation measures for the EU's objectives on climate change and renewable energy for 2020 thus responding to the invitation of the European Council. The proposal for a decision on the effort of Member States to reduce their GHG emissions to meet the Community's GHG emission reduction commitments up to 2020[15] was part of that package, which also included proposals for a directive amending the EU ETS directive[16] and a directive on the promotion of the use of renewable energy sources.[17] An appropriate understanding of the Effort-Sharing Decision requires putting it in the context of this package.

As the Effort-Sharing Decision formed part of the overall climate and energy package, the debate about sharing the effort could consider more elements than in the case of the preceding stand-alone burden-sharing decision. The principles guiding this debate, efficiency and equity/fairness, thus became an issue for the overall climate and energy package. They are reflected in the six key principles that underpin the policy approach put forward by the European Commission:

• Cost-effectiveness of the policy instruments deployed, so as to minimise the economic impacts of achieving the agreed objectives;
• Flexibility in the manner that the targets are achieved, so as to accommodate variations from underlying assumptions of the modelling exercise on which the proposals are based;

14. See the chapter by Oberthür and Pallemaerts in this volume.
15. Commission 2008c.
16. See the chapter by Skjærseth and Wettestad in this volume.
17. See the chapter by Howes in this volume.

- Internal market and fair competition, so as to ensure consistency and create a level playing field in the EU that ensures fair competition among EU industries in the context of the internal market;
- Subsidiarity, so that action is taken at the most appropriate decision-making level;
- Fairness, so as to take into account Member States' different circumstances and the reality that differing levels of prosperity have an impact on Member States' capacity to invest;
- Competitiveness and innovation, so as to address concerns of international competitiveness, which could undermine the overall environmental objective of EU climate and energy policies.[18]

As the Effort-Sharing Decision was integrated into the broader package, the impact assessment that accompanied the Commission proposal also addressed the issue in an integrated way. Hence, the cost-efficiency scenario included in the assessment was defined as the option that would simultaneously deliver the 20 per cent renewable target and the 20 per cent reduction commitment for GHG emissions. In order words, the scenario aimed to equalise marginal costs across all Member States and all sectors, both for GHG emission reductions as well as for the deployment of renewable energy.[19] The Effort-Sharing Decision thus formed only one part in the broader attempt to achieve a cost-efficient and fair distribution of the effort to achieve the targets for both renewable energy consumption and GHG emission reduction.

In the design of the overall package, flexibility and subsidiarity both took second stage to cost-effectiveness and internal market and fairness. The partitioning into ETS and non-ETS sectors limited Member States' flexibility of realising emission reductions in various sectors, while providing for a fairer sectoral distribution of efforts by impeding free-riding of sectors and requiring all sectors to contribute. Flexibility was discussed within these parameters focusing in particular on the use of international offsets (see next section). Subsidiarity took second stage to internal market and fair competition considerations as a result of experience from the implementation of the 2005-2007 EU ETS trading period.

The demand to balance cost-efficiency with fairness considerations was reinforced because it would impinge more severely on Member States with the lowest levels of GDP per capita and hence with the least capability to pay, thus contravening guidance from EU leaders in March 2007.[20] The

18. Commission 2008a.
19. Commission 2008a.
20. European Council 2007, 12.

increased membership of the EU in both numbers and diversity further fortified the demand for equity and fairness, since economic and social differences across the EU increased considerably with EU enlargement. In 2001, only two of the then 15 Member States had a GDP per capita below 75 per cent of the Community's average, while five Member States were above the EU-15 average. In 2006, 13 Member States of the EU-27 were above average (all from the previous EU-15) and nine Member States were below 75 per cent of EU average GDP per capita. Furthermore, in 2001 the difference between the wealthier and the poorest EU-15 Member States was three-fold. In 2006, this difference in the EU-27 was around seven-fold.[21]

Against this backdrop, the Commission contemplated specific policy options to address these differences and ensure a fairer distribution of efforts among Member States. At the same time, the targets needed to be delivered and a fair contribution by all sectors maintained. As identified in the impact assessment, three major policy design choices for differentiation were assessed and picked up in the package proposal:

• Differentiation between Member State targets in the sectors not covered by the EU ETS;
• Partial redistribution of the right to auction allowances under the EU ETS among Member States;
• Differentiation between Member States' national targets set for the deployment of renewable energy.[22]

While the redistribution of auctioning rights under the EU ETS and differentiated national targets for deployment of renewable energy fall out of the scope of this chapter,[23] it is important to understand that equity and fairness were not only pursued within the Effort-Sharing Decision. Instead, and in contrast to the earlier efforts to distribute the costs of climate policy among EU Member States in the 1990s, they were a crosscutting theme and objective of the overall climate and energy package.

Perhaps the most important difference between the previous burden-sharing agreements and the "effort sharing" of 2009 concerns the scope of the agreements. Whereas the previous burden-sharing agreements had established economy-wide targets (with the exception of international aviation and shipping emissions which are not covered under the Kyoto

---

21. See Eurostat data on GDP per capita in the EU http://epp.eurostat.ec.europa.eu/tgm/table.do?tab=table&init=1&plugin=1&language=en&pcode=tsieb010 (Accessed: 4 November 2009).
22. Commission 2008a.
23. See the chapters by Skjærseth and Wettestad and by Howes in this volume, respectively.

Protocol), the 2009 Effort-Sharing Decision only applies to the sectors not covered by the EU ETS. This limitation was a direct consequence of the establishment of an EU-wide cap under the ETS as a result of the experiences with the EU ETS in its first phase from 2005 to 2007. While considered politically difficult by some due to the implied transfer of political power to the EU level,[24] Member States did not seriously dispute the centralised approach proposed by the Commission.[25] The harmonisation of rules in the EU ETS inevitably led to a downsizing of Member States' direct responsibility over emission control to sectors outside the EU ETS. Since the EU ETS roughly applies to large-point source facilities, covering most energy and industry emissions, the scope of the Effort-Sharing Decision was limited to sectors which are arguably the least tractable but represent somewhat less than 60 per cent of current total EU GHG emissions. These sectors cover mostly small-scale diffuse emitters such as transport, residential and office buildings, services, agriculture and waste (accountable for the lion's share of non-CO_2 emissions) and also smaller industrial installations, which were considered to be mainly covered by Member States' actions.[26]

As a consequence of the split between ETS and non-ETS, a burden sharing between the sectors covered in the EU ETS and the sectors not covered needed to be established at the EU level. For reasons of cost-effectiveness and fairness, both the ETS and the non-ETS sectors would need to contribute to the overall emission reduction efforts. The partition between them was determined through the cost-efficient scenario elaborated by the Commission. This scenario rendered an EU-wide reduction for current EU ETS sectors of some 21 per cent compared to 2005 by 2020 and a reduction of around 10 per cent compared to 2005 by the sectors not covered by the EU ETS. Together, the reductions in the ETS and non-ETS sectors amounted to a 14 per cent economy-wide reduction by 2020 compared to 2005. This reduction is equivalent to a 20 per cent reduction by 2020 compared to 1990, as committed to by the European Council in March 2007. The partition implies that some 60 per cent of the reductions would be achieved in EU ETS sectors, reflecting the larger cost-effective potential of these sectors and in particular of the electricity generation sector. In addition to this, it was estimated that more than half of the 20 per cent renewable energy would be achieved in these sectors.[27]

24. Sijm et al. 2007.
25. See the chapter by Skjærseth and Wettestad in this volume.
26. There are, of course, EU-level actions in the Effort-Sharing part of the package. By and large, however, the package was designed so that the non-ETS part would include mostly national-level actions in sectors such as transport and housing.
27. Commission 2008a, 8; see also Figure 1.

The split between ETS and non-ETS and the centralisation of the ETS introduced a certain level of fairness into the package. From a strictly theoretical economic point of view, and assuming a competitive carbon market, the same price signal would be available to everyone and higher emissions reductions would result where mitigation costs were lower. This theoretical analysis masks, however, in the European case, the significant distortions arising from different access to capital markets and wealth-related effects. Still, all participants are affected by the same rules and similar installations are subject to the same constraints/rules thus preventing competition distortions. In this way, the ETS facilitates emission reductions and lowers mitigation costs across the EU, thus also lowering the overall burden on Member States.

Furthermore, the formal split between ETS and non-ETS increases pressure on Member States to address emissions in the non-ETS sectors. Previously, Member States could overburden the ETS sectors, where the mitigation potential is higher, and be less stringent on non-trading sectors. The Member States' economy-wide targets, under the 1998 burden-sharing agreement, allowed Member States to balance emission reductions in ETS sectors and non-ETS sectors themselves. In the framework of the package, Member States have specific responsibility for achieving targets for emission reductions in the non-trading sectors. Action addressing these sectors can no longer be evaded by targeting ETS sectors. Given the stringency of targets and the strict compliance procedures (see below), this requires a significant effort from Member States to establish policies that can deliver in sectors such as transport, housing and services, and agriculture.

4. Key issues in the negotiations and key elements of the Decision

On the basis of the Commission proposal, political agreement on the overall climate and energy package, including the Effort-Sharing Decision, was reached at the European Council meeting in December 2008. In October 2008, the European Council had agreed to come back to the issue in December, with a view to concluding on the matter. As a consequence, agreement on the climate and energy package had to be achieved by unanimity, while the Environment Council could have decided by qualified majority. Operating under a unanimity decision rule gave additional negotiating leverage to individual Member States. In the end, however, the notion that an agreement on these issues would benefit all prevailed.

In contrast to Decision 2002/358/EC on the ratification of the Kyoto Protocol, which codified the 1998 burden-sharing agreement, the Effort-Sharing Decision was based on Article 175(1) of the EC Treaty and thus adopted in a co-decision procedure requiring agreement by both the Council and the European Parliament. The European Parliament agreed to the effort-sharing proposal in their first reading on 17 December 2008.[28] The Decision, as agreed during the first reading of the Parliament, was formally adopted by the Council on 23 April 2009 and published in the Official Journal on 5 June 2009.

4.1 The overall design

The Commission's proposal changed the terminology from "burden sharing" to "effort sharing". Even though the new term "effort sharing" carries more positive connotations, it means the same in practice. However, the new terminology reflects that the climate-change storyline has evolved from one where action on climate change is considered only a costly "burden", to one where it is considered an opportunity – for jobs, for innovation, for development and for clean growth. The 2006 Stern Review on the Economics of Climate Change spearheaded such change by stating that the costs of dealing with the challenge of climate change are manageable and, in any event, far less than the costs of the impacts from a changing climate.[29] The change in discourse is also a reflection of the potential and opportunities that the carbon market, especially driven by the EU ETS, created in the 2000s. In this context, the change from "burden sharing" to "effort sharing" also marks the attempt to instil a more positive message in the issue. Nevertheless, costs and perceptions of costs remained key in the discussions of EU Member States on the "effort sharing". In this context, notions of solidarity and fairness among Member States were important ingredients.[30]

A prominent feature of the Commission proposal for all elements of the climate and energy package was the choice of 2005 as the base year against which GHG emission reductions and increases in renewable energy shares are presented. This was the most recent year for which reliable emissions data existed at Member State level for both the EU ETS sectors and for

---

28.   See European Parliament 2008b.
29.   Stern 2007.
30.   Stephenson 2008.

sectors not covered by the ETS. In particular, 2005 was the first year for which independently verified emission data existed under the ETS. It thus configured the most recent, complete and adequate starting point on which 2020 scenarios could be built, including assessment of cost-effective reduction potentials.[31]

On this basis, the Commission proposal introduced a differentiation of Member State targets according to the relative level of GDP per capita. It reflected the so-called principle of solidarity between Member States coupled with the recognition of the need for sustainable economic growth across the Community, and taking into account the relative per capita GDP of Member States.[32] Member States with a GDP per capita below the EU average would need to reduce less than the EU average, or, in some cases, would even be allowed to increase their emissions above 2005 levels in the non-ETS sectors. Member States with a GDP per capita above the EU average would need to reduce more than the EU average. Boundaries of +20 per cent and -20 per cent were established in each case for those Member States with respectively the lowest and the highest GDP per capita. Whereas countries with a low GDP per capita would thus be allowed to emit more than they did in 2005 in the non-ETS sectors, ensuring that their short-term higher GDP growth expectations and hence growing emissions trajectory can be accommodated, they would still need to limit their emissions to the cap (see Figure 1). With this approach, the Commission estimated that overall costs for implementing the package would increase from 0.58 per cent to 0.61 per cent of GDP, but cost reductions in countries with relatively low GDP per capita would be significant.[33]

In addition to the 2020 target, the proposal also established a linear reduction or limitation pathway from 2013 to 2020 for each Member State to achieve its target. Member States were to receive annual emission allocations that would gradually decrease until 2020, replicating to some extent the approach under the EU ETS. Rather than a 2020 target, the proposed Effort-Sharing Decision in effect established eight targets for the years 2013-2020 for each Member State. Going beyond their annual emission allocation would render the Member State liable to infringement procedures under Articles 226 et seq. of the EC Treaty.

---

31. Commission 2008a, 5.
32. European Council 2007, 12.
33. Commission 2008a, 9.

Figure 1 – 2020 GHG emission targets of EU Member States and GDP per capita

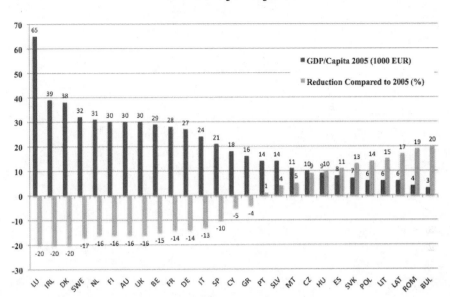

Source: adapted from Commission 2008a, 9.

Even though this overall set-up proposed by the Commission, including the 2005 baseline and the differentiated targets, was upheld in the final agreement, it was subject to serious criticism. In particular, a group of central and eastern European Member States, led by Hungary, claimed that the 2005 baseline did not adequately take into account early efforts to reduce emissions undertaken by Member States. They proposed to use 1990 as a baseline instead and to establish economy-wide flat rate targets for each Member State of minus 18 per cent below their respective Kyoto targets, instead of the differentiated targets proposed by the Commission.[34] These demands of the new Member States were hardly feasible, not least because they were incompatible with the overall design of the package, including the split between ETS and non-ETS sectors. However, they served to retrieve concessions in the ETS part of the overall package in the form of an increased share of auctioning rights being granted to Member States with 2005 emissions already below the overall -20 per cent target for 2020.[35] Negotiations on the Effort-Sharing Decision did not lead to changes of the proposed targets of individual Member States, but focused

---

34. ENDS Europe Daily 2008a and b.
35. See chapter by Skjærseth and Wettestad in this volume.

on other elements, especially on the degree of flexibility available to Member States in achieving their non-ETS targets.

4.2   Increasing flexibility

The main focus in the effort-sharing negotiations was on how much flexibility the Member States would have in achieving their annual targets from 2013 to 2020. The trade-off for not disputing the individual targets and even the intermediate annual targets was intense efforts to secure sufficient flexibility for Member States in implementing their commitments. In essence, this meant that a majority of Member States demanded – and received – more flexibility than proposed by the Commission.

The original Commission proposal included three kinds of flexibility. First, when a Member State was above its annual target, it could *carry forward or borrow* from the following year a quantity of up to two per cent of its GHG emission allocation for that year. Second, when a Member State was below its annual target, it could *carry-over* the excess emissions reductions to the subsequent years. Finally, Member States could make use of international credits from the project-based flexible mechanisms of the Kyoto Protocol, the Clean Development Mechanism (CDM) and Joint Implementation (JI). The Commission proposed an annual limit for the use of such *CDM/JI credits* defined as the equivalent of three per cent of each Member State's individual 2005 emissions in the non-ETS sectors (i.e. a total of 24 per cent of 2005 emissions over the period 2013-2020). In this context, the proposal also provided continuity for the international carbon market after 2012 by allowing the continued use of credits generated in existing CDM projects (registered and implemented during the 2008-2012 period) beyond 2012. Any part of the limit unused in one year could be transferred to other Member States, but the Commission proposal did not foresee any banking of unused parts of the allowed quantity of international credits. The limit amounted, according to the Commission, to a potential reduction of the domestic emission reduction efforts of the EU in the non-ETS sectors by a third in 2020. Over the whole period 2013-2020, the allowance for international credits, if exploited in full, equalled about half of the overall emission reductions required.[36]

The limits on flexibility proposed by the Commission became a major focus of attention in the negotiations, with the limits to CDM/JI credits

36.   Commission 2008a and b.

becoming particularly controversial. On the one side, several Member States looked at CDM/JI credits as the most effective flexibility mechanism. They argued that these credits provided an important tool not only for the implementation of commitments but also for promoting sustainable development in third countries, in particular in developing countries through the CDM. On the other side, the European Parliament and environmental groups pointed out a number of rationales for strict limits on international emission credits. In particular, unconstrained access to these credits could disincentivise and delay much needed changes in domestic systems, in particular the energy system. As a result, the EU would fail to realise much-needed oil and gas savings and perpetuate its energy dependence on third countries. The result would be a lack of incentives for technological innovation in the EU and increased difficulties in achieving the 20 per cent renewable energy target, which would become more expensive, as more support for renewable energy technologies would be required. In addition, excessive use of international credits would render the EU vulnerable to criticism of "buying its way to the targets" by international partners. Thus, the use of these credits should be consistent with the EU's goal of climate leadership through significant domestic GHG emission reductions, the goal of generating 20 per cent of its energy from renewable sources by 2020, promoting the EU's energy security and promoting innovation and the EU's competitiveness. To this end, the European Parliament's Environment Committee demanded that the use of international offsets should be limited to eight per cent of 2005 emissions for the whole period 2013-2020 (down from the Commission's proposed total of 24 per cent).[37]

While this criticism and pressure helped to contain Member States' demands for more flexibility, especially with regard to international emission credits, more extensive flexibility found its way into the final agreement. The carry-forward limit was increased to five per cent. In addition, Member States that experience extreme meteorological conditions in 2013 and 2014 were allowed to go beyond the five per cent for these two years, because factors that are not foreseeable and beyond the control of Member States may require additional flexibility in the early years of implementation.[38] Furthermore, even though the annual limit of CDM/JI credits use was maintained at three per cent, full banking of these limits was introduced and the potential use of such credits for the 2013-

---

37. ENDS Europe Daily 2008c; European Parliament 2008a, 34-37.
38. Decision 406/2009/EC, Article 3(3).

2020 period thus increased.[39] The use of credits from forest projects under the CDM was also added, thus replicating the conditions on the use of credits by Member States in the 2008-2012 Kyoto commitment period.[40]

Also, Member States fended off attempts to strengthen quality safeguards with respect to international emission credits. The European Parliament's Environment Committee had advocated limiting the use of CDM and JI to credits from high-quality projects.[41] Several Member States argued, however, that the EU should avoid creating an additional level of complexity in the market. Instead, the EU should try to improve the environmental effectiveness of the market-based mechanisms at the international level. The final agreement thus allows the use by Member States of GHG emission reduction credits resulting from project types that were eligible for use in the ETS during the period 2008 to 2012.[42]

As the negotiation proceeded, additional flexibility options were proposed and established. In particular, each Member State was allowed to transfer up to five per cent of its annual GHG emissions allocation to other Member States.[43] Also, the use of credits resulting from Community-level projects defined under Article 24a of the new Emissions Trading Directive was allowed. This new article in essence enables Member States to apply for the inclusion of additional installations/emission sources into the EU ETS on a project basis.[44] Finally, 12 Member States that face a particular burden in the implementation of the climate and energy package (listed in a new Annex III) were granted access to an additional amount of CDM credits from projects in least developed countries and small island developing states of up to one per cent of their verified emissions in 2005. Member States that benefit from this additional level of flexibility have to fulfil at least one of four conditions:
- The direct costs of the overall package exceed 0.7 per cent of GDP according to the Commission's impact assessment;
- The costs of implementing the target of the Member States is at least 0.1 per cent higher than if the cost-efficient scenario defined in the Commission's impact assessment had been followed;

39. Decision 406/2009/EC, Article 5(4) and 5(6).
40. Decision 406/2009/EC, Article 5(1).
41. European Parliament 2008a.
42. Decision 406/2009/EC, Article 5(1).
43. Decision 406/2009/EC, Article 3(4).
44. Decision 406/2009/EC, Article 5(7).

- Transport-related emissions account for more than 50 per cent of the non-ETS emissions; or
- The Member State concerned has a renewable energies target for 2020 of more than 30 per cent under the Renewable Energy Directive 2009/28/EC.[45]

These criteria further reinforce the interlinkages between the different elements of the package. In this case, additional flexibility was granted under the Effort-Sharing Decision as a means of enhancing fairness and balancing the costs of the package as a whole.

4.3   Other provisions

The very scope of the effort-sharing proposal was disputed, as the Commission proposal did not include emissions and removals from land use, land use change and forestry. The rational for this was the inherent uncertainty regarding the rules to which the sector will be bound under an international agreement. A large part of the rules for the accounting of emissions and removals from land use, land use change and forestry under the Kyoto Protocol only apply until 2012 and have therefore formed part of discussions on the future international climate change regime post-2012. The non-inclusion of this sizeable sector raised concerns by some Member States. Ireland, in particular, was adamant about including this sector in the decision. In the final agreement, Article 8(6) of the Decision obliges the Commission to propose the inclusion of the sector as part of the adjustments to move to the 30 per cent reduction commitment in the context of an international agreement, to be proposed within three months of the signature of such agreement. The proposal shall be based on the then agreed international rules and according to modalities ensuring permanence and environmental integrity. In the absence of approval of an international agreement by the end of 2010, the Commission has to put forward a proposal on how to include the sector as part of the 20 per cent reduction commitment, complementing the current Effort-Sharing Decision.[46]

How to organise the transition to the 30 per cent reduction in GHG emissions by 2020 compared to 1990 as the EU's contribution to a global

---

45. Decision 406/2009/EC, Article 5(5). The following Member States are listed accordingly in Annex III of the Decision: Belgium, Denmark, Ireland, Spain, Italy, Cyprus, Luxembourg, Austria, Portugal, Slovenia, Finland, and Sweden. For more detail on the Renewable Energy Directive, see the chapter by Howes in this volume.
46. Decision 406/2009/EC, Article 9.

and comprehensive agreement for the period beyond 2012 constituted a major point of discussion (with respect to both the Effort-Sharing Decision and the ETS revision). The Commission had proposed to establish an automatic adjustment to accommodate the transition. Member State emission limits would be adjusted on the basis of the new GHG emission reduction commitment set out in the international agreement. The partition of the additional overall effort for the EU between the ETS and sectors not covered by the ETS would remain the same, and the limits for the use of international credits would be increased so as to cover half the additional reduction effort due to the international agreement. This approach was initially supported by some Member States on the grounds that it would provide a strong signal to third parties of the EU's commitment. It also received support from the European Parliament.[47] However, the sensitivity around the issues to be considered in the transition from 20 to 30 per cent, including the distribution of the additional efforts and thus the determination of the new targets, meant a short life for the automatic approach. It was soon replaced by provisions for a new co-decision procedure to take place following the conclusion of a new international climate change agreement in future. Both the partition between the ETS and non-ETS sectors and the limits for the use of international credits will need to be addressed in the related proposal by the Commission (while not pre-determined in the Effort-Sharing Decision).[48]

A particularly noteworthy feature of the Effort-Sharing Decision is that it allocates binding emission targets to both Cyprus and Malta, currently non-Annex I countries under the UNFCCC and thus with no targets under the Kyoto Protocol. This inclusion reflects the self-conceptualisation of the EU as a union of developed countries and the acceptance of the new Member States that joining the EU changes political circumstances. This approach was further consolidated in March 2009 when EU Environment Ministers agreed that they expected future Member States to accept economy-wide binding GHG emission reductions or limitation commitments, thus joining the group of developed countries.[49]

47. European Parliament 2008a.
48. Decision 406/2009/EC, Article 8.
49. The Council stressed "that the Copenhagen agreement should contain binding quantified emission limitation or reduction commitments for at least all Parties listed in Annex I to the UNFCCC and all current EU Member States, EU candidate countries and potential candidate countries that are not included in Annex I to the UNFCCC"; Council 2009, 5.

The major achievement of the European Parliament in the negotiations on the Decision was the introduction of a particular compliance mechanism on top of the regular EU infringement procedures. While other demands by the Parliament (including the establishment of long-term reduction targets) left no imprint, the Decision translates the consequences of non-compliance applicable under the Kyoto Protocol to the EU level. A Member State exceeding its annual emission allocation under the Effort-Sharing Decision faces three particular measures. First, every tonne of excess emissions will lead to a deduction of 1.08 tonnes from the Member State's emission allocation of the following year. Second, the Member State concerned will have to develop and submit to the Commission a "corrective action plan" identifying further action to meet its emission target and a timetable for implementation. Third, it will face a temporary suspension of the eligibility to transfer part of its emission allocation and JI/CDM rights to another Member State until its emission levels are once again in line with the established pathway.[50]

5. Conclusions

Understanding the Effort-Sharing Decision adopted in 2009 requires taking into account the particular framework and political environment in which it was embedded. First of all, the prominence of climate change on the European and international political agenda has shaped the process and its outcome. While the burden-sharing agreements of 1997 and 1998 were agreed by environment ministers, the 2008 climate and energy package was a matter for Heads of State or Government assembled in the European Council (with involvement of the European Parliament as required by the co-decision procedure). Furthermore, the Effort-Sharing Decision formed part of the broader package, which allowed various trade-offs across its different components. Finally, the outcome could not have but reflected the uncertain economic times, especially in the later stages in the negotiations. A package which started its life at the European Council in March 2007 and in times of relative economic optimism, eventually was finalised as reports on the collapse of the financial system stole the headlines from the negotiations on the climate and energy package. In the end, the agreement on the package achieved in December 2008 is a testimony to the importance attached to climate change by Europeans.

50. Decision 406/2009/EC, Article 7. On the Kyoto Protocol's compliance mechanism, see Holtwisch 2006; Oberthür and Lefeber 2010; on the demands of the European Parliament, see European Parliament 2008a.

The changes that took place since the burden-sharing agreements of the 1990s further contribute to the understanding of the Effort-Sharing Decision. Experience gained in implementing climate policy since the 1990s, and in particular experience with the ETS, played a crucial role in the design of the 2013-2020 effort sharing. Whereas the 1990s did not witness the implementation of specific and coordinated EU climate policies, the 2000s saw, among other things, the establishment of the EU ETS. The "teething problems" of the ETS created demand for further harmonisation and centralisation. As a result, and in contrast to the economy-wide burden-sharing agreement underpinning the ratification of the Kyoto Protocol, the Effort-Sharing Decision therefore only covers the non-ETS sectors. As a further consequence of this approach, the negotiations on the Effort-Sharing Decision took second stage to the negotiations on the ETS. The targets ascribed to each Member State were hardly questioned and remained the same throughout the negotiations. Instead, Member States focused on ensuring an adequate degree of flexibility in achieving the targets.

A significant difference between the 1997 burden-sharing agreement and the 2008 effort sharing, especially as regards the EU's international credibility, concerns their legal status. The 1997 agreement reflected a political agreement in the Council of Environment Ministers contained in Council Conclusions. It thus represented a negotiating position rather than a commitment. Even the 1998 revised agreement remained soft-law until codified in 2002. In contrast, the Effort-Sharing Decision represents a commitment that is binding under EU law. In contrast to the situation in the negotiations on the Kyoto Protocol in 1996 and 1997, the EU has thus, through the Effort-Sharing Decision and the other parts of the climate and energy package, put in place part of its commitment. Rather than starting from scratch, ratcheting up the independent commitment of a reduction of GHG emissions of 20 per cent to an international commitment of 30 per cent could build on the existing legislative framework, which would only need to be strengthened.

As part of the new climate policies of the EU, the Effort-Sharing Decision also contributes to what can be considered a significant centralisation and Europeanisation of climate and energy policy. The weaknesses in the implementation of both the 2003 Emissions Trading Directive and the 2001 Green Electricity Directive (Directive 2001/77/EC) created demand for, and eventually paved the way for, a greater degree of harmonisation at the European level in these fields.[51] As a functional spill-over, the non-ETS

51.   See the chapters by Skjærseth and Wettestad, and by Howes in this volume.

part of the package may also see a higher degree of Europeanisation in its operationalisation. While the Effort-Sharing Decision carves out a significant portion of economic sectors from direct EU control and leaves the development of emission reduction policies addressing these sectors to Member States, pressure is likely to build for a greater EU role with respect to the non-ETS sectors also. Delivering on the 20 per cent reduction target will require the coordination of 28 different caps across the EU: one "ETS cap", and 27 national "effort sharing caps". The demand for further coordination and harmonisation at EU level may further mount with an international agreement on climate change. The preference of the EU for binding international emission targets backed by a strong compliance system suggests that we may see increasing calls for a further role for the EU institutions, and the Commission in particular, in keeping Member States in check on their emissions. Already over the past years, EU legislative activity addressing emissions in non-ETS sectors has grown dynamically.[52]

It is therefore likely that we shall see movement towards a wider coordination of climate policy at the EU level in the near future. Considering the growing reluctance of Member States to relegate power to the European level in the name of subsidiarity and "better regulation" since the 1990s, the climate and energy package itself constitutes a remarkable resurrection of hierarchical and harmonised European regulation. Building on the package, and its Effort-Sharing Decision, this trend may well be reinforced. Initially, the GHG monitoring mechanism of the EU will need to be strengthened, to expand on current reporting by Member States on policies and measures in non-ETS sectors and to help implement the climate and energy package. Over time, the EU may confront the need for a wider role in Member State policy assessment. The climate and energy package may thus set the stage for reshaping the roles of the European institutions and the role of the EU in the world.

References

Aidt, Toke and Sandra Greiner. 2002. Sharing the climate policy burden in the EU. Discussion paper 176. Hamburg: Hamburgisches Welt-Wirtschafts-Archiv (HWWA), Hamburg Institute of International Economics.

---

52. See the chapters by Oberthür and Pallemaerts and by ten Brink in this volume.

Commission (EC). 1997. Communication from the Commission to the Council, the European Parliament, the Economic and Social Committee and the Committee of the Regions: Climate Change – The EU Approach for Kyoto. COM (97) 481 final. Brussels: European Commission.

Commission (EC). 2000. Communication from the Commission to the Council, the European Parliament on EU Policies and Measures to Reduce Greenhouse Gas Emisions: Towards a European Climate Change Programme (ECCP). COM (2000) 88 final. Brussels: European Commission.

Commission (EC). 2008a. Impact Assessment. Document Accompanying the Package of Implementation Measures for the EU's Objectives on Climate Change and Renewable Energy for 2020. SEC (2008) 85/3. Brussels: European Commission.

Commission (EC). 2008b. Communication from the Commission to the European Parliament, the Council, the European Economic and Social Committee and the Committee of the Regions. 20 20 by 2020. Europe's Climate Change Opportunity. COM (2008) 30 final. Brussels: European Commission.

Commission (EC). 2008c. Proposal for a Decision of the European Parliament and of the Council on the Effort of Member States to Reduce their Greenhouse Emissions to Meet the Community's Greenhouse Gas Reduction Commitments up to 2020. COM (2008) 17 final. Brussels: European Commission.

Council of the European Union (Energy and Environment). 1990. Press Release. 1436th Joint Council Meeting: Energy/Environment. 29 October 1990. 9482/90. Luxembourg: Council of the European Communities.

Council of the European Union (Environment). 1997. Council Conclusions, 3 March 1997. 6309/97. Brussels: Council of the European Union.

Council of the European Union (Environment). 2009. Council Conclusions, 3 March 2009. 7128/09. Brussels. Council of the European Union.

Decision 2002/358/EC of the Council of the European Union of 25 April 2002 Concerning the Approval, on Behalf of the European Community, of the Kyoto Protocol to the United Nations Framework Convention on Climate Change and the Joint Fulfilment of Commitments Thereunder. *Official Journal of the European Union*, 15 May, L 130/1.

Decision No 406/2009/EC of the European Parliament and of the Council of 23 April 2009 on the Effort of Member States to Reduce their Greenhouse Gas Emissions to Meet the Community's Greenhouse Gas Emission Reduction Commitments up to 2020. *Official Journal of the European Union*, 5 June, L 140.

Directive 2001/77/EC of the European Parliament and of the Council of 27 September 2001 on the Promotion of Electricity Produced from Renewable Energy Sources in the Internal Electricity Market. *Official Journal of the European Communities*, 27 October, L 283/33.

Directive 2009/28/EC of the European Parliament and of the Council of 23 April 2009 on the Promotion of the Use of Energy from Renewable Sources and Amending and Subsequently Repealing Directives 2001/77/EC and 2003/30/EC. *Official Journal of the European Union*, 5 June, L 140/16.

ENDS Europe Daily. 2008a. Renewable Energy Plans to Occupy EU Ministers. Issue 2551. 28 May 2008. London: Environmental Data Services.

ENDS Europe Daily. 2008b. Ministers Make Scant Progress on EU Climate Plan. Issue 2557. 5 June 2008. London: Environmental Data Services.

ENDS Europe Daily. 2008c. MEP Clamps Down on International Carbon Credits. Issue 2566. 18 June 2008. London: Environmental Data Services.

European Council. 2007. *Presidency Conclusions*. 7224/1/07 REV 1. Brussels: Council of the European Union.

European Parliament. 2008a. Committee on the Environment, Public Health and Food Safety. Report on the Proposal for a Decision of the European Parliament and of the Council on the Effort of Member States to Reduce their Greenhouse Gas Emissions to Meet the Community's Greenhouse Gas Emission Reduction Commitments up to 2020. A6-0411/2008. 15 October 2008. Brussels: European Parliament.

European Parliament. 2008b. *Legislative Resolution of 17 December 2008 on the Proposal for a Decision of the European Parliament and of the Council on the Effort of Member States to Reduce their Greenhouse Gas emissions to Meet the Community's Greenhouse Gas Emission Reduction Commitments up to 2020*. http://www.europarl.europa.eu/sides/getDoc.do?pubRef=-//EP//TEXT+TA+P6-TA-2008-0611+0+DOC+XML+V0//EN. Accessed: 5 November 2009.

Eyckmans, Johan, Jan Cornillie and Denise Van Regemorter. 2002. Efficiency and Equity in the EU Burden Sharing Agreement. Working paper series no. 2000-02. Energy, Transport & Environment.

Haug, Constanze and Andrew Jordan. 2010, forthcoming. Burden Sharing: Distributing Burdens or Sharing Efforts? In *Climate Change Policy in the European Union: Confronting the Dilemmas of Adaptation and Mitigation?* Edited by Jordan, Andrew, David Huitema, Harro van Asselt, Tim Rayner and Frans Berkhout. 83-110. Cambridge: Cambridge University Press.

Holtwisch, Christoph. 2006. *Das Nichteinhaltunsverfahren des Kyoto-Protokolls, Entstehung – Gestalt – Wirkung.* Berlin: Duncker & Humblot.

IPCC (Intergovernmental Panel on Climate Change). 1996. *Climate Change 1995. The Science of Climate Change.* Contribution of Working Group I to the Second Assessment Report of the Intergovernmental Panel on Climate Change. Cambridge: Cambridge University Press.

Lyons, Paul K. 1998. *EU Energy Policies Towards the 21st Century.* EC INFORM. http://uk.geocities.com/ec_inform/21stCont.html.

Marklund, Per-Olov and Eva Samakovlis. 2004. What is Driving the EU Burden-Sharing Agreement: Efficiency or Equity? *Umeå Economic Studies,* No. 620, Umeå University.

Oberthür, Sebastian, and Hermann E. Ott. 1999. *The Kyoto Protocol. International Climate Policy for the 21st Century.* Berlin: Springer.

Oberthür, Sebastian and René Lefeber. 2010. Key Features of the Compliance System of the Kyoto Protocol. *Climate Law* 1(1) (forthcoming).

Phylipsen G.J.M, Jeffrey W. Bode, Kornelis Blok, H. Merkus and B. Metz. 1998. A Triptych Sectoral Approach to Burden Differentiation: GHG Emissions in the European Bubble. *Energy Policy* 26: 929-43.

Ringius, Lasse. 1999. Differentiation, Leaders, and Fairness: Negotiating Climate Commitments in the European Community. *International Negotiation* 4(2): 133-66.

Sijm, J.P.M., M.M. Berk, M.G.J. den Elzen and R.A. van den Wijngaart. 2007. Options for Post-2012 EU Burden Sharing and EU ETS Allocation. Bilthoven: Netherlands Environmental Assessment Agency.

Stephenson, Paule. 2008. Climate Change, Equity and European "Effort Sharing". Working paper 08/07. Institute of Policy Studies.

Stern, Nicholas. 2007. *The Economics of Climate Change. The Stern Review.* Cambridge: Cambridge University Press.

The EU's New Renewable Energy Directive (2009/28/EC)

Tom Howes[1]

1.   Introduction

The EU has had an explicit renewable energy policy, distinct from climate policy, since the launch of the White Paper "Energy for the Future" in 1997.[2] The Community's renewable energy policy then focused on the goal of achieving a doubling of the share of renewable energy in primary energy consumption (the standard measure of energy at the time) to twelve per cent by 2010.

This policy has always had three distinct justifications. First, the production of renewable energy displaces fossil fuel based energy and thus contributes directly to the reduction of emissions from energy consumption. So, renewable energy policy clearly has a link to climate and sustainability policy. Second, the growth of renewable energy directly reduces the consumption of fossil fuels. It therefore improves the trade balance and diversifies Europe's energy supplies both in terms of the type of energy developed and the sources used. Often, renewable energy sources are indigenous, which is another factor that can contribute to improving the security of energy supplies. Third, the growth of renewable energy depends on new technologies and processes, and ongoing efforts to improve the technology and bring down costs. Consequently, there is a clear technology innovation drive from the sector and a clear economic and employment benefit: the sector employs over 1.4 million people, with this expected to rise by over 400,000 (net) jobs by 2020. It also creates a value added of 58 billion Euro per year, which is expected to rise to 129 billion Euro by 2020.[3] Thus, for some time, the economic stimulus impact of green measures in the renewable energy sector has been acknowledged.

---

1.   Directorate General for Energy and Transport, European Commission. The views expressed in this chapter are those of the author and in no way constitute a view, official or otherwise, of the European Commission.
2.   Commission 1997.
3.   Ragwitz et al. 2009.

Whilst all of these elements could be pursued at a national level, the need for tackling them from a European perspective, in a coordinated fashion, has become increasingly clear. This is especially true given the global nature of the sustainability benefits of renewable energy, the dawning realisation of the need to act collectively to ensure the security of Europe's energy supplies, and the integration of national markets into the single European market that ensures economic development, employment and innovation flow more smoothly between Member States.

However, it was political and economic events that drove renewable energy and climate policy to the top of the policy agenda in the 2000s. The need for a coherent, consistent and unified European approach to setting the global regulatory regime to deal with climate change "post Kyoto" was becoming apparent and led to a stronger European dimension to environmental policy more broadly. In addition, record energy prices were highlighting the energy supply vulnerability of all Member States. Finally, the UK's Stern Review on the Economics of Climate Change of 2006 contributed to the global recognition that there is a strong economic case to be made for taking action to prevent further climate change. Thus, immediate political and economic concerns moved climate change and renewable energy policy up the policy agenda.

Addressing renewable energy policy, this chapter proceeds in four steps. The following section covers the historical development of renewable energy and renewable energy policy in the EU. Section 3 ensues with a discussion of the resulting climate and energy package of 2008. Section 4 addresses the details of the new Renewable Energy Directive. The chapter ends with a brief conclusion.

2. Background

On the basis of the broad policy goal of promoting renewable energy, a number of Member States have made further efforts to develop their domestic resources, but progress has been limited. The share of renewable energy of what is now the EU-27 rose from 7.2 per cent in 1997 to 7.55 per cent in 2000 (see Table 1).

Table 1 – Share of renewable energy (in per cent)

	1997	1998	1999	2000	2001	2002	2003	2004	2005	2006
Sweden	36,7	36,5	36,4	37,7	37,2	36,6	37,3	38,2	39,5	41,4
Latvia	31,2	32,1	33,9	33,4	33,2	32,4	32,9	33,3	32,6	31,4
Finland	26,6	26,6	27,6	28,9	27,9	28,5	27,9	29,2	28,5	28,9
Austria	25,1	24,1	25,0	25,1	25,1	24,1	23,2	23,9	23,5	25,1
Portugal	22,0	20,9	20,4	19,5	19,1	19,3	19,4	18,2	20,3	21,5
Denmark	9,2	9,6	10,2	11,7	12,2	13,3	14,9	16,0	17,3	17,1
Romania	14,9	15,3	17,1	16,9	14,0	14,8	16,3	16,4	17,6	17,1
Estonia	15,3	14,2	15,6	16,0	15,4	15,6	16,6	18,8	17,8	16,6
Slovenia	11,3	11,6	11,4	16,4	16,2	16,7	16,4	16,2	16,0	15,6
Lithuania	10,5	12,5	13,3	15,0	15,3	15,2	15,3	15,2	14,8	14,6
France	10,8	10,8	10,6	10,6	10,1	10,1	10,2	10,2	10,3	10,5
Bulgaria	4,1	5,5	6,8	7,7	7,6	8,5	8,3	8,8	9,1	9,0
Spain	8,5	8,3	8,2	8,2	8,1	8,2	8,5	8,3	8,5	8,7
Germany	3,2	3,5	3,3	3,7	4,2	4,8	4,9	5,7	6,5	7,8
Poland	5,7	6,3	6,1	6,5	6,9	7,2	7,1	7,1	7,2	7,5
Greece	7,3	7,1	7,1	7,2	7,1	7,0	6,6	6,8	6,9	7,2
Slovakia	3,1	3,2	3,3	3,2	5,8	4,9	5,5	5,0	6,5	6,8
Czech Republic	2,2	2,3	2,5	2,1	2,3	3,0	4,3	6,0	6,1	6,4
Italy	4,6	4,6	4,6	4,8	4,9	5,5	4,7	5,2	5,8	6,3
Hungary	2,8	2,6	2,6	2,8	2,6	4,8	4,8	4,4	4,3	5,1
Ireland	1,9	2,1	2,0	2,0	2,1	2,1	2,0	2,3	2,8	3,0
Belgium	0,9	1,1	1,2	1,1	1,3	1,3	1,5	1,7	2,3	2,7
Cyprus	2,8	2,7	2,7	2,6	2,6	2,6	2,6	2,6	2,6	2,7
Netherlands	1,5	1,6	1,5	1,6	1,6	1,6	1,8	2,0	2,5	2,7
United Kingdom	1,0	1,0	0,9	0,9	0,9	1,0	1,1	1,2	1,3	1,5
Luxembourg	0,7	0,9	0,9	0,9	0,9	0,9	0,9	0,9	1,0	1,0
Malta	0,0	0,0	0,0	0,0	0,0	0,0	0,0	0,0	0,0	0,0
EU-27	7,2	7,3	7,3	7,6	7,5	7,8	7,9	8,2	8,7	9,2

Source: Eurostat (http://epp.eurostat.ec.europa.eu/portal/page/portal/energy/data/database).

Note: Share of renewable energy in gross final energy consumption (including consumption of the energy branch for electricity and heat generation and distribution losses) with normalised hydroelectricity.

The various barriers to the growth of renewable energy were enumerated in the 1997 White Paper and included high costs (in particular relative to the external costs of competing energy sources), a lack of consumer information, and administrative barriers in plant siting, other planning matters and grid management. Furthermore, when total energy consumption is rising rapidly, even significant growth in renewable energy may not alter the percentage share. Given these barriers and the slow progress in increasing the share of renewable energy, the European Commission proposed legislation on the matter in 2000. The subsequent Directive 2001/77/EC focused on the electricity sector. Modelled on this Directive, Directive 2003/30/EC was adopted for the transport sector in 2003.

2.1 The "Green Electricity" Directive and the "Biofuels" Directive

Directive 2001/77/EC established targets for 2010 for the share of electricity from renewable energy sources for each Member State and also aimed to remove barriers in terms of grid management and administrative procedures. It created "guarantees of origin"-certificates that constituted proof of the provenance of the electricity in question, which could then be traded. This trade could be in the "green consumer" market, where electricity suppliers wish to identify the fact that they are selling "renewable electricity" to their customers. In addition, the trade could be between Member States, allowing an exchange that would count towards their target compliance. This latter trade was deemed necessary, as, with the establishment of national targets, obligations were fixed that could not be guaranteed to be "optimal" targets under all circumstances, although they attempted to reflect national resource potential. The creation of a trading mechanism, to be used as necessary, thus gave flexibility to Member States.

A further and final component of this Directive was the framework it provided for national support schemes. Since the late 1990s, an increasing number of Member States were establishing support schemes – subsidy regimes – to develop renewable energy, particularly in the electricity sector. By 2002, following Member States' implementation of the Directive, nearly all Member States had such support schemes. These included investment support (capital grants, tax exemptions or deductions on the purchase of goods) and operating support (price subsidies, green certificates, tender schemes and tax exemptions or reductions on the production of electricity). Operating support measures were the commonest form of support. Of these, "feed-in tariffs" were used in 18

Member States, while obligations/green-certificate regimes were in place in seven Member States.[4]

Feed-in tariffs and premiums, fixed prices higher than market prices or mark-ups in addition to the market price, are granted to operators of eligible domestic renewable electricity plants for the electricity they feed into the grid. The preferential, technology-specific feed-in tariffs and premiums paid to producers are regulated by the government. Feed-in tariffs take the form of a total price per unit of electricity paid to the producers whereas the premiums are paid to the producer on top of the electricity market price. An important difference between the feed-in tariff and the premium payment is that the latter introduces competition between producers in the electricity market. The cost for the grid operator is normally covered by a cross-subsidy through the overall tariff structure. The tariff or premium is normally guaranteed for a period of 10–20 years. In addition to the level of the tariff or premium, the guaranteed duration provides a strong degree of certainty, which lowers the financial risk faced by investors. Both feed-in tariffs and premiums can be structured to encourage specific technology promotion and cost reductions (the latter through stepped reductions in tariffs/premiums).

Quota obligations with green certificates are applied by a government imposing an obligation on consumers, suppliers or producers to source a certain percentage of their electricity from renewable energy. This obligation is usually accompanied by green certificates, which can be sold by producers separately or with the electricity and used by suppliers to meet their obligations.

These different schemes were developed in the 1990s – with some Member States using a combination of a range of instruments. In the Directive, the establishment of national targets and a guarantee of origin trading regime meant that more efforts would be needed to support the growth of renewable energy, and that a more coherent European approach would be needed as the market grew. For that reason, Member States included a framework in the new Directive to guide the harmonisation of these various national support schemes. This framework highlighted that harmonisation of support schemes would improve the efficiency of the market and so generate significant cost savings. It also emphasised that policy stability was an important element in ensuring market-based mechanisms worked, and proposed that to maintain investor confidence, a transition period of at least seven years was appropriate.[5]

---

4.   Commission 2008e.
5.   Directive 2001/77/EC, Article 4(2).

Following up on what was deemed a successful European legal framework for the electricity sector, the Commission proposed a similar arrangement for the transport sector. The resulting Directive 2003/30/EC established targets for the share of renewable energy in transport, and reporting requirements to monitor the sustainability of biofuels in particular (as biofuels were, and are, expected to be the dominant form of renewable energy available to the transport sector for some time to come). The proposed target was to reach a share of two per cent of biofuels in overall transport fuel by 2005 and 5.75 per cent by 2010. The target was the same for all Member States, as a European market for biofuels existed and national resource potential was not relevant.

These two Directives, which formed the legal basis for Community renewable energy policy, reflect a phase in the development of European environmental and climate policy overall. The policy has evolved significantly over the last decade, in particular moving from highly regulated sectoral or industrial approaches for limiting various emissions, to a much looser approach, embracing market mechanisms – and in particular, the emissions trading system (ETS).[6] Renewable energy policy grew out of environmental policy, and out of the environmental articles of the EC Treaty (namely Article 175). With the Directives, a market orientation and flexibility are evident: overall sectoral targets rather than industry-specific objectives were established, while, in the absence of specific regulatory instruments, the measures were left to be determined by each Member State as appropriate.

Regular reporting by Member States and monitoring by the Commission followed the implementation of these Directives.[7] These reports monitored the slow progress in developing renewable energy, the expected failure to meet the 2010 targets and the failure to take adequate measures to remove the various barriers to developing renewable energy technologies. Despite having targets (of an indicative, rather than mandatory, nature), and Commission requests to address specific barriers, growth in renewable energy has been dominated by a few keen Member States. Table 1 shows that between 2000 and 2006, only Denmark, the Czech Republic, Germany, Slovakia and Hungary increased their shares of renewable energy by more than two percentage points. What's more, growth in overall energy consumption meant that some countries' shares actually *declined*, despite some growth in the absolute amount of renewable energy being produced. (These countries are Latvia, Slovenia, Lithuania, France, Greece and Finland.)

6.   See the chapter by Skjærseth and Wettestad in this volume.
7.   Commission 2004; 2005; 2006; 2008e.

Thus, at a time when the "teething problems" of the ETS were becoming clear, it was clear that the framework for the promotion of renewable energy also needed improving, not least to set a new timeframe. The timeframe is important because it is a key element in providing policy stability for industry. Knowing that, for a fixed period, goals, measures and instruments will be established to achieve an agreed objective gives industry the assurance needed to undertake the necessary investments. It also gives the financial sector reassurance, reduces the assessed risk, and so helps reduce the cost of capital for those industries involved.

2.2 The international dimension to European renewable energy policy

Whilst the legal framework outlined above covers the EU, concerted efforts have been made to spread best practice regarding the development of renewable energy across the world, and particularly to developing countries. As with greenhouse gas (GHG) emission reduction policies, this international dimension of renewable energy policy has a number of goals: the increased use of renewable energy in third countries cuts emissions of GHGs and other harmful substances, increases the diversity, and thus the security, of energy supply, and also provides a local economic stimulus. It thus contributes to developing countries' economic growth as well as whatever climate and energy policies they might operate.

A range of measures was established or harnessed by the Commission to promote renewable energy. These include increasing the priority of renewable energy under European funding mechanisms: the European Investment Bank, the European Bank for Reconstruction and Development, funding under the multiannual framework programmes for research and development, a new Global Energy Efficiency and Renewable Energy Fund (GEEREF) focusing on leveraging private capital into developing renewable energy markets, the EU Energy Initiative (EUEI), the Renewable Energy and Energy Efficiency Partnership (REEEP), the Mediterranean Renewable Energy Partnership (MEDREP), the Global Village Energy Partnership (GVEP), and the Basel Agency for Sustainable Energy (BASE).[8] All these mechanisms are means of providing a direct, development-oriented benefit to recipient countries, but they also play a role in highlighting and demonstrating the benefits of developing renewable energy projects locally.

---

8. See the following websites for more information: http://ec.europa.eu/environment/
    climat/pdf/key_elements.pdf; http://www.euei.org; http://www.reeep.org; http://
    www.medrep.it; http://www.gvep.org; http://www.energy-base.org.

From the "practical advocacy" of these mechanisms, third countries are able to understand the concrete benefits of a renewable energy policy and are encouraged to adopt similar practices themselves, thus also helping combat global climate change.

2.3   The policy proposals of 2007

Having acknowledged the inadequacies of the existing regimes, and the need to establish a new time horizon, the Commission came forward with its proposals for "An Energy Policy for Europe"[9] in January 2007. For renewable energy, the details of the plan were contained in the renewables "Roadmap" of 2006.[10] This explored various feasible scenarios and their costs and concluded that a 20 per cent goal for renewable energy for the EU by 2020 was ambitious, demanding, but feasible. Thus, together with the reviews of energy efficiency policy and emissions reductions plans, the famous 20-20-20 by 2020 was born.[11]

The Roadmap directly examined the question of continuing with a separate renewable energy policy at all, or abandoning it on the assumption that it was part of climate policy overall and that growth in the use of renewable energy would be driven by climate policy instruments such as the ETS. The Roadmap makes it clear that separate renewable energy policies and targets provide the stability necessary to guarantee growth. The review of the ETS had highlighted the role that price volatility had played in undermining the effectiveness of the scheme in the first phase. In comparison, the simple structure of targets geared to a specific sector appeared to prove more effective in achieving growth.

The Roadmap also proposed other significant modifications to the existing renewable energy policy regime. Chief amongst these was the decision to strengthen the targets. The Green Electricity Directive of 2001 and the Biofuels Directive of 2003 had both contained reference values to be taken into account by Member States when setting indicative targets. Most of the targets set were based on the reference values (though some were lower), but all were *indicative*. Whilst initially this was seen as positive terminology – giving stakeholders, industry and investors an indicative sense of plans and priorities – the slow progress and lack of action by Member States over the years highlighted that the indicative nature of the targets actually weakened them. Setting targets is intended to give clear signals and provide

9.   Commission 2007.
10.   Commission 2006a.
11.   See the chapter by Oberthür and Pallemaerts in this volume.

a sense of policy stability. The indicative targets clearly did not provide that stability. The Roadmap therefore proposed that the targets to be established should be legally binding in order to ensure confidence and encourage investment.

The Roadmap also proposed that rather than continuing with a sectoral approach (electricity, transport and the heating sector), which could result in up to 81 different targets (three targets for each of the 27 Member States), a more flexible arrangement would be appropriate. Thus, targets would be established for renewable energy overall. This would both remove the existing major distortion to the market by including the heating sector for the first time and would help reduce costs by leaving the choice of sectoral emphasis to each Member State.

The "Energy Policy for Europe" and the Roadmap were discussed at length throughout 2007, together with the plans for the modification of specific GHG policies such as the ETS, carbon capture and storage legislation and energy efficiency policy. In In particular, these discussions resulted in the European Council's endorsement of the Roadmap, in March 2007, and the European Parliament's similar endorsement in September 2007.[12]

3. The climate and energy package of January 2008

Whilst the Council of Ministers constitutes the primary European legislative chamber (the other being the European Parliament), the European Council, consisting of Heads of State or Government, is the foremost forum for setting the European policy agenda and priorities. Thus the endorsement of "An Energy Policy for Europe" by both the European Council and the European Parliament constitutes the strongest possible political endorsement of a policy.

On this basis, the European Commission published its "climate and energy package" on 23 January 2008. The climate and energy package presented measures that acknowledged the integrated nature of, and interrelationships between, energy policy (energy efficiency, security of supply, renewable energy policy) and climate policy (revised ETS, GHG emission reduction targets for the sectors of the economy not included in the ETS, and a legal framework for carbon capture and storage). It consisted of the

---

12. European Council 2007.

impact assessment, four pieces of draft legislation, new state aid guidelines and a review of Member States' national energy efficiency action plans.[13]

The impact assessment of the package included a range of modelled economic and policy scenarios.[14] These covered different oil prices, different scales of the use of international offsets from the Clean Development Mechanism of the Kyoto Protocol and sensitivity tests of different target levels (including the impacts of no renewables target and of no GHG emission reductions target). The impact assessment found that for the package overall, the direct annual costs by 2020 could be 0.45 per cent of the EU's GDP (roughly 70 billion Euro), with a carbon price of between 30-43 Euro per tonne of CO_2. Similar analysis undertaken in the renewable energy Roadmap impact assessment[15] found that for the renewable energy target alone, the annual cost by 2020 could range from 10.6-18 billion Euro (depending on oil price assumptions of 48-78 US dollars per barrel) and that the 20 per cent renewable energy would generate annual CO_2 emission reductions of between 600-900Mt, reduce annual fossil fuel demand by 250 million tonnes of oil equivalent and generate employment adding to the 300,000 jobs already existing in the renewable energy industry in Europe in 2005.

The impact assessment of the package also went into detail about all the key choices made in developing the Commission's proposal. These elements will be discussed below as each aspect of the final version of the new Renewable Energy Directive is analysed.

4.   The Renewable Energy Directive

Based on the Commission's proposal of January 2008, the Council of Ministers finalised the text of the Directive in April 2009. Together with the other elements of the legislative package, Directive 2009/28/EC was published in the Official Journal on 5 June 2009 and entered into force on 25 June 2009. It contains five distinct elements: obligatory national targets for 2020, national action plans, cooperation mechanisms, administrative and regulatory reforms, and biofuels sustainability criteria. These are discussed in the following sections.

---

13. See the chapter by Oberthür and Pallemaerts in this volume.
14. Commission 2008g.
15. Commission 2006b.

4.1 Setting the national targets

In the transition from separate electricity and transport targets to a new single "renewable energy target", a most notable switch was made from primary to final energy consumption as the basis of statistics and measurement. Energy has traditionally been measured and presented in terms of primary energy consumption (typically "gross inland consumption"), which accounts for the energy consumed prior to transformation into final energy – typically the coal, gas or oil used to generate electricity or heating. Such measurement puts renewable energy sources at a disadvantage, as there are no measured conversion or transformation losses. For example, one unit of electricity might require three units of coal, because two units of the coal are lost in the transformation of the energy into electricity, while it would require only one unit of wind (or hydro) power, as there are no transformation losses. For both, the amount of electricity generated and consumed is the same. But in primary energy terms, coal constitutes three units and wind just one. The Community's 2010 target of twelve per cent had been presented in those terms. However, the Green Electricity Directive and the Biofuels Directive dealt with energy in terms of final consumption. Thus, for consistency with the existing legislative arrangements and because of the desire to avoid discrimination against non-thermal energy sources, the 2020 targets are all in terms of final energy consumption. In fact the statistical term used in the measurement is "gross final energy consumption" which is Eurostat's traditional "final energy consumption" increased by consumption of the energy branch for electricity and heat generation and distribution losses.

Having determined the units of measurement, the next key task of the Directive was to allocate the EU's renewable energy target of 20 per cent amongst the 27 Member States. A traditional approach to establishing targets has been to base them on projected future potential resource availability. Economic models are often used, and were used in the Commission's analysis, to assess the resource potential of the EU – and the feasibility of the 20 per cent target. The results of one study undertaken for the Commission are presented in Figure 1.

Figure 1 – 2005 share and 2020 potential (per cent)

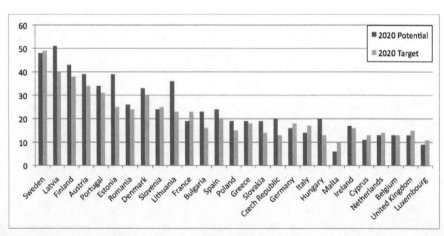

Source: Eurostat (2005) and Commission 2008f (PRIMES modelling of 2020 potential).

However, as with the analysis undertaken for the GHG reduction strategy, there appears to be a mismatch between the resource potential of several Member States and their ability to exploit such potential – i.e. their relative wealth. Giving high targets to countries with relatively low levels of GDP/capita was considered to be unfair and unrealistic. Instead, a GDP weighting was introduced. This weighting, combined with an "early starter bonus" (for Member States that had achieved reasonable growth in recent years) resulted in targets that differed from potential (Figure 2):

Figure 2 – 2020 potential and target (per cent)

Source: Directive 2009/28/EC and Commission 2008f.

In the discussions between Member States in the Council and with Parliament, little time was given to altering the approach to target setting. Establishing an alternative approach to sharing the EU target, whereby some countries have a lower target, would necessarily require some Member States to accept a higher target – which was too difficult to achieve. Thus, the targets agreed by Member States and Parliament were those proposed by the Commission (apart from a statistical correction for Latvia). The targets are indicated in Table 2.

Whilst the targets themselves were not altered, the details of how they would be calculated were modified. Both hydropower and wind power will be "normalised", i.e. averaged, to avoid volatile results due to annual climatic variations. In addition, the total gross final energy consumption will be capped such that the aviation share is not more than 6.18 per cent (4.12 per cent for Malta and Cyprus). Because widespread penetration of renewables in the aviation sector is unlikely to be achieved, Member States with above average aviation shares should not be "penalised".[16]

In addition to the 20 per cent renewable energy target, the Commission proposed, and Member States accepted, a ten per cent target for renewable energy in the transport sector. The earlier Biofuels Directive 2003/30/EC had first established such a target. While flexibility in determining sectoral shares is a necessary part of a cost-effective approach to developing renewable energy resources, a minimum effort is needed specifically in the transport sector as a crucial element of the modern European economy, because it is the sector in which energy consumption is forecast to grow most rapidly in the coming years. Also, this sector has the lowest level of fuel diversification of any sector (over 99 per cent is oil), and so has the least flexibility in achieving emission reductions and in reducing its exposure to supply shock risks. An "Energy Policy for Europe" that left the transport sector untouched would therefore hardly be credible. Thus Member States and Parliament retained the proposed minimum target of ten per cent.

As with the overall target, however, the calculation method was changed. In particular, it was agreed that biofuels from second-generation sources (biofuels produced from wastes, residues, non-food cellulosic material, and ligno-cellulosic material), which often generate higher GHG emissions

---

16. Directive 2009/28/EC, Article 5(6).

savings and compete less for land with agricultural crops, should have a bonus and count double towards the target. In addition, the electricity from renewable energy sources used in road transport should also receive a bonus and count 2.5 times their actual quantity for target calculation purposes. Finally, only biofuels that meet the sustainability criteria established by the Directive (discussed below) may count towards the target.[17]

4.2 Pathway to the targets

Targets are an effective policy instrument for providing a degree of certainty to investors or other stakeholders about a particular policy goal. The 2020 targets are meant to provide such stability. However, their effectiveness depends on their credibility, which is strengthened if there is an understanding of how the targets will be reached. It is for this reason that the Commission proposed a trajectory for each Member State (Table 2).

The trajectory as agreed by Member States is relatively flat: Member States should achieve 20 per cent of the growth towards the target by 2012, 30 per cent by 2014, 45 per cent by 2016 and 65 per cent by 2018. Whilst the trajectory offers "indicative targets", Member States are required to introduce measures "effectively designed" to ensure that the trajectory is reached.[18] Thus, any deviation from the trajectory should not be by design and national plans must demonstrate that a credible growth path will be established for reaching the target.

The recent trends in some Member States suggest that the planned trajectory is well balanced: some Member States have actually seen a decline in their share in the years to 2006; others (notably Sweden, Denmark, Austria, Czech Republic) have had recent growth rates higher than those proposed by the trajectory.

17. Directive 2009/28/EC, Article 3(4).
18. Directive 2009/28/EC, Article 3(2).

Table 2 – Proposed trajectory for reaching the renewables targets (per cent of final energy consumption)

	2000	2001	2002	2003	2004	2005	2006	2007	2008	2009	2010	2011	2012	2013	2014	2015	2016	2017	2018	2019	2020
Sweden	37,4	37,2	36,5	37,3	38,2	39,8	41,4	41,4	41,5	41,6	41,6	41,6	41,6	42,6	42,6	43,9	43,9	45,8	45,8	47,4	49,0
Latvia	35,5	34,8	34,4	33,6	34,8	32,6	31,4	31,9	32,6	33,3	33,9	34,1	34,1	34,8	34,8	35,9	35,9	37,4	37,4	38,7	40,0
Finland	29,0	28,0	28,5	28,0	28,2	28,5	28,9	29,2	29,6	30,0	30,3	30,4	30,4	31,4	31,4	32,8	32,8	34,7	34,7	36,3	38,0
Austria	25,6	25,4	24,7	23,8	22,8	23,3	25,2	25,2	25,3	25,4	25,4	25,4	25,4	26,5	26,5	28,1	28,1	30,3	30,3	32,1	34,0
Portugal	19,6	19,2	19,4	19,5	18,3	20,5	21,5	21,7	22,0	22,3	22,5	22,6	22,6	23,7	23,7	25,2	25,2	27,3	27,3	29,2	31,0
Denmark	11,7	12,3	13,4	14,9	16,1	17,0	17,1	17,6	18,2	18,9	19,5	19,6	19,6	20,9	20,9	22,9	22,9	25,5	25,5	27,7	30,0
Estonia	16,0	15,3	14,9	14,9	19,0	18,0	16,6	17,2	17,9	18,6	19,3	19,4	19,4	20,1	20,1	21,2	21,2	22,6	22,6	23,8	25,0
Slovenia	16,4	16,2	16,7	16,4	16,2	16,0	15,6	16,0	16,6	17,1	17,7	17,8	17,8	18,7	18,7	20,1	20,1	21,9	21,9	23,4	25,0
Romania	16,9	14,0	14,8	16,3	16,3	17,8	17,1	17,5	18,0	18,5	18,9	19,0	19,0	19,7	19,7	20,6	20,6	21,8	21,8	22,9	24,0
France	10,6	10,4	10,3	10,3	10,1	10,3	10,5	11,0	11,6	12,1	12,7	12,8	12,8	14,1	14,1	16,0	16,0	18,6	18,6	20,8	23,0
Lithuania	16,7	16,8	16,8	16,9	15,4	15,0	14,6	15,0	15,5	16,0	16,5	16,6	16,6	17,4	17,4	18,6	18,6	20,2	20,2	21,6	23,0
Spain	8,3	8,2	8,3	8,6	8,5	8,7	8,7	9,2	9,7	10,3	10,8	11,0	11,0	12,1	12,1	13,8	13,8	16,0	16,0	18,0	20,0
Germany	4,0	4,2	4,8	4,6	4,7	5,8	7,8	7,9	8,0	8,1	8,2	8,2	8,2	9,5	9,5	11,3	11,3	13,7	13,7	15,9	18,0
Greece	7,4	7,3	7,2	6,8	6,8	6,9	7,2	7,6	8,1	8,5	9,0	9,1	9,1	10,2	10,2	11,9	11,9	14,1	14,1	16,1	18,0
Italy	4,8	4,9	5,5	4,7	5,0	5,2	6,3	6,6	6,9	7,2	7,5	7,6	7,6	8,7	8,7	10,5	10,5	12,9	12,9	14,9	17,0
Bulgaria	8,2	8,1	9,0	8,8	9,4	9,4	9,0	9,3	9,8	10,2	10,6	10,7	10,7	11,4	11,4	12,4	12,4	13,7	13,7	14,8	16,0
Ireland	2,2	2,3	2,3	2,4	2,7	3,1	3,0	3,5	4,2	4,9	5,5	5,7	5,7	7,0	7,0	8,9	8,9	11,5	11,5	13,7	16,0
Poland	6,5	6,9	7,2	7,1	7,1	7,2	7,5	7,8	8,1	8,4	8,7	8,8	8,8	9,5	9,5	10,7	10,7	12,3	12,3	13,6	15,0
United Kingdom	0,9	0,9	1,0	1,1	1,2	1,3	1,5	2,0	2,6	3,3	3,9	4,0	4,0	5,4	5,4	7,5	7,5	10,2	10,2	12,6	15,0
Netherlands	1,6	1,6	1,6	1,8	2,0	2,4	2,7	3,1	3,6	4,1	4,6	4,7	4,7	5,9	5,9	7,6	7,6	9,9	9,9	12,0	14,0
Slovakia	3,2	5,7	5,1	5,8	6,3	6,7	6,8	7,1	7,4	7,8	8,1	8,2	8,2	8,9	8,9	10,0	10,0	11,4	11,4	12,7	14,0
Belgium	1,2	1,3	1,4	1,6	1,8	2,2	2,7	3,0	3,4	3,9	4,3	4,4	4,4	5,4	5,4	7,1	7,1	9,2	9,2	11,1	13,0
Cyprus	2,6	2,5	2,5	2,4	2,6	2,9	2,7	3,1	3,7	4,3	4,8	4,9	4,9	5,9	5,9	7,4	7,4	9,5	9,5	11,2	13,0
Czech Republic	2,4	2,7	2,9	4,3	5,9	6,1	6,4	6,6	6,9	7,2	7,4	7,5	7,5	8,2	8,2	9,2	9,2	10,6	10,6	11,8	13,0
Hungary	2,8	2,6	4,8	4,7	4,4	4,3	5,1	5,3	5,5	5,8	6,0	6,0	6,0	6,9	6,9	8,2	8,2	10,0	10,0	11,5	13,0
Luxembourg	0,9	0,8	0,7	0,8	0,9	0,9	1,0	1,4	1,9	2,3	2,8	2,9	2,9	3,9	3,9	5,4	5,4	7,5	7,5	9,2	11,0
Malta	0,0	0,0	0,0	0,0	0,0	0,0	0,0	0,4	0,9	1,4	1,9	2,0	2,0	3,0	3,0	4,5	4,5	6,5	6,5	8,3	10,0
EU 27	7,6	7,6	7,9	7,9	8,1	8,5	9,2	9,5	9,9	10,3	10,7	10,8	10,8	12,0	12,0	13,7	13,7	16,0	16,0	18,0	20,0

Source: Directive 2009/28/EC, Annexes IA and IB.

Note: Figures for 2000-2006 represent collected, Eurostat data. Figures from 2007 onwards represent the indicative trajectory towards the 2020 target, as set in Annex IB of the new Directive.

4.3   Cooperation mechanisms

Intra-European trade has always been a source of growth and development for Europe, and this is no less the case with renewable energy. Under Directive 2001/77/EC, targets were set for each Member State for the 2010 share of electricity from renewable energy sources. Even though these targets were established on the basis of estimates of national resource potential, a regime for mutually recognised guarantees of origin was established and trade in such certificates was envisaged, to ensure that the resources could be exploited across Europe in a cost effective manner. Such trade never occurred. It appears Member States were keener to develop their own resources (contributing to their own emissions reductions, reducing fossil fuel imports and generating jobs). However, as the cheaper renewables potentials are exploited and costs start to rise, the need to seek out cheaper renewables in other Member States will rise. Analysis by the European Commission suggests that such trade could save Member States billions of Euro per year and thus should be encouraged.[19] For this reason, the Directive created a number of "cooperation mechanisms" that allow a cross-financing between Member States for the achievement of the EU target.

Statistical transfers

Article 6 of the Directive creates "statistical transfers". These are agreements between Member States to transfer a quantity of renewable energy produced in one Member State to another Member State for target compliance purposes. The transfer is purely virtual; there is no accompanying energy flow.

This mechanism exists so that Member States with considerable renewable energy sources, or with effective support schemes that help develop such sources cost effectively, can offer any renewable energy production surplus to their requirements (either to their target or trajectory) to other Member States. The "other" Member States interested in purchasing such transfers would be those with limited domestic renewable energy sources or with inadequate support schemes for developing the available domestic resources. The transfer would normally be agreed for a number of years, for a price per MWh. In fact, most Member States wanting to buy the energy would likely want the supply to continue until at least 2020, in order to comply with their targets, or until their own domestic resources can be brought into production at a later stage.

19.   Commission 2008g.

Once such an agreement is reached between two or more Member States, the European Commission will be notified, and at the end of each year the production statistics of the relevant Member States will be adjusted accordingly.

Joint projects for Member States

Articles 7 and 8 create "joint projects". A "joint project" is a broad concept covering the building or co-financing of infrastructure or even an energy purchase agreement. The intention behind the mechanism is the same as for statistical transfers: to help build new plants and infrastructure in a Member State and sharing the resulting energy towards two or more Member States' national targets, in order to reduce the overall cost of reaching the targets.

One key difference between joint projects and statistical transfers is the proposed inclusion of "private entities" in joint projects. A private entity, such as a power generator, infrastructure company, energy equipment manufacturer, a banking consortium, can identify projects in any Member State. Financing such a project could occur under the normal and existing domestic arrangements, but if such arrangements are insufficient, because the support is too low or does not qualify according to domestic priorities, the project would not be built. In such a case, the project developer could broker an agreement whereby another Member State agrees to help finance the project; again, this could be through loans, grants, tenders or access to national support schemes such as feed-in tariffs or green-certificate regimes. In exchange for this co-financing, the Member State would receive credit for a share of the renewable energy that was produced as a result of the project.

As in the case of "statistical transfers", the European Commission will again be notified of the details of the joint project, and each year the agreed quantity of energy will be virtually exchanged. Such an arrangement does not preclude a project being completed and the actual energy, the heat or electricity generated, being sold physically, and exported to another country. In this case, the Member State would be buying the energy itself as well as its "green characteristics".

Joint support schemes

The third element of the cooperation mechanisms established under the Directive is called "joint support schemes" created by Articles 10 and 11. Under these articles, Member States may agree to join or coordinate their national support schemes (e.g. a common feed-in tariff or green-certificate/

obligation regime). The European Commission has regularly reported on the structure and functioning of support schemes and has maintained that efforts are needed to improve the coordination and cooperation amongst different national schemes – and eventually, harmonisation of support schemes. Thus these articles of the Directive ensure that in the event of Member States coordinating or joining their support schemes, the targets can be adjusted to reflect the change.

In the event of the joining of schemes, the renewable energy produced under such conditions is considered "pooled" and shared out either as a "statistical transfer" or according to an agreed distribution rule of which the Commission has been notified. So whilst the Commission does not require any harmonisation of support schemes, it expects national support schemes to continue to evolve and will facilitate increasing cooperation and coordination.

Third-country participation

The above three mechanisms (statistical transfers, joint projects and joint support schemes) were all created for Member States' use, because the renewable energy policy and target are focused on consumption *in the EU*. However, the Directive explicitly highlights that some non-Member States – "third countries" – may also take part in the use of these mechanisms. These include the European Economic Area (EEA) countries of Norway, Liechtenstein and Iceland (who would normally adopt this Directive in the course of applying EU legislation of relevance to the EEA). It also includes the Contracting Parties to the Energy Community Treaty, an association of South-East European countries[20] providing a legal framework for the gradual adaptation of these countries' energy markets to EU energy market laws. The Directive explicitly encourages the Energy Community to adopt the Directive (including the establishment of ambitious 2020 targets) so that the contracting parties to the Treaty would thereupon be eligible to make use of the cooperation mechanisms to help develop their energy production or energy infrastructure.[21]

In addition to the cooperation mechanisms available to Member States, the Directive also creates an instrument (under Articles 9 and 10) that would enable third countries to take part in developing renewable energy sources

---

20. These countries are Albania, Bosnia and Herzegovina, Croatia, former Yugoslav Republic of Macedonia, Montenegro, Serbia and the United Nations Interim Administration Mission in Kosovo. Georgia, Moldova, Norway, Turkey and Ukraine take part as observers.
21. Directive 2009/28/EC, Article 9(8).

and contributing to the EU target, irrespective of their membership of the EEA or Energy Community Treaty. Accordingly, "joint projects" between Member States and third countries – similar in structure to the joint projects between Member States described above – can be established under Article 9 of the Directive. However, whilst joint projects between Member States can be purely "virtual trade" arrangements, joint projects with third countries have strict conditions attached to them to ensure that the arrangements generate new renewable energy production of electricity that is actually consumed in the EU. In particular, as proof of importation, the Directive requires that:

- the electricity is firmly nominated to the allocated interconnection capacity by all responsible Transmission System Operators in the country of origin, the country of destination and, if relevant, each third country of transit;
- the electricity is firmly registered in the schedule of balance by the responsible Transmission System Operator on the Community side of an interconnector; and
- the nominated capacity and the production of electricity from the designated installation refer to the same period of time.

In addition, the energy that is produced and exported to the EU under the agreement may not receive operating support. This rule is applied to reduce the risk of paying double subsidies and over-compensating producers.

A limited exception to the requirement of physical importation of electricity is included in Article 9(3). This article allows for the virtual transfer of electricity from a new plant if interconnector capacity is being built (construction started by 2016), if it will be operational after 2020 but no later than 2022 and if it will be used to export the electricity to the EU.

As with the other types of cooperation mechanisms, following notification of such schemes, the Commission will adjust the energy statistics.

With this instrument, the way is opened for trading arrangements not unlike the Clean Development Mechanism under the Kyoto Protocol and EU ETS for GHG emissions. The requirement to import the electricity into the EU limits the scope of the instrument: it depends on new plants being built and electricity being exported through interconnector capacity between the country of production and the EU (including any transit countries). However, together with the ability to produce other renewable energy fuels (biomass, biofuels, biogas) and export them to the EU, this mechanism allows third countries access to a source of finance to help develop their infrastructure (which is badly needed), whilst at the same time helping to contribute to EU energy policy objectives.

4.4   Administrative measures

In the discussion on climate change and other environmental concerns, economic analysis has often focused on the external costs of fossil fuels and the market failure and discrimination against clean alternatives that follows. However, such market failure is not the sole problem. The administrative, regulatory and information failures also distort the market and need addressing.

In the past, in European legislation and in the reports of the Commission examining the barriers to the growth of renewable energy, "administrative and regulatory barriers" have been highlighted as a significant problem. Legislation has, in broad terms, required Member States to "take action" and Commission reports have included more specific recommendations for such action. That said, the monitoring of Member States and the analysis undertaken for the Commission consistently highlight the administrative barriers faced by the renewable energy sector. Whether it is in national building codes, planning regimes, planning timetables, public consultation processes, in builder, planner or architect certification schemes, in the provision of information to consumers, or in the provision of equipment installation and maintenance regimes by manufacturers and installers etc., the costs, uncertainties about results and quality are intolerably high.

It is for this reason that the Commission proposed, and the Council and Parliament accepted (in a weaker form), a range of recommendations and requirements covering all of the above areas. These are all addressed in Articles 13 and 14 of the new Renewable Energy Directive.

These articles go into quite some detail in explaining what Member States need to do. For the first time in European legislation, Member States have agreed to coordinate their approaches to a range of planning, certification and educational issues associated with the renewable energy sector. Some elements are obligatory while others are recommendations. In either case, Member States are obliged to reflect on their procedures and other institutional and administrative arrangements and to ensure that they are improved. In particular, they require Member States to ensure that:

- authorisation, certification and licensing procedures for plants and infrastructure are streamlined, proportionate and necessary, with simplified procedures for small or decentralised projects where appropriate;

- responsibilities for such procedures are defined and coordinated between local, regional and national bodies, with transparent timetables and provision of information on processing and assistance;
- rules for these procedures are objective, transparent, proportionate and non-discriminatory and that associated administrative charges are transparent and cost related.

In addition, technical specifications of equipment (for support) must be clearly defined, based on European standards, and should not constitute a barrier to trade.

In addition to the planning-oriented requirements, the Directive requires reforms to building codes, administrative coordination, promotion of energy efficiency of renewable energy equipment certification regimes for equipment installers and information campaigns to inform consumers. National action plans to be submitted by each Member State by June 2010 (see below) will describe how each Member State will implement the relevant legal provisions based on a template prepared by the Commission.

4.5 Consumer market for green energy

Another element of the Directive focuses on the further development of the "green consumer market" as a stimulus for the renewable energy sector. Directive 2003/54/EC on the internal market in electricity requires that electricity suppliers give a breakdown of the primary energy mix of their electricity to all their customers in their electricity bills. It also requires that Member States ensure the reliability of the system, but gives no further instruction. As the key interest in providing such information to consumers derives from the growing use of electricity from renewable energy sources, the "guarantees of origin" introduced by the Green Electricity Directive of 2001 first established a common form of proof for electricity producers in all Member States. The 2001 Directive did not, however, prescribe in detail how the guarantees of origin would be issued and used. Since some Member States required electricity suppliers to use them to meet their energy mix disclosure requirements and others did not, a coherent system was not developed. Doubts arose about the reliability of the system and stories of double counting of electricity abounded (for instance following the sale of guarantees of origin to a third party who was acquiring the "green rights" to the electricity, the producer of the electricity would continue to tell their clients that the electricity came from a renewable energy source).

Given these inadequacies in the existing regime, the new Directive strengthens the legislation on guarantees of origin by imposing standardisation, greater and more uniform provision of information, guards against double counting of the same energy, and by providing scope for using the guarantees of origin to generate "additionality".[22]

The "additionality" arguments arose during discussions of the text in the Council and Parliament. Some saw guarantees of origin as simple proof of origin of the energy mix – demonstrating that the energy is from old hydro plants or new photovoltaic farms. Others felt that as the consumer market grows and consumers pay extra "green electricity", consumers will expect their additional expenditure to contribute to the growth in renewable energy, to the building of new capacity and even to ensuring that the new capacity is additional to the Member State's target. It is for this reason that information about the age and type of plant and receipt of subsidy are now included on the guarantee of origin. This information can be used by Member States either to provide more accurate information to consumers when the energy mix is disclosed, or, if a country so chooses, to establish particular requirements to promote new growth of renewable energy capacity (e.g. by requiring that electricity suppliers selling "100 per cent green" electricity provide a minimum fraction from new production capacity).

It is in the use of guarantees of origin that the greatest change occurred between the Commission's proposal and the final text of the Directive as agreed by the Council and Parliament. In the Commission's proposal, the guarantees of origin were to be standardised and their use regularised as described above, but they were also to be used as a tradable instrument for target compliance. In the course of discussions with Member States and Parliament, this approach was modified: the "cooperation mechanisms" were established, as described above, as the sole means of flexibility or trade for target compliance, and the instrument of the guarantee of origin was explicitly rendered a tool for the green consumer market.

4.6 Grid reform

In the creation and management of the electricity grid, administrative, regulatory and market barriers are combined. The electricity grids of Europe were built for centralised power production from government monopolies. The restructuring and market liberalisation which have been

---

22. Directive 2009/28/EC, Article 15.

ongoing since the 1990s have begun the process of creating a competitive market in the electricity sector, where new entrants – such as renewable energy producers – may enter and compete fairly. But the process is still very much underway. Given the market dominance of incumbents and the traditional grid management structures in place, ensuring smooth access to the grid and to the electricity market for renewable energy producers has not been straightforward. This issue was addressed in Directive 2001/77/EC that established guaranteed access (connections) for renewable energy producers and encouraged priority access such as in electricity dispatching. In general, system operators and regulators were meant to ensure that charging regimes and administrative arrangements were reformed and improved so as to avoid barriers to the entry of new market players, such as renewable electricity producers.

The reports of the Commission have consistently highlighted that not enough is being done to improve the system of grid management in most Member States,[23] and for this reason the new Renewable Energy Directive strengthened these elements. Under Article 16, Member States must now take appropriate steps to develop the grid to be able to absorb the expected growth in electricity from renewable energy sources, while also accelerating authorisation procedures, guaranteeing transmission and distribution of green electricity and providing priority or guaranteed grid access. As with other elements of the Directive, the measures the Member States will take to implement this Article will be included in the national action plan.

Knowing the rules is crucial when producers are planning their investments. So it is important that rules on how costs are determined and allocated are clear and public. When it comes to actually establishing connections, it is also important to have a good understanding of the costs involved, and of the potential delays and timetable. If this type of information is available to new producers and would-be investors, the risks of the investment are reduced; the cost of capital may even be lower. All this helps improve the investment environment for new investments in plant and infrastructure.

Article 16(4) of the Directive also requires a review of cost rules and charges: adaptations might be needed to meet the challenging demands on a new grid. A regular review provides a stable and predictable means of updating the rules.

---

23.   Commission 2004, 2006, 2008e.

Finally, the Directive makes it clear that Member States may, but are not obliged to, put the cost burden on the system operators. This "socialised" or "shallow" connection cost model ensures that all consumers share the extra costs of developing the network. The opposite type of charging regime ("deep" cost model) leaves producers bearing the costs themselves (although generally they would receive a higher subsidy from the relevant renewable energy support instrument).

4.7 Sustainability criteria

Since the adoption of the Biofuels Directive, the discussion on biofuels in transport has gone from a discussion of a panacea, to that of a possibly beneficial alternative energy, to an energy source that has negative climate, environmental, agricultural, biodiversity and social impacts. Thus, this final element of the new Renewable Energy Directive was probably the most controversial element.

The European Community has been promoting biofuels since 2003. Quantities are still very small (the 2007 share of biofuels was still only 2.6 per cent).[24] However, environmental concerns surrounding the production of biofuels have been significant, and at one point entirely dominated the debate about renewable energy. The concerns raised included fundamental ones such as whether, considering the lifecycle of biofuels (that is the production processes and agricultural practices associated with each type of biofuel), they actually generated a net GHG emission saving. Other concerns included the impact on competition for land and the consequent impact on food prices, the use of water and land resources, the impact on labour conditions, on possible loss of biodiversity (such as through rainforest destruction), and so on. On the question of net GHG emission savings, the vast bulk of literature[25] confirms that nearly all crop types and modern agricultural and refining processes ensure that biofuels produce a clear and net saving in emissions, compared to the use of petrol and diesel. On other issues, such as the impact on food prices, the empirical evidence suggests that European production of biofuels has had an insignificant impact.

In the course of negotiating the Directive, Member States and Parliament discussed all these issues at length and in the end concluded that the need to establish alternatives to fossil fuels in the transport sector was

24. Commission 2009b.
25. Commission 2009b.

paramount: the ten per cent minimum target for renewable energy in the transport sector remained in the Directive, although bonuses were added for the use of electricity from renewable energy sources and second generation biofuels,[26] given the fears of some of the possible negative impact of first generation biofuels. In addition, the Directive requires Member States both to closely monitor the impacts of biofuels consumption and also to explore the application of sustainability criteria for biomass in general. This debate in turn has stimulated calls for broad sustainability criteria, consistent with and applicable to the agricultural sector overall.

In order to ensure that the growth of biofuels in the transport sector is a major source of GHG savings, and does *not* generate any of these negative consequences, the Commission was clear that strict sustainability criteria need to be applied. The agreed sustainability criteria for biofuels and bioliquids produced in, or imported into, the EU are contained in Articles 17–19 and associated annexes of the Directive. All biofuels must achieve a lifecycle GHG emission saving of a minimum of 35 per cent. Existing plants are required to reach this limit from 2013. In 2017, the required level increases to 50 per cent for existing plants and 60 per cent for new installations. The savings relative to fossil fuel use and, to ease the administrative burden of such calculations, default values and calculation methods are given in Annex V of the Directive.

To safeguard land with high carbon stocks, no conversion of wetlands, undrained peatland or continuously forested areas is allowed, and the Commission's 2010 report will examine indirect land use change. To safeguard biodiversity, no raw materials may be grown on sensitive areas (primary forest, grasslands, protected areas). Biofuels produced in the EU must also meet environmental rules under "cross-compliance" obligations of the Common Agricultural Policy (where farmers in receipt of payments are obliged to meet good environmental standards).

The regime requires close monitoring not only by the Commission but also by producers, who must report on measures taken for water, air and soil protection as well as on social aspects (such as labour standards). In addition, Member States must report on commodity price developments, land use changes, impacts on biodiversity, soil and water, and GHG emission savings achieved. The Commission will publish this information in its reports, including environmental and socioeconomic impacts,

---

26. Directive 2009/28/EC, Articles 3(4)c and 21(2).

environmental costs and benefits, availability of second generation biofuels. By 2014, it will also review the level of lifecycle GHG emission savings.

With the sustainability criteria imposed, and with close monitoring of the situation by all parties concerned, biofuels can be the first significant step in weaning the transport sector off fossil fuels. Despite the bonuses for electric cars and second-generation biofuels, biofuels are the only significant form for reducing the dependence on oil in this sector in the short-term.

4.8   National Renewable Energy Action Plans

The earlier Green Electricity and Biofuels Directives contained monitoring requirements, but simply as a requirement to produce a report. Such a model had been followed in other areas as well, most notably in requiring the production of national energy efficiency action plans and biomass action plans. In all cases, the submission of monitoring or planning data was poor, because different Member States took different approaches and applied different reporting styles. As a result, not all the useful or necessary information was provided and the data were rarely comparable.

For these reasons, the Council and Parliament agreed early on in the process not merely to require Member States to submit such plans, as proposed by the Commission, but to comply with an obligatory template. This template was to be prepared by the Commission, in accordance with some minimum reporting requirements contained in Annex VI of the Directive (which was inserted by Parliament).[27] The Commission has produced a template for the national action plan[28] and Member States must submit complete plans to the Commission by June 2010.

These plans must contain national sectoral targets and trajectories (electricity, transport, heating and cooling), describe the adequate measures to achieve the overall target, the means of cooperation between national, regional and local authorities and planned statistical transfers or joint projects. In addition, to help Member States assess their use of planned statistical transfers or joint projects, six months prior to the due date of the national action plans (i.e. by December 2009), Member States must submit "forecast documents" to the Commission, containing estimates of future renewable energy production in excess of their

27.   Directive 2009/28/EC, Article 4(1).
28.   Commission 2009c.

trajectory and potential for "joint projects", together with the expected domestic production /import split.

In its proposal, the Commission tried to illustrate the nature of the "pathways" that were needed and the information that needs to be provided. Its analysis and modelling work included projections of the technologies that could be used to reach the target. Figure 3 illustrates a simplified technology and sectoral breakdown of the future development of renewable energy in the EU (as aggregated from data for individual Member States and for more than 20 renewable energy technologies). The data are based on an estimate developed for the Commission. Other models, forecasts and projections are of course possible. Member States' action plans should provide detailed information of a similar kind per renewable energy technology, which essentially requires each Member State to undertake analysis about its potential and to explore the pathways it can follow to reach its target.

Figure 3 – Renewable energy technology trends to 2020 – EU25 scenario (in GWh)

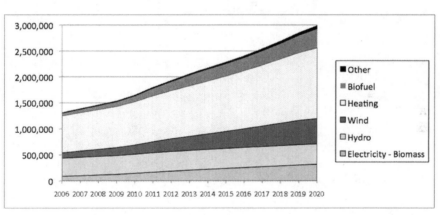

Source: Resch et al. 2008.[29]

29. *Other* = Electricity Geothermal, Photovoltaics, Electricity – Solar Thermal, Tide & Wave; *Biofuel* = Traditional Biofuels, Advanced Biofuels, Biofuel Import; *Heating* = Heating Biogas (grid), Heating Solid Biomass (grid), Heating Biowaste (grid), Heating Geothermal (grid), Heating Solid Biomass (non-grid), Heating Solar Thermal and Hot Water, Heat Pumps; *Wind* = Wind Onshore, Wind Offshore; *Hydro* = Hydro Large-Scale, Hydro Small-Scale; *Electricity – Biomass* = Electricity – Biogas, Electricity – Solid Biomass, Electricity – Biowaste.

It is expected that national renewable energy action plans will form a key element in the implementation and monitoring of the Directive. This is important for the European Commission, as it has the duty to ensure the Directive is properly implemented and applied. However, it will also be an important document for stakeholders with an interest in the development of renewable energy. The plan will be a "roadmap" for each Member State and from it, project developers, investors, manufacturers, and others will be able to assess the sectoral or technology priorities, plans, and measures of every Member State. Having such a wealth of detailed knowledge of a sector for the next ten years provides a uniquely clear picture and basis for investment. Such clarity and certainty is the core goal of the Directive and is seen as a core element in providing policy stability to encourage investment and the "green economic recovery" that governments talk of after the onset of the economic crisis of 2008/09.

5.   Conclusion

Climate and energy policy goals are both served by the growth of the renewable energy sector. The growth of Europe's renewable energy sources has been "patchy" and the legislative framework has proved inadequate.

The analysis and policy discussions the European Commission undertook in 2007 highlighted that a 20 per cent target for the share of renewable energy in 2020 was demanding but necessary, and an important part of a cost-effective strategy to address climate change and security of energy supply concerns. Since the European Commission made its proposals, the worsening macroeconomic situation has also highlighted the economic stimulus a "green recovery" can have. Major efforts to boost renewable energy production have become a key part of all economic stimulus packages around the world.

The legal framework provided by the new Renewable Energy Directive builds on the experience of earlier renewable energy legislation, but also on climate change legislation. As a result, the new Directive establishes national targets on the basis of GDP per capita or ability to pay (much like GHG emission reduction targets for Member States for sectors not covered by the ETS). Furthermore, the same experience and basis led to the introduction of some kind of flexibility mechanism to ensure Member States can exploit their comparative advantages and achieve the policy goals in a cost-effective manner.

144

The implementation of the new Directive, and in particular the application of Member States' national action plans, will provide the strongest basis yet for consistent growth in renewable energy production – yielding significant GHG emission reductions, energy supply diversification and technological innovation.

References

Brandstetter, Friedrich, Josef Buchinger and Susanne Gosytonyi. Without date. *Case Study EARTH Extended Accredited Renewables Training for Heating.* Vienna: Österreichisches Forschungs- und Prüfzentrum, Arsenal Ges.m.b.H. http://www.arsenal.ac.at. Accessed: 3 August 2009.

Coenraads, Rogier, Monique Voogt, Atilla Morotz. 2006. Analysis of Barriers for the Development of Electricity Generation from Renewable Energy Sources in the EU25. *Intelligent Energy Europe OPTRES Report.* Utrecht: Ecofys.

Coenraads, Rogier, Gemma Reece, Monique Voogt, Mario Ragwitz, Anne Held, Gustav Resch, Thomas Faber, Reinhard Haas, Inga Konstantinaviciute, Juraj Krivošík and Tomáš Chadim. 2008. *PROGRESS: Promotion and Growth of Renewable Energy Sources and Systems. Final Report.* Utrecht: Ecofys.

Commission (EC). 1996. *Energy for the Future: Renewable Sources of Energy.* Green Paper for a Community Strategy. COM (96) 576. Brussels: European Commission.

Commission (EC). 1997. *Energy for the Future: Renewable Sources of Energy.* White Paper for a Community Strategy and Action Plan. COM (97) 599. Brussels: European Commission.

Commission (EC). 2004. *The Share of Renewable Energy in the EU. Commission Report in Accordance with Article 3 of Directive 2001/77EC, Evaluation of the Effect of Legislative Instruments and Other Community Policies on the Development of the Contribution of Renewable Energy Sources in the EU and Proposals for Concrete Actions.* Communication from the Commission to the Council and the European Parliament. COM (2004) 366. Brussels: European Commission.

Commission (EC). 2005. *The Support of Electricity from Renewable Energy Sources.* Communication from the Commission. COM (2005) 627. Brussels: European Commission.

Commission (EC). 2006a. *Renewable Energy Road Map. Renewable Energies in the 21st Century: Building a More Sustainable Future.* Communication from the Commission to the Council and the European Parliament. COM (2006) 848. Brussels: European Commission.

Commission (EC). 2006b. *Renewable Energy Road Map. Renewable Energies in the 21st Century: Building a More Sustainable Future.* Commission Staff Working Document. Accompanying Document to the Communication from the Commission to the Council and the European Parliament. SEC (2006) 1719. Brussels: European Commission.

Commission (EC). 2006c. *Green Paper Follow-Up Action. Report on Progress in Renewable Electricity.* Communication from the Commission to the Council and the European Parliament. COM (2006) 849. Brussels: European Commission.

Commission (EC). 2007. *An Energy Policy for Europe.* Communication from the Commission to the European Council and the European Parliament. COM (2007) 1. Brussels: European Commission.

Commission (EC). 2008a. *Towards a Secure, Sustainable and Competitive European Energy Network.* Green Paper. COM (2008) 782. Brussels: European Commission.

Commission (EC). 2008b. *Second Strategic Energy Review. An EU Energy Security and Solidarity Action Plan.* Communication from the Commission to the European Parliament, the Council, the European Economic and Social Committee and the Committee of the Regions. COM (2008) 781. Brussels: European Commission.

Commission (EC). 2008c. *Offshore Wind Energy Action Needed to Deliver on the Energy Policy Objectives for 2020 and Beyond.* Communication from the Commission to the European Parliament, the Council, the European Economic and Social Committee and the Committee of the Regions. COM (2008) 768. Brussels: European Commission.

Commission (EC). 2008d. *Proposal for a Directive of the European Parliament and of the Council on the Energy Performance of Buildings.* COM (2008) 780. Brussels: European Commission.

Commission (EC). 2008e. *The Support of Electricity from Renewable Energy Sources. Accompanying Document to the Proposal for a Directive of the European Parliament and the Council on the Promotion of the Use of Energy from Renewable Sources.* Commission Staff Working Document. SEC (2008) 57. Brussels: European Commission.

Commission (EC). 2008f. *Annex to the Impact Assessment. Document Accompanying the Package of Implementation Measures for the EU's Objectives on Climate Change and Renewable Energy for 2020.* Commission Staff Working Document. SEC (2008) 85/1. Brussels: European Commission.

Commission (EC). 2008g. *Summary of the Impact Assessment. Document Accompanying the Package of Implementation Measures for the EU's Objectives on Climate Change and Renewable Energy for 2020.* Commission Staff Working Document. SEC (2008) 85/2. Brussels: European Commission.

Commission (EC). 2008h. *Impact Assessment. Document Accompanying the Package of Implementation Measures for the EU's Objectives on Climate Change and Renewable Energy for 2020.* Commission Staff Working Document. SEC (2008) 85/3. Brussels: European Commission.

Commission (EC). 2009a. *Report on Progress in Creating the Internal Gas and Electricity Market.* Communication from the Commission to the Council and the European Parliament. COM (2009) 115. Brussels: European Commission.

Commission (EC). 2009b. *The Renewable Energy Progress Report: Commission Report in Accordance with Article 3 of Directive 2001/77/EC, Article 4(2) of Directive 2003/30/EC and on the Implementation of the EU Biomass Action Plan, COM (2006) 628.* Communication from the Commission to the Council and the European Parliament. COM (2009) 192. Brussels: European Commission.

Commission (EC). 2009c. *A Template for National Renewable Energy Action Plans under Directive 2009/28/EC of the European Parliament and of the Council.* Commission Decision of 30 June 2009 (2009/548/EC). Brussels: European Commission.

Directive 2001/77/EC of the European Parliament and of the Council of 27 September 2001 on the Promotion of Electricity Produced from Renewable Energy Sources in the Internal Energy Market. *Official Journal of the European Communities,* 27 October, L 283.

Directive 2002/91/EC of the European Parliament and of the Council of 16 December 2002 on the Energy Performance of Buildings. *Official Journal of the European Communities,* 4 January, L 1.

Directive 2003/30/EC of the European Parliament and of the Council of May 2003 on the Promotion of the Use of Biofuels or Other Renewable Fuels for Transport. *Official Journal of the European Union,* 17 May, L 123.

Directive 2003/54/EC of the European Parliament and of the Council of 26 June 2003 Concerning Common Rules for the Internal Market in Electricity and Repealing Directive 96/92/EC. *Official Journal of the European Communities*, 15 July, L 176.

Directive 2009/28/EC of the European Parliament and of the Council of 23 April 2009 on the Promotion of Energy from Renewable Sources and Amending and Subsequently Repealing Directives 2001/77/EC and 2003/ 30/EC. *Official Journal of the European Union*, 5 June, L 140.

Directive 2009/31/EC of the European Parliament and of the Council of 23 April 2009 on the Geological Storage of Carbon Dioxide and Amending Council Directive 85/337/EEC, European Parliament and Council Directives 2000/60/EC, 2001/80/EC, 2004/35/EC, 2008/1/EC and Regulation (EC) No 1013/2006. *Official Journal of the European Union*, 5 June, L 140.

Ecoheatcool and Euroheat & Power. 2006. *Reducing Europe's Consumption of Fossil Fuels for Heating and Cooling. Project Results.* Brussels: Euroheat & Power.

European Council. 1997. Council Resolution of 27 June 1997 on Renewable Sources of Energy. *Official Journal of the European Communities*, 27 June, C210/01.

European Council. 2006. Brussels European Council 23 and 24 March 2006. *Presidency Conclusions.* 7775/1/06 REV 1. Brussels: Council of the European Union.

European Council. 2007. Brussels European Council 8 and 9 March 2007. *Presidency Conclusions.* 7224/07. Brussels: Council of the European Union.

European Parliament. 2007. *Report on the Roadmap for Renewable Energy in Europe.* (2007/2090(INI)). A6-0287/2007. Brussels: European Parliament.

European Renewable Energy Council (EREC). 2007. *Action Plan for Renewable Heating and Cooling.* Action Plan – Project "Key Issues for Renewable Heat in Europe". Brussels: European Renewable Energy Council.

European Renewable Energy Council (EREC). 2008. EREC Position Paper. *Report of Claude Turmes on the Directive on the Promotion of the Use of Energy from Renewable Sources.* Brussels: European Renewable Energy Council. http://www.erec.org/fileadmin/erec_docs/Documents/Position_ Papers/Turmes.pdf. Accessed: 4 August 2009.

European Wind Energy Study (EWIS). 2008. *European Transmission System Operators. European Wind Integration Study (EWIS)*. EWIS-Interim Report. Brussels: EWIS.

International Energy Agency (IEA). 2007. *Renewables for Heating and Cooling – Untapped Potential*. Paris: OECD/IEA.

International Energy Agency (IEA). 2008a. *World Energy Outlook 2008*. Paris: OECD/IEA.

International Energy Agency (IEA). 2008b. *Empowering Variable Renewables – Options for Flexible Electricity Systems*. Paris: OECD/IEA.

Intergovernmental Panel on Climate Change (IPCC). 2007. Climate Change 2007: Mitigation. *Contribution of Working Group III to the Fourth Assessment Report of the Intergovernmental Panel on Climate Change*. Cambridge and New York: Cambridge University Press.

MVV Consulting. 2007a. *Technical Assistance on the Standards and Codes Applied to Heating and Cooling from the Renewable Energies Sector. Final Report*. Mannheim: MVV decon GmbH.

MVV Consulting. 2007b. *Heating and Cooling from Renewable Energies: Costs of National Policies and Administrative Barriers. Final Report*. Mannheim: MVV decon GmbH.

Owens, Daey R., Francesco Belfiore, Rob Bijsma, Franck van Dellen Ramon, Ava Georgieva, Willem Hettinga, Piotr Kociolek, Malgorzata Lechwacka, Livia Manzone, Daniela Musciacchio, Anne Palenberg, Pietro Rescia, Sebastian Rivera, Jasper van der Staaij and Ursel Weissleder. 2009. *Benchmark of Bio-Energy Permitting Procedures in the European Union*. Utrecht: Ecofys/Golder.

Ragwitz, Mario, Mario Schleich, Claus Huber, Gustav Resch, Thomas Faber, Monique Voogt, Rogier Coenraads, Hans Cleijne and Peter Bodo. 2005. *FORRES 2020: Analysis of the Renewable Energy Sources' Evolution up to 2020. Final Report*. Karlsruhe: Fraunhofer ISI.

Ragwitz, Mario, Wolfgang Schade, Barbara Breitschopf, Rainer Walz, Nicki Helfrich, Max Rathmann, Gustav Resch, Christian Panzer, Thomas Faber, Reinhard Haas, Carsten Nathani, Matthias Holzhey, Inga Konstantinaviciute, Paul Zagamé, Arnaud Fougeyrollas and Boris Le Hir. 2009. *EmployRES The Impact of Renewable Energy Policy on Economic Growth and Employment in the European Union. Final Report*. Karlsruhe: Fraunhofer ISI.

Renewable Energy Policy Network for the 21st Century (REN21). 2008. *Renewables 2007 Global Status Report*. Paris: REN21 Secretariat and Washington D.C.: Worldwatch Institute.

Resch, Gustav, Thomas Faber, Mario Ragwitz, Anne Held, Christian Panzer and Reinhard Haas. 2008. *20 % RES by 2020 – a Balanced Scenario to Meet Europe's Renewable Energy Target*. Vienna: Vienna University of Technology, Institute of Power Systems and Energy Economics, Ebergy Economics Group (EEG).

TradeWind. 2009. *Integrating Wind – Developing Europe's Power Market for the Large Scale Integration of Wind Power. Final Report*. Brussels: TradeWind.

Vasconcelos, Jorge. 2008. *Survey of Regulatory and Technological Developments Concerning Smart Metering in the European Union Electricity Market*. Policy Papers, RSCAS 2008/01. San Domenico di Fiesole: European University Institute.

Werner, Sven. 2008. *Benefits with More District Heating and Cooling in Europe*. Göteborg: Chalmers University of Technology Department of Energy and Environment.

The Legal Framework for Carbon Capture and Storage in the EU (Directive 2009/31/EC)

Joana Chiavari[1]

1. Introduction

"Carbon capture and storage" (CCS) refers to a system of technologies that integrates CO_2 capture, transport and geological storage. CCS is seen as the only promising option to reduce the global warming impact from large scale fossil fuel usage, on which the world will continue to rely for decades to generate electricity, while alternatives to fossil fuels are developed further and gradually deployed. Analysis from the International Energy Agency (IEA) concludes that CCS will need to contribute one-fifth of the necessary efforts to achieve a 50 per cent reduction in energy-related CO_2 emissions from 2005 levels by 2050, and suggests that without CCS, overall costs to achieve a halving of emissions will increase by 70 per cent.[2]

Although questions and concerns remain about some of the benefits and impacts of CCS, discussion of this technology made its way onto the EU's agenda. A number of recent regulatory and legal developments have clearly reflected the increasing attention being given to CCS in Europe. This includes the 2009 CCS Directive (Directive 2009/31/EC), which is the world's first example of dedicated CCS legislation.

This chapter begins by describing the policy context for CCS in Europe in section 2. Section 3 presents some of the main arguments for and against this technology, and also discusses EU involvement in the development of CCS technology. Section 4 then reviews the negotiation process that culminated in the adoption of Directive 2009/31/EC on the geological storage of CO_2. This section also outlines the key elements of the Directive and addresses the need to secure financing to get CCS up and running.

---

1. The contents of this chapter are the sole responsibility of the author and do not necessarily reflect the views of the IEA.
2. IEA 2009, 5.

2. Setting the context: the two degree challenge

The EU's agreed policy objective is to limit the rise in global average temperature to two degrees Celsius above pre-industrial levels, a threshold beyond which irreversible and catastrophic climate changes become far more likely. The EU's first reference to the need to stay below two degrees Celsius appeared in 1996,[3] based on the Second Assessment Report of the Intergovernmental Panel on Climate Change – the most recent scientific assessment at that time.[4] The two-degrees target implies global greenhouse gas (GHG) emission reductions of at least 50 per cent globally by 2050 compared to the emissions in 1990, and 80 to 95 per cent emission reductions for developed countries.[5]

The EU's commitments depend to a large extent on the cooperation of other big GHG emitters, and more prominently, on the agreement on the post-2012 climate framework at international level. However, it is clear that these targets cannot be achieved without significant domestic reductions of GHG emissions from the energy sector, which is heavily dependent on fossil fuels and accounts for 80 per cent of the total GHG emissions (with the electricity generation and heat production sectors as the largest emitters).[6]

The use of fossil fuels in power generation produces approximately 40 per cent of all CO_2 emissions in the EU, with coal and gas accounting for about 50 per cent of electricity production.[7] Recent trends and projections show that the use of coal in electricity generation is likely to increase in the EU up to 2030, due to concerns about security of energy supply, as well as concerns over high and volatile prices of imported fossil fuels.[8]

Furthermore, approximately 75 per cent of the coal-fired power plants in Europe are over 25 years old, and over 45 per cent are over 30 years old, and, hence, have to be replaced or upgraded in the next 10 to 15 years.[9] This gives rise to the possible resurgence of coal as a power source, as evidenced by the power company E.ON UK's recent application to build the first large coal-fired power station in the UK since the late 1980s, and

3. Council of the European Union 1996.
4. IPCC 1995.
5. European Council 2009, 3; see also the chapter by Oberthür and Pallemaerts in this volume.
6. EEA 2009, 119.
7. Commission 2008b, 2; EEA 2008, 43.
8. EEA 2008, 7.
9. Commission 2006b, 14.

plans to bring about 50 coal-fired plants into operation in Europe in 2008-2013.[10] The European Commission notes that: "Replacement of these plants with coal-fired generating capacity to maintain a diverse energy mix will only be publicly acceptable, compatible with the EU's climate change objectives, and may only be economically viable if specific CO_2 emissions are reduced drastically".[11]

Fossil fuels account for such a large portion of global energy use that shifting away from them is difficult for structural reasons. The Commission notes that: "While increased use of energy efficiency measures and greater penetration of renewable energy sources are expected to contribute to meeting the increased demand, even ambitious scenarios foresee that most electricity will still be supplied by the traditional thermal power plants, both fossil fuel and nuclear".[12] This is reinforced by the estimation that fossil fuels will comprise roughly 60 per cent of European electricity generation up to 2030.[13]

With fossil fuel power generation continuing to be an important part of the electricity-generating mix in the EU for at least several decades, a new generation of low-emissions technologies has to come online as soon as possible to avoid high-carbon lock-in. This is where CCS shows its potential. In the absence of a more comprehensive low-carbon energy solution, it can contribute significantly to preventing climate change, if installed quickly enough, in great enough quantities, and at a reasonable cost. CCS is currently the only technology available to mitigate GHG emissions from large-scale fossil fuel usage in fuel transformation, industry and power generation, and can therefore bridge the gap between increasing demand for fossil fuel use and the need to decrease CO_2 emissions.

3. Carbon dioxide capture and storage explained

3.1 The potential and criticism of CCS

Carbon Capture and Storage is one of the few energy technologies being developed as a direct response to climate change. It refers to an emerging group of technologies that capture carbon dioxide (CO_2) from the gases emitted by large, concentrated stationary sources, such as coal and gas power

10. Rosenthal 2008.
11. Commission 2006b, 14.
12. Commission 2006b, 14.
13. Hämäläinen 2009, 59.

plants and CO_2-intensive industrial processes. The CO_2 is then compressed into liquid form and transported by tanker truck, ship, train or (most likely) high-pressure pipeline networks, just like any other gas, to a site where it can be injected deep underground. The gas is stored in geological formations about one kilometre below the Earth's surface, such as in depleted oil and gas reservoirs, unmined coal beds, and saline aquifers, which will trap it for a long period of time (probably thousands of years or more).[14]

Depending on the type of power plant and the CO_2 capture process (i.e. pre-combustion, post combustion, or oxyfuel combustion, depending on whether the separation of the CO_2 from other gases occurs either before or after the fuel is burned[15]), it is possible to reduce emission by 80-90 per cent compared to the emissions of a conventional plant. The International Energy Agency estimates that CCS could deliver one-fifth of the total CO_2 emission savings needed to cut global emissions by 50 per cent by 2050.[16] Analysis by the European Commission indicates that around 18 per cent of global power generation from fossil fuels would have to be fitted with CCS technology by 2030 to achieve an emissions scenario compatible with meeting the two degree Celsius target.[17] In addition, preliminary estimates indicate that some 15 per cent of the EU's required reductions by 2030 could come from CCS.

The Intergovernmental Panel on Climate Change (IPCC) special report on CCS identified the technology as part of "a portfolio of measures that will be needed" to achieve the stabilisation of GHG emissions.[18] The IPCC report was part of a larger wave of research activity being pushed by both industry and policy initiatives. Efforts to expand CCS research and development and demonstration include projects under the EU's Research Framework Programme, the US Department of Energy Carbon Sequestration Programme, collaborative CCS research projects involving academia, industry and government representatives,[19] as well as research programmes

14. It is expected that saline formations will provide the opportunity to store the greatest quantity of CO_2; see IEA 2008a, 103. Most countries, including those in the European Union, exclude storage in ocean waters for environmental reasons.
15. At the time of writing, these technologies are at a different degree of maturity and are competing to be the low-cost solution. It is not yet clear which option(s) will prove to be more viable in the long term.
16. IEA 2008a, 28.
17. Commission 2009a, 9.
18. IPCC 2005, 3.
19. Such as CO_2CRC in Australia (http://www.co2crc.com.au/), the Dutch national CCS programme CATO$_2$ (http://www.co2-cato.nl/cato-2/program-overview), and US-led FutureGen public-private initiative (http://www.futuregenalliance.org/about.stm) (Accessed: 21 October 2009).

at Stanford, Princeton, the Massachusetts Institute of Technology (MIT), and other universities. Industrial consortia like the CO_2 Capture Project, a partnership of eight of the world's leading energy companies and three government organisations, including the EU,[20] also play large roles in the development of CCS. In addition, there are a number of other important CCS research and demonstration projects and activities around the world, beginning with Statoil's Sleipner project in Norway, the first large scale commercial application of CO_2 storage in a deep saline aquifer in the world, which has been operating successfully since 1996. Furthermore, international collaboration efforts on research, development and demonstration have served an important role as platform and forum for sharing early project results, best practices and lessons learned relating to CCS technologies. Relevant initiatives include the Carbon Sequestration Leadership Forum, an international framework for cooperation on research and development of CCS;[21] the IEA Greenhouse Gas R&D Programme, an Implementing Agreement of the International Energy Agency aimed at assessing technologies capable of achieving deep reductions in GHG emissions;[22] and the new Global CCS Institute, an initiative launched by the Australian Government in April 2009 aimed at collaborating on projects and allowing knowledge to be shared.[23]

Although there are not yet any large scale power plants fitted with CCS technology,[24] many of the CCS components are generally regarded as mature enough for deployment, based on decades of studies in analogous hydrocarbon systems, natural gas storage operations and enhanced oil recovery projects. Now the challenge is to demonstrate an integrated system of capture, transportation, and storage of CO_2 on a commercial scale. Demonstration projects are thus needed to validate the technology, to discover the true cost of CCS and to begin the process of bringing costs down.

However, CCS remains a subject of controversy in policy debate. Some stakeholders have expressed concern that CCS will justify the building of

---

20. See http://www.co2captureproject.org/ (Accessed: 21 October 2009).
21. See http://www.cslforum.org/ (Accessed: 21 October 2009).
22. See http://www.ieagreen.org.uk/ (Accessed: 21 October 2009).
23. See http://www.globalccsinstitute.com/ (Accessed: 21 October 2009).
24. At the time of writing, there are only four fully integrated commercial-scale CCS projects in operation (Sleipner and Snøvit in Norway, In Salah in Algeria, and the Weyburn-Midale project in North America. See http://sequestration.mit.edu/tools/projects/map_projects.html). However, there are currently no large scale, integrated CCS projects in the power generation sector, which should be the focus for early demonstration and larger scale projects.

new coal-fired power plants at a time when CCS has not been demonstrated to work. Another argument raised is that CCS will distract both political attention and funding away from renewables, which use technologies that are ready now, and are more sustainable and safer options. In addition, critics have also brought attention to the long-term risks of CCS, in particular regarding potential impacts of leakage on global atmospheric levels of CO_2, on crops and on animal and human health.[25]

Some of the drawbacks of CCS are that it reduces efficiency, adds both additional capital investment and additional operational costs, and lowers energy output. Large-scale CCS technologies require significant amounts of energy, due to the energy absorbed in the capture process, and decrease the average efficiency of power plants by up to 20 per cent. This drives an increase in fuel consumption and requires an over-sizing of the plant to ensure the same net electricity output.[26] As a result, this could increase upstream environmental pressure. Furthermore, the US Department of Energy calculates that installing carbon capture systems, which represent the main cost block for CCS, will almost double plant costs, making CCS uneconomical.[27] According to estimates of McKinsey, fitting a non-CCS 900-megawatt coal power plant built around 2020 with CCS would raise capital investment by roughly 50 per cent.[28]

Many believe that the efficiency loss and financial cost of CCS do not make sense when we have renewable energy technologies available. However, the costs of CCS are forecast to fall over time with increased demonstration of integrated projects and technology cost reductions. McKinsey estimated in September 2008 that the costs for integrated CCS projects could come down to 30-45 Euro per tonne of CO_2 abated for new coal-fired power by 2030. In such a price range, CCS may be able to compete with other low-carbon technologies, including renewables.[29] Because of its compatibility with the current fossil energy infrastructure, CCS could become one of the most promising options to reduce emissions from power generation and industry at a reasonable cost. Including CCS as an option for energy generation could be cheaper than relying on renewables and energy efficiency alone. According to the IEA, the overall cost to achieve a halving of CO_2 emissions by 2050 would rise by 70 per cent, if CCS technologies are not available.[30]

25. Greenpeace International 2008.
26. McKinsey & Company 2008, 18.
27. NETL 2007.
28. McKinsey & Company 2008, 10.
29. McKinsey & Company 2008, 16.
30. IEA 2008a, 16.

An important justification regularly cited for implementing CCS is the growing use of coal in emerging economies. The IEA World Energy Outlook 2008 projects that world demand for coal advances by two per cent a year on average, with its share in global energy demand climbing from 26 per cent in 2006 to 29 per cent in 2030. Some 85 per cent of the increase in global coal consumption comes from the power sector in China and India.[31] Many believe that the EU's commitment towards the development and deployment of CCS could help maximise the potential for CCS in emerging economies. In this respect the EU and China have developed a project with the aim of developing and demonstrating advanced near-zero emission coal technology through CCS.[32]

In recent years, with the reality of the technology on the ground increasing, CCS has emerged as an essential part of the portfolio of technologies to achieve deep global emission reductions, thus intensifying the need to develop suitable CCS regulatory and policy frameworks. Important progress was made in relation to international marine environment protection treaties to advance CCS development.[33] In parallel, many countries started to develop domestic regulatory frameworks for CCS, either at national or province/state level. The EU was pressed into considering how it could regulate CCS to allow the first demonstration projects to move forward, and facilitate CCS commercialisation for the longer term. The evolution of CCS in the EU policy debate is presented below.

3.2   CCS in the EU

CCS has made its way onto the EU's agenda, and it is expected that it will continue to be considered a serious mitigation option in Europe. The EU's interest in CCS first took the form of technology research, through the Fifth, Sixth and, more recently, Seventh Framework Programmes for Research and Development administered by the Directorate General (DG) for Research of the European Commission.[34]

---

31.   IEA 2008b, 39.
32.   See http://ec.europa.eu/environment/climat/china.htm (Accessed: 21 October 2009).
33.   The London Protocol was amended in 2006 to allow for offshore CO_2 storage, and in 2007, the Convention for the Protection of the Marine Environment of the North-East Atlantic (OSPAR Convention) adopted similar provisions; see IEA 2008a, 132.
34.   See http://www.cordis.lu/sustdev/energy/ml-term/home.html (Accessed: 12 August 2009).

The recognition of the need for a policy context to facilitate and influence CCS deployment resulted in the inclusion of a working group on CCS in the second phase of the European Climate Change Programme, established by the Commission in 2005.[35] This working group convened a series of stakeholder meetings on CCS in the first five months of 2006 focusing on:

- Reviewing the potential, economics and risks of CCS;
- Identifying regulatory needs and barriers and exploring the elements of an enabling legal and regulatory framework for the development of environmentally sound CCS technologies;
- Identifying barriers other than regulatory ones that could impede the development of CCS, and enabling policies to advance the development of environmentally sound CCS.[36]

The working group's final report was published in June 2006 and stressed the need to develop the policy and regulatory framework for CCS.[37] In particular, the report requested the Commission to address:

- Permitting of geological storage sites, including risk management, site selection, operation, monitoring, reporting, verification, closure and post-closure;
- Liability for leakage from storage sites during operation and post-closure;
- Clarification of the role of CCS under EU legislation (and proposal of appropriate amendments), in particular concerning waste and water;
- The recognition of CCS projects under the EU Emissions Trading System (ETS);
- The need and possible options for incentivising CCS in a transitional period;
- The status of CCS projects under rules and guidelines for State Aid.

In November 2006, the Technology Platform for Zero Emission Fossil Fuel Power Plants (ZEP) advocated funding mechanisms for the implementation of 10-12 integrated, large-scale CCS demonstration projects in Europe by 2015, and outlined the need for an enabling regulatory framework.[38] The Platform's creation had resulted from meetings of industrial stakeholders, the research community and non-governmental organisations towards the end of 2004, in the wake of research carried out under the EU's Framework Programme for Research in the field of clean power generation. The initial

---

35. Commission 2005.
36. Documents from the Carbon Capture and Geological Storage working group (WG 3) are available at http://circa.europa.eu/Public/irc/env/eccp_2/library?l=/geological_storage&vm=detailed&sb=Title.
37. European Climate Change Programme 2006, 1.
38. See http://www.zeroemissionsplatform.eu/index.html (Accessed: 21 October 2009).

concept and guiding principles of the Technology Platform were developed by the Commission's DG Research with the support of a group of industrial associations, and its main objective was to better coordinate industry-driven activities to enable zero CO_2 emissions from European fossil fuel power plants by 2020. The Platform was officially launched on 1 December 2005 and a Vision Paper was published in May 2006.[39]

CCS is also one of the six "technologies avenues" promoted under the European Strategic Energy Technology Plan (SET-Plan), an initiative launched by the European Commission in January 2007 and recognised as the technology pillar of the EU's energy and climate policy.[40] The plan identifies those technologies for which it is essential to mobilise resources at European level in order to accelerate development and deployment, and describes concrete actions to build a coherent energy research landscape under the coordination of the European Commission. In a related Communication published in 2009, the Commission recognises the pressing need to demonstrate at industrial scale the full CCS chain for a representative portfolio of different capture, transport and storage options, and estimates the total public and private investment in research and development needed in Europe over the next ten years to reduce the costs of CCS as 13 billion Euro.[41]

The Commission further adopted a Communication on 10 January 2007,[42] as part of its climate and energy strategy to achieve at least a 20 per cent reduction of GHG emissions by 2020 compared to 1990 levels outlined in its 2006 Green Paper on "A European Strategy for Secure, Competitive and Sustainable Energy".[43] The Communication set out the EU approach with respect to CCS and identified two major tasks for the deployment of CCS technology:
• To develop an enabling legal framework and economic incentives for CCS within the EU;
• To encourage a network of demonstration plants across Europe and in key third countries.

The European Council endorsed this strategy during its meeting in March 2007, and urged the Member States and the Commission to develop the necessary technical, economic and regulatory framework to ensure the deployment of environmentally safe CCS for new fossil-fuel power plants

39. Commission 2006d.
40. Commission 2007.
41. Commission 2009b.
42. Commission 2006c.
43. Commission 2006a.

by 2020.[44] This set the stage for the legislative process that ensued in 2008 and is reviewed in the next section.

4. The Directive on the Geological Storage of Carbon Dioxide

The "climate and energy package"[45] published by the Commission on 23 January 2008 included a number of documents that clearly showed the rising attention given to CCS. In particular, a Directive for the geological storage of CO_2 was proposed to enable the safe operation of CCS in Europe,[46] and a communication put forward on the realisation and funding of 10-12 CCS demonstration projects by 2015.[47] At the same time, an impact assessment report concerning the environmental, safety and health implications of CCS as a large-scale mitigation option was published.[48]

4.1 The negotiations

According to the Commission's proposal, the only inducement to implement CCS was the deduction of the stored CO_2 from the emissions of facilities covered by the EU ETS.[49] CCS would not become mandatory, though this idea had been floated in earlier drafts. Operators would thus not have to purchase emissions allowances, which translates to a financial advantage equal to the prevailing carbon price. The carbon price resulting from the ETS should eventually (by 2020 according to the Commission's expectations) provide the incentive for CCS. However, there is no guarantee that the ETS will deliver a carbon price that will make CCS cost-effective.

Following the publication of the Commission proposal, the European Parliament assigned Chris Davies, a British Liberal MEP from the Environment Committee, as rapporteur for the CCS dossier. Mr. Davies took a strong public position on his intended amendments to the Directive – shifting the tone of the legislative debate from one focused almost entirely on regulatory issues associated with risk management, licensing and liability, to a broader consideration of how CCS will be financed and commercialised more generally.

44. European Council 2007.
45. Commission 2008a. See also the chapter by Oberthür and Pallemaerts in this volume.
46. Commission 2008d.
47. Commission 2008b.
48. Commission 2008c.
49. See the chapter by Skjærseth and Wettestad in this volume.

The main battle in the Parliament over CCS therefore revolved around what was *not* in the proposed Directive, i.e. a requirement to use CCS, a subsidy system higher than the value of the ETS credits, or a combination of both. Mr. Davies supported a system of "double crediting" under the EU ETS, giving operators a tradable carbon credit for every tonne of CO_2 they store. This "double crediting" would have been applied over a limited time period for initial demonstration facilities, after which CCS would become mandatory (i.e. in 2015).

In the months leading up the vote of the Parliament's Environment Committee, Mr. Davies cooperated closely with his fellow MEP Ms. Avril Doyle, rapporteur for the parallel Commission proposal for a Directive revising the EU ETS. Ms. Doyle's amendments created a funding mechanism that set aside 500 million carbon allowances from the new entrants' reserve, a special pool of emission rights earmarked for new installations joining the ETS, to co-finance the construction of CCS demonstration plants. One of the advantages of this system is that the overall cap on CO_2 emissions would not be increased. In addition, a CO_2 emission-limit value for new coal-fired power plants of 500g per kilowatt-hour was proposed under Mr. Davies' amendments. This value was based on a similar measure introduced in California and aimed to essentially force the use of CCS for coal power.[50] The advantage of emission-limit values is that they provide much greater regulatory certainty regarding technology deployment, as well as predictable results regarding environmental protection. Doyle's amendment on the use of funds from the ETS new entrants' reserve combined with Davies' amendment for a CO_2 emission limit on power stations. On 7 October 2008, the Parliament's Environment Committee backed these amendments.[51]

These proposed amendments were contested by a number of Ministers at the October 2008 Environment Council,[52] particularly those from Member States where CCS would be much more expensive because of their specific geography and geology (such as several coal-dependent new Eastern European Member States). A number of Ministers expressed their opposition to the Parliament's proposal to allocate a proportion of emission allowances to co-finance the construction of CCS demonstration plants, questioning why the EU should use a specific funding mechanism for one particular technology and not another, such as renewables. Member State

---

50. It is estimated that a newer, more efficient coal plant would emit around 700g CO_2 per kilowatt-hour if built without CCS; Clean Coal Task Group 2006, 6.
51. European Parliament 2008a.
52. Council of the European Union 2008a.

governments also opposed an emission limit for large power plants.[53] Instead, they favoured the Commission's original proposal to make all new large power plants "CCS ready" where technically and economically feasible. Furthermore, Mr. Davies' amendment requiring geological storage sites and means of transport to be specified for all newly constructed power plants before authorisation was granted was rejected in favour of the Commission's proposal requiring operators to "assess the availability" of suitable storage sites and transport facilities for allowing the construction of new power plants.[54]

After taking over the rotating EU Council Presidency in the second half of 2008, France initiated bilateral negotiations with certain Member States which had expressed serious reservations about various components of the CCS proposal, as well as informal discussions between Council, Parliament and Commission, as part of their "trialogue" talks, trying to reach an agreement at first reading. The French Presidency proposed to lower the number of carbon allowances to be set aside for CCS under the EU ETS to 100-200 million, less than half of what the European Parliament proposed. The Presidency argued that the ETS new entrants' reserve would no longer be able to serve its intended purpose if the Parliament's plan went ahead. The intended reduction was in line with the Commission's argument that CCS demonstration plants should not be entirely financed through the new entrants' reserve, and that funds should come from a combination of sources at EU and national level, including private investment and government money.[55] Many environmental groups, sceptical about the use of public funds in support of fossil fuel-based energy production, also supported reducing public funding for CCS demonstration, due to feared windfall profits for power companies.

On 17 December 2008, in a first reading vote in plenary, the European Parliament formally adopted a legislative resolution on the CCS Directive,[56] based on the outcome of the trialogue negotiations. That same day a compromise text was adopted to improve and extend the EU ETS,[57] calling for up to 300 million carbon allowances from the ETS new entrants' reserve

---

53. Although the CO_2 emission-limit standards for coal-fired power plants were omitted from the final text of the CCS Directive, the European Parliament continues to push for emission values (e.g. within negotiations for a new Directive on Industrial Emissions, (IED): COM (2007) 844 final).
54. ENDS Europe 2008.
55. Council of the European Union 2008b.
56. European Parliament 2008b.
57. European Parliament 2008c.

to be made available until 31 December 2015 to co-finance the construction and operation of up to twelve commercial CCS demonstration projects as well as demonstration projects of innovative renewable energy technologies. Although the value of this support will depend on the price of allowances at the time, it could amount to approximately 6-9 billion Euro, which was described by Mr. Davies as the "bare minimum" and only a starting point.[58]

The CCS Directive was formally adopted by the Council on 6 April 2009, and published in the *Official Journal* as Directive 2009/31/EC on 5 June 2009, entering into force 20 days later. Member States have two years from that date to transpose it into their national legislation. In the meantime, the Commission will prepare and adopt guidelines on a number of crucial issues[59] to help Member States implement the Directive, and will establish an information exchange between the competent authorities of the Member States.

4.2   Final compromise

The CCS Directive focuses primarily on the regulation of geological storage of CO_2 and on the removal of unintended barriers in existing legislation to CCS. Since capture and transportation are more conventional business practices, legislation is largely already in place for them as explained below.

While Directive 2009/31/EC applies to the territory of Member States, both onshore and offshore (Article 2(1)), Member States retain the right not to allow any storage in parts or on the whole of their territory (Article 4(1)). However, those Member States that decide to allow storage are required to undertake an assessment of the storage capacity available within their territory (Article 4(2)).

The Directive establishes criteria for the selection of appropriate storage sites to ensure that the stored CO_2 will be completely and permanently contained (Article 4(3)). A detailed process of site characterisation involving the entire storage complex[60] is outlined in Annex I of the Directive, and may include more invasive activities, such as drilling into

---

58.   ALDE Group 2008.
59.   Including the composition of the CO_2 stream, transfer of responsibility, and the calculation of the financial contribution for the post-transfer period.
60.   The "storage complex" means the storage site and surrounding geological domain which can have an effect on overall storage integrity and security; that is, secondary containment formations (Article 3(6)). Therefore it is broader than the "storage site", defined under Article 3(3).

the subsurface, to obtain the necessary information (Article 3(8)). However, this process of exploration, that is activities intruding into the subsurface, will not be allowed without an exploration permit issued by the Member State concerned (Article 5(1)). This exploration permit should be granted for a limited volume, area and time (Article 5(3)) on the basis of objective, published and transparent criteria (Article 6(2)).

After the suitability of the storage site is demonstrated, operators can apply for a storage permit, based on the minimum criteria for the permit application outlined in the Directive (Article 7). In addition to proving technical competence, operators are required to provide financial security before starting injection, to cover the costs of operation and post-closure of the storage site, until responsibility is transferred to a competent authority (Article 7(10) and Article 19). Importantly, Member States are required to ensure that storage sites are not operated without a storage permit (Article 6(1)).

As part of the application process, a series of plans concerning the operations and closure of the site need to be prepared by the operator (i.e. methodology for monitoring the site designed in accordance with Annex II of the Directive, corrective measures to be adopted in the case of leakage or when there is a risk of leakage, and proposed plan for the post-closure period) (Article 9). The approved version of these plans will be part of the granted storage permit (Article 13).

Details on the "CO_2 stream", that is the flow of substances that results from the CO_2 capture processes (Article 3(13)) to be injected in the storage site are also to be included in the storage permit. This includes information on the quantity of CO_2 to be stored, its source and transport method, and the composition of the liquefied gas stream injected (Article 9(4)), which may include some incidental substances (Article 12(1). Operators are required to perform a risk assessment regarding the stream composition, and maintain a register of the quantities, properties and composition of the stream injected (Article 12(3)).

All draft storage permits are to be submitted by national competent authorities to the Commission within one month after receipt for a non-binding opinion on it (Article 10(1)). Member States may depart from the Commission's opinion, but are required to provide reasons for such a decision (Article 10(2)).

During the operational phase, storage permits are subject to periodic reviews, and may be changed, updated or withdrawn based on technological developments or problems affecting the operation of the site

(Article 11). In particular, detection of leakage or irregularities requires a review and update of the storage permit (Article 11(3)). If a storage permit is withdrawn, the competent authority may decide either to issue a new permit or to close the site, in which case it will assume all responsibility for the management of the site (Article 11(4)).

Once a storage permit is issued, the injection of CO_2 into the storage site may begin. During the operation, monitoring is to be carried out in accordance with the approved monitoring plan (Article 13), and operators are required to submit reports at least on an annual basis (Article 14). Any leakage or significant irregularities need to be reported to the competent authority immediately (Article 16(1)). In addition, competent authorities will carry out routine inspections at least annually as well as non-routine inspections, under certain circumstances listed in the Directive (Article 15). Findings from these inspections will be documented in reports to be made available to the public (Article 15(5) and Article 26). These provisions are intended to ensure early detection of any problem with the integrity of the storage site.

Any significant leakage or irregularity obliges the operator to take corrective measures to prevent or stop the release of CO_2 from the complex (Article 16 (1)). If an operator fails to take the necessary measures, the competent authority is entitled to take these measures and recover the costs incurred from the operator (Article 16(4)).

The closure of a storage site, following the cessation of CO_2 injection, is carried out in accordance with a reviewed post-closure plan approved by the competent authority (Article 17). The Directive provides for the transfer of responsibility for the storage site from the operator to the competent authority, provided that: (i) "all available evidence indicates that the stored CO_2 will be completely and permanently contained"; (ii) a minimum default period of twenty years from when the site is closed has passed – unless the competent authority decides to decrease this time period; (iii) a financial contribution is made available by the operator to the competent authority covering at least the anticipated cost of monitoring for a period of 30 years, in the terms of Article 20; (iv) the site has been sealed and injection facilities removed (Article 18(1)).

Once the above conditions are met, the competent authority will adopt a draft decision approving the transfer (Article 18(3)), which has to be submitted to the Commission within one month after receipt for a non-binding opinion (Article 18(4)). Where the competent authority departs from the Commission opinion, it shall state its reasons (Article 18(5)). Following the transfer of responsibility, routine inspections will end, and monitoring may be reduced to a minimum level while still allowing for the detection of leakage and irregularities (Article 18(6)).

The transfer of site responsibility releases the operator from monitoring and corrective obligations, as well as from any liabilities under the EU ETS and the environmental liability Directive. However, the CCS Directive refers to a number of situations where costs incurred by the competent authority are eligible to be reimbursed by the operator, notably in the cases of wilful deceit, negligence, lack of due diligence or the provision of deficient data (Article 18(7)).

Various amendments have furthermore been made to explicitly include CCS activities within the scope of existing legal provisions.[61] Thus, Article 31 of the CCS Directive ensures that the capture of CO_2, its transport by pipeline and storage are made subject to requirements under the Environmental Impact Assessment (EIA) Directive (Directive 85/337/EEC). The assessment of the likely significant (direct and indirect) effects on the environment of a storage site will need to be submitted as part of the storage permit application outlined under Article 7 of the CCS Directive. In addition, following the inclusion of capture installations in Directive 85/337/EEC, an EIA has to be carried out in the capture permit procedure.

Article 37 of the CCS Directive determines that Directive 2008/1/EC (formerly Directive 96/61/EC) concerning integrated pollution prevention and control (IPPC)[62] should be applied to the capture of CO_2 streams from CCS capture installations. In addition, this provision ensures that best available techniques to improve the composition of the CO_2 stream have to be established and applied.

Article 34 of the CCS Directive ensures that liability for environmental damage (damage to protected species and natural habitats, water and land) is regulated by the Environmental Liability Directive 2004/35/EC, which should be applied to the operators of CO_2 storage sites in case of local environmental damage.

Liability for local environmental damage under the 2004 Directive is complemented by the inclusion of storage sites under the ETS Directive 2003/87/EC, by Article 17(2) of the CCS Directive, which requires operators to surrender emission-trading allowances in the event of leaked CO_2. In addition, liabilities concerning the injection phase, the closure of

---

61. UCL Carbon Capture Legal Programme 2009; Brockett 2009.
62. In light of a number of amendments, a new codified version of the IPPC Directive 96/61/EC has been issued as Directive 2008/1/EC.

the storage site and the period after transfer of legal obligations to the competent authority not covered by the CCS Directive, the ETS Directive and the Environmental Liability Directive, in particular for damage to human health, other forms of personal injury, as well damage to private property, should be dealt with at national level.

Furthermore, Article 33 of the CCS Directive amends Directive 2001/80/EC on the limitation of emissions of certain pollutants into the air from large combustion plants to require operators of new power plants with an output of more than 300 Megawatts to assess whether suitable storage sites and transport facilities are available and if it is technically and economically feasible to retrofit the power station for the capture of CO_2. If these conditions are met, authorities in Member States are required to guarantee that "suitable space on the installation site for the equipment necessary to capture and compress CO_2 is set aside".

This provision represents the "capture ready" concept, which has raised a lot of opposition, since it allows new coal-fired power stations to be built without providing any specific guarantee that CCS technology will be added, or that a robust study of real transport and storage opportunities will take place.[63] The Commission will carry out an assessment of this provision by 2015, and present a proposal for revision, if appropriate. The inclusion of CO_2 emission-limit values will likely be considered at that stage, as an alternative to "carbon capture readiness".

Where existing EU legislation represented a barrier to CCS because it was drafted without specific consideration of CO_2 storage, CCS activities were specifically removed from the scope of such legislation. Amendments were made to the Water Framework Directive (Directive 2000/60/EC) to exempt CO_2 injections for storage purposes into geological formations from certain prohibitive provisions, as long as it is shown that underground pore spaces are "permanently unsuitable" for non-CCS purposes (Article 32). Amendments were also made to the Waste Framework Directive (Directive 2006/12/EC) excluding captured CO_2 from its scope, provided it is captured for the purposes of CCS and geologically stored in accordance with the CCS Directive (Article 35). This amendment ensures that CO_2 is not considered a waste, and that storage activities do not constitute "discarding" under the meaning of the Directive. The classification of CO_2 as waste would have had a number of implications for CCS activities, determining specific conditions under several Directives that use the same definition of waste.[64]

---

63. Markusson and Haszeldine 2008, 4.
64. Such as the Landfill Directive (Directive 1999/31/EC) and the Hazardous Waste Directive (Directive 91/689/EEC).

This classification would also have had an effect on the treatment of CO_2 under the IPPC Directive and the EIA Directive. An additional amendment included to facilitate the progress of CCS also excluded shipments of CO_2 from the scope of Regulation (EC) No 1013/2006 on the transfrontier shipment of waste (Article 36).

4.3   The next step – securing financing

The infrastructure for mature fuels benefited significantly from support received under state ownership, in the form of funding of research and development, capital investment and the subsidisation of operating costs. This indicates that the development of innovative energy has historically required public support.[65] However, there are serious issues to consider in terms of how to direct funding for particular energy sources, and whether the priorities are correct.

Early CCS deployment will not take place in Europe without some policy intervention, such as guaranteed CO_2 prices to enable domestic implementation, feed-in subsidies for CCS-based electricity supply, or some means of cost recovery. Given the large revenues of the fossil fuel industry, the subsidies that encourage fossil fuels,[66] and public enthusiasm for renewable energy and efficiency, there is a major debate about subsidising CCS in Europe. However, CCS would not develop on a commercial basis if left entirely to the private sector because, aside from specific opportunities for enhanced hydrocarbon recovery, CCS is purely a GHG mitigation technology. Kick-start funding is therefore a key requirement for enabling European action on CCS.

According to the CCS Directive, operators will decide whether to use CCS on the basis of the conditions in the carbon market. CCS deployment would therefore depend on two factors – the carbon price and the cost of the technology. However, while trading is referred to as a priority for CCS, it may not be sufficient to get the technology off the ground. The reason for this, besides the volatility and uncertainty of trading prices, is that cap-and-trade approaches, such as the ETS, are unlikely to provide the incentives

---

65. For instance, nuclear energy garnered subsidies during its development in Europe (1947-1961) that were the equivalent of 15 US dollars per kilowatt-hour: 30 times the support level of renewable energy today; see EEA 2004, 16.
66. For instance, the coal extraction industry in Germany enjoys far more subsidies than the wind industry, while preferable tax treatment for oil and gas in several European countries amounts to an off-budget subsidy of around 8.5 billion US dollars annually; see EEA 2004, 14.

needed to compensate innovators for inducing technological change, particularly for those technologies that involve high development and demonstration costs (such as CCS), as the return on investment in innovation is unlikely to be sufficient.[67] According to economic theory, government intervention can be justified in such cases, in order to optimise technological advance.[68]

In addition, in order to deliver up to twelve operational demonstration projects by 2015, as endorsed by the European Council, most of the funding will be required between 2012 and 2014 when the cost of CCS is expected to be higher than the cost of emitting carbon. The time delay between the potential support from emissions trading from 2013 and the necessary planning and construction phase of demonstration facilities reinforces the case for targeted and limited public funding.

The Commission considered several options on how to stimulate investment from industry and individual Member States to enable early full-scale demonstration.[69] The funding mechanisms discussed to cover the incremental capital requirements and increased operating costs of early demonstrations, estimated at 7-12 billion Euro,[70] can be grouped under three main categories, notably:

• Those relying on the price of carbon, such as (i) earmarking part of the income from auctioning EU emission allowances for the third phase of the EU ETS (2013 onwards) to create a special CCS fund; (ii) allocating credits for CO_2 stored underground through CCS (the so-called "double credit" system); and (iii) making CCS projects eligible for generating carbon credits under the Clean Development Mechanism (CDM) and Joint Implementation (JI) Kyoto flexible mechanisms;[71]
• Shifting subsidies towards CCS demonstrations at Member State level[72] or through reallocating the EU budget;
• Promoting other types of support measures, similar to ones being applied to low carbon energy sources, such as investment incentives,

---

67. Coninck and Groenenberg 2007.
68. Sorrell and Sijm 2003.
69. Bellona Europa 2008.
70. Hill 2009, 2857-2861.
71. The last option would require agreement at the international level under the UN Framework Convention on Climate Change (UNFCCC).
72. Such policies would need validation under EU state aid regulations. In January 2008 the Commission published an updated version of its environmental state aid rules, which entered in force on 1 April 2008, allowing Member States to grant state aid to CCS projects.

feed-in tariffs, quota obligations based on tradable green certificates, production tax incentives, tendering systems and voluntary agreements.

Funding from other sources could complement the 300 million emission allowances allocated to CCS and innovative renewable technologies from the ETS new entrants' reserve until the end of 2015. In particular, the European Economic Recovery Plan[73] allocates 1.05 billion Euro to CCS projects until 31 December 2010. The European Commission has proposed seven individual CCS projects in seven Member States (notably Germany, UK, the Netherlands, Poland, Spain, Italy and France) based on a list of 13 projects listed in the Recovery Plan that were deemed eligible for funding. The Commission's plan was presented to Member States and needs to be approved by the European Parliament. Additional funds could come from the Member States, who have indicated that they are willing to use part of their auctioning revenues under the ETS to mitigate and adapt to climate change.[74]

The decision on how to allocate funding from the 300 million carbon allowances from the EU ETS new entrants' reserve between renewables and CCS has raised intense debate in Europe. While large Member States, such as Germany, France and the UK are willing to have more control over the selection of projects, environmental organisations like Greenpeace and the Greens[75] have expressed concern about most of the 300 million allowances going to CCS.

The interaction between support from the ETS new entrants' reserve, the Recovery Plan stimulus and additional domestic and EU mechanisms,[76] each operating over different time horizons and supporting individual CCS projects, will ultimately determine both the fate of the EU commitment to build up to twelve CCS demonstration projects and the speed of deployment and ultimate viability of CCS.

73. Regulation (EC) No 663/2009.
74. Governments agreed to the principle that "at least 50 per cent" of the proceeds from auctioning "should" be used for climate-related adaptation and mitigation purposes.
75. Greenpeace 2008; The Greens 2009.
76. Additional sources of financing for CCS demonstration are available at EU level from the Seventh Framework Programme for Research. Although resources in the context of the Framework Programme projects cannot go directly to demonstration projects, they can be applied in research to support these demonstrations. Furthermore, European financial institutions, such as the European Investment Bank, and other specific mechanisms, such as the Structural Funds, could also provide financial support for these projects.

5. Conclusion

CCS technologies may be necessary for transforming Europe into a low-carbon economy in the short- to medium-term, but the climate benefits of CCS must be assessed in the context of the potential risks it presents to the environment and human health. Like any large-scale industrial activity, CCS brings with it a number of environmental concerns, both at the global and local level. Some of these are analogous to similar activities, such as natural gas storage. But others are new in nature and related to the long-term leakage potential from underground storage. In order to ensure safety and security of the CO_2 storage, the key is to find sites that are able to contain the injected CO_2 for a long period of time, and this requires understanding the particular risks which are linked to specific sites (through risk assessment techniques), and managing those risks.

The CCS Directive outlines a proper risk management framework. This secures at least equivalent levels of environmental protection as those applied to analogous activities. In order to minimise leakage, the Directive provides regulation on the selection and management of storage sites, based on the characterisation of the site, and appropriate requirements on operation, monitoring, site closure and post-closure obligations.

Measures in place to avoid leakage do not guarantee it will be avoided, especially if there are management failures (although the same can be said of any industrial activity). For rectification of any leakage that does occur, though, the Directive imposes a strict liability regime for local environmental damage, and liability obligations with regard to emissions of CO_2 into the atmosphere, by removing ETS allowances. The Directive leaves any liability for damage to human health, other forms of personal injury, as well damage to private property to be dealt with under existing national tort laws.

In addition to regulating environmental risks and promoting the security of storage, the CCS Directive seeks to ensure a second purpose: to incentivise the technology and stimulate demonstrations through the carbon market. Clearly, the ETS is not sufficient to get CCS off the ground. Additional funding mechanisms have been put forward to finance CCS demonstration projects in Europe, but greater clarity on how these mechanisms can interact is required. Since the future of CCS will be judged by the successful demonstration of the first projects within the next decade, such clarification may be crucial.

References

ALDE Group. 2008. European Council Delivers on Three Fronts. 12 December 2008. http://www.alde.eu/index.php?id=42&no_cache=1&tx_ttnews[tt_news]=10012&L=0. Accessed: 21 October 2009.

Bellona Europa. 2008. *Paying for a Decent Burial*. Funding Options for an EU Programme for Full-Scale Demonstration of CO_2 Capture and Storage. http://www.bellona.no/filearchive/fil_Paying_for_a_descent_burial2.pdf. Accessed: 12 August 2009.

Brockett, Scott. 2009. The EU Enabling Legal Framework for Carbon Capture and Storage. *Energy Procedia* 1(1): 4433-4441.

Clean Coal Task Group. 2006. A Framework for Clean Coal in Britain. Paper prepared by Clean Coal Task Group. 7 June 2006.

Commission (EC). 2005. *Winning the Battle Against Global Climate Change*. Communication from the Commission to the Council, the European Parliament, the European Economic and Social Committee and the Committee of the Regions. COM (2005) 35 final. Brussels: European Commission.

Commission (EC). 2006a. *Green Paper. A European Strategy for Sustainable, Competitive and Secure Energy*. COM (2006) 105 final. Brussels: European Commission.

Commission (EC). 2006b. *Sustainable Power Generation from Fossil Fuels: Aiming for Near-Zero Emissions from Coal after 2020*. Commission Staff Working Document Accompanying the Communication from the Commission to the Council and the European Parliament. SEC (2006) 1722. Brussels: European Commission.

Commission (EC). 2006c. *Sustainable Power Generation from Fossil Fuels: Aiming for Near-Zero Emissions from Coal after 2020*. Communication from the Commission to the Council, the European Parliament, the European Economic and Social Committee and the Committee of the Regions. COM (2006) 843 final. Brussels: European Commission.

Commission (EC). 2006d. *A Vision for Zero Emission Fossil Fuel Power Plants*. Report by the Zero Emission Fossil Fuel Power Plants Technology Platform. Luxembourg: Office for Official Publications of the European Communities.

Commission (EC). 2007. *A European Strategic Energy Technology Plan (SET Plan) – Towards a Low Carbon Future*. Communication from the

Commission to the Council, the European Parliament, the European Economic and Social Committee and the Committee of the Regions. COM (2007) 723 final. Brussels: European Commission.

Commission (EC). 2008a. *20 20 by 2020: Europe's Climate Change Opportunity*. Communication from the Commission to the Council and the European Parliament. COM (2008) 30. Brussels: European Commission.

Commission (EC). 2008b. *Supporting Early Demonstration of Sustainable Power Generation from Fossil Fuels*. Communication from the Commission to the European Parliament, the Council, the European Economic and Social Committee and the Committee of the Regions. COM (2008) 13 final. Brussels: European Commission.

Commission (EC). 2008c. *Impact Assessment*. Document Accompanying the Proposal for a Directive of the European Parliament and of the Council on the Geological Storage of Carbon Dioxide. Commission Staff Working Document. SEC (2008) 54. Brussels: European Commission.

Commission (EC). 2008d. Proposal for a Directive of the European Parliament and of the Council on the Geological Storage of Carbon Dioxide and Amending Council Directives 85/337/EEC, 96/61/EC, Directives 2000/60/EC, 2001/80/EC, 2004/35/EC, 2006/12/EC and Regulation (EC) No 1013/2006. COM (2008) 15. Brussels: European Commission.

Commission (EC). 2009a. *Demonstrating Carbon Capture and Geological Storage (CCS) in Emerging Developing Countries: Financing the EU-China Near Zero Emissions Coal Plant Project*. Commission Staff Working Document accompanying the Communication from the Commission to the Council and the European Parliament. SEC (2009) 814. Brussels: European Commission.

Commission (EC). 2009b. *Investing in the Development of Low Carbon Technologies (SET-Plan)*. Communication from the Commission to the European Parliament, the Council, the European Economic and Social Committee and the Committee of the Regions. COM (2009) 519 final. Brussels: European Commission.

Coninck, Heleen de and Heleen Groenenberg. 2007. *Incentivising CO_2 Capture and Storage in the European Union*. Report to the European Commission. Brussels: DG Environment.

Council of the European Union (Environment). 1996. 1939th Council Meeting of 25 June 1996. Luxembourg: Council of the European Union.

Council of the European Union (Environment). 2008a. Press Release. 2898th Council Meeting of 20 October 2008. Luxembourg. http:// www.consilium.europa.eu/ueDocs/cms_Data/docs/pressData/en/envir/ 103492.pdf. Accessed: 21 October 2009.

Council of the European Union. 2008b. Note from Presidency 15713/08. Interinstitutional File: 2008/0013 (COD) 2008/0014 (COD). 13 November 2008. Brussels. http://www.euractiv.fr/fileadmin/Documents/13_november _climat.pdf. Accessed: 21 October 2009.

Directive 85/337/EEC of the Council of the European Communities of 27 June 1985 on the Assessment of the Effect of Certain Public and Private Projects on the Environment. *Official Journal of the European Union*, 5 July, L 175.

Directive 91/689/EEC of the Council of the European Communities of 12 December 1991 on Hazardous Waste. *Official Journal of the European Communities*, 31 December, L 377.

Directive 1999/31/EC of the Council of the European Union of 26 April 1999 on the Landfill of Waste. *Official Journal of the European Communities*, 16 July, L 182/1.

Directive 2000/60/EC of the European Parliament and of the Council of 23 October 2000 Establishing a Framework for Community Action in the Field of Water Policy. *Official Journal of the European Communities*, 22 December, L 327.

Directive 2001/80/EC of the European Parliament and of the Council of 23 October 2001 on the Limitation of Emissions of Certain Pollutants into the Air from Large Combustion Plants. *Official Journal of the European Communities*, 27 November 2001, L309/1.

Directive 2003/87/EC of the European Parliament and of the Council of 13 October 2003 Establishing a Scheme for Greenhouse Gas Emission Allowance Trading within the Community and Amending Council Directive 96/61/EE. *Official Journal of the European Union*, 25 October, L 275/32.

Directive 2004/35/EC of the European Parliament and of the Council of 21 April 2004 on Environmental Liability with Regard to the Prevention and Remedying of Environmental Damage. *Official Journal of the European Union*, 30 April, L 143/56.

Directive 2006/12/EC of the European Parliament and of the Council of 5 April 2006 on Waste. *Official Journal of the European Union*, 2 April, L 114/9.

Directive 2008/1/EC of the European Parliament and of the Council of 15 January 2008 Concerning Integrated Pollution Prevention and Control. *Official Journal of the European Union*, 29 January, L 24/8.

Directive 2009/31/EC of the European Parliament and of the Council of 23 April 2009 on the Geological Storage of Carbon Dioxide and Amending Council Directives 85/337/EEC, European Parliament and Council Directives 2000/60/EC, 2001/80/EC, 2004/35/EC, 2006/12/EC, 2008/1/EC and Regulation (EC) No 1013/2006. *Official Journal of the European Union*, 6 June, L 140/114.

ENDS Europe Daily. 2008. Still No Consensus in Sight on EU Climate Plans. Issue 2639. 20 October 2008. London: Environmental Data Services.

European Climate Change Programme. 2006. *Carbon Capture and Storage, the Second European Climate Change Programme*. Final Report of Working Group 3 of the European Climate Change Programme.

European Council. 2007. Brussels European Council 8 and 9 March 2007. *Presidency Conclusions*. 7224/07. Brussels: Council of the European Union.

European Council. 2009. Brussels European Council 29 and 30 October 2009. *Presidency Conclusions*. 15265/09. Brussels: Council of the European Union.

EEA (European Environment Agency). 2004. *Energy Subsidies in the European Union: A Brief Overview*. EEA Technical report 1/2004. Luxembourg: Office for Official Publications of the European Communities.

EEA (European Environment Agency). 2008. *Energy and Environment Report 2008*. EEA Report No 6/2008. Luxembourg: Office for Official Publications of the European Communities.

EEA (European Environment Agency). 2009. *Annual European Community Greenhouse Gas Inventory 1990-2007 and Inventory Report 2009. Submission to the UNFCCC Secretariat*. Technical report No 04/2009. Copenhagen: EEA.

European Parliament. 2008a. Equipping Power Plants to Store CO_2 Underground. Press Release. 7 October 2008. http://www.europarl.europa.eu/sides/getDoc.do?type=IM-PRESS&reference=20081006IPR38802&language=EN. Accessed: 21 October 2009.

European Parliament. 2008b. Legislative Resolution of 17 December 2008 on the Proposal for a Directive of the European Parliament and of the Council on the Geological Storage of Carbon Dioxide and Amending Council Directives 85/337/EEC, 96/61/EC, Directives 2000/60/EC, 2001/80/EC, 2004/35/EC, 2006/12/EC and Regulation (EC) No 1013/2006. http://www.europarl.europa.eu/sides/getDoc.do?pubRef=-//EP//TEXT+TA+P6-TA-2008-0612+0+DOC+XML+V0//EN&language=EN. Accessed: 12 August 2009.

European Parliament. 2008c. Legislative Resolution of 17 December 2008 on the Proposal for a Directive of the European Parliament and of the Council Amending Directive 2003/87/EC so as to Improve and Extend the Greenhouse Gas Emission Allowance Trading System of the Community. http://www.europarl.europa.eu/sides/getDoc.do?pubRef=-//EP//NONSGML+TC+P6-TC1-COD-2008-0013+0+DOC+PDF+V0//EN. Accessed: 12 August 2009.

Greenpeace. 2008. *Briefing on the Allocation of New Entrants' Reserve Funding for Innovative Renewable Technologies & CCS*. Position Paper. http://www.endseurope.com/docs/90610b.pdf. Accessed: 12 August 2009.

Greenpeace International. 2008. *False Hope. Why Carbon Capture and Storage won't Save the Climate*. http://www.greenpeace.org/raw/content/international/press/reports/false-hope.pdf. Accessed: 12 October 2009.

Hämäläinen, Jouni. 2009. Role of Fossil Fuels in the Future. In *VTT Intelligence Forum 2009 "Towards Zero Emission Energy Production"*, edited by Lind, Irma, Olli Ernvall and Sari Halme, 52-75. Helsinki: Edita Prima Oy.

Hill, Gardiner. 2009. Implementing CCS in Europe: ZEP's Vision of Zero Emissions Power by 2020. *Energy Procedia* 1(1): 2857-2861.

IEA (International Energy Agency). 2008a. *CO_2 Capture and Storage. A Key Carbon Abatement Option*. Paris: IEA/OECD.

IEA (International Energy Agency). 2008b. *World Energy Outlook 2008*. Paris: IEA/OECD.

IEA (International Energy Agency). 2009. *Technology Roadmap. Carbon Capture and Storage*. Paris: IEA/OECD.

IPCC (Intergovernmental Panel on Climate Change). 1995. IPCC Second Assessment Report (SAR) of Working Group I. Cambridge: Cambridge University Press.

IPCC (Intergovernmental Panel on Climate Change). 2005. *Carbon Dioxide Capture and Storage*. Special Report. Cambridge: Cambridge University Press.

Markusson, Nils and Stuart Haszeldine. 2008. *How Ready is "Capture Ready"? – Preparing the UK Power Sector for Carbon Capture and Storage*. A report written by the Scottish Centre for Carbon Storage for WWF-UK. http://www.geos.ed.ac.uk/sccs/
Capture_Ready_CCS_power_plant_Report_for_WWF_%28FINAL%29_May08.pdf. Accessed: 21 October 2009.

McKinsey & Company. 2008. Carbon Capture & Storage: Assessing the Economics. http://www.mckinsey.com/clientservice/ccsi/pdf/CCS_Assessing_the_Economics.pdf. Accessed: 12 August 2009.

NETL (National Energy Technology Laboratory). 2007. *Cost and Performance Baseline for Fossil Energy Plants*. DOE/NETL-2007/1281. http://www.netl.doe.gov/energy-analyses/pubs/
Bituminous%20Baseline_Final%20Report.pdf. Accessed: 12 October 2009.

Regulation (EC) No 1013/2006 of the European Parliament and of the Council of 14 June 2006 on Shipments of Waste. *Official Journal of the European Union*, 12 July, L 190.

Regulation (EC) No 663/2009 of the European Parliament and of the Council of 13 July 2009 Establishing a Programme to Aid Economic Recovery by Granting Community Financial Assistance to Projects in the Field of Energy. *Official Journal of the European Union,* 31 July, L 200/31.

Rosenthal, Elisabeth. 2008. Europe Turns Back to Coal Raising Climate Fears. The New York Times 23 April 2008. http://www.nytimes.com/2008/04/23/world/europe/23coal.html. Accessed: 21 October 2009.

Sorrell, Steven and Jos Sijm. 2003. Carbon Trading in the Policy Mix. *Oxford Review of Economic Policy* 19(3): 420-437.

The Greens. 2009. New Entrants Reserve: Coal Strikes Gold as EU Commission Favours Funding CCS over Renewables. http://www.greens-efa.org/cms/pressreleases/dok/289/289286.new_entrants_reserve@en.htm. Accessed: 12 August 2009.

UCL Carbon Capture Legal Programme. 2009. *Directive 2009/31/EC on the Geological Storage of Carbon Dioxide*. http://www.ucl.ac.uk/cclp/ccsdedlegstorage.php. Accessed: 12 August 2009.

Mitigating CO_2 Emissions from Cars in the EU (Regulation (EC) No 443/2009)

Patrick ten Brink[1]

1. Introduction and background

CO_2 emissions from cars are a major contributor to greenhouse gas (GHG) emissions and urgently need to be addressed in order to combat climate change effectively. Energy use and GHG emissions in the transport sector are rising at a time when emissions need to fall. In the EU, the transport sector's GHG emissions increased by 28 per cent between 1990 and 2006 compared with a three per cent reduction in emissions across all sectors.[2] CO_2 emissions from passenger cars in the EU-27 amounted to 0.92 gigatonnes in 2006, 29 per cent higher than the 1990 level of 0.72 gigatonnes. The share of transport in overall CO_2 emissions rose from 21 per cent in 1990 to 27 per cent in 2005.

Cars remain the most dominant source of emissions in the transport sector, accounting for 73 per cent of emissions in 2006. Private cars represent 50 per cent of total transport emissions. Also, CO_2 emissions from passenger cars account for around twelve per cent of total CO_2 emissions in the EU, although this is a figure that continues to rise.[3]

Although the energy efficiency of the car fleet has been improving (with a 14 per cent fuel efficiency improvement between 1995 and 2006),[4] CO_2 emissions have continued to increase. The increase in car ownership and the distance driven by car owners per year have offset the vehicle-efficiency gains. Car ownership in the EU-27 increased by 22 per cent (equivalent to

---

1. Many thanks to Sirini Withana and Emma Watkins for their comments and suggestions, and to Malcolm Fergusson, Ian Skinner and Richard Smokers, with whom I have worked for many years. Thanks also to Guenther Hörmandinger for comments on an earlier draft. The views expressed in this chapter are purely those of the author and may not in any circumstances be regarded as stating an official position of those who have been involved in commenting on the early draft or the organisations to which they belong.
2. EEA 2009, 17.
3. See http://ec.europa.eu/environment/air/transport/co2/co2_home.htm. (Accessed: 29 October 2009).
4. Commission 2007b, 9.

an increase of 52 million cars), and passenger car use increased by 18 per cent during the same period. The number of kilometres travelled by passengers in the member countries of the European Environment Agency[5] grew by one per cent (equivalent to 65 million kilometres) in 2006, slightly down from the annual average of about 1.3 per cent per year of the previous decade.[6] Since more people drive cars greater distances, focusing policy developments on the energy efficiency and reduction of CO_2 emissions from cars is critical.

This chapter explores the development of Regulation (EC) No 443/2009 to limit CO_2 emissions from passenger cars. The process has been long and intense. Automotive industries, Member States, European Commission directorates, non-governmental organisations (NGOs) and institutes have been working in a complex interplay in order to achieve significant and measurable progress on CO_2 emissions from passenger cars without compromising the competitiveness of EU automotive industries in a European and global market. The legislation adopted in 2009 represents a real step forward, yet it is still insufficient for achieving the goal of largely decarbonising transport by 2050,[7] which will require a range of instruments, including EU legislation, measures at national level and engagement by manufacturers.

The development of policy on CO_2 emissions from newly registered passenger cars was part of a wider, and intense, process of analysis and negotiation leading to the adoption of the EU's climate and energy package in 2009. The package has several targets for 2020, including reducing the EU's GHG emissions by 20 per cent by 2020 (or 30 per cent in the context of an adequate international agreement); increasing the share of renewable energy in the overall primary energy supply to 20 per cent (including a ten per cent target for the share of renewable energy in transport fuels); and to increase energy efficiency by 20 per cent. This in turn is part of the even more intense international negotiations for an international climate regime post-2012.[8]

The EU is unlikely to be able to meet its 20 per cent GHG emission reduction target without addressing the rising emissions from the transport sector. Thus, the credibility of the EU's leadership role in international climate talks is in part dependent on the ambition of its domestic legislation

---

5. EEA member countries include the 27 members of the EU as well as Iceland, Liechtenstein, Norway, Switzerland and Turkey.
6. EEA 2009, 14.
7. Commission 2008.
8. See the chapter by Oberthür and Pallemaerts in this volume.

to reduce CO_2 emissions from cars. If the CO_2 emission-reduction target for passenger cars is seen as too weak, then this reduces the EU's credibility as a bloc committed to doing its share. Furthermore, the EU's credibility is also damaged if the target does not make an adequate contribution to meeting the eight per cent GHG emission reduction target for the EU under the Kyoto Protocol.

This chapter proceeds as follows. The next section discusses and analyses the voluntary agreements with car manufacturers to reduce CO_2 emissions from passenger cars concluded in the second half of the 1990s. These predecessors of the 2009 Regulation failed to achieve their objective. Section 3 outlines the preparations for a legislative proposal that aimed to limit average specific CO_2 emissions from newly registered passenger cars to 120g of CO_2 per kilometre (CO_2/km) by 2012, the long-established EU objective. Section 4 analyses the process of agreeing on the Regulation to limit CO_2 emissions from passenger cars and the eventual outcome that is significantly different to the initial proposal tabled by the European Commission. The concluding section outlines some future challenges for the transport sector.

2. The first attempt to address the challenge: voluntary agreements

2.1 Voluntary agreements and complementary measures

In December 1994, a proposal to limit CO_2 emissions from passenger cars to 120g CO_2/km was tabled at the Environment Council meeting. This proposal came as a result of the lack of improvement in the fuel economy of vehicles in the 1990s, and against the backdrop of the 1993 EU ratification of the UN Framework Convention on Climate Change (UNFCCC). As early as 1995, the European Parliament formally supported the objective that, by 2005, any new cars registered in the EU should emit a mean of only 120g CO_2/km. This would mean an average consumption of 5 litres per 100 km for cars with petrol engines and 4.5 litres per 100 km for diesel engines.[9] The Commission's CO_2 emission reduction strategy, also published in 1995,[10] noted the goal of 120g CO_2/km. As the average CO_2 emissions per kilometre from cars was at 186g in 1995, the target

---

9. The 120g CO_2/km target was tabled by Germany at the Environment Council meeting in December 1994; see TNE 2007. Note that one litre of petrol consumption leads to about 2.36 kg of CO_2, one litre of diesel consumption to approx. 2.62 kg of CO_2.
10. Commission 1995.

therefore represented a 35 per cent reduction from 1995 levels. The Environment Council endorsed the target in June 1996, but added some flexibility by stating that "should it appear that it is not possible fully to achieve the objective by 2005, the phasing could be extended, but in no case beyond 2010".[11]

EU institutions held divergent views as to which policy instrument would be preferable. The European Parliament was initially against a voluntary agreement and called on the Commission to propose CO_2 emission limit values, while supporting fuel-economy labelling and fiscal measures.[12] In response, the Commission agreed that in the event that negotiations with automotive manufacturers were not to come to a successful conclusion it would consider legislation.[13]

As the major tool to achieve the target, the automotive manufacturers agreed to sign "self-commitments" (or "voluntary agreements"),[14] after the European Commission "threatened" legislation in 1997 and kept up pressure in 1998. The European Automobile Manufacturers Association (ACEA)[15] was the first to commit to a voluntary agreement in 1998.[16] JAMA (Japan Automobile Manufacturers Association)[17] and KAMA (Korea Automobile Manufacturers Association)[18] followed suit in 1999.[19] These agreements committed the associations to limit average specific emissions from newly registered passenger cars to 140g CO_2/km by 2008 for ACEA, and by 2009 for JAMA and KAMA. This represented, on average, a 25 per cent reduction in emissions. At the same time, efforts began to be made to weaken the 2010 target date. ACEA noted that, in any possible extension to the agreement, it would review the potential for further CO_2 emission reductions with a view to moving to 120g CO_2/km by 2012, which the Commission "warmly welcomed".[20] The original target of 120g CO_2/km

11. See Council Conclusions 25 March 1996. http://www.consilium.europa.eu/ueDocs/cms_Data/docs/pressData/en/envir/011a0006.htm (Accessed: 29 October 2009).
12. Commission 1998, 2.
13. See Commission 1998.
14. See ten Brink 2002 for a wider discussion on this instrument.
15. European car manufacturers in ACEA: BMW AG, DaimlerChrysler AG, Fiat S.p.A., Ford of Europe Inc., General Motors Europe AG, Dr. Ing. H.c.F. Porsche AG, PSA Peugeot Citroën, Renault SA, Volkswagen AG, AB Volvo.
16. Commission 1998.
17. Japanese car manufacturers in JAMA: Daihatsu, Fuji Heavy Industries (Subaru), Honda, Isuzu, Mazda, Nissan, Mitsubishi, Suzuki, Toyota.
18. Korean car manufacturers in KAMA: Daewoo Motor Co. Ltd., Hyundai Motor Company, Kia Motors Corporation.
19. Commission 1999a.
20. Commission 1998, 4.

proposed for 2005, which had already moved to 2010, was thus in the process of being moved to 2012.[21]

The two most important aspects of the voluntary agreements are the above-mentioned 140g CO_2/km target and the associated non-binding "intermediate target ranges" for 2003/2004.[22] In addition, ACEA and JAMA committed themselves to introducing car models emitting 120g CO_2/km or less onto the EU market by 2000, while KAMA agreed to do so as soon as possible. The focus of the agreements was furthermore on technological developments, and they stated that "ACEA, JAMA and KAMA commit themselves to achieving the CO_2 target mainly by technological developments and related market changes".[23]

In 1999 and 2000, the European Commission "recognised" these commitments,[24] which were subsequently referred to as "voluntary agreements". Since the European Commission did not at the time have the right to formally enter into agreements with associations, the correct term for these "agreements" is rather "recognised self-commitments". However, they are usually called "voluntary agreements" (the term also used in this chapter) since there *was* an agreement, which de facto was voluntary as no one was forced by legislation. Instead, the associations were simply "encouraged" to make commitments under the threat of legislation.

The voluntary agreements were one of three key pillars of the Commission's CO_2 emission reduction strategy for passenger cars in the 1990s.[25] The other two pillars were CO_2 labelling and (Member State) fiscal measures. Both these instruments were aimed at the demand side and were intended to provide additional reductions below the 140g CO_2/km target of the voluntary agreements. In addition, a monitoring mechanism was launched in order to track progress (see below).

Directive 1999/94/EC (adopted in December 1999 and amended in 2003) on CO_2 labelling of vehicles came into effect in 2001. This Directive required mandatory CO_2 labels to be clearly visible on vehicles in show rooms. The vehicle promotional materials needed also to note the CO_2 emissions and fuel consumption, so as to assist consumers to make an informed choice. In the interests of subsidiarity, the Directive left the right

21. T&E 2009.
22. For ACEA 165–170g CO_2/km in 2003; for JAMA 165–175g CO_2/km in 2003; for KAMA 165–170g CO_2/km in 2004. The intermediate target ranges are indicative and did not constitute a commitment of any sort.
23. Commission 1999a, 3; 1998, 4.
24. Commission 1999b; 2000a; 2000b.
25. Commission 1995.

to decide on the form of the labels to Member States, which meant that some countries' labelling approaches were more effective at communicating CO_2 emissions to consumers than others.[26]

The fiscal measures of the Member States included taxes on petrol and diesel (also biofuels and compressed natural gas); registration and annual circulation taxes; congestion charging and road pricing; subsidies and their reform, whether for low emission vehicles or company cars; or (later) scrappage schemes to take old cars off the road and encourage the purchase of newer, cleaner and more efficient models. A wide range of instruments has been used across Member States and some have been reformed to better reduce CO_2 emissions.[27]

The Monitoring Mechanism (Decision 1753/2000/EC) – set up for annual data collection and complemented by a commitment by the automobile associations and the European Commission to submit joint reports – forms the core of the Commission's annual Communication to the Parliament and Council on progress. The data covered by Decision 1753/2000/EC included specific CO_2 emissions, the number of vehicle registrations and also a range of technical details from mass (kilograms) and power to engine capacity. Initially this data was based on information provided by the automobile associations. However, once the data systems were operational, the Member States provided the required data in order to ensure more impartiality.

The result was a valuable basis for tracking the development of emissions, and assessing progress towards the target. It also allowed for public scrutiny and public pressure, even though only a subset of the data was presented in the annual and publicly available Commission Communications to the Council and Parliament.[28] The key item that was *not* disclosed in the public reports was that of manufacturer-specific data. This omission was considered a necessary compromise in order to ensure competitiveness among manufacturers and gain agreement on the reporting method. The EU access to documents law does, however, allow public access to the

---

26. This issue was one of the reasons for the call for the revision of the CO_2/cars labelling Directive 1999/94/EC. For the concept paper prior to the Stakeholders meeting on 5 June 2008, see http://ec.europa.eu/environment/air/transport/co2/pdf/background 050608.pdf (Accessed: 29 October 2009).
27. See EEA 2005; EEA 2006; IEEP 2007a; 2009.
28. For the latest report, see Commission 2009a. For older reports, see http://ec.europa.eu/ environment/air/transport/co2/co2_monitoring.htm (Accessed: 29 October 2009).

collected manufacturer data.[29] The NGO *Transport and the Environment* (*T&E*) has made use of this provision and data presented in Table 1 below is a result.[30]

2.2 Initial progress and eventual failure of the voluntary agreements

Some initial progress towards meeting the targets under the voluntary agreements was achieved. The average specific emissions of ACEA, KAMA and JAMA fell over the whole period of the agreements (see Figure 1). ACEA started with the lowest average specific emissions for their new registrations (ca. 171g CO_2/km) and KAMA with the highest (184g CO_2/km) in 2000. By 2007, the averages for the three associations were similar: 157.2g CO_2/km for ACEA, 159.1g CO_2/km for JAMA and 161.1g CO_2/km for KAMA, with an overall average of 157.7g CO_2/km. The total average is close to the ACEA average given the predominance of ACEA sales in the EU-15 (see Table 1). According to unofficial data for 2008, average specific emissions have fallen further to 152g CO_2/km for ACEA, 154g CO_2/km for JAMA, and 150g CO_2/km for KAMA in 2008 (see Figure 1).[31]

Table 1 – Registrations and average specific CO_2 emissions of new passenger cars in the EU-15 in 2007

	Sum of Registrations	Average CO_2 Emissions (g/km)
ACEA	11,438,448	157.2
JAMA	1,880,842	159.1
KAMA	622,697	161.1
Other	15,275	196.2
Total	**13,957,262**	**157.7**

Source: IEEP calculations based on Passenger Car CO_2 Monitoring Mechanism data (EU-15) 2000-2007

29. Article 255 of the treaty establishing the European Community, implemented through Regulation 1049/2001 of 30 May 2001, grants a right of access to European Parliament, Council and Commission documents to any Union citizen and to any natural or legal person residing, or having its registered office, in a Member State. See http://ec.europa.eu/transparency/access_documents/index_en.htm (Accessed: 29 October 2009).
30. See T&E 2009 and 2007.
31. T&E 2009. At the time of writing the author only had partial information on 2008, hence detailed discussions are on 2007. Some updates are already noted for 2008 values, where possible.

**Figure 1 – Average specific CO_2 emissions of newly registered
vehicles 2000-2008 in the EU-15 (g CO_2/km)**

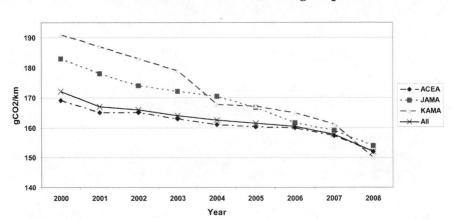

Source: IEEP calculations based on Passenger Car CO_2 Monitoring Mechanism data (EU-15); 2008 numbers from T&E (2009).

Throughout the period 2000-2007, fleet characteristics were changing with the shift of market share away from high emitting towards lower emitting vehicles.[32] Such a shift resulted from a mix of the automotive manufacturers' efforts to introduce fuel-efficient models onto the market; signals from Member State tax schemes; labelling; and consumer demand. It is difficult to identify a single specific cause for the improvements, but the technological developments by manufacturers were definitely important. However, manufacturers made few efforts to include CO_2 emission reductions in their advertising campaigns as many were still focused on making profits on sports utility vehicles. Hence, the European Commission proposed an EU code of good practice on car marketing and advertising to promote more sustainable consumption patterns in its 2007 revision of the strategy for CO_2 emissions from passenger vehicles.[33] The approach in advertising has changed visibly with the financial crisis and higher oil prices, with fuel efficiency and CO_2 emissions playing a more prominent role than before.

In the early years of the voluntary agreements, manufacturers repeatedly made statements that the 2008/2009 targets would be met. Accordingly, some vehicles with emissions of less than 120g CO_2/km were indeed put

32. See Commission 2007b.
33. See http://www.europa-eu-un.org/articles/en/article_6747_en.htm (Accessed: 29 October 2009).

on the market by 2000,[34] as promised. The market share of such vehicles grew quickly until they became more than a "fringe segment" of the market.[35]

A comparative assessment of the performance of the manufacturers between 2000 and 2007 in achieving the target may be based on either of two criteria. Firstly, best performers can be identified in terms of lowest emissions (i.e. PSA Peugeot Citroën and Fiat), or secondly, they can be identified in terms of the greatest emission reductions achieved (i.e. Mitsubishi, Honda and BMW). Conversely, Porsche and MG Rover are the worst performers in terms of level of emissions and emission trajectory, as both actually increased their average CO_2 emissions per km. Table 2 outlines manufacturers' average specific CO_2 emissions in 2000 and 2007 as well as the relative changes in their emissions over the period.

From 2007 to 2008, further substantial, but still insufficient, progress in reducing emissions was made. Overall emissions for newly registered cars decreased from 157.7g CO_2/km in 2007 to 152g CO_2/km in 2008. Average specific CO_2 emissions of Fiat and PSA Citroën fell to 138g CO_2/km and 139g CO_2/km respectively. BMW further augmented its relative improvement since its average specific CO_2 emissions dropped from 170g CO_2/km in 2007 to 154g CO_2/km in 2008.[36]

Although most manufacturers made progress each year, this progress varied considerably across manufacturers and was inadequate for reaching the target. As the gap towards the target of 140g CO_2/km widened, it was already clear that the automobile associations would have difficulty honouring their voluntary agreements. The Commission undertook a review of the passenger car CO_2 emission reduction strategy in 2005/2006. Work began on exploring the options for a potential follow up to the voluntary agreements, as further described in the next section. By 2007, the failure was undeniable since it was impossible for ACEA to reduce emissions by 17.2g CO_2/km, for JAMA to reduce by 19.1 g CO_2/km and for KAMA by 21.1g CO_2/km in the time remaining to 2008/2009 (Figure 1 and Table 1), as confirmed for ACEA by 2008 data.

34. Commission 1999a.
35. See Commission 2007b and earlier Joint Reports.
36. Data from T&E 2009.

Table 2 – Manufacturer Group average specific CO_2 emissions (g/km) in 2000 and 2007 (ranked by 2007 emissions from lowest to highest)

	2000	2007	2000 to 2007
PSA Peugeot Citroën	161.1	141.1	-12.40 %
Fiat	156.4	141.3	-9.60 %
Renault	160.3	146.4	-8.70 %
Toyota	169.7	149.2	-12.10 %
Honda	194.4	155.8	-19.90 %
General Motors	163.5	155.9	-4.70 %
Hyundai	186.2	160.5	-13.80 %
Ford	183.1	161.8	-11.60 %
Volkswagen	165.3	163.4	-1.10 %
Suzuki	172.2	164.1	-4.70 %
Nissan	173.4	166.6	-3.90 %
BMW	205.8	170.3	-17.30 %
Mazda	187	170.9	-8.60 %
Mitsubishi	217.1	173	-20.30 %
Daimler	200.2	180.9	-9.60 %
MG Rover	177.5	186.3	5.00 %
Subaru	223.2	218.6	-2.10 %
Porsche	277	285.3	3.00 %
Average	170.9	157.7	-7.80 %

Source: IEEP calculations based on Passenger Car CO_2 Monitoring Mechanism data (EU-15) 2000-2007.

3. Preparations for a legislative proposal

In the beginning of the voluntary agreements in the early 2000s, the responsible services of the European Commission focused on the implementation of the monitoring mechanism under Decision 1753/2000. In the annual Communications to the Council and Parliament on the CO_2 strategy and in the joint reports on ACEA, JAMA and KAMA's progress, annexed to the annual Communications, they constantly reviewed progress made by the automotive manufacturers. Apart from highlighting inadequate progress towards the target, the joint reports also increasingly featured footnotes qualifying progress. By raising, for example, the implications of the end-of-life-vehicles directive and of security requirements for vehicle mass and hence CO_2 emissions, preparations were apparently being made for explaining failure.[37]

Since the failure of the voluntary agreements had always been a possibility and it became clear that another instrument might well be needed to address CO_2 emissions from passenger cars, DG Environment and DG Enterprise of the Commission began analysing other policy tools to follow on from the 2008/2009 voluntary agreements. Studies were conducted in 2002/2003 for DG Environment and for DG Enterprise in 2006, and a first business impact assessment of different tools was carried out for DG Environment in 2004/2005.[38] These were complemented by further analyses for DG Environment in 2006 and for both DG Environment and DG Enterprise in 2007.[39] This analysis culminated in the European Commission's Impact Assessment accompanying the proposed regulation.[40] Analysis was also carried out at the Member State level. This section focuses on the analysis initiated by the European Commission, which looked at a wide range of options with different targets, instruments and assumptions and provided the background for the final Regulation.[41]

3.1 Targets and instruments

Three different types of targets were addressed in the analysis:
- A fixed emission target to be met by all – i.e. 120g CO_2/km (in the first analysis) or 130g CO_2/km (in later analysis; see below). This type of target, typical for emission limit values for pollutants from vehicles, would be achieved more easily by smaller vehicles.
- A percentage reduction target from a reference year, which would make it easier for those that had not been early movers before the reference year; and
- A "utility"-based "sloped-line" target (see Figure 2) – i.e. a reduction for CO_2 per kg of vehicle (or other utility parameter; see discussion further below).

---

37. See Commission 2007a; 2001.
38. See IEEP 2003; 2005; TNO 2006.
39. ZEW 2006; IEEP 2007b.
40. Commission 2007b; see http://ec.europa.eu/environment/air/transport/co2/pdf/sec_2007_1723.pdf (Accessed: 29 October 2009).
41. The discussion in the remainder of this section is based on IEEP 2003; 2005; 2007b; TNO 2006; ZEW 2006.

From different possible utility parameters, mass was eventually chosen as the parameter for the legal target. CO_2 emissions from all models and variants can be plotted against a range of technical parameters, such as vehicle mass (kerb weight or maximum payload), power (maximum or specific power), engine capacity, footprint (wheelbase area multiplied by track width), pan area (vehicle length multiplied by width), internal volume, number of seats, and/or combinations of these.[42] A range of these parameters was assessed for their relative advantages and disadvantages (potential applicability for a target in legislative proposal, data availability, understandability, positive incentives, perverse incentives, practicability, etc.). The two utility parameters retained as most potentially applicable were footprint and mass. While technical merits spoke for footprint, understandability and practicability tipped the scales in favour of mass (see further below).

Figure 2 – A utility-based CO_2 curve – a basis for a "sloped-line target"

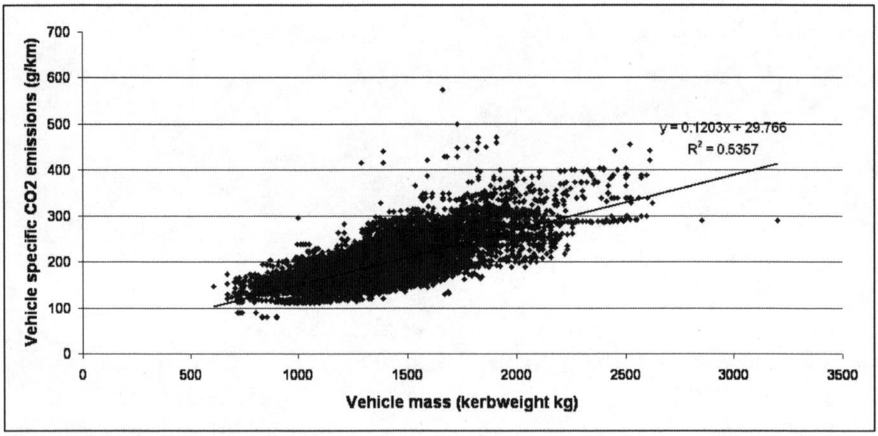

Note: example for EU-15, 2002.

Source: adapted from IEEP 2005; building on data purchased from Polk Marketing systems.

Figure 2 shows the distribution for CO_2 emissions across the range of models, versions and variants on the market versus mass (kg). There is a sufficiently good statistical relationship between mass and CO_2 emissions and also a fair amount of variation between vehicles on the market (vertical range), indicating it is possible to build a car with the same utility but lower CO_2 emissions. With the spread giving the range of potential for improvement,

42.   See Fergusson et al. 2008 for a discussion of the options.

190

manufacturers do not have to change focus on market segment to reduce CO_2 emissions.

The CO_2 utility statistical relationship (the "best-fit line") indicated in Figure 2 would form the basis of a "sloped-line target".[43] One way of defining the target is simply shifting down this line in parallel to the reference line to create a target line. This would imply the same g CO_2/km reduction for all vehicles whatever their utility. This would tend to reward efficient technologies: the winners would be best in their class, or more precisely the best for the given utility. An alternative to shifting straight down in parallel to the original line would be tilting the line (see also Figure 4), which could also be done at different points (e.g. at zero point in x-y axis, or elsewhere). The flatter the line, the more difficult achieving the target becomes for the heavier vehicles. As will be seen below, how much the line is shifted down and the exact slant of the curve became points of intense debate, given the differential impact on small cars and more luxury brands.

Other variants in early discussions included having ceilings (i.e. no more emissions than above a certain limit, e.g. 240g CO_2/km) to give clear signals to high emission vehicles and floors (e.g. no legal requirements below a certain emission level) to give additional incentives to develop low-emission vehicles. These were, however, dropped as it was recognised that it would make the negotiations too complex and, in any case, could be addressed by complementary national incentives schemes.

In addition to different target types and variants, three different types of instruments involving different degrees of flexibility were assessed:
- Emission reduction requirements for individual vehicles constitute the least flexible approach, which would have important impacts on which vehicles could be put on the market.
- A manufacturer "bubble" where the manufacturer can meet the target on average, allowing a differential distribution across models, offers important flexibility (similar to the car average fleet efficiency targets used in the US).
- A trading scheme between manufacturers could allow additional flexibility.

---

43. The reason the line is at the lower part of the "cloud" is because more of the vehicles models, versions and variants are clustered lower in the "cloud".

In practice, the following combinations of targets and instruments were analysed:

- **Car-based:** (i) Each car reaching 120g CO_2/km by 2012 (early analysis) or 130g CO_2/km by 2012 (later analysis; see below), and (ii) each car meeting a utility-based limit.[44]
- **Manufacturer-based:** each manufacturer meeting, for its fleet average, (iii) a 130g CO_2/km target, (iv) a percentage reduction from the reference year; (v) its own utility-based target on average.
- **Fleet-based:** (vi, vii and viii) the same as for manufacturer-based, but with trading – i.e. trading within an automotive manufacturer-specific system and not linked to the EU Emissions Trading Scheme (ETS) (see section 5).

3.2   Analysis

There are both benefits and costs for each target/instrument combination, when examined from different perspectives. For each of the combinations, assessing the benefits and costs involves examining factors including: the likely effectiveness of the target/instrument; fairness (including reflection of past efforts); costs; practicability and enforceability; internal market considerations and avoiding unjustified distortion of competition (i.e. reflecting the diverse positions of present and future manufacturers in the market); innovation interests; equitability across manufacturers; social equity; consumer choice; and sustainability.

On the cost side, the analysis looked at the costs to manufacturers, to society and government, and to consumers under different assumptions of how costs are passed on. Any move to reduce emissions from vehicles would result in rising manufacturer costs in the short to medium-term. This cost would most likely be passed on to consumers to some extent in the form of a price rise for the vehicle, since it is unlikely that the manufacturer would absorb 100 per cent of the cost. Reducing emissions would also lead to a loss of tax revenue for governments (from lower fuel sales). Finally, the fuel-savings could compensate (in part or wholly) or even over-compensate consumers for the increased up-front cost.

There were two particularly critical issues in the analysis: firstly, the cost to manufacturers (before any passing of costs onto consumers), and secondly, which manufacturers would face greater costs, and hence be at a

---

44. Car-based per-cent reduction targets do not make sense since new versions and variants are continuously produced and there will not be a practical way of comparing the 2012 model, version and variant with one for the reference year.

competitive disadvantage. The costs to manufacturers varied in the studies as more data was obtained and assumptions were refined. By the end of the analysis, the target changed from 120g CO_2/km to 130g CO_2/km, as the "integrated approach", that allowed other measures to reduce CO_2 emissions to be counted towards the 120g CO_2/km target, gained political favour (see further below). Interestingly, the option that offered important cost savings – full trading across manufacturers – was rejected. This reflected *inter alia* the competitive viewpoint that it is better to pay more oneself than to pay a competitor. The manufacturer bubble, on the other hand, was welcomed as an essential way of limiting costs and not affecting which vehicles could be placed on the market.

To address competitiveness concerns, the aforementioned utility curve (sloped-line target) became the focus of attention and analysis. Different curve angles were tested to understand who would be the winners and losers under different conditions.[45] Intense debate and lobbying ensued, as the potential implications for different manufacturers became clear.

The initial emissions of the different manufacturer groups were quite varied in 2000 and also in 2007 (see Table 2). Porsche (sports cars) and Subaru (4x4) emitted over 200g CO_2/km and would face a great challenge to meet a 120/130g CO_2/km target, as would other German premium brands (Mercedes and BMW). Renault, Fiat and PSA Peugeot Citroën, in contrast, would find the target significantly easier to achieve. The aim of the legislation was to encourage CO_2 emission reductions without distorting competition, thus a common target was impractical (and politically impossible). The percentage reduction target faced problems of how to deal with "earlier action" and perceptions of fairness. For the utility curve, the more it was "flattened" (i.e. made more horizontal), the more difficult it would be for heavier vehicles, or luxury brands, to reach the target. Consequently, some argued for a flatter curve, others for a steeper curve.

4.   Regulation (EC) No 443/2009 on Emission Performance Standards for New Passenger Cars

4.1 Commission proposal

While the original focus of work on the legislative proposal was for a target of 120g CO_2/km of average specific CO_2 emissions from new passenger car

---

45.   See Commission 2007b, 28.

registrations by 2012, this target was weakened over time through the introduction of a so-called "integrated approach". This integrated approach had gained traction especially through the Competitive Automotive Regulatory System for the 21st Century High Level Group (CARS21) that was set up in 2005 by the Enterprise and Industry Commissioner Günter Verheugen. CARS21 was (and remains) a process to support the competitiveness of the automotive industry, whilst at the same time working to clarify strategic and practical ways forward. During this process, interest grew in the "integrated approach", a term used to combine technology-based efforts to reduce CO_2 emissions with other measures. This broadened the scope of the target, allowing the benefits of other measures to be taken into account, including efficiency requirements for air-conditioning systems, tyre pressure monitoring systems, low rolling-resistance tyres, gear-shift indicators, mandatory fuel-efficiency targets for light-commercial vehicles, and increased use of biofuels.

The discussions on the "integrated approach" had material influence on the move to reflect wider efforts to reduce specific CO_2 emissions from vehicles within the CO_2 target. In addition, calls were made for investment in measures to support hydrogen infrastructure and the transition to a more electrified fleet, including investment in infrastructure and support for common charge sockets to facilitate the internal market.[46]

In 2007, the Commission launched a revised CO_2 and cars strategy,[47] along with a Communication on CARS21.[48] This revised strategy proposed a legislative approach rather than voluntary agreements, reflecting the widely-held view that the voluntary agreements did not deliver and could not achieve the necessary emissions reductions. It also included the above-mentioned "integrated approach". While some regarded this as necessary for the targets to be achievable and to encourage other measures, the "integrated approach" weakened the earlier target of 120g CO_2/km. The average CO_2 emissions of any new car fleet were to be 130g CO_2/km, and no longer 120g CO_2/km. The strategy nevertheless formally maintained the overall target of 120g CO_2/km by 2012 as an average emission target for new passenger cars. The additional 10g CO_2/km was to be achieved by other technological improvements noted above. Overall, the move to the "integrated approach" can be seen on the one hand as a necessary compromise to achieve a legislative outcome, and on the other hand as a major lobbying victory for the industry.

46. Commission 2008.
47. Commission 2007c.
48. Commission 2007d.

The Commission proposal for a Regulation to reduce CO_2 emissions from cars, published on 19 December 2007, consequently also embraced the "integrated approach" (see Figure 3).[49] It proposed setting a binding target of 130g CO_2/km on average by 2012 on CO_2 emissions from newly registered passenger cars in the EU market, with an additional 10g CO_2/km to be made up by contributions from measures under the "integrated approach" (see Figure 3 for the timeline). Despite this weakening, setting a binding target marked an end of the voluntary approach.[50] In principle, proposing mandatory limits on manufacturers for CO_2 emissions from new passenger cars was a radical measure. The proposal also included a broad aim for reducing emissions to 95g CO_2/km by 2020, although this was not called a "target".

Figure 3 – Past evolution and future targets of EU policy on CO₂ emissions from passenger cars

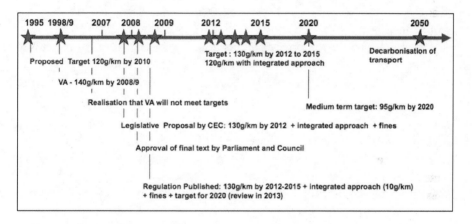

The proposal placed the obligation to reduce emissions on car manufacturers, and not on individual brands or individual vehicles. The obligation was in the form of a utility function based on vehicle weight (mass). It adopted the sloped-line target idea noted above and proposed a somewhat flattened target: a slope at 60 per cent of the best-fit line of CO_2 to mass. Manufacturers of heavy vehicles reportedly preferred a slope of nearer 80 per cent, and those of smaller cars a slope of 20-30 per cent.[51] Had there been a "zero per cent slope", this would have been a horizontal line and

49. Commission 2007a.
50. The ACEA/JAMA/KAMA agreements had been seen as somewhat of a flagship to voluntary agreements as a new form of governance (see ten Brink 2002), and their failure was perceived as a blow to the wider approach of voluntary governance.
51. Hörmandinger 2008.

hence the same as a common target. A "100 per cent target" would be parallel to the best-fit line. The 60 per cent slope is slightly more favourable towards smaller vehicle manufacturers, and it partly addresses the perverse incentive for manufacturers to increase the weight of their cars in order to avoid significant emission reductions, which can result from using a mass-based utility curve. The curve is also shifted down and pivoted at the 1,372kg point in the curve (see also Figure 4). The line is then used to calculate a corporate target that is to be met by the annual sales-weighted g CO_2/km values (as given in certificates of conformity) of new cars.

The analysis carried out as part of the Impact Assessment suggested that the overall savings from lower fuel costs would exceed the costs to consumers from higher vehicle purchase costs. Consumers would save, on average, 2,700 Euro on fuel over the car's lifetime (based on average 2006-2007 fuel prices). At the same time, they would face an average price increase of 1,100-1,300 Euro per car. The whole life cost of the vehicle would be lower. The analysis does not take into account any potential savings from innovation or economies of scale, since these are difficult to predict, although the cost to manufacturers and consumers could be even lower with such factors included.[52]

The Commission furthermore proposed to levy fines on manufacturers who did not meet their targets. These fines would rise steeply, from 20 Euro per g CO_2/km emitted beyond the target for every car sold in 2012, to 95 Euro in 2015. The latter figure was based on the expected marginal cost of a high level of CO_2 reduction, and aimed to provide a major disincentive to non-compliance.[53] Building on the precedent existing with respect to competition, it would be the Commission that would levy the fine. Monies raised in this way would not create new revenues for the Commission, but would go to the Community budget and, through the normal budgetary management procedures, back to the Member States at the end of a financial year.

In addition to proposing setting the targets for manufacturers (rather than individual cars), the proposal allowed for several additional elements of flexibility. For example, pooling targets between several manufacturers would be allowed. Detailed reporting requirements were to be imposed upon the Member States, and unlike the current Monitoring Mechanism

52. Commission 2007b.
53. Davis et al. 2007.

arrangement (under Decision 1753/2000), it was envisaged that the reported results of manufacturers would be made public.

4.2 Towards agreement

As was expected, the proposal was the target of intense lobbying, both from the automotive industry and Member States in which the manufacturers concerned are based. At its launch, the future of the proposal was, therefore, uncertain.[54] There was a range of areas of focus for lobbying during the Slovenian Presidency and, particularly, the French Presidency of the EU in 2008.

The manufacturers and concerned Member States agreed on the need to water down the proposal. The 2012 target date came under fire, with arguments that industry would not be able to meet this, given the time it takes to design and put new products on the market (the product cycle). Instead of challenging the target date head on, the preference was to delay practical implementation by arguing for a "substantial phasing-in" of compliance. In addition, there were efforts to block the idea of a medium-term (2020) target and also to weaken it (e.g. to have a wide range of 95-110g CO$_2$/km). Furthermore, lobbyists also focused their efforts on reducing the fines proposed for not meeting the target. Finally, there were efforts to have a wider set of "eco-innovations" eligible for inclusion under the "integrated approach".

The use of weight as the "utility criterion" also led to criticism from NGOs and institutes. Firstly, it does not directly represent utility (unlike power, internal volume or number of seats), and, secondly, the use of mass as a criterion reduces the incentive to use weight reduction as a means of reducing emissions (and may potentially result in the "perverse incentive" for manufacturers to increase the weight of their cars in order to avoid significant emission reductions). The proposed target (with its 60 per cent slope) only partly addressed the latter concern.

Obtaining an agreement on the cars and CO$_2$ Regulation was a priority for the French Presidency and was important as a demonstration of EU commitment to addressing climate change in the context of UN negotiations on climate change. Within the European Council, France and Germany dominated the discussions. They spearheaded a major debate on the form that the target should take, given the varying impacts on different manufacturers in their countries. The UK and the Netherlands argued

---

54. See the chapter by Hey in this volume.

against excessively watering down the proposal. There was also a divergence of opinion within the European Parliament, with the Environment Committee fighting to save the essentials of the proposal. Negotiations were very heated, with disagreements rife given the different interests of the Environment and Industry Committees. In response to the weakening of the text in the early vote in the Industry Committee the Environment Committee voted on 25 September 2008 and backed the more stringent initial proposal, notably on the 120g CO_2/km target for 2012. The Committee voted 46 in favour and 19 against the more stringent proposal, despite committee members' certainty that it would face considerable resistance.[55]

The European Parliament approved the final text of the Regulation on 17 December 2008 when MEPs adopted the legislative resolution on the proposed Regulation setting emission performance standards for new passenger cars.[56] The resolution was adopted with 559 votes in favour, 98 votes against and 60 abstentions following the conclusion of negotiations between the Parliament, the Council and the Commission on 1 December 2008.

The legislation was officially published as Regulation (EC) No 443/2009 of the European Parliament and of the Council of 23 April 2009 setting emission performance standards for new passenger cars as part of the Community's integrated approach to reduce CO_2 emissions from light-duty vehicles on 5 June 2009. Green groups saw this final deal, the result of months of negotiations and lobbying, as a poor compromise.[57] In all areas of focused lobbying, some compromise was added to the text.

The Regulation sets an average CO_2 emission limit for new cars of 130g CO_2/km by improving vehicle motor technology. This target will be gradually phased in: limits will apply to 65 per cent of each manufacturer's new fleet in 2012, increasing to 75 per cent by 2013, 80 per cent by 2014 and 100 per cent of the fleet by 2015. In effect, therefore, the target is no longer for 2012, but for 2015.[58]

55. ENDS Daily 2008.
56. See http://www.europarl.europa.eu/sides/getDoc.do?pubRef=-//EP//TEXT+TA+P6-TA-2008-0614+0+DOC+XML+V0//EN&language=EN#BKMD-15 (Accessed: 29 October 2009).
57. See http://www.euractiv.com/en/transport/cars-co2/article-162412 (Accessed: 29 October 2009).
58. Regulation (EC) No 443/2009, Article 4.

Figure 4 – Performance of manufacturers against the CO_2-mass trend line

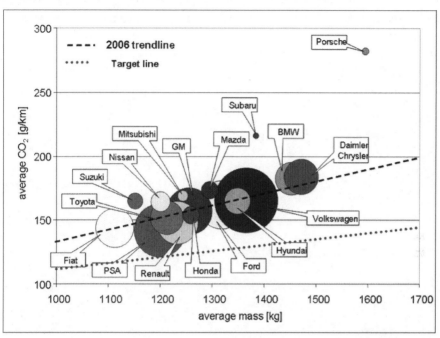

Source: adapted from Hörmandinger 2008; IEEP 2007b; target line added by author.

The final slope of 60 per cent tries to find a balance between the perspectives of premium car manufacturers and manufacturers of smaller vehicles. As can be seen from Figure 4, different manufacturers have different average mass, different average specific CO_2 emissions and different positions vis-à-vis the statistically identified 2006 trendline for the CO_2/km/mass utility curve. The bigger the bubble, the larger the number of vehicles put on the market. It also shows the target line.[59]

Additional flexibility was given to "niche" manufacturers. Manufacturers producing up to 300,000 units per year can apply for individual targets. For manufacturers producing 10,000 to 300,000 units per year, the target should be a reduction of 25 per cent on the average specific emissions of CO_2 in 2007.[60] This additional flexibility appears to be potentially relevant in particular to Jaguar and Range Rover.

59. The exact equation is: specific emissions of CO_2 = 130 + a × (M – M0), where: M = mass calculated as "mass in running order" which equals mass of the empty vehicle plus 75kg for the driver; M0 = 1,372kg; a = 0.0457.
60. Regulation (EC) No 443/2009, Article 11. Earlier, only manufacturers producing less than 10,000 units were granted a special derogation; see Hörmandinger 2008.

Additional measures corresponding to CO_2 emission reductions of 10g CO_2/km will be part of the Community's integrated approach. The use of innovative technologies, such as efficiency improvements, tyre pressure monitoring systems etc., is to contribute up to 7g CO_2/km of the 10g CO_2/km needed to bridge the gap between the 130g CO_2/km target and the 120g CO_2/km overall objective.

The fines for carmakers that do not comply with their targets were also adapted. While the fine will uniformly amount to 95 Euro for every g CO_2/km in excess of the target times the number of new passenger cars from 2019, fines for carmakers that narrowly miss their targets over the period 2012 to 2018 were reduced as follows:

- For the first g CO_2/km of excess emissions: penalty of five Euro × number of new passenger cars;
- For the second g CO_2/km: additional penalty of 15 Euro × number of new passenger cars;
- For the third g CO_2/km: additional penalty of 25 Euro × number of new passenger cars; and
- For any excess emission beyond 3g CO_2/km above target: additional penalty of 95 Euro per g CO_2/km × number of new passenger cars.[61]

The new legislation was strengthened, however, with the inclusion of a medium-term target of 95g CO_2/km for 2020.[62] The Commission will review the "modalities for reaching" the target, such as utility parameter and slope, but not the target itself, by 2013, opening the door for additional lobbying and negotiations. A formal new legislative proposal is expected in 2014.[63]

5. Conclusion and future challenges

The process of moving from recognition of the problem of CO_2 emissions from passenger cars, to formal statements of ambition (the 120g CO_2/km target), to voluntary agreements, to legislation, has been long. Throughout this process, actual commitments have fallen short of stated ambitions. A range of serious efforts to analyse the pros and cons of different solutions has supported progress. Lobbying was intense, and built on the work of the CARS21 High Level Group, which has focused more on the (short-term) automotive industry interests than on practical steps to meet the recognised

---

61. Regulation (EC) No 443/2009, Article 9.
62. Regulation (EC) No 443/2009, Article 1.
63. Regulation (EC) No 443/2009, Article 13(5) and 13(6).

need to largely decarbonise passenger transport by 2050. Figure 5 provides an overview of the process towards the long-term goal of decarbonisation.

The Regulation on CO_2 emissions from passenger cars is a significant step forward. However, from a climate change perspective, the Regulation does not fully address the enormity of the challenge of passenger car CO_2 emissions. There is a growing recognition that passenger transport has to be largely decarbonised by 2050, although how best to achieve this aim remains uncertain. What instruments can be used in what combination? What technologies are appropriate and how can they be encouraged? What is the balance of effort needed between manufacturers, fuel suppliers, retailers, national government, European institutions and consumers?

Figure 5 – Stages in reducing specific CO_2 emissions from passenger cars

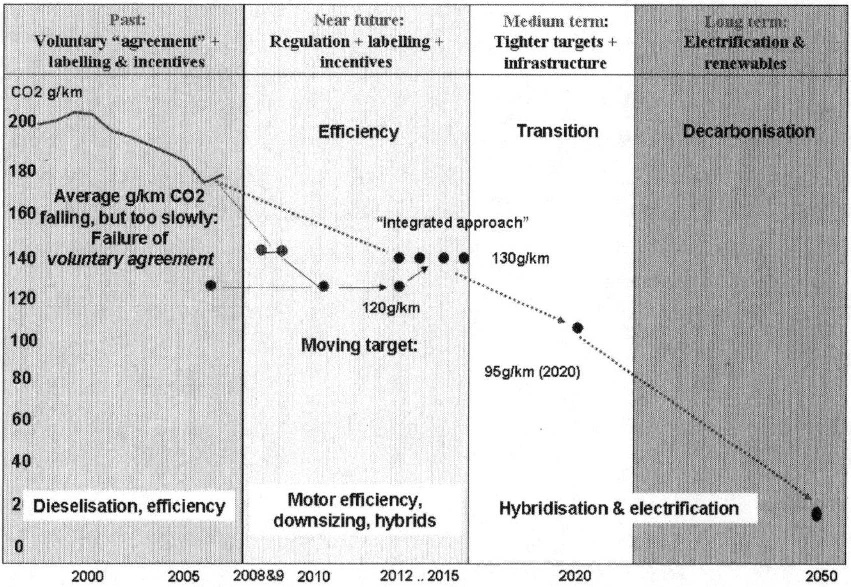

The decline in specific CO_2 emissions over the past decade has been due to a mix of the increased use of diesel, efficiency gains in technologies and market changes (downsizing). In the short term (to 2015), one can expect further efficiency improvements, downsizing (engine and vehicle) and more hybrid vehicles. In the medium term, electrification (plug-in hybrids, followed by full electrification) is expected to make a sizeable contribution to progress. In the long term, if the vision of decarbonised transport is to become a reality, we will need electrification or fuel cells linked to non-CO_2 emitting sources of electricity (as well as greater use of public transport) (see Figure 5).

The type of target enshrined in the new Regulation on CO_2 emissions from passenger cars does not necessarily need to remain unchanged in the longer term. The utility-based curve was only one of the options available, and the choice reflects an interest in preserving the diversity of the car industry. As regards the similar case of air pollution, in contrast, it has generally been accepted that each car has to respect the same limit. The cost and competitiveness implications for reducing CO_2 emissions made such an approach impossible for the current Regulation. It may also be unlikely to change for the 2020 target, even if the modalities of meeting this target are still to be determined. For the 2050 horizon, however, things might look different.

While there is a continued need for legislative approaches to ensure progress, requiring lower specific CO_2 emissions per km will be only one of a range of instruments needed. Reducing CO_2 emissions from passenger cars constitutes a formidable challenge also because the richer the population becomes, the higher the level of car ownership and the greater the distance travelled. Improvements in the average specific CO_2 emissions of new vehicles thus risk being outstripped by increased passenger car use. In short, there need to be fewer cars, driven over shorter distances, and emitting less CO_2 per km. Technology that reduces the CO_2 emissions of the vehicle per km is necessary but not sufficient. A wider "integrated approach" that combines a broad set of instruments is therefore imperative (but with separate targets to ensure clarity of responsibility and ability to monitor, verify and enforce progress). A schematic of the wide range of tools available in the short and medium term is provided in Figure 6, including instruments that affect the technology supply side and others that impinge on the demand for vehicles and actual use of vehicles.

Both consumer information (labelling, advertising, on-board CO_2 measurement) and driver information (driver training, gear shift indicators, information on fuel use and CO_2 emissions) will be critical. It would, for example, be useful for on board CO_2 measurement to be combined with annual vehicle checkups and for the average CO_2 emissions and fuel use per km to be recorded in the vehicle log so that the current owner has this information easily available. This could be useful for the current owner to help with driver behaviour and tyre pressure management. It would also be useful for potential purchasers of the vehicle to have real information on emissions and fuel use, which they could integrate into their cost calculations. It would thus support the transparency and efficiency of the second-hand market.

Taxes, charges and subsidies will be equally vital, including fuel taxes, registration taxes, annual circulation fees, road pricing (e.g. Euro vignette), and subsidies for low-emitting vehicles, as well as scrappage subsidies. The more these are differentiated according to CO$_2$ emissions, the more they will offer due signals that will support CO$_2$ emission reductions.[64]

Figure 6 – Tools available for a fully integrated approach to CO$_2$ emissions reductions

Well ⟶	Manufacture ⟶	Road ⟶	Wheel
Fuels	**Vehicle Technology Supply**	**Demand type of vehicle**	**Demand km travel & CO2**
Auto-oils	CO2 legislation	Advertising	Fuel tax
UNECE standards	R&D	Incentives ("bonus-malus")	Road pricing
Biofuels standards	Investment	Green public procurement	Congestion charge
	Standards: UNECE		Parking fees
	Certificates of Conformity	Scrappage schemes	Subsidy: Company cars
	Test Cycle	Labelling	Subsidy Private cars use for business
		Fuel taxes	Driver information
	↑	Registration tax	Public transport
		Circulation tax	
	Finance	Company car tax	↑
	Own finance, loans (EIB, commercial banks); grants: TENS/SF Research grants →	Infrastructure (electric, hydrogen) ←	**Infrastructure investment**

Demand-side measures will also be important, particularly to help encourage innovation by creating sizeable demand for low-emitting vehicles and hence encouraging innovation and progress. Similarly, how much demand for personal mobility (kilometres travelled) will be met by private vehicles or public transport will also be a fundamental factor affecting CO$_2$ emissions. A move to "mobility services" should arguably be part of a fully integrated approach, and for this, public transport will have to be a full part of the equation.

The above instruments are in the hands of a range of different actors, who each need to be fully engaged if the transport sector's contribution to addressing the climate challenge is to be achieved. Vehicle manufacturers are central as regards research and development, bringing technologies onto the market, and advertising. Member States have an important

---

64.   See IEEP 2007b and 2009.

contribution to make in the jurisdiction of fiscal incentives, infrastructure investment (e.g. for electricity points) and other areas (e.g. labelling, congestion charges). The EU institutions' responsibilities include the regulatory framework (technical standards, labelling and some fiscal issues: fuel excise tax regime and Eurovignette), and they also contribute with support for research. On the standards side, the role of the UN and international standardisation bodies is important. Banks also play a critical role, as many vehicle manufacturers relied on credit facilities and received loans from the European Investment Bank (EIB) to help restructure in the financial crisis. Finally, consumers have a fundamental responsibility regarding their choice of vehicle, choice of driving and driving style.

Trading is no longer an option for the foreseeable future with respect to CO_2 and cars (and is thus not included in Figure 6). Trading among car manufacturers has met with a lack of interest by the automotive industry (presumably because of competitiveness concerns) and was not pursued in the process leading to the 2009 Regulation. It may also run into liquidity problems given the limited number of players and competitiveness concerns. Trading integrated into the EU ETS faces serious challenges as regards practicability and effectiveness. Firstly, such integration is practically difficult, since specific CO_2 emissions per km for a vehicle are not easily converted to actual CO_2 emissions tradable in a year. Secondly, linking an automotive CO_2 trading scheme to the EU ETS could, under current prices, make it easier for the automotive manufacturers to do less, and increase the burden on other sectors of the economy. A trading scheme on the basis of specific CO_2 emissions would also not offer incentives to reduce mileage or change driver behaviour. Some of these concerns might be addressed by moving to the upstream fuel refiners/suppliers. The resulting price signal, however, would be unlikely to be strong enough: an allowance price of 20 to 40 Euro per tonne of CO_2 translates into 5-10 cents per litre of fuel. Judging from past fuel price increases, this would be unlikely to trigger the reductions required and would presumably result in pressure to balance the price increase for consumers. Finally, drivers could in principle trade directly, enabled maybe through an information processing software in the car. This would lead to several hundred million participants in the EU-ETS and could be part of a move to individual CO_2 rights or quotas. While interesting in principle, it is, however, unimaginable for the foreseeable future.

An effective response to the challenge of CO_2 emissions from passenger transport requires progress on all fronts and a coordinated response, with signals pointing in the same direction and with all actors having responsibilities and possibilities. Whatever the share of public transport in the future portfolio, interest in private mobility will stay to 2050, when it will have to be largely decarbonised if the wider climate challenge is to be met. Technical measures to reduce specific CO_2 emissions of vehicles are a critical part of the solution. Ambitious but achievable progress that stimulates and exploits manufacturers' innovation skills will be essential for the long-term viability of European automotive industry. Lobbying to reduce the bite of related legislation might support short-term competitiveness, but it risks making it easier for competitors from abroad to challenge EU manufacturers in their home market. Medium and long-term competitiveness requires fuel efficiency and decreasing the CO_2 intensity of vehicles. To this end, EU regulation on specific CO_2 emissions from vehicles is key.

References

Commission (EC). 1995. *A Community Strategy to Reduce CO₂ Emissions from Passenger Cars and Improve Fuel Economy*. Communication from the Commission to the Council and the European Parliament. COM (1995) 689 final. Brussels: European Union.

Commission (EC). 1998. *Implementing the Community Strategy to Reduce CO₂ Emissions from Cars: an Environmental Agreement with the European Automobile Industry*. Communication from the Commission to the Council and the European Parliament. COM (1998) 495 final. Brussels: European Commission.

Commission (EC). 1999a. *Implementing the Community Strategy to Reduce CO₂ Emissions from Cars: Outcome of the Negotiations with the Japanese and Korean Automobile Industries*. Communication from the Commission to the Council and the European Parliament. COM (1999) 446 final. Brussels: European Commission.

Commission (EC). 1999b. Commission Recommendation of 5 February 1999 on the Reduction of CO₂ Emissions from Passenger Cars. Under Document Number C (1999) 107). 1999/125/EC. *Official Journal of the European Communities*, 13 February, L 40/49.

Commission (EC). 2000a. Commission Recommendation 2000/303/EC on the Reduction of CO₂ Emissions from Passenger Cars (KAMA). Under Document Number C (2000) 801). 2000/303/EC. *Official Journal of the European Communities*, 20 April, L 100/55.

Commission (EC). 2000b. Commission Recommendation 2000/304/EC on the Reduction of CO_2 emissions from passenger cars (JAMA). Under Document Number C (2000) 803). 2000/304/EC. *Official Journal of the European Communities,* 20 April, L 100/57.

Commission (EC). 2001. *Implementing the Community Strategy to Reduce CO_2 Emissions from Cars. Second Annual Report on the Effectiveness of the Strategy (Reporting Year: 2000).* Communication from the Commission to the Council and the European Parliament. COM (2001) 643 final. Brussels: European Commission.

Commission (EC). 2007a. *Proposal for a Regulation of the European Parliament and of the Council Setting Emission Performance Standards for New Passenger Cars as Part of the Community's Integrated Approach to Reduce CO_2 Emissions from Light-Duty Vehicles.* COM (2007) 856 final. Brussels: European Commission.

Commission (EC). 2007b. *Impact Assessment. Accompanying Document to the Proposal from the Commission to the European Parliament and Council for a Regulation to Reduce CO_2 Emissions from Passenger Cars.* Commission Staff Working Document. SEC (2007) 1723. Brussels: European Commission.

Commission (EC). 2007c. *Results of the Review of the Community Strategy to Reduce CO_2 Emissions from Passenger Cars and Light-Commercial Vehicles.* Communication from the Commission to the Council and the European Parliament. COM (2007) 19 final. Brussels: European Commission.

Commission (EC). 2007d. *A Competitive Automotive Regulatory Framework for the 21st Century. Commission's Position on the CARS 21 High Level Group Final Report. A Contribution to the EU's Growth and Jobs Strategy.* Communication from the Commission to the Council and the European Parliament. COM (2007) 22 final. Brussels: European Commission.

Commission (EC). 2008. *CARS 21 Mid-Term Review High Level Conference – Conclusions and Report.* European Commission, DG Enterprise and Industry. Brussels: European Commission.

Commission (EC). 2009a. *Monitoring the CO_2 Emissions from Cars in the EU: Data for the Years 2005, 2006 and 2007.* Communication from the Commission to the Council and the European Parliament. COM (2009) 9 final. Brussels: European Commission.

Commission (EC). 2009b. DG Environment website http://ec.europa.eu/environment/air/transport/co2/co2_home.htm. Accessed: 22 October 2009.

Council of the European Union (Environment). 1996. Council Conclusions 25 March 1996. Brussels: Council of the European Union. http://www.consilium.europa.eu/ueDocs/cms_Data/docs/pressData/en/ envir/011a0006.htm. Accessed: 29 October 2009.

Council of the European Union (Environment). 1999. Brussels 25 June 1999. *Pollution Standards for the Engines on Non-Road Mobile Machinery. Press Release*. 8518/96. Brussels: Council of the European Union.

Davis, Adrian, Carolina Valsecchi and Malcolm Fergusson. 2007. *Unfit for Purpose: How Car Use Fuels Climate Change and Obesity*. London: Institute for European Environmental Policy.

Decision 1753/2000/EC of the European Parliament and of the Council of 22 June 2000 Establishing a Scheme to Monitor the Average Specific Emissions of CO₂ from New Passenger Cars. *Official Journal of the European Communities*, 10 August, L 202/1.

Directive 1999/94/EC of the European Parliament and of the Council of 13 December 1999 Relating to the Availability of Consumer Information on Fuel Economy and CO₂ Emissions in Respect of the Marketing of New Passenger Cars. *Official Journal of the European Communities*, 18 January, L 012/16.

EEA (European Environment Agency). 2005. *Market-Based Instruments for Environmental Policy in Europe*. EEA Technical Report No 8/2005. Luxembourg: Office for Official Publications of the European Communities.

EEA (European Environment Agency). 2006. *Using the Market for Cost-Effective Environmental Policy*. EEA Technical Report No 1/2006. Luxembourg: Office for Official Publications of the European Communities.

EEA (European Environment Agency). 2009. *Transport at a Crossroads. TERM 2008: Indicators Tracking Transport and Environment in the European Union*. EEA Report No 3/2009. Luxembourg: Office for Official Publications of the European Communities.

ENDS Europe Daily. 2008. *MEPs Reject Attempt to Dilute Car CO₂ Proposals*. Issue 2622. 25 September 2008. London: Environmental Data Services.

European Parliament. 2008. *Legislative Resolution of 17 December 2008 on the Proposal for a Regulation of the European Parliament and of the Council Setting Emission Performance Standards for New Passenger Cars as Part of the Community's Integrated Approach to Reduce CO₂ Emissions from Light-Duty*

Vehicles. http://www.europarl.europa.eu/sides/getDoc.do?pubRef=-//EP//TEXT+TA+P6-TA-2008-0614+0+DOC+XML+V0//EN&language=EN. Accessed: 29 October 2009.

Fergusson, Malcolm, Richard Smokers, Gerben Passier and Maurice Snoeren. 2008. *Footprint as Utility Parameter. A Technical Assessment of the Possibility of Using Footprint as the Utility Parameter for Regulating Passenger Car CO_2 Emissions in the EU.* Brussels: IEEP.

Hörmandinger, Günther. 2008. *The EU Policy on CO_2 and Cars. FIA Foundation – Towards a Global Approach to Automotive Fuel Economy – 2008 Symposium Paris, 15-16 May 2008.* http://www.internationaltransportforum.org/Proceedings/FIA2008/FIA-Hoermandinger.pdf. Accessed: 4 September 2009.

IEEP (Institute for European Environmental Policy). 2003. *Service Contract on the Future of the Passenger Car CO_2 Strategy, DG Environment, 2002-3.* A report to the European Commission's DG Environment. Brussels: IEEP, TNO and CAIR.

IEEP (Institute for European Environmental Policy). 2005. *Service Contract to Carry Out Economic Analysis and Business Impact Assessment of CO_2 Emissions Reduction Measures in the Automotive Sector.* A report to the European Commission's DG Environment. Brussels: IEEP, TNO and CAIR.

IEEP (Institute for European Environmental Policy). 2007a. *Reforming Environmentally Harmful Subsidies.* A report to the European Commission's DG Environment. Brussels: IEEP, Ecologic, FEEM and IVM.

IEEP (Institute for European Environmental Policy). 2007b. *Possible Regulatory Approaches to Reducing CO_2 Emissions from Cars.* A report to DG Environment. Brussels: IEEP, CE and TNO.

IEEP (Institute for European Environmental Policy). 2009. *Environmentally Harmful Subsidies (EHS) – Identification and Assessment.* A report to the European Commission's DG Environment. Brussels: IEEP, Ecologic, IVM.

Regulation (EC) No 1907/2006 of the European Parliament and of the Council of 18 December 2006 Concerning the Registration, Evaluation, Authorisation and Restriction of Chemicals (REACH), Establishing a European Chemicals Agency, Amending Directive 1999/45/EC and Repealing Council Regulation (EEC) No 793/93 and Commission Regulation (EC) No 1488/94 as well as Council Directive 76/769/EEC and Commission Directives 91/155/EEC, 93/67/EEC, 93/105/EC and 2000/21/EC. *Official Journal of the European Union*, 29 May, L 136/3.

Regulation (EC) No 443/2009 of the European Parliament and of the Council of 23 April 2009 Setting Performance Standards for New Passenger Cars as Part of the Community's Integrated Approach to Reduce CO_2 Emission from Light-Duty Vehicles. *Official Journal of the European Union*, 5 June, L 140/1.

Ten Brink, Patrick, ed. 2002. *Voluntary Environmental Agreements: Process and Practice, and Future Trends.* Sheffield: Greenleaf Publishing.

T&E (European Federation for Transport and Environment). *Reducing CO_2 Emissions from New Cars: A Study of Major Car Manufacturers' Progress in 2006.* Brussels: T&E.

T&E (European Federation for Transport and Environment). 2009. *Reducing CO_2 Emissions from New Cars: A Study of Major Car Manufacturers' Progress in 2008.* Brussels: T&E.

TNO Science and Industry. 2006. *Review and Analysis of the Reduction Potential and Costs of Technological and Other Measures to Reduce CO_2 Emissions from Passenger Cars.* Final Report. http://ec.europa.eu/enterprise/automotive/projects/report_co2_reduction.pdf. Accessed: 29 October 2009.

ZEW (Centre for European Economic Research). 2006. *Service Contract in Support of the Impact Assessment of Various Policy Scenarios to Reduce CO_2 Emissions from Passenger Cars.* Report by the Centre for European Economic Research for the European Commission (DG Environment). Mannheim: ZEW.

The German Paradox:
Climate Leader and Green Car Laggard

Christian Hey

1.   Introduction

Germany is an important player in EU environmental policies.[1] Without the encouragement and full support of Germany, the European Commission would hardly have dared to propose the climate and energy package in January 2008 – a proposal that set the ambitions for the negotiations on an international post-Kyoto climate regime.[2] Although the Directive on limiting CO_2 emissions from cars[3] was proposed before the official climate and energy package it should still, substantially, be considered as part of this package.

Germany not only has one of the most ambitious national CO_2 emission reduction commitments in Europe, including a broad national package of measures (the Integrated Climate and Energy Programme from 2007), but it also played a very active role during its double EU and G8 presidencies in 2007 in order to maintain and reinforce the momentum of the previous presidencies on the climate agenda.

It may therefore come as a surprise to many observers that this same country has mobilised a strong and effective opposition to the targets and the timetable of the Commission proposal on limiting CO_2 emissions from cars. The political agreement achieved on 1 December 2008 reflects mainly German industrial policy interests.

In the following chapter, I explain the paradox of a government simultaneously pushing and slowing down a policy agenda. My argument is that it would be too simplistic to denounce the German climate agenda as "symbolic" or to explain this in terms of political economy merely as a reflection of the industrial structure. The industrial structure, as such, would also allow for a more innovative approach. The explanation rather

1.   Andersen and Liefferink 1997; Héritier et al. 1994; Schreurs 2002; Sachverständigenrat für Umweltfragen 2008.
2.   Oberthür and Roche Kelly 2008.
3.   Commission 2007a.

lies in Germany's political system and the influence of certain advocacy coalitions, namely the strong influence of a historically successful car industry, the very strong corporatist traditions and the specifics of German Federalism. The overall perception on the links between innovation driving climate policies and competitiveness has radically changed in Germany in recent years. There is also some evidence that in the energy sector corporatist ties have been slightly loosened and have become more pluralistic – but this is not the case in the automobile sector. This asymmetry of influence may explain the paradox of being at the same time an overall climate-policy leader and a climate laggard in one or the other sector.

2. The new wave of EU climate policies and Germany's paradoxical role

EU climate policies over the last 20 years have followed a cyclical process of trial and error. There have been attempts to centralise rule-making, as well as long phases of national control and softer forms of intergovernmental or multi-stakeholder coordination.

An early attempt of a top-down approach, imposing a relatively centralised regime, was the Commission proposal on an energy/CO_2 tax in 1992. This proposal failed.[4] The Commission had underestimated both national objections, based on distributive and sovereignty arguments, as well as the strength of the institutional barrier limiting EU competence on taxation issues.[5] During most of the 1990s, therefore, the Commission relied on softer modes of coordination, namely networking and voluntary agreements. The most important voluntary agreement was the commitment by the European Automobile Manufacturers' Association (ACEA) in 1998 to limit CO_2 emissions from cars to 140g per km by 2008.[6] This voluntary agreement was not only a sectoral instrument, but also a pilot, if not a flagship project for "better regulation" relying on means other than the traditional regulatory approach.[7] European climate policy was hence an early experimenting ground for the so-called new modes of governance, relying on soft policy instruments, shared national and private responsibility, and networking, as advocated by the better regulation agenda.[8] The

4. See the chapter by Oberthür and Pallemaerts in this volume.
5. Haigh 1996; Jachtenfuchs 1996.
6. Michaelis and Zerle 2006.
7. Commission 2001.
8. Meuleman et al. 2003; Pallemaerts et al. 2006; Radaelli 2007.

Commission launched the European Climate Change Programme (ECCP), the most important multi-stakeholder networking exercise, in 2000.

In January 2008, the European Commission proposed a package of measures aimed at reducing CO_2 emissions by at least 20 per cent by 2020 compared to 1990 levels with a view to reducing emissions by 30 per cent if other countries sign up to an international agreement. The package consisted, among others, of proposals for:[9]

- a revised Emission Trading System (ETS) for the period 2012–2020 and beyond,
- national greenhouse gas (GHG) emission reduction targets for the non-trading sector,
- a revised Renewable Energy Directive containing differentiated overall targets for renewable energies and a uniform target for renewable energies in the transport sector (mainly biofuels),
- a legal framework for carbon capture and storage (CCS).

Further initiatives need to be considered as part of this package. In particular, in December 2007, the Commission proposed regulation to limit CO_2 emissions from passenger cars, replacing the voluntary agreement with ACEA from 1998. Furthermore, an energy efficiency plan, aiming for a 20 per cent increase in energy efficiency, and a respective set of implementing measures had already been proposed in early 2006.[10] All these measures were part of the triple 20 per cent targets for climate mitigation, renewable energy shares and energy efficiency.

The approach of the Commission must be interpreted as a far-reaching deviation from past prevailing patterns of environmental policy making.[11] Due to the socio-economic and ecosystem diversity of Member States and the respective different national interests, most environmental legislation left considerable discretion to Member States to adjust overall frameworks to national conditions. In the 2000s, "better regulation" was associated with less bureaucracy, less prescription, renationalisation of responsibility and open-ended programming approaches. It was not associated with the re-emergence of top-down regulation, with a radical recentralisation and

---

9.   Olivier et al. 2008; see also the chapters by Oberthür and Pallemaerts; Chiavari; Skjaerseth and Wettestad; ten Brink; and Lacasta et al. in this volume.
10.   European Commission 2006a.
11.   On the debate on old and new modes of governance see Knill and Lenschow 2004.

re-Europeanisation of policy design. These are exactly the features of many of the legislative acts of the climate and energy package.[12]

The two most radical elements of centralisation were the reform of the EU ETS and of the limits of CO_2 emissions from cars. In the case of the reform of the ETS most Member States' discretion on distributing free emission rights to their power sector was abolished and substituted by a uniform European emission cap and the principle of allocating emission rights via auctioning. Member states' discretion for hidden subsidies to their power sector was thus restricted.[13] In the case of the car legislation, the leap towards a Europeanisation of the policy was even greater, as the voluntary approach, which during the previous decade had been the flagship of "better regulation", was declared ineffective. In its February 2007 communication, the European Commission stated that the voluntary agreement with the car industry had not delivered and that a flexible command-and-control instrument would be chosen instead.[14] Essentially the European Commission had to admit that regulation is better than the earlier "flagship project" of better regulation.

The core element of the proposal was a call for an average emission value of 130g CO_2 per km to be achieved by the fleet of new passenger cars as a whole by 2012. The proposed regulation allowed producers of heavier cars to exceed the average emission value, as their allowed emission budget was to be calculated on the basis of a weight-based emission limit value curve and the number and structure of their sold new cars. The weight-based emission limit value curve, which allowed more emissions for heavier cars, was calculated by a formula that ensures the achievement of the average 130g CO_2/km. So, in essence, the regulation introduced a differentiated European standard. While this general approach was confirmed in the legislative process, the original proposal of the Commission was watered down considerably especially in response to German pressure, as discussed below.

The change in the overall governance approach by the Commission would have been inconceivable without the support of at least a number of core Member States, including, to a large extent, Germany. The EU climate agenda was prepared by high-level activities of EU and/or G8 presidencies, namely the British, German and French presidencies in the years 2005, 2007 and 2008.[15] During the German presidency, the spring European

12. Hey 2009a.
13. See the chapter by Skjærseth and Wettestad in this volume.
14. Commission 2007b.
15. Schreurs et al. 2009.

Council in March 2007 agreed the triple 20 per cent targets for 2020, which guided the ambitions of the climate and energy package proposed by the European Commission. Also, domestically, Germany has an ambitious and credible climate agenda for 2020.[16] The Integrated Energy and Climate Programme adopted by the Federal Cabinet in August 2007 is a broad set of measures, which will reduce total GHG emissions by at least a further 200 mega tonnes of CO_2 equivalent by 2020, thus reaching a national GHG emission reduction of about 36 per cent compared to 1990 levels. Important elements of that package are efficiency standards and investments for buildings; the further extension of the successful system for feed-in tariffs for electricity from renewable energy; the intensified promotion of installations for combined heat and power; and national biofuel promotion. The programme also calculates a supportive framework for the expected GHG emission reductions, with the successful adoption of the EU climate and energy package.

It seems contradictory of its dynamic international and national role for Germany to defend some conservative industry interests so strongly in the case of limiting CO_2 emissions from cars. I have rarely observed such a furious, hostile and unified response from nearly all quarters of the German political spectrum, including most mass media, when the Commission proposal was published in late 2007. Environmental NGOs and the Green Party formed rare exceptions to this general reaction. The Commission was reproached from nearly all sides for launching an attack against the German car industry and for creating competitive advantages for French and Italian producers. Later, during the French EU presidency, the government and industry played with anti-French sentiment, blaming France for adopting a one-sided industrial policy. The German car industry and the government called for a "competition-neutral solution", meaning a solution that did not disadvantage the high fuel-consuming German market segment. Only a few voices tried to adopt a more balanced and differentiated view.[17]

According to the analysis of the German Advisory Council on the Environment (SRU), the European Commission had already made far-reaching concessions to accommodate the special concerns of the German car industry in its own proposal from late 2007:
- The objective of achieving average emissions of 120g CO_2/km was diluted by the so-called "integrated approach", developed with the car industry and endorsed by the Commission.[18] The target was weakened

16. Sachverständigenrat für Umweltfragen 2008, Item 104.
17. Sachverständigenrat für Umweltfragen 2008, Item 161ff.
18. Commission 2006b.

to 130g CO_2/km, with the remaining ten grams to be achieved by other measures, including biofuels.[19]

• The weight-dependent limit value curve was introduced, which allowed higher emissions for the considerably heavier German car fleet.
• Relatively low penalties for exceeding company CO_2 emission budgets in the first two years of the system were proposed, which allowed for some transitional flexibility.

Germany responded effectively in opposition to this balanced proposal. In June 2008, President Sarkozy and Chancellor Merkel agreed a compromise delaying the achievement of the official target to 2015 and weakening the commitment by including eco-innovations, which are not considered by the official test-cycle, as contributing to the 130g target. This agreement formed the basis of the common position adopted by the Environment Council on 1 December 2008, and subsequently accepted by the European Parliament.

The German paradox can be interpreted as an unresolved battle between two advocacy coalitions in Germany on the link between environment and competitiveness. Since 2005, the coalition government has advocated and promoted ideas of a "green new deal" and of "ecological industry policy" with an unprecedented profile. According to the concept, strong environmental policies drive ecological modernisation and create tremendous new market opportunities.[20] The concept is supported by much scientific evidence, as summarised in several reports of the German Advisory Council on the Environment.[21] Germany will be able to sell the solutions to a carbon constrained and high-energy price world. This fundamental idea also found much support within the government, especially with the German Chancellor. She has advocated the idea of Germany as "trend setter".[22] The fundamental innovation in this concept is that there is no need for trade-offs between environmental regulation and competitiveness. Instead, synergy exists between them: the one helps the other. In my view, this new frame explains the German support for a revival of EU climate policies. However this does not mean that the advocates of the old frame have disappeared. The idea that strong environmental policy kills competitiveness still prevails in business, and also within the ministry of economics. The Commission proposal on CO_2

19. For a critical analysis of German and EU biofuel policy, see Sachverständigenrat für Umweltfragen 2007.
20. Jänicke 2008.
21. Sachverständigenrat für Umweltfragen 2002; 2008.
22. Bundesministerium für Umwelt, Naturschutz und Reaktorsicherheit 2007.

and cars was the first occasion when the old frame was rearticulated. Suddenly, the public accepted the idea that Italy and France, with the support of the European Commission, intended to kill the premium car industry in Germany. The environment minister had the tricky task of striking the balance between the old and a new industrial policy. The solution seems to be that the "green new deal" applies everywhere, but only partially in the car industry.

This is the core of what I would like to call "the German Paradox": how can a country be simultaneously a motor of a policy process and also an obstacle to its development? How can we understand this stop and go?

3.   More than symbolic policy

One simple answer to the German Paradox might be that climate policy in Germany is simply a symbolic policy to appease an alarmed public, while simultaneously gaining a reputation as a hero of the international climate agenda. "Symbolic policy", according to Edelman,[23] is a way of cheating the public by pretending to do one thing, while instead doing something else.

Such a critique, however, cannot hold in the face of facts. There are considerable actions both at national and international levels, which may not live fully up to the level of aspirations, but which are, from a comparative perspective, more comprehensive, more serious and more radical than you would expect from a purely symbolic policy. There is scarcely any country with such an ambitious national climate mitigation programme, which even according to the sceptics will reduce GHG emissions by more than 30 per cent by 2020.[24] So, the overall commitment is serious.

Neither can the role of Germany be characterised as blocking any progress on cars and climate change. Its approach is rather one of commitment and concession. There is a policy commitment to a legal standard, to the 120/130g target and to further progress by 2020. Germany was also supportive of the switch from a voluntary agreement to a regulatory approach, while at the same time arguing for considerable concessions to German car makers as regards:
• The deadline for achieving the target: 2015 instead of 2012. A later deadline was justified with the "innovation cycle" argument, stating

23.   Edelman 1971; Hansjürgens and Lübbe-Wolf 2000.
24.   Sachverständigenrat für Umweltfragen 2008, Item 104ff.

that manufacturers need time to invest in model changes, and thereby avoid "sunk capital costs";

• The specific structure of German car industry with its heavy, over-motorised and oversized car models ("premium cars"), with a call for a much steeper weight-based limit value curve and many loopholes (called technical innovations);

• Strong opposition to any flexible mechanisms, which might lead to a situation where German car-makers would be forced to buy emission reductions from competitors in other countries; and

• An attack against high penalties in cases where the limit is exceeded: the penalties proposed by the European Commission, reaching levels of 95 Euro per g CO_2 per km over the limit, were criticised as being excessive. In polemic and unfair critiques, the penalty was compared with the price for emission certificates, which oscillated at around 20 Euro per t CO_2, thus confusing the concept of effective enforcement of a standard by penalty with a market-based economic instrument.

In sum, Germany was also committed to reducing CO_2 emissions from cars, but with a later target date and with weaker commitments than those suggested by the Commission. This gap, however, was officially and politically communicated, and widely supported. There was no double bind behind it.

4. Beyond industrial structure

One of the most widely shared explanations for the German paradox is the contradiction between the industrial structure and Germany's climate policy trajectory, i.e. the specialisation of the German car industry on upper class vehicles with high energy consumption. Due to this specialisation (focused on the "premium" market), German producers have to achieve higher relative reductions than their foreign competitors. Mercedes and BMW have to achieve reductions of 24 and 25 per cent respectively, whereas Fiat, Peugeot and Citroën only have to achieve 12-14 per cent.[25] The average fuel consumption of the German car fleet is second in Europe, directly after Sweden: Daimler, Audi and BMW lead with average emissions between 181 and 170g CO_2/km; Volkswagen is closer to the EU average with 163g CO_2/km.[26] Despite the many concessions in the Commission proposal to German manufacturers, they nonetheless have

25. Verband der Deutschen Automobilindustrie 2008.
26. European Federation Transport and Environment (T&E) 2008.

the highest relative reduction shares. The market trend over the last decade has favoured heavier and stronger motorised cars (Figure 1). The average weight of German cars has increased by 15 per cent (170 kg) over the last decade. Without such increases in power and weight the German car industry would be much closer to achieving the target level under the voluntary agreement with ACEA of 140g CO_2/km.

Figure 1 – Developments in German car production 1990-2007

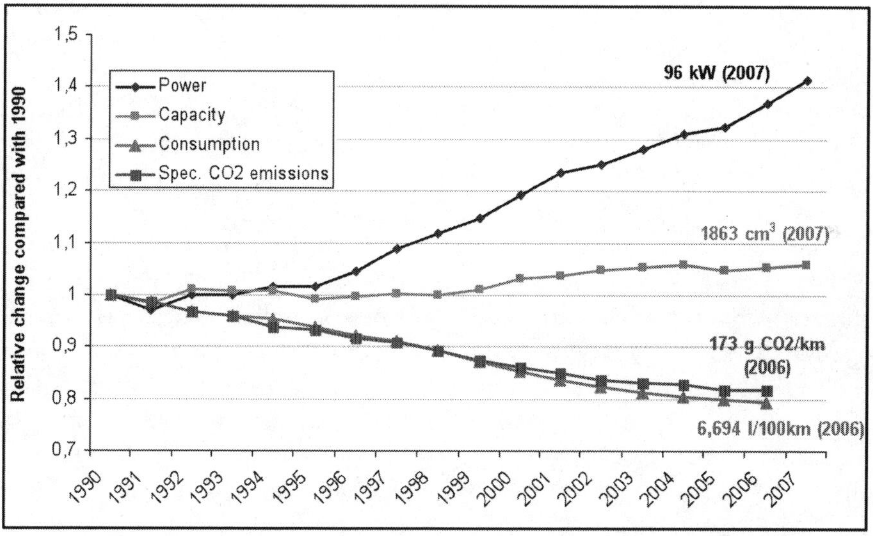

Source: SRU 2008.

There is little doubt that the world market success of the German car industry has relied on this premium market segment specialisation.[27] This may also explain the determination of the German car manufacturers to defend their success.

However, an historic success story is no guarantee for future success, especially if the market context is about to change radically. It is also no argument against innovation, if the changing market context requires such innovation in any case.

There are four major trends, which at least raise considerable doubts over the assumption that the past trajectory will continue to be successful. First, long-term trends show that energy prices will continue to rise. Second, the transport sector will not be able to resist the overall trend of drastically

27.   Verband der Deutschen Automobilindustrie 2008.

reducing GHG emissions in the long run. Third, markets and regulation in emerging countries – the fastest growing markets – are set to introduce tougher environmental regulation on cars. Finally, fuel efficiency is a driver for innovation and producers in high-wage regions will only survive if they continue to be the first movers in innovation.[28]

The German car industry is, in principle, well prepared to match these secular market challenges. Proactively taking on these challenges would also allow a much more innovation-oriented path. The German car industry has the potential to contribute to climate mitigation. According to the German Car Industry Federation itself, Germany has the highest market share in the EU of cars emitting less than 130g CO_2/km, with a market share of 57 per cent. German producers already produce 77 models that emit less than 120g CO_2/km and many middle-class cars emitting in the range of 100g CO_2/km.[29] Furthermore, Germany has very innovative supply industries. This industry is even more important, since close to 80 per cent of added value of the German car industry comes from suppliers. They employ 322,000 workers, a figure close to the 380,000 workers in the direct production of cars and motors.[30] These suppliers claim that they are already capable of providing elements to reduce the average CO_2 emissions of the German car fleet to below 140g CO_2/km. The only problem is that this would have a cost. The Federal Environment Ministry made an inquiry among suppliers in 2007 on the feasibility of rapidly retrofitting the car fleet. Suppliers responded positively. In that case, the innovation cycle argument of the car industry does not stand under closer scrutiny.

The Federal Environment Agency has concluded that a reduction of CO_2 emissions by 20 per cent would be feasible at a production cost in the range of 280–330 Euro for petrol cars and 680–900 Euro for diesel passenger cars. This is equal to avoidance cost levels for producers in the range of between 48 and 214 Euro per tonne of CO_2 – considerably less than the 100 to 5000 Euro per tonne of CO_2 calculated by McKinsey and cited by the German Car Industry Federation. It is half the costs calculated in the report that provided the data for the impact assessment of the European Commission.[31] It is to be noted that such figures imply negative CO_2 avoidance costs, as life-cycle fuel cost savings are higher than additional production costs.

28. Hey 2009b.
29. Wissmann 2008.
30. Verband der Deutschen Automobilindustrie 2008, 78.
31. Commission 2007; Netherlands Organization for Applied Scientific Research (TNO), Institute for European Environmental Policy (IEEP) and Laboratory of Applied Thermodynamics (LAT) 2006.

BMW provides a good example of the innovative capacity of the German car industry. BMW has improved the fuel efficiency of its overall car fleet by 22g CO_2/km, or 15 per cent, within three years (2005-2007)[32] and, in 2009, was able to offer a broad range of models that emit between 100 and 140g CO_2/km.[33] This recent track record in innovation is factually penalised by a regulatory policy that aims to soften GHG emission standards for cars and fails to link tax subsidies to GHG emission performance.

Looking into a life cycle cost calculation, including fuel cost savings, the original Commission proposal constitutes a "no regrets" policy, which, according to the calculations of the German Federal Environment Agency, leads to net benefits. Such calculations are very much in line with more general empirical analyses that real life costs after implementation are frequently much lower than the ex-ante cost assessments,[34] mainly due to strategic overestimation and neglected innovation dynamics. The aforementioned cost calculations show another key result, namely that the bigger the size of the vehicle, the lower the specific reduction costs. In other words, requiring steeper reductions from bigger cars is more efficient and reduces the overall cost of meeting the 130g target of the EU. In this context, the higher reduction efforts required by the producers of bigger cars are not unfair, but efficient. A flat reduction curve would require higher relative reduction costs for smaller cars and hence make achieving the target more expensive.

In sum, there is evidence that the capacity and ability of the German industry to adjust without major damage is higher than claimed by the lobby arguments, or, in other words, a pure political-economic explanation of the paradox would not be sufficient. The data even suggest that the German car industry has some potential for modernisation and that a tough regulatory framework could improve market opportunities for fuel-efficient models that are in the pipeline or even already on the market.

So why would the car industry not accept a technology-forcing, innovation-oriented regulation, and why does the government not have the autonomy to enforce such an enlightened innovation-oriented approach?

32. European Federation Transport and Environment (T&E) 2006; 2008.
33. BMW 2008.
34. Oosterhuis 2006.

5. Perverse tax incentives

Policy intervention in favour of the car industry has a long and uncontroversial tradition in Germany. VW is still at least partly state–owned, and, in the economic and financial crises of 2008/2009, with Opel and its mother company General Motors suffering, even some form of nationalisation of Opel was under discussion. This policy intervention has supported and reinforced the specialisation of the German car industry in premium cars and hence is an integral element of the technical trajectory of German car manufacturing. The interlinkages between special and supportive government policies can clearly be seen in the policy of tax relief for company cars – a policy that survived the German Integrated Energy and Climate Programme of 2007.

62 per cent of new cars sold in Germany in 2007 received some form of tax relief as company cars. This percentage has considerably increased in the 2000s and has compensated for the decline of private car purchases. A car used as a company car can be fully or partially declared as a business cost.

There are two forms of company cars:
- The car is used both for private and business purposes: as long as the car is needed for daily business, running costs can be deduced as a business cost. The "private" share cannot be deduced.
- The car is bought by a company and given to employees as part of their salary.

In both cases, both the purchase cost and the running costs can be deduced from payable income tax without regard to the energy performance of the car. Since tax relief is related to cost and as premium cars are more expensive than middle-class cars, a premium car gets more tax relief than a middle-class car. As the government pays at least a part of the purchase and running costs of the car, company buyers will likely opt for heavier and more fuel-consuming models than a private person who has to pay the full cost. The total estimated annual tax relief amounts to about nine billion Euro. This is a perverse subsidy with considerable impact. Even though all types of cars can benefit from this relief, the share of institutional buyers of new cars (benefiting from the tax relief) is as much as 80 per cent in the premium car segment. Premium cars would undoubtedly have much lower domestic sales without such a subsidy, or at least with a qualified tax relief system. It is also interesting to observe, in this context, that the market share of new company cars has increased considerably over recent years. As we can see, national fiscal policy is actually subsidising an industry structure, and, hence indirectly, a lobby. With such policies, it becomes increasingly difficult to resist the arguments of the industry lobby against EU-driven innovation.[35]

The environment ministry, as well as some green groups, have tried to introduce an environmental qualification to this perverse subsidy, relating the level of tax relief to GHG emission performance. This environmental qualifier failed to be adopted by the government when it negotiated the Integrated Energy and Climate Programme in 2007.[36]

It would be too strong to argue that the tax relief explains the specialisation of the German car industry since a large share of German cars is exported. In fact, the success in exporting largely explains the specialisation of the industry. However, the fact that the state does not use its means for a more foresighted preparation of the sector to future challenges remains an issue. Instead, the fiscal policy approach has integrated and stabilised the national specialisation.

6.   Political influence of the car industry

Germany has a federal political system with strong corporatist traditions offering sectoral industry interests and trade unions privileged access to the political system, resulting in attempts to find consensual arrangements within this triangle.[37] Along with the extreme institutional division of powers, this is one factor explaining why Germany has been labelled a "semi-sovereign state" by political scientists.[38] These close ties between industry and the state largely explain the original radicalism of the early environmental movement – seen as an outsider fighting for access[39] – and also the strong criticism from political scientists analysing environmental policies.[40] In his 2008 book on environmental innovation as a "megatrend", Martin Jänicke criticises the resulting power structures. According to him, "power is the privilege not to have to learn". He calls this the "tank syndrome" – in contrast to the "bicycle syndrome". The bicycle needs to anticipate every problem in order to avoid an accident – the tank forces everybody else to adjust.[41]

35. Görres and Meyer 2008.
36. Sachverständigenrat für Umweltfragen 2008, Item 104.
37. Jeffery 2005; Lehmbruch and Schmitter 1982; Wurzel 2008.
38. Katzenstein 1987.
39. Hey and Brendle 1994.
40. Jänicke 2008; 1986.
41. Jänicke 2008.

Although the political system in Germany has experienced a modernisation process over the last 20 years, corporatist ties have remained strong in the automobile sector. The German political system has gradually become more pluralist and more open to environmental interests. This not only applies to the environment ministry, but also to the agriculture ministry and the chancellor's office (e.g. the open consultation processes on the national Sustainable Development Strategy in 2008). More pluralism can also be observed in the energy sector, where the emerging renewable energy sector has become an influential political player.[42] The importance of the green energy sector can be seen in the fact that the decision to phase out nuclear power, taken in 2000, was upheld even after the government changed and the green party was no longer in power. One of the most important results of the energy summit that was held in June 2007 between the government and the energy sector was the clear unwillingness of the Chancellor to bow to industry demands for a weaker national and European climate regime. Therefore, there are signs that the corporatist ties have become looser even in such a strategic sector as the power sector. However, the ties have remained strong in the automobile sector. The links with the car industry are special, mainly due to the reasons elaborated below.

The federalist structure of the German political system plays an important role. Several German states (Bundesländer), such as Bavaria, Baden-Württemberg, Hessen, North Rhine-Westphalia, and Lower Saxony are important sites for the car industry. The situation of a strategic employer is felt more strongly at the local and regional levels, closer to the employer, than at a higher level. Therefore, local and regional politicians tend to defend the specific industry interests within their constituency more strongly than those at a higher level who might adopt a more aggregate approach. Some of those states are potential swing states, where no political party wants to risk its majority by losing car workers' support. Therefore, these states tend to be stronger advocates of their respective local industry interests, independent of the actual political party in power. Social Democrats and Christian Democrats equally advocate defending the car industry's interests.

Furthermore, political carriers at the federal level frequently have their roots in the Länder. The former Social Democratic German chancellor Gerhard Schröder, for example, previously served as prime minister of the state of Lower Saxony that owns part of VW. His successor as prime minister of Lower Saxony, Sigmar Gabriel, subsequently became federal

42. Hirschl 2008.

minister for the environment in 2005. It is evident that his close ties to VW persist even in his new function.

It seems that corporatist ties to the car sector have also been more effectively reinforced than to other sectors. The German Car Industry Federation elected a new president in 2007. The incoming president, Matthias Wissmann, is not only an excellent communicator, but he also has outstanding political connections. Not least, he formerly held the position of transport and research minister and had a leading role within the Christian Democratic party. In public, he has successfully cultivated the image of himself as a green car advocate, while fighting related regulation.

7.   Conclusion

The German paradox is the result of an unstable power balance between an advocacy coalition built around the idea of a positive link between climate mitigation, innovation and competitiveness, and a traditional industrial policy coalition, emphasising the trade-offs between the environment and competitiveness. The first coalition showed considerable power in the agenda-setting phase. The second coalition won control over minds in the second phase and successfully managed to re-establish the old corporatist ties between government and industry.

The German paradox is also the result of different dynamics in the modernisation of sectoral corporatist networks. Basically, with the emergence of a relevant renewable energy industry and the nuclear phase-out decision of 2000, the policy network of the German power sector has become more pluralist. The government won some autonomy from the interests of the power sector – an autonomy that was also used to promote the recent national and, especially, European climate agendas. Climate issues have ranked high on the national political agenda since the first national Parliamentary Enquiry Commission was established in the late 1980s. With regard to the car industry, however, the old corporatist ties still prevail. This, in essence, assures the car industry's control over the government. The strong role of the Länder within the federalist decision-making system further strengthens those ties. The result is a policy that protects the industry against regulation-driven innovation.

The German Advisory Council on the Environment has been advocating ideas of a green leadership, as well as the need for environmental policies that drive innovation since 1978. Costs are frequently lower after the adoption of a policy than estimated by most studies beforehand. There is little evidence to show that problems of competitiveness result from environmental legislation, but there are huge market opportunities for trend-setting environmental regulation. In its 2008 report, the Council suggested a stricter objective for the average car fleet for 2012 and 2020 (130g and 80-95g CO_2/km) should be enforced by a more flexible instrument (trading within the car industry). Such an approach would place the European car industry at a long-term competitive edge in a carbon constrained and high-energy price world economy. It would drive vehicle innovation and promote the penetration of fuel-efficient cars into the market. Resisting such an approach could backfire.

References

Andersen, Mikael Skou and Duncan Liefferink. 1997. *European Environmental Policy. The Pioneers*. Manchester: Manchester University Press.

BMW Group. 2007. *Sustainable Value Report 2007/2008*. Munich: Bayerische Motorenwerke.

Bundesministerium für Umwelt, Naturschutz und Reaktorsicherheit (BMU). 2007. Bilanz und Perspektiven – Handlungsfelder der deutschen Umweltpolitik. *Tagungsband zum Symposium "20 Jahre Bundesumweltministerium"*. Berlin: Bundesministerium für Umwelt, Naturschutz und Reaktorischerheit. http://www.bmu.de/files/pdfs/allgemein/application/pdf/20jahre_bmu_doku.pdf. Accessed: 14 July 2009.

Commission (EC). 2001. *European Governance. A White Paper*. COM (2001) 428 final. Brussels: European Commission.

Commission (EC). 2006a. *Action Plan for Energy Efficiency: Realising the Potential*. Communication from the Commission. COM (2006) 545 final. Brussels: European Commission.

Commission (EC). 2006b. *Cars 21. A Competitive Automotive Regulatory System for the 21st Century*. Final Report. Luxembourg: Office for Official Publications of the European Communities.

Commission (EC). 2007a. Proposal of 19 December 2007 for a Regulation of the European Parliament and of the Council Setting Emission Performance Standards for New Passenger Cars as Part of the Community's

Integrated Approach to Reduce CO$_2$ Emissions from Light-Duty Vehicles. Brussels: European Commission.

Commission (EC). 2007b. Communication of the Commission to the Council and the European Parliament. *Results of the Review of the Community Strategy to Reduce CO$_2$ Emission from Passenger Cars and Light-Commercial Vehicles and on the "Competitive Automotive Regulatory Framework for the 21st Century"*. COM (2007) 22. Brussels: *European Commission*.

Edelman, Murray. 1971. *Politics as Symbolic Action. Mass Arousal and Quiescence*. Chicago: Markham.

European Federation Transport and Environment (T&E). 2006. *How Clean is Your Car Brand? The Car Industry's Commitment to the EU to Reduce CO$_2$ Emissions. A Brand-by-Brand Progress Report*. Brussels: T&E (European Federation Transport and Environment).

European Federation Transport and Environment (T&E). 2008. *Reducing CO$_2$ Emissions from New Cars: A Study of Major Car Manufacturers' Progress in 2006*. Brussels: T&E (European Federation Transport and Environment).

Görres, Anselm and Bettina Meyer. 2008. *Firmen- und Dienstwagenbesteuerung modernisieren: Für Klimaschutz und mehr Gerechtigkeit*. Munich: Forum Ökologisch-Soziale Martktwirtschaft. http://files.foes.de/de/downloads/ links/ Pr%E4siDienstwagen05_2SBS_hoch.pdf. Accessed: 14 July 2009.

Haigh, Nigel. 1996. Climate Change Policies and Politics in the European Community. In *Politics of Climate Change*, edited by Tim O'Riordan and Jill Jäger. 155-185. London: Routledge.

Hansjürgens, Bernd and Gertrude Lübbe-Wolf, eds. 2000. *Symbolische Umweltpolitik*. Frankfurt a.M.: Suhrkamp.

Héritier, Adrienne, Susanne Mingers, Christoph Knill and Martina Becka. 1994. *Die Veränderung von Staatlichkeit in Europa. Ein regulativer Wettbewerb: Deutschland, Großbritannien und Frankreich in der Europäischen Union*. Opladen: Leske + Budrich.

Hey, Christian. 2009a. Rediscovery of Hierarchy: The New EU Climate Policies. In *EU Environmental Policies and Governance: Climate Change and Beyond*, edited by Annette Bongardt and Francisco Torres. Cheltenham: Edward Elgar (in press).

Hey, Christian. 2009b. Klimaschutz&Kfz. *Forum Wissenschaft*. No. 2. May 2009. 17-21.

Hey, Christian and Uwe Brendle. 1994. *Umweltverbände und EG. Strategien, politische Kulturen und Organisationsformen.* Opladen: Westdeutscher Verlag.

Hirschl, Bernd. 2008. *Erneuerbare Energien-Politik. Eine Multi-Level Policy-Analyse mit Fokus auf den deutschen Strommarkt.* Wiesbaden: VS Verlag für Sozialwissenschaften.

Jachtenfuchs, Markus. 1996. Regieren durch Überzeugen: Die Europäische Union und der Treibhauseffekt. In *Europäische Integration*, edited by Beate Kohler-Koch and Markus Jachtenfuchs. 429-454. Opladen: Leske + Budrich.

Jänicke, Martin. 1986. *Staatsversagen. Die Ohnmacht der Politik in der Industriegesellschaft.* München: Piper.

Jänicke, Martin. 2008. *Megatrend Umweltinnovation. Zur ökologischen Modernisierung von Wirtschaft und Staat.* München: oekom.

Jeffery, Charlie. 2005. Federalism: The New Territorialism. In *Governance in Contemporary Germany. The Semisovereign State Revisited*, edited by Simon Green and William E. Paterson. 78-93. Cambridge: Cambridge University Press.

Katzenstein, Peter J. 1987. *Policy and Politics in Western Germany. The Growth of the Semi-Sovereign State.* Philadephia: Cornell University Press.

Knill, Christoph and Andrea Lenschow. 2004. Modes of Governance in the European Union. Towards a Comprehensive Evaluation. In *The Politics of Regulation. Institutions and Regulatory Reforms for the Age of Governance*, edited by Jacint Jordana and David Levi-Faur. 218-244. Cheltenham: Elgar.

Lehmbruch, Gerhard and Philippe Schmitter, eds. 1982. *Patterns of Corporatist Policy Making.* London: Sage.

Meuleman, Louis, Ingeborg Niestroy and Christian Hey, eds. 2003. *Environmental Governance in Europe.* Edited by EEAC. The Hague: Lemma.

Michaelis, Peter and Peter Zerle. 2006. From Acea's Voluntary Agreement to an Emission Trading Scheme for New Passenger Cars. *Journal of Environmental Planning and Management* 49(3): 435-453.

Oberthür, Sebastian and Claire Roche Kelly. 2008. EU Leadership in International Climate Policy: Achievements and Challenges. *The International Spectator* 43(3): 35-50.

Olivier, Jos G., W. Tuinstra, H. E Elzenga, R. A. van den Wijngaart, P. R. Bopsch, B. Eickhout, and M. Visser. 2008. *Consequences of the European Policy Package on Climate and Energy. Initial Assessment of the Consequences for the Netherlands and Other Member States*. In MNP report 500094009. AH Bilthoven: MNP (Milieu en Natuur Planbureau).

Oosterhuis, Frans. 2006. *Ex-Post Estimates of Costs to Business of EU Environmental Legislation. Final Report*. Amsterdam: Institute for Environmental Studies.

Pallemaerts, Marc, David Wilkinson, Catherine Bowyer, James Brown, Andrew Farmer, Martin Farmer, Martina Herodes, Peter Hjerp, Clare Miller, Claire Monkhouse, Ian Skinner, Patrick ten Brink and Camilla Adelle. 2006. *Drowning in Process? The Implementation of the EU's 6th Environmental Action Programme*. An IEEP Report for the European Environmental Bureau (EEB). London: IEEP.

Radaelli, Claudio M. 2007. Whither Better Regulation for the Lisbon Agenda? *Journal of European Public Policy* 14(2): 190-207.

Schreurs, Miranda. 2002. *Environmental Politics in Japan, Germany, and the United States*. Cambridge: Cambridge University Press.

Schreurs, Miranda, Henrik Selin and Stacy D. van Deveer, eds. 2009. *Transatlantic Environment and Energy Politics: Comparative and International Perspectives*. Aldershot: Ashgate.

Sachverständigenrat für Umweltfragen (SRU). 2002. *Umweltgutachten 2002. Für eine neue Vorreiterrolle*. Stuttgart: Metzler-Poeschel.

Sachverständigenrat für Umweltfragen (SRU). 2007. *Climate Mitigation by Biomass*. Berlin: http://www.umweltrat.de/02gutach/downlo02/sonderg/Climate_Change_Mitigation_by_Biomass_web_2007.pdf. Accessed: 14 July 2009.

Sachverständigenrat für Umweltfragen (SRU). 2008. *Umweltgutachten 2008. Umweltschutz im Zeichen des Klimawandels*. Berlin: Erich Schmidt.

Netherlands Organization for Applied Scientific Research (TNO), Institute for European Environmental Policy (IEEP) and Laboratory of Applied Thermodynamics (LAT). 2006. *Review and Analysis of the Reduction Potential and Costs of Technological and Other Measures to Reduce CO_2-Emissions from Passenger Cars*. Delft, London, Thessaloniki: TNO, IEEP, LAT.

Umweltbundesamt (UBA). 2008. *Technikkostenschätzung für die CO_2-Reduktion bei Pkw*. Dessau: UBA.

Verband der Deutschen Automobilindustrie (VDA). 2008. *Autojahresbericht 2008*. Frankfurt a. M.: VDA (Verband der Deutschen Automobilindustrie).

Wissmann, Matthias (VDA President). 2008. Die Automobilindustrie steht an einer Weggabelung. *Die Welt*. 6 October 2008.

Wurzel, Rüdiger K.W. 2008. *The Politics of Emissions Trading in Britain and Germany*. London: Anglo-German Foundation Report.

Assessing EU Assistance for Adaptation to Climate Change in Developing Countries: a Southern Perspective

Jessica Ayers, Saleemul Huq and Achala Chandani

1.   Introduction

The Fourth Assessment Report from the Intergovernmental Panel on Climate Change (IPCC) showed clearly that climate change is a reality, that its impacts are being felt, and that those most vulnerable to climate change are the poorest communities in developing countries.[1] While "mitigation" (the limiting of greenhouse gas (GHG) emissions into the atmosphere) is an undeniable priority, all countries, but particularly the most vulnerable developing countries, are facing the need to adapt to the now inevitable impacts. "Adaptation" describes the process of adjustment in natural or human systems in response to actual or expected climatic stimuli or their effects, to moderate harm or exploit beneficial opportunities.[2] Since the publication of the IPCC Fourth Assessment Report, evidence has emerged of greater and more rapid impacts of climate change, and we now face the realistic possibility of climate warming up to four degrees, two degrees more than is currently considered a dangerous level of climate change.[3] Providing vulnerable developing countries with adequate assistance to help them adapt to the impacts of such warming is therefore becoming increasingly urgent.

The European Union and its 27 Member States have shown good leadership in engaging in global dialogue and action for managing climate change, both through the United Nations Framework Convention on Climate Change (UNFCCC) processes, and also independently of the UNFCCC. To date, the emphasis of EU action on climate change has been on mitigation, which indeed reflects global trends in the climate change arena. More recently, both internationally and at the level of the EU, the need to provide more and better assistance to developing countries to adapt

---

1.   Intergovernmental Panel on Climate Change 2007.
2.   Intergovernmental Panel on Climate Change 2007.
3.   Parry et al. 2008.

231

has been recognised, and adaptation has begun to play a key role in recent EU climate policy and planning. This paper will begin by considering what kind of assistance developing countries require from international sources, including the EU. We will then discuss recent key developments in EU action on climate change, and consider whether the EU is taking the right steps towards meeting adaptation needs in the South.

2.   Adaptation needs in developing countries

2.1   The costs of adapting to climate change

Global estimates for the costs of adaptation vary hugely from between four to over 100 billion US dollars per year.[4] These estimates are even vaguer for developing countries, where data is often sparse and variables remain uncertain. Existing attempts to measure adaptation costs differ according to the assumptions they are based on (for example, some estimates include climate proofing existing development);[5] time frames; the definition of adaptation used and the "types" of adaptation included (ranging from "hard" technological responses to climate change, through "soft" development-based measures that also address vulnerability to climatic variability); as well as the level of climate change being assumed.

Estimates generated by the UNFCCC suggest the total funding needed for adaptation in developing countries by 2030 will be 27-66 billion US dollars annually.[6] Oxfam put the figure at 50 billion US dollars annually,[7] while the United Nations Development Programme (UNDP) has suggested 86 billion US dollars annually by 2015.[8] A recent review of these cost estimates suggests that these are underestimates, based on similar assumptions that exclude some sectors (e.g. ecosystems, energy, manufacturing, retailing and tourism), only partially cover others, and calculate costs as "climate mark-ups"[9] against low levels of assumed investment. The authors point out that in some parts of the world low levels of investment have led to a current

---

4.   Parry et al. 2009, 20.
5.   "Climate proofing" means integrating risk reduction and adaptation to climate change in development and poverty reduction planning, thus ensuring opportunities for building adaptive capacity through development are maximised, and maladaptive planning is avoided.
6.   UNFCCC 2007.
7.   Oxfam International 2007.
8.   UNDP 2007.
9.   Parry et al. 2009, 7.

"adaptation deficit", and this deficit will need to be made up by full funding for development, without which the funding for adaptation will be insufficient.[10] More recent estimates by the World Bank put the costs of adaptation to climate change in developing countries in the order of 75-100 billion US dollars per year for the period 2010-2050, considering a temperature increase of two degrees Celsius.[11]

Importantly, the longer it takes to implement an effective international agreement to halt and then reduce GHG emissions, the higher these costs of adaptation will be and the more likely that the limits to adaptation will be reached and exceeded.[12] The cost estimates mentioned above use a highest level of two degrees Celsius temperature increase for climate change projection. However, if global temperature increases reach three degrees or even four degrees Celsius, as is considered increasingly likely,[13] then the costs of adaptation will increase exponentially. IPCC scientists are currently working on more realistic future climate change scenarios of above two degrees Celsius. These are likely to reveal much greater costs for adaptation in developing countries, and globally.[14]

2.2   Modes of financing adaptation in developing countries

There are essentially two "types" of financial assistance that are being used to help developing countries meet the costs of climate change: first, under existing channels of official development assistance (ODA); and second, through dedicated climate change funds under the UNFCCC.

Providing assistance through ODA makes sense,[15] because the objectives of development overlap considerably with those of adaptation, given that vulnerability to climate change depends on the capacity of a society to cope with and adapt to climate-related hazards. This assistance is constrained by factors such as lack of resources, poor institutions and governance, inadequate infrastructure and other economic constraints related to a lack of development.[16] ODA should, at least in principle, target some of the poorest and most vulnerable who are also the most in need of adaptation assistance, and so ODA provides a channel to build adaptive capacity where it is needed most. It is therefore tempting to use existing channels of

10.   Ibid.
11.   World Bank 2009.
12.   Ayers 2009.
13.   Parry et al. 2008.
14.   Parry, M., personal communication to Saleemul Huq, March 2009.
15.   Dodman et al. 2009.
16.   Huq and Ayers 2008.

development assistance for filling the gap in adaptation funding and support.[17]

However, using ODA for adaptation in developing countries is contentious because, firstly, not all adaptation is development, and not all development reduces vulnerability to climate change. Long-term adaptation priorities may conflict with near-term development priorities. For example, economic development strategies, which do not take into account the long-term implications of climate change, could increase dependency on climate-sensitive resources and ultimately prove maladaptive.[18] Likewise, "climate-proofing" development interventions may give rise to a conflict of interest between external donors, wishing to ensure the longer-term resilience of their investments, and recipient countries, wishing to maintain ownership over their development priorities and control over national development budgets.[19]

Secondly, because climate change is the result of unsustainable development pathways, those countries that are least developed (and most vulnerable) to climate change, are also the least responsible, whilst the industrialised nations are responsible for the increasing vulnerability of the South.[20] The responsibility of developed countries to assist the most vulnerable countries to cope with the impacts of climate change is *additional* to existing aid commitments.[21]

It is therefore a widely agreed principle for adaptation assistance that finance should be additional to existing aid commitments. This is not a universally adhered to principle, however. The World Bank-managed multilateral fund, the "Pilot Programme on Climate Resilience", for example, with a target budget of one billion US dollars, is aimed at increasing climate resilience in developing countries. The fund has been heavily criticised for allowing contributions from donors in the form of both ODA loans and additional funding grants. However, revised proposals from the Bank allow developing countries to choose whether to take both loans and grants, with many developing countries to date opting for the "grant only" portion of funding in principle.[22]

17. Ayers and Huq 2009.
18. Ayers 2009. Maladaptations are actions or investments that enhance, rather than reduce, vulnerability to impacts of climate change. This can include the shifting of vulnerability from one social group or place to another; it also includes shifting risk to future generations and/or to ecosystems and ecosystem services.
19. Ayers and Dodman 2010.
20. Ayers and Huq 2009.
21. Oxfam 2007; Ayers 2009.
22. Ayers 2009.

At the same time, it is recognised that there are synergies between adaptation and development, and adaptive capacity will be built where these synergies can be exploited. This has led to calls for adaptation to be "mainstreamed" into development policies, programmes and projects where possible, ensuring that development efforts are both "climate-proofed", and also consciously aimed at reducing vulnerability, by including priorities that are essential for successful adaptation.[23]

The second avenue for financing adaptation is through the UNFCCC funds. There are four funds relevant to adaptation under the UNFCCC: The Least Developed Countries Fund (LDCF) was established under the UNFCCC to help developing countries prepare and implement their National Adaptation Programmes of Action (NAPAs). The Special Climate Change Fund (SCCF) also operates under the UNFCCC to support a number of climate change activities such as mitigation and technology transfer, but prioritises adaptation. The Global Environment Facility (GEF) Trust Fund's Strategic Priority for Adaptation pilots "operational" approaches to adaptation. Finally, the Adaptation Fund sits under the Kyoto Protocol.[24]

However, the total funds available under the GEF are far from enough to meet the costs of adaptation discussed above. All three GEF-managed funds (the LDCF, the SCCF, and the Trust Fund) are based on ODA-type voluntary pledges and bilateral contributions from donors. This type of contribution is unlikely ever to be able to generate the required levels of funding – especially given that contributions are meant to be additional to ODA – when many high-income nations are failing to meet their 0.7 per cent commitments to ODA in the first place. According to the most recent status report (October 2008), 172.4 million US dollars were pledged to the LDCF, 106.6 million to the SCCF and 50 million to the GEF Trust Fund's Strategic Priority for Adaptation, resulting in pledges totalling 328 million US dollars.[25] Furthermore, donors are delaying on meeting their pledged commitments because of an alleged lack of adequate and accountable mechanisms in developing countries for receiving and disbursing money.[26] In addition, many donors are including contributions to UNFCCC funds in their ODA reporting.

The Adaptation Fund does offer more promising levels of funding. Unlike the GEF-managed funds described above, the Adaptation Fund is not based

23. Klein 2008.
24. See www.gefweb.org.
25. GEF 2008.
26. Ayers 2009.

on voluntary pledges, but on a two per cent "levy" on emission credits generated under the Clean Development Mechanism (CDM), which allows developed countries to invest in projects in developing countries in order to earn emission credits. The revenue generated from the CDM levy alone is projected to be between 160 and 190 million US dollars, and potentially much more depending on the volume of CDM emission credits generated and prices on the carbon market, as emission targets are set.[27] There is also potential to significantly scale up financing under the Adaptation Fund mechanism by applying the levy to other activities. One idea launched in 2006, for example, was to create an International Air Travel Adaptation Levy, which has the potential to generate an estimated four to ten billion US dollars per annum of additional funding for adaptation in low- and middle-income countries. There have also been proposals to apply the levy to maritime bunker fuels.[28]

In the following sections, we will discuss EU assistance to developing countries on adaptation, and consider how they relate to the issues surrounding international adaptation assistance highlighted above. These issues are, first, that adaptation assistance should be additional to ODA; second, that adaptation should, where possible, also be mainstreamed into ODA and development assistance should be "climate-proofed"; and finally, whether the EU is taking steps to meet the significant shortfall in adaptation funding.

3. EU assistance for adaptation in developing countries

The European Union is at the forefront of promoting international action on climate change. In particular, the EU has recognised the need for better engagement with, and support for, developing countries on both mitigation and adaptation. Since the 2000s, the importance of adaptation has risen on the EU climate agenda, and the EU has included adaptation in both its development and also its climate change initiatives. In terms of integrating adaptation into development, the EU Action Plan on Climate Change and Development (2004) and, more recently, the Global Climate Change Alliance (2007), provide support for integration, and climate change is also being mainstreamed into EU development cooperation. With regards to climate policy, the key policy documents that will be discussed here are the Green Paper (2007) and White Paper (2009) on

---

27. Müller 2007.
28. Ayers 2009.

adaptation from the Commission to the European Council and Parliament; and the European Commission's Communication "Towards a Comprehensive Climate Change Agreement in Copenhagen" (2009). We will set the context for this section by describing one of the main financial mechanisms for climate change action in the EU, the Environment and Natural Resources Thematic Programme, which provides funding for both the Action Plan and the Global Climate Change Alliance.

3.1 The Thematic Programme for Environment and Sustainable Management of Natural Resources including Energy

The Thematic Programme for Environment and Sustainable Management of Natural Resources including Energy is a four-year strategy that addresses environmental challenges that affect the lives of poor people. These environmental challenges include rapidly degrading key ecosystems, climate change, poor global environmental governance and inadequate access to and security of energy supplies. The Thematic Programme is the main instrument for climate change related funding in EC development cooperation. It has a global budget of 804 million Euro, allocated for the period 2007-2013, of which 469.7 million Euro is allocated for the period 2007-2010.[29] Financial allocations are broken down into five themes:[30]

1. Working upstream on Millennium Development Goal (MDG) seven: promoting environmental sustainability (14.2 million Euro allocated for 2007-2010);
2. Promoting implementation of EU initiatives and internationally agreed commitments, including the EU Action Plan and the Global Climate Change Alliance (273.8 million Euro allocated for 2007-2010);
3. Improving expertise for integration and coherence (8.2 million Euro allocated for 2007-2010);
4. Strengthening environmental governance and EU leadership (38.5 million Euro allocated for 2007-2010);
5. Support for sustainable energy options in partner countries and regions (115.4 million Euro allocated for 2007-2010).

All of the above priorities are directly or indirectly relevant to supporting climate change activities in developing countries, and could be linked to adaptation one way or another, particularly if we think more broadly in terms of adaptive capacity. However, the second priority is most relevant

29. See http://www.welcomeurope.com/default.asp?id=1110&idpgm=11820 (Accessed: 6 November 2009).
30. Behrens 2008.

237

to adaptation. Under this priority 23.3 million Euro has been included for the implementation of the EU Action Plan on Climate Change and Development and around 50 million Euro to support the Global Climate Change Alliance, discussed below.

3.2 The EU Action Plan on Climate Change and Development (2004) and the Global Climate Change Alliance

The EU Action Plan on Climate Change and Development arose from a growing understanding within the EU that climate change threatened the achievement of development priorities in EU partner countries, and should be integrated into development assistance. This was formally recognised in the 2003 Communication from the Commission to the European Council and Parliament, entitled "Climate Change in the Context of Development Cooperation", which states that "climate change concerns and its potentially disastrous long-term implications need to be fully mainstreamed into EU development co-operation so that they receive a higher profile in priority-setting in a way that is completely coherent with the overarching objective of poverty reduction".[31] The Communication includes a proposal for an Action Plan, adopted in November 2004, to support partner countries. The overall objective of the Action Plan is "to assist EU partner countries in meeting the challenges posed by climate change, in particular by supporting them in the implementation of the UN Framework Convention on Climate Change and the Kyoto Protocol".[32] This includes four strategic priorities: raising the profile of climate change; support for adaptation to climate change; support for mitigation of climate change; and capacity development.[33]

The EU Action Plan reflects a significant step in the EU's thinking on climate change and development. By explicitly linking the two, the EU appreciates their interdependence: that impacts of climate change will adversely affect progress in the achievement of development objectives, whilst sustainable development can reduce vulnerability to climate change. However, while indeed a reflection of progress, a closer look at the Action Plan shows that there were no financial commitments attached. This was one of the fundamental criticisms that non-governmental organisations

31. Commission 2003, 4.
32. Commission 2003, 4.
33. Commission 2003, 4.

(NGOs) communicated to the Commission and Member States, since implementation will crucially depend on the resources to back the Plan.[34] The Action Plan was also criticised by NGOs for not going far enough on encouraging development NGOs in partner countries to integrate climate change into their work, and the EU was requested to provide greater support to the exchange of information and experience in this respect among the different stakeholders.[35]

In 2007, the European Commission announced the Global Climate Change Alliance, renewing the commitment of the EU Action Plan on Climate Change and Development, to systematically integrate climate change into development cooperation. The Alliance became fully operational in 2008. It is intended to provide a platform for dialogue and exchange as well as practical cooperation between the EU and those developing countries most vulnerable to climate change, particularly the Small Island Developing States and the Least Developed Countries. The Alliance will also provide technical and financial support for adaptation and mitigation measures, and for integrating climate change into development. In doing so, the Alliance aims to increase developing countries' capacity to adapt to climate change and support their participation in global mitigation efforts.[36]

The Global Climate Change Alliance provides assistance under five focal areas: developing and implementing concrete adaptation strategies; reducing emissions from deforestation; helping poor countries to take advantage of the CDM; helping developing countries be better prepared for natural disasters; and integrating climate change into development cooperation and poverty strategies. While the Alliance therefore provides assistance in both mitigation and adaptation, priority is given to adaptation, disaster risk reduction, and climate change integration.[37] Around 60 million Euro has been provided for the Alliance under the Environment and Natural Resources Thematic Programme to cover the period 2008-2010, while over 300 million Euro is available from various budget lines to fund its objectives.

---

34. See, for example, criticisms by the Climate Action Network http://www.climnet.org/ EUenergy/eu_action_plan.html (Accessed: 6 November 2009).
35. NGO comments on the draft text of the revised Action Plan of the Communication "Climate Change in the Context of Development Cooperation" COM (2003) 85 final. EU Consultation Workshop, 14 June 2004, German Ministry of Environment, Bonn.
36. Behrens 2008.
37. Commission 2007a.

The Alliance is a welcome development from the EU in terms of acknowledging the need to improve dialogue between North and South, particularly on adaptation. Its launch at the end of 2007 was also timely as it could feed into the UNFCCC negotiations in Poznan in December 2008, and also ahead of the negotiations in Copenhagen in December 2009, where the fostering of relationships and trust-building between developed and developing counties is essential to achieve concrete action on both mitigation and adaptation in any post-2012 agreements. The Alliance also contributes to filling the huge gap between knowledge and action on climate change, particularly in terms of achieving synergies between development and climate change on the ground.[38]

However, while the Alliance certainly indicates a strengthening in the discourse of the EU around climate change and development, this has yet to be matched by firm commitments in terms of additional action and finance. 60 million Euro is a drop in the ocean compared to what is needed to meet the adaptation needs of developing countries as highlighted in section 2 of this chapter. A resolution by the European Parliament calls on the Commission to clarify the "added value" of the Alliance, and also considers the financial contribution under the Alliance as "woefully inadequate", suggesting that a longer term financial commitment is needed of at least two billion Euro annually by 2010 and five to ten billion annually by 2020.[39]

There are two additional issues with the assistance provided under both the Alliance and the Action Plan. First, while one of the main purposes of the Alliance is to provide a platform for promoting political dialogue on climate change between the EU and developing countries, and facilitating the integration of climate change concerns into poverty reduction plans on local and national levels, there was remarkably little involvement of developing country governments, civil society and local communities in the programming process of the Alliance.[40] Second, as noted in section 2, while integrating assistance for adaptation into development can fall under the remit of ODA, funding for adaptation activities should be additional to ODA. This principle is specifically recognised by the climate convention in Article 4(4), which states that developed countries have committed to helping "particularly vulnerable" developing countries meet the costs of adaptation and that this funding is additional to existing aid commitments. The two initiatives highlighted above, while a step in the right direction for

38. European Parliament 2008.
39. European Parliament 2008.
40. European Parliament 2008.

integrating adaptation into development, overshadow the need for the EU to meet its responsibility to provide *additional* assistance for adaptation.

3.3   The European Commission's Green Paper and White Paper

In 2007, the European Commission released the Green Paper "Adapting to Climate Change in Europe – Options for EU Actions". Whilst the Green Paper focuses on adaptation within EU Member States, it also contains a section on integrating adaptation into external EU actions. Here, the Green Paper specifically recognises the vulnerability of developing countries, and in particular the LDCs in Africa, Latin America and Asia. The Paper also highlights the responsibility of developed countries for funding adaptation, stating:

> "Being responsible for most of the historic accumulation of anthropogenic greenhouse gas emissions in the atmosphere, developed countries will need to support adaptation actions in developing countries".[41]

This statement highlights the EU's recognition of this fundamental principle. Yet, the paper does not outline a transparent, principle-based allocation framework of responsibility for adaptation funding that would result in adequate, new and additional money for adaptation in developing countries.[42]

Nevertheless, the Green Paper is progressive in terms of EU assistance. It states clearly that the EU must further integrate adaptation to climate change into existing external policies and funding instruments, strategies for poverty reduction, as well as development planning and budgeting. The Green Paper also commits to strengthening the inclusion of adaptation measures in geographical programming. The emphasis on integrating adaptation and development is much stronger in the Green Paper than in the EU Action Plan, indicating that, since the Action Plan, support for mainstreaming adaptation into development has grown.[43] Therefore, while the Green Paper falls short of proposing specific policy measures, it nevertheless steers the debate on EU assistance to developing countries on adaptation towards an integrated approach.

On 1 April 2009, the EU presented its White Paper "Adapting to Climate Change: Towards a European Framework for Action".[44] The paper

41.   Commission 2007b, 22.
42.   Klein 2008.
43.   Klein 2008.
44.   Commission 2009a.

summarises the likely impacts of global warming and sets out an EU framework to help the bloc and its Member States prepare for the consequences. In many ways, the White Paper seems a step back from the Green Paper in terms of addressing shortfalls in EU commitments on adaptation in the South. However, this may simply be a reflection of the greater internal focus of the White Paper. Nevertheless, there is some mention of supporting adaptation in developing countries. The particular vulnerability of developing countries is once again noted, and the EU restates its commitment to working with developing countries on climate change through its various bilateral cooperation agreements and in multilateral forums, and acknowledges that it should do more to meet the ever-increasing adaptation needs of the most vulnerable countries.

One aspect of the White Paper, which could sound alarm bells, is the emphasis placed on the need for "reliable data on the likely impact of climate change"[45] in order to develop appropriate policy responses. In the past, the focus on an "impacts-based" approach to adaptation, particularly in developing countries where such data is unavailable or extremely difficult to access, has resulted in delays in commitments on adaptation support. This was because of concerns over the uncertainty of the threat being adapted to, since investing in action pre-emptively against an uncertain threat could actually be maladaptive.[46]

The particular vulnerability of the South is a result of the lack of adaptive capacity of the poorest groups to deal with the impacts of climate change, and therefore not exclusively a result of the impacts themselves. Following on, it should not be necessary to wait for data on impacts before taking action to reduce vulnerability. Addressing the underlying "drivers" of vulnerability, such as low socio-economic status, over-reliance on uncertain livelihood options, poor governance structures and low levels of health and education, will help people to become more resilient to the impacts as and when they occur, regardless of the nature or extent of the impact. Taking a more open approach to vulnerability reduction is urgent in the South both to build development and to improve adaptive capacity before the worst impacts occur. The EU should not avoid commitments to investing in adaptation on such grounds.

45. Commission 2009a, 7.
46. Ayers et al. 2009.

3.4 European Commission Communication on the Copenhagen Climate Agreement

On 28 January 2009, the European Commission released a Communication setting out proposals to contribute to the achievement of a successful conclusion of the international climate negotiations at Copenhagen at the end of 2009. The Communication was then debated by representatives of Member State governments in three formations of the Council of Ministers of the EU: the Environment Council on 2 March, the Economic and Financial Affairs Council (ECOFIN) on 10 March, and the General Affairs and External Relations Council on 17 March. The conclusions from each session were taken as contributions to discussion by EU Heads of State and Government at the European Spring Summit (or European Council) on 19-20 March 2009. The Communication sends a strong political message to the international arena, and to some extent predefines Europe's negotiating position up to and including Copenhagen. It sets out three key challenges: targets and actions; financing; and building an effective global carbon market. It also presents a strategy for scaling up finance and investment flows for both emission reductions and adaptation.[47] This section will focus on the parts of the Communication relevant to adaptation in developing countries.

The first significant discussion on adaptation within the Communication is under the heading of "Financing low-carbon development and adaptation".[48] Here, the Communication recognises the need to significantly scale up, redirect and optimise finance and investment. Yet, the Communication also states that "the costs of capacity building and priority action in most vulnerable countries could, to a large extent, be covered by the existing Adaptation Fund".[49]

This is simply not the case, and the National Adaptation Programmes of Action (NAPAs) illustrate the shortfalls of this claim. The Least Developed Countries Fund supports all Least Developed Countries to develop their NAPAs, to identify "urgent and immediate needs... relating to adaptation",[50] which we will use here as a proxy for "priority action". As of April 2009, 40 Least Developed Countries have completed their NAPAs, each of which provides a (by no means exhaustive) list of activities that would contribute to meeting "urgent and immediate" adaptation needs. The total cost of all

---

47. Commission 2009b.
48. Commission 2009b, 7.
49. Commission 2009b, 9.
50. Least Developed Countries Expert Group, 2002.

the projects of the 40 NAPAs submitted totals around 2 billion US dollars. The Adaptation Fund, however, is currently projected to generate only 160 million to 190 million US dollars. While proposals exist to boost the fund by applying a levy to other activities, such as bunker fuels, these options were still under discussion at the time of writing. As these discussions will likely take some time, the suggestion that the Adaptation Fund can be used to pay for "priority actions", which are by definition near-term, is rather overly ambitious. In addition, the Adaptation Fund is not replenished through contributions from developed countries, and so does not contribute to meeting developed countries' obligations to finance adaptation in developing countries.

However, the Communication does take steps towards progress on adaptation, stating that the Copenhagen agreement should provide a framework on adaptation that includes:[51]

- The need for all to adapt: Support for doing so should be provided to the most vulnerable and the poorest. Only by anticipating potential adverse effects early enough and adapting accordingly can very costly damage be avoided.
- A commitment to systematically integrate adaptation strategies into national strategies: This should be the shared responsibility for both developed and developing countries.
- Improving the tools to define and implement adaptation strategies, including methodologies and technologies for adaptation, capacity building and a strengthened role for the UNFCCC process by mobilising stakeholders, including international organisations, and ensuring a more coordinated approach to risk management/disaster risk reduction.

In the Communication, the European Commission seems to recognise the need to adapt in developing countries *now,* anticipating effects rather than waiting for impact-scientists to "say go", as the White Paper seems to suggest.

The Communication does, however, fall short on commitments to funding any action on adaptation in developing countries, despite the repeated recognition that these needs must be met. The Climate Action Network-Europe co-ordinated and published an open letter from over 50 global civil society organisations, calling on the EU to commit to an annual sum in the order of 35 billion Euro. They considered this amount to be the EU's fair share, based on the principles of historic responsibility for emissions and

---

51. Commission 2009b, 7.

the capacity to pay.[52] The 2009 Spring European Council Conclusions did confirm the EU's willingness to pay its fair share of the total financing requirements for climate action in developing countries. Further discussions took place on novel international finance-raising mechanisms. However, concrete decisions on these questions were pushed back until the positions of other developed countries are made clear.[53]

Another issue with the Communication is that the text does not specify anywhere that finance for adaptation must be additional to existing ODA contributions. As noted in section 2, the principle that funding for adaptation is additional is fundamental and based on maintaining justice and equity within the negotiations. It is a principle that must be upheld if trust is to continue between developing and developed country parties. The Communication also makes a rather confusing statement that the burden of integrating adaptation into development should be a "shared responsibility for both developed and developing countries".[54] Given that the Communication also acknowledges that the historic responsibility for climate change falls to the North, the suggestion that the South should share responsibility for dealing with the impacts seems misplaced. As stated by the Third World Network, "by converting a right to develop into an obligation to adapt, and transforming 'common but differentiated responsibilities' into 'shared' ones, it would shift legal as well as practical responsibility for the rising impacts of climate change to developing countries thus limiting Europe's exposure to climate-related claims of cost and damage".[55]

In March 2009, the Economic and Financial Affairs (ECOFIN) Council of the EU met to conclude on the future financial architecture for managing climate change, including adaptation, to strengthen the EU's position ahead of Copenhagen. The Council adopted several conclusions that, again, indicate recognition of the urgency of providing adaptation funding for developing countries. The Council outlined that it is "aware of the challenge of adaptation for developing countries and their possibly limited fiscal leeway in the near future", and that "the Council (ECOFIN) stresses the important role of existing financial mechanisms".[56] Crucially however, the Council left in bracketed text any decision relating to financial commitments to these financial mechanisms, stating only: "The Council is ready to develop in more detail the practical options for financing

---

52. Climate Action Network Europe 2009a.
53. Climate Action Network Europe 2009b.
54. Commission 2009b, 8.
55. Third World Network 2009, 9.
56. Council 2009, 14.

mitigation, adaptation, technology support and capacity building".[57] The Council was heavily criticised by the non-governmental community for "failing to put concrete sums on the table".[58] Delays in discussions over financial commitments send the wrong signals to developing countries regarding the EU's commitment to a fair and equitable deal on adaptation in Copenhagen, undermining the trust between the EU and developing countries so essential for an effective agreement on both adaptation and mitigation. The EU appears to be repeatedly dawdling on translating the rhetoric of responsibility into action on meeting its obligations to support adaptation in vulnerable developing countries.

4.   Conclusions

The EU has made significant progress on adaptation to climate change in developing countries, and in many respects is "ahead of the game" compared to other international actors and parties to the UNFCCC. The EU has clearly recognised the need for adaptation; the scale of the need; and the responsibility for the North to provide adaptation assistance to the South that is additional to ODA commitments.

Yet, these achievements in policy discourse have not been adequately translated into concrete action. First, in all of the policy documents described above, the emphasis of each remains on mitigation, with a much smaller weight and space given to adaptation. At the international level, adaptation has risen on the policy agenda and is now recognised as equally important as mitigation. The Bali Action Plan under the UNFCCC in 2007, for example, ensured that adaptation was placed on an equal footing with mitigation, making it one of four equal "building blocks" required in response to climate change, alongside mitigation, technology cooperation and finance.[59] Yet, if we go by the relative attention given to mitigation and adaptation under EU action and policy, the EU appears still to consider adaptation as less important than mitigation. It is vital that the EU gives adaptation equal weight especially since the possibility of a temperature increase of more than four degrees Celsius is increasingly likely.

---

57. Ibid.
58. Euractiv.com 2009. EU summit postpones climate decision until June. http://www.euractiv.com/en/eu-summit/eu-summit-postpones-climate-decision-june/article-180526 (Accessed: 6 November 2009).
59. Ayers et al. 2009.

Second, the EU is failing to commit to firm and adequate financial obligations for adaptation, and is not clear on whether it considers funding for adaptation as additional to ODA in practice as well as in principle. Furthermore, the EU has not been active enough in engaging developing countries while elaborating its strategies for adaptation assistance, which may result in a rejection of the EU strategy by the very countries that are in need of assistance.

The EU should therefore be commended for the progress it has made on recognising the need to assist developing countries in meeting their adaptation needs. However, the EU must address these shortfalls, and make firm commitments on adaptation with the full engagement of developing country partners, in order to ensure that the trust between the North and South, that is so vital to a successful outcome at Copenhagen and beyond, is maintained.

References

Ayers, Jessica. 2009. International Funding to Support Urban Adaptation to Climate Change. *Environment and Urbanization* 21(1): 225-240.

Ayers, Jessica and David Dodman. 2010. Climate Change Adaptation and Development: the State of the Debate. Accepted for publication by *Progress in Development Studies*. Sage Publications.

Ayers, Jessica and Saleemul Huq. 2009. Supporting Adaptation through Development: what Role for ODA? *Development Policy Review* 27(6): 675-692.

Ayers, Jessica, Mozaharul Alam and Salemuul Huq. 2009. Adaptation in a Post-2012 Regime: Developing Country Perspectives. In *Global Climate Governance Post 2012: Architecture, Agency and Adaptation,* edited by Biermann Frank, Philipp Pattberg and Fariborz Zelli. Cambridge: Cambridge University Press.

Behrens, Arno. 2008. Financing for Climate Change Mitigation and Adaptation in EC Development Cooperation. *Financing Climate Change Policies in Developing Countries*, edited by European Parliament. Brussels: European Parliament.

Climate Action Network Europe (CAN-Europe). 2009a. Less than 300 Days: An Open Letter to EU Heads of State and Government about the Climate Crisis. 20 February 2009. http://www.climnet.org/Position%20papers/NGO_economist_ad.pdf. Accessed: 6 April 2009.

Climate Action Network Europe (CAN-Europe). 2009b. EU Kyoto Protocol Implementation: New Developments. http://www.climnet.org/EUenergy/eu_kyoto.htm. Accessed: 6 April 2009.

Commission (EC). 2003. Climate Change in the Context of Development Cooperation. Communication from the Commission to the Council and the European Parliament. COM (2003) 85. Brussels: European Commission.

Commission (EC). 2007a. Building a Global Climate Change Alliance between the European Union and Poor Developing Countries Most Vulnerable to Climate Change. Communication from the Commission to the Council and the European Parliament. COM (2007) 540. Brussels: European Commission.

Commission (EC). 2007b. Adapting to Climate Change in Europe – Options for EU Action. Green Paper from the Commission to the Council, the European Parliament, and the European Economic and Social Committee and the Committee of the Regions. SEC (2007) 849. Brussels: European Commission.

Commission (EC). 2009a. Towards a European Framework for Action. White Paper: Adapting to Climate Change. COM (2009) 147. Brussels: European Commission.

Commission (EC). 2009b. Towards a Comprehensive Climate Change Agreement in Copenhagen. Communication from the Commission to the European Parliament, the Council, the European Economic and Social Committee and the Committee of the Regions. COM (2009) 39. Brussels: European Commission.

Council of the European Union (Economic and Financial Affairs). 2009. 2931st Meeting of the Council. Brussels, 10 March 2009. Press Release. 7048/09 (Presse 54). Brussels: Council of the European Union.

Dodman, David, Jessica Ayers and Saleemul Huq. 2009. Building Resilience. In *State of the World 2009: Into a Warming World,* edited by Worldwatch Institute, 150-168. Washington, D.C.: Worldwatch Institute.

European Parliament. 2008. European Parliament Resolution of 21 October 2008 on Building a Global Climate Change Alliance between the European Union and Poor Developing Countries Most Vulnerable to Climate Change. (2008/2131(INI)). Brussels: European Parliament.

Global Environment Facility (GEF). 2008. Status Report on the Climate Change Funds October 2008. Report from the Trustee. Washington D.C.: GEF.

Huq, Saleemul and Jessica Ayers. 2008. Streamlining Adaptation to Climate Change into Development Projects at the National and Local Level. *Financing Climate Change Policies in Developing Countries*, edited by European Parliament. Brussels: European Parliament.

Intergovernmental Panel on Climate Change (IPCC). 2007. Summary for Policymakers. In *Climate Change 2007: Impacts, Adaptation and Vulnerability. Contribution of Working Group II to the Fourth Assessment Report of the Intergovernmental Panel on Climate Change*, edited by Martin Parry, Osvaldo F. Canziani, Jean P. Palutikof, Paul J. van der Linden, and Clair Hanson. 7-22. Cambridge: Cambridge University Press.

Klein, Richard T. J. 2008. Mainstreaming Climate Adaptation into Development Policies and Programmes: A European Perspective. *Financing Climate Change Policies in Developing Countries*, edited by European Parliament. Brussels: European Parliament.

Least Developed Countries Expert Group. 2002. Annotated Guidelines for the Preparation of National Adaptation Programmes of Action. Bonn: UNFCCC.

Müller, Benito. 2007. The Nairobi Climate Change Conference: a Breakthrough for Adaptation Funding. *Oxford Energy and Environment Comment* January 2007. Oxford: Oxford Institute for Energy Studies.

Oxfam International. 2007. Adapting to Climate Change: What's Needed in Poor Countries, and Who Should Pay. *Oxfam Briefing Paper*, 104. Washington D.C., Brussels, Geneva and New York: Oxfam.

Parry, Martin, Jean P. Palutikof, Clair Hanson, and Jason Lowe. 2008. Climate Policy: Squaring up to Reality. *Nature Reports Climate Change* 2: 68-70.

Parry, Martin, Nigel Arnell, Pam Berry, David Dodman, Samuel Fankhauser, Chris Hope, Sari Kovats, Robert Nicholls, David Satterthwaite, Richard Tiffin, Tim Wheeler. 2009. *Assessing the Costs of Adaptation to Climate Change: A Review of the UNFCCC and Other Recent Estimates*. London: International Institute for Environment and Development and Grantham Institute for Climate Change.

Third World Network. 2009. Understanding the European Commission's Climate Communication. http://www.twnside.org.sg/title2/climate/info. service/2009/climate.change.20090301.htm. Accessed: 14 July 2009.

UNFCCC (UN Framework Convention on Climate Change). 2007. *Investment and Financial Flows to Address Climate Change.* Bonn: UNFCCC

United Nations Development Programme (UNDP). 2007. *Human Development Report 2007/2008. Fighting Climate Change: Human Solidarity in a Divided World.* New York: UNDP.

World Bank. 2009. *Economics of Adaptation to Climate Change.* Washington D.C.: World Bank.

The Sustainability of the EU's Model for Climate Diplomacy

Louise van Schaik[1]

1.   Introduction

Politicians concerned with the institutional developments of the European Union (EU) regularly emphasize the importance of unity in the EU's external representation in international affairs. In the field of climate change, EU Member States remain remarkably united. Despite US opposition, the EU successfully convinced other countries to ratify the Kyoto Protocol, thereby ensuring its entry into force in 2005. Subsequently, the EU sought to continue its leadership by actively promoting the issue of climate change in various international discussions, such as the G8 summits and the UN General Assembly. It aimed to take the lead in, and set the agenda for, the negotiations on a future climate deal in Copenhagen in December 2009.

The success of the EU in the future climate negotiations depends on a number of factors, including the extent to which other countries are willing to commit to meaningful emission reduction commitments (in times of economic downturn), the EU's own ability to reduce emissions at a low cost and its ability to offer resources for adaptation and technology transfer to developing countries.[2] Its performance will obviously also be influenced by the way it organises its climate diplomacy. The focus of this chapter is on the way the EU decides internally on its international climate negotiation position. Is it operating as a state-like entity or a strong coalition of its Member States? What are the internal procedures to decide upon the negotiation stance and strategy, and do these procedures enable or constrain its performance in the negotiations? How did the EU's system operate in previous climate conferences and can we expect it to function well in the future? The focus will be on factors that explain the EU's strong climate diplomacy of recent years and whether this is likely to continue in the future.

---

1.   The author would like to thank Bart Kerremans and the two editors of this book for their useful comments on earlier versions of this chapter.
2.   Van Schaik and Van Hecke 2008.

The chapter proceeds as follows. Section 2 discusses how the EU operates as a global actor and which factors are most likely to influence its performance in international negotiations. Factors identified are the degree of EU competence, the homogeneity of preferences among the EU Member States and processes of EU socialisation among those representatives involved in the negotiations. The degree of EU competence influences how processes of EU coordination and external representation are organised. It could be considered an enabling factor for unity, but it does not provide a guarantee that Member States will agree upon a common position.[3] Therefore it is also relevant to analyse the homogeneity of preferences of the Member States (and the Commission), and EU socialisation, such that national delegates involved in the negotiations consider it most appropriate to operate with a common European position.

Section 3 describes how the EU organises its external representation in the international climate negotiations. On the basis of a brief analysis of European interests and preferences, it discusses why EU Member States have agreed relatively easily on a common international position and whether this is likely to continue. The section will then analyse how informal processes contribute to EU cooperation in the international climate negotiations. The analysis is based on a document and literature study and a small number of interviews with civil servants involved in EU coordination of international climate policy.[4] Moreover, the research builds upon earlier work by the author on the EU's institutional and governance features in the field of climate change for which a larger number of interviews were conducted, and on a number of similar studies by others.[5]

Section 4 looks at whether the current model for coordination and external representation is likely to be sustained into the future. It will discuss alternative models and under which circumstances they may become relevant (in legal and political terms). It will discuss in particular what changes may occur after the entry info force of the Lisbon Treaty.

The concluding section elaborates on what the experiences in the climate negotiations can teach us with regard to how we can conceive of the EU in international affairs and what lessons can be drawn for other negotiations.

---

3.   Gstöhl 2009.
4.   About five interviews were held with representatives of EU Member States who have been involved in the climate negotiations.
5.   Van Schaik and Egenhofer 2005; Groenleer and Van Schaik 2007; Oberthür and Roche Kelly 2008; Costa 2008; Damro 2008; Delreux 2008; Birkel forthcoming.

2. The EU as a global actor

2.1 The EU and the multilateral system

Since the end of the twentieth century, there has been a rapid expansion in international organisations and institutions. In an increasingly globalised world, international cooperation is considered a necessity to safeguard and increase the problem-solving capacity of nation states. The EU is a staunch supporter of the multilateral system. It believes it is possible to establish international agreements with which states comply, as is done within the EU in a most advanced form. It considers international policy cooperation the preferred option, rather than policy competition, oppression or conflict. It, moreover, often considers international agreements to be in its interest, since it enables the EU to export its own (frequently high) standards. International agreements can guarantee the level playing field that helps (European) companies to compete on equal terms in the world.

However, the international system can still be largely characterised as anarchic, where nations have significant freedom to decide their own course. They attach much importance to their sovereignty, meaning the freedom from outside interference and the legitimate right of states to decide upon their own internal and external policies. When sovereign states do not abide by international rules, there is often little that can be done. Only the UN Security Council has some official status in condemning governments violating the rights of other states. The International Criminal Court and International Court of Justice provide a channel of last resort in legal terms, but rely very much on the cooperation of states. Finally, compliance systems of international organisations and treaties, such as the WTO dispute settlement system and the Kyoto compliance committee, seem to indicate that some hierarchy is adhered to. Their effectiveness, however, still very much depends on states accepting their authority and abiding by their rules.

Within the EU, international agreements are taken very seriously. EU legislation is often directly derived from international agreements, particularly in trade-related policy areas, such as food safety and environmental protection. Once European laws are adopted, they supersede the laws of the EU Member States. Compliance is ensured by the European Court of Justice, which can impose financial penalties on Member States that infringe EU law. A conviction by the Court is also considered a breach of EU solidarity, which damages the reputation of a

Member State as a reliable partner. As a result, even though the EU system is very much dependent upon the proper implementation and enforcement of EU policies by the Member States, the level of compliance with EU law is relatively high. The EU believes that it is possible to have similar compliance mechanisms at the international level. In that case, international agreements contribute to the EU's ability to set ambitious regulatory standards without damaging competitiveness. For other states it may also be advantageous to join such international agreements, for instance because they also want to set higher standards, or because they want to improve trade relations with the EU. Also, the costs of compliance are easier to bear with the knowledge that competitors will stick to the same rules and thus will face similar costs.

In this context, it is particularly interesting to see how the EU, itself a *sui generis* system between an international organisation and a supranational state, operates within the international system. Laatikainen and Smith label this phenomenon "intersecting multilateralisms".[6] Looking at the interface between the EU and various UN organisations, they consider it essential to question whether the EU is an actor in its own right within the UN or whether the EU merely serves as a diplomatic forum for Member States.[7] Indeed, in some international organisations (e.g. the WTO, FAO and Codex Alimentarius) the EU behaves like a state party, enjoying membership and a uniform representation, whereas in other international organisations, the Member States are the most important EU actors (e.g. UN Security Council, IMF, World Bank).

2.2   EU external unity

Most researchers studying EU foreign policy assert that the way the EU decides upon its international positions and organises its external representation influences its effectiveness in international negotiations.[8] It would influence its capacity to negotiate and, thereby, its bargaining power.[9] The argument that EU foreign policy-making needs to be reformed to make the EU a more effective actor in world affairs has also been a prevailing rationale in the discussions on EU institutional reform leading eventually to the Lisbon Treaty. Agreed reform proposals, such as the

6. Laatikainen and Smith 2006, 3.
7. Laatikainen and Smith 2006.
8. Keukeleire and MacNaughton 2008; Cameron 2007; Sapir 2007; Bretherton and Vogler 2006; Vanhoonacker 2005.
9. Meunier 2000; Frieden 2004; Gstöhl 2009.

establishment of an EU foreign policy coordinator, or High Representative, focus on establishing a more uniform external representation.[10]

Although it seems reasonable to assume that a more unified EU stance in international affairs would increase its influence, only a small number of case studies[11] have systematically analysed the EU's effectiveness or performance in international negotiations and have related it back to its institutional set-up. This is not surprising, since it is rather complicated to measure the EU's effectiveness in international negotiations.[12] Whether the EU is effective is very much influenced by its negotiating partners and subject to the perceptions of those who were involved in the negotiations, or of those who observed them (e.g. media). Here we will also focus on these perceptions of effectiveness. Where possible, specific examples are given of issues in which the EU managed to convince negotiating partners to follow its preferred option.

In general, it is expected that the EU is more effective when it can keep its ranks closed. This is confirmed by other research,[13] but it is not clear whether more involvement of the European Commission strengthens EU unity, or whether the rotating EU Presidency is in a better position to do this. The Commission would be a more permanent partner able to build up more stable contact, invest in diplomatic skills and capacity, and work on the basis of a common European interest. The alternative of the rotating Presidency leading the EU in international affairs has the benefit that this actor is one of the Member States and is less able to build up an autonomous position, since it only leads for half a year.[14] Neither the Commission, nor the Presidency can be expected to obtain a *carte blanche* from the Member States. Control systems by the Member States will be established making it likely that tension will occur (as in all "principal-agent" constellations). Such tension is more likely to occur with the Commission since it would function on a permanent basis and is not one of the Member States. It is not fully clear how these trade-offs between the (possible) advantages and disadvantages of the Commission or the Presidency in the lead affect EU unity and, by extension, EU performance in the international negotiations.

With this in mind, the degree of unity displayed by the EU in its external representation in the climate negotiations will be analysed. To identify and

10. Avery et al. 2007; Aggestam et al. 2007; Duke 2008; Van Schaik 2008.
11. E.g. Smith 2006; Rhinard and Kaeding 2006.
12. Oberthür 2009.
13. Laatikainen and Smith 2006; Bretherton and Vogler 2006; Jørgensen 2009.
14. Schout and Van Schaik 2008.

understand the degree of unity in external representation, three issues will be examined: the degree of EU competence, the degree of preference homogeneity, and the degree of EU socialisation evident among represent-atives of the EU Member States. It is particularly interesting to question the extent to which EU Member States consider it a deliberate choice to unite in their external representation, or whether they consider it merely a legal obligation. Under which conditions do they consider it advantageous, and does it improve their effectiveness in international negotiations? According to a realist or intergovernmentalist view, for example, EU Member States would only agree to bundle their positions to the extent it is in their interest to do so.[15] They would consider that operating jointly strengthens their bargaining power in the negotiations, while bundling expertise and resources brings further benefits.

2.3   Competence

Scholars looking at the influence of institutions have pointed out that Member States' options and preferences are influenced by the legal rules and procedures and by the informal institutional features that may be at work.[16] In the field of EU external relations, procedures for external representation are strongly related to the degree of EU competence. When EU Member States transfer legislative powers to the EU level, its institutions also obtain a competence to represent the EU externally ("principle of implied powers").[17] Deciding who acts as lead negotiator depends on whether the main thrust of the matter lies with the EU, in which case the Commission is in the lead, or with the Member States, in which case the rotating Presidency of the EU Council is in charge. Member States may not always realise the implications for international negotiations when (internal) competences are transferred through amending what is now the Treaty on the Functioning of the EU (TFEU) or adopting EU legislation. With an issue such as climate change, where both the EU and the Member States possess competence ("shared competence"), external representation is taken care of jointly, with Member States usually preferring to appoint the rotating Presidency as lead negotiator.

In political terms, authority over external representation is a key feature of state sovereignty. Having a single representative to speak on behalf of the EU in international negotiations could hence be viewed as a sign of

15. Smith 2006; Frieden 2004.
16. Vanhoonacker 2005.
17. Eeckhout 2004; Hoffmeister 2007.

statehood. Within the inter-state system of international organisations, involvement of the EU often leads to questions on how to treat this "unidentified political object". The transfer of competence to the EU in international settings is also not always welcomed by the EU Member States. The political-sensitive issues of war and peace, for example, have led Member States to prevent "an EU take-over" of foreign and security policy. With other external policy issues the transfer of competence is also sensitive. If Member States consider it is to their advantage to operate as a European bloc, for instance because they can relatively easily agree on a joint stance, they may see the advantages of a unified external representation even when it is not legally obligatory. However, if they believe that operating with a joint stance only leads to a lowest common denominator position or no agreement at all, they may be less enthusiastic. In such circumstances, they may also call legal provisions into question. In fact, many cases have been brought to the European Court of Justice in which the Commission and Member States have fought over who had the authority of external representation in international organisations.[18]

2.4 Preference homogeneity

Whether the EU can operate in unity also depends upon outside recognition and upon the willingness of Member States to agree upon a common view.[19] Inconsistencies are likely to exist between the demands and interests of 27 Member States at differing levels of economic development and political preferences.

Nevertheless, there are a number of reasons why we can expect EU Member States' positions to be homogeneous. First of all, EU Member States share a considerable part of their cultural heritage. This influences their political preference on certain issues, such as the role of democracy, the death penalty, the position of women, etc. Secondly, on the world scale EU Member States tend to have a relatively similar geographic interest. For the EU, the Balkans, Africa, the Middle East and Russia represent regions it needs to engage with closely. Thirdly, despite differences in levels of prosperity, none of the EU Member States are developing countries, or fragile states. Instead they have relatively well-functioning democratic governance systems. Fourthly, and perhaps most importantly, EU Member States have a common internal market governed by extensive common regulation. This means that EU Member States have a common interest in

18. Eeckhout 2004.
19. Gstöhl 2009; Vogler 2005, 838.

promoting their regulatory standards in international bodies. It also means that unity in external representation is a necessity the moment common EU legislation is in place or could be decided upon, since legal uncertainty could otherwise emerge with regard to whether European or international agreements should be adhered to. This is why the European Court of Justice established the principle of parallel competences.[20] Lastly, there can be issue-specific interests. In the field of climate change, energy mix and infrastructure, for instance, greatly influence the interest of states.

On the basis of the factors outlined above, we can expect the preferences of EU Member States to be rather homogeneous in international affairs. However, on some issues, EU Member States can be very much divided. Prominent examples include the divisions over the war in Iraq and more recently over the recognition of Kosovo as an independent state. A complicating factor is that common EU positions, frequently, have to be decided by consensus, meaning that, in theory, any one Member State can veto an international position. In practice the veto is considered a "nuclear option", but the mere possibility of using it can at times prevent the EU from adopting ambitious and progressive common positions. Diplomats often complain about having to operate with a lowest common denominator position. Hence, when voting can be used to adopt a negotiating mandate, the likelihood of agreeing upon a more ambitious position is greater, at least in theory.[21] Preference homogeneity among all EU Member States is in that scenario less important, since a minority can be outvoted.

2.5   EU socialisation

The influence of informal norms on EU unity becomes clear when looking at processes of EU socialisation emerging from institutionalised coordination practices between the Member States. Regardless of which legal rules are in place for external representation, diplomats may just consider it "appropriate" to collaborate with their European partners in international negotiations.[22] Outsiders may for instance always approach them as a European actor. Processes of EU coordination and meetings may reinforce their allegiance.

Previous research has demonstrated that experts participating in EU working groups and committees can feel more affiliated with their

20.   Eeckhout 2004.
21.   Frieden 2004.
22.   Smith 2006.

European counterparts than with their national colleagues from other departments.[23] Often they share a common policy-specific orientation. Sometimes they consider that a considerable part of their work consists of explaining and promoting a commonly agreed European policy to national colleagues. Of course, there are also national representatives who operate in Brussels and jealously guard their national interests and positions, but it can be expected that, particularly with regard to international affairs, the moment an international position can be agreed upon, EU Member States will be keen to work together to promote their view to national colleagues and non-EU states. Here we see the close relationship between preference homogeneity and socialisation; both can reinforce each other, but if one is lacking, EU unity in external representation is unlikely to be strong.

2.6 Other factors influencing EU performance in international negotiations

EC competence, preference homogeneity and EU socialisation can thus be expected to substantially affect the EU's unity in external representation and therefore influence the EU's effectiveness in the negotiations. In this chapter somewhat less attention is devoted to other, more contextual, or incidental factors that may influence the EU's performance, such as the acceptance of a unified external representation by non-EU actors,[24] issue-specific power such as commercial interests,[25] the negotiating environment,[26] and the influence of key individuals involved in the negotiations. These are considered less structural or subordinate to the factors outlined above. For example, commercial interests can be reflected in preferences and an influential person usually relies on a strong team. Where relevant, these factors are still elaborated in the section on the general characteristics on the EU's internal procedures for operating in the climate negotiations, but they are not the main focus of this chapter.

23. Beyers and Trondal 2005.
24. Groenleer and Van Schaik 2007.
25. Gstöhl 2009.
26. Meunier 2000; Rhinard and Kaeding 2006.

3. EU coordination and external representation in the international climate negotiations

Climate change, by definition, is an international issue and is one of the key priority issues of the EU's external relations. Like many other environmental issues, it is a policy problem that crosses national borders. Its "public good" character implies a need for inter-state cooperation; otherwise self-interested states may opt to let other states invest in greenhouse gas (GHG) emission reductions, whilst benefiting from the result. Even though scientists indicate swift action to avoid dangerous climate change is required, international agreement on an international climate deal should not be taken for granted.[27] National governments may focus on short-term interests, may consider the costs of climate policies burdensome, may argue that other states have to carry more of the burden, or have other reasons not to agree to take action. This makes international climate negotiations a challenging endeavour, and also at time jeopardises the ability of EU Member States to agree to an ambitious climate policy.

In this section we will analyse to what extent EU competence exists with regard to international climate policy, how homogeneous the preferences of EU Member States have been and whether EU socialisation processes have emerged in the EU's climate diplomacy. The degree of unity in external representation evident in the formal negotiations, and in the corridors and informal negotiation groups, will be analysed in more depth and considered with regard to the EU's effectiveness in the negotiations.

3.1 Competence

Climate change, like other environmental policies, is an area where Member States share competence with the EC. The EU is a Party to regional and international environmental agreements, alongside states, including the EU Member States. This practice has evolved since the late 1970s when the then EEC joined the 1979 UNECE Convention on Long-Range Transboundary Air Pollution and, later, the 1985 Vienna Convention for the Protection of the Ozone Layer at the global level.[28] At the Earth Summit in Rio de Janeiro in 1992 (the United Nations Conference on Environment and Development), it was agreed that the then EC could also become a party to the United Nations Framework Convention on Climate Change

27. Intergovernmental Panel on Climate Change 2007.
28. Vogler and Stephan 2007, 296.

(UNFCCC).[29] As in the other environmental agreements mentioned, the EU does not have separate voting rights in the UNFCCC and participates as a Regional Economic Integration Organisation (REIO), a category created especially for the EU.[30]

Although more and more EU climate legislation has been adopted over time, the shared competence has been translated into a rather intergovernmental model in the international negotiations. Member States decide by consensus and the half-yearly rotating EU Presidency is the EU's main spokesperson.[31] In the most important bilateral negotiations and smaller negotiating sessions (e.g. "friends of the chair sessions"), the Presidency is assisted by the Commission and the incoming EU Presidency. Jointly they are called the EU troika, which is sometimes complemented by the Council Secretariat, as well as the bigger EU Member States.

The Commission's contribution is mostly related to it leading the formulation of new climate legislation within the EU, which is adopted through the normal Community method of decision-making (Commission proposes, Council and European Parliament co-decide). Because it initiates new legislation and oversees its implementation, the Commission is in the best position to monitor whether the EU will be able to meet international climate commitments and to testify to its negotiating partners about the effectiveness of EU climate policies. Although the European Parliament has co-decision power with regard to EU climate legislation, it only has an advisory role when it comes to the EU's position in the international climate negotiations. Members of the European Parliament attend the international climate conferences, but they are neither allowed to attend the meetings where the Member States and the Commission decide upon the EU position, nor to speak on behalf of the EU to the press or negotiating partners.

The EU position is adopted in the Council of Ministers. Within the Council, climate change is the prerogative of the Environment Ministers, but other Council formations and the Presidents and Prime Ministers meeting in the European Council also discuss the issue. The Council

---

29. Damro 2006.
30. The REIO formulation was invented within the context of the 1979 Long Range Transboundary Air Pollution Convention (LRTAP), and afterwards used in other environmental conventions and international institutions, cf. Vogler and Bretherton 2006. In theory, other regional integration organisations may also use the construction in future (e.g. Mercosur, ASEAN), provided their Member States delegate relevant powers to them.
31. Oberthür and Roche Kelly 2008; Groenleer and Van Schaik 2007.

Working Party on International Environmental Issues (WPIEI, Climate Change formation) and about eight expert groups on specific issues carry out the preparatory work. The WPIEI is composed of senior officials from Environment Ministries and the Commission's DG Environment.[32] During climate negotiation sessions, adjustments can be made in EU coordination meetings where delegates of the Member States meet on a daily basis. The same officials that form the WPIEI usually also attend the EU coordination meetings, unless the Ministers arrive and take over from the senior officials.

Since the Presidency is in the lead, the EU position, or negotiating mandate, is recorded in the Council Conclusions of the Environment Council and, more recently, in the Presidency Conclusions of the European Council, as well as in issue-specific EU submissions and position papers. The conclusions are publicly available, but fallback positions and the negotiating strategy that accompany them and are also discussed in the Council, are not disclosed. The Presidency takes the lead in drafting the conclusions. The Commission provides input through Communications in which it outlines its position and suggestions to the Council. During the UN climate conference in Copenhagen in December 2009, Sweden holds the EU Presidency.

Since the workload for the Council Presidency has at times been overwhelming, and because it was deemed important to ensure continuity in the negotiations, other Member States in the past have assisted or taken over parts of the external representation. Since 2004 a more formalised system is in place in which the EU appoints "lead negotiators" and "issue leaders".[33] These are officials from Member States and the Commission who cover a specific issue for a longer term. Under the auspices of the Presidency they take care of most of the negotiations at the working level. There is, for instance, a lead negotiator for GHG mitigation and one for climate change adaptation. Each lead negotiator is supported by about three issue leaders, who serve as back up and help in developing positions and negotiating strategies. The appointment of lead negotiators and issue leaders is formally the responsibility of the Presidency to whom they report, but informally the relevant expert groups and the WPIEI are consulted on who should lead the EU on which issues. In the distribution of positions a balance is aimed for among the Member States and the Commission.[34]

---

32. Costa 2008.
33. Oberthür and Roche Kelly 2008; Birkel forthcoming.
34. Oberthür 2009.

In line with their competence to negotiate internationally on environmental issues, as now stipulated in the Treaty on the Functioning of the EU (TFEU), Member States adopt their position by consensus. Article 191(4) TFEU (ex-Article 174(4)) provides the legal basis for EU activities in international environmental negotiations. It stipulates that the Union and the Member States shall cooperate with third countries and with the competent international organisations. The last sentence of this Article further stipulates that "the previous subparagraph shall be without prejudice to Member States' competence to negotiate in international bodies and to conclude international agreements". This has been used not only to refuse handing over authority to the Commission, as it requested in 1996,[35] but also to argue that consensus should be used for decision-making. Others have argued that the position could also be adopted by means of qualified majority voting, since this is the rule for adoption of European climate policies. Yet others argue that unanimity would be needed since climate policy affects the choice of energy sources and this has remained an area where the national veto applies (Article 192(2)(c) of the TFEU). For the adoption of GHG reduction or renewable energy policies, however, the Treaty article referring to the national veto over the energy mix has not been used.[36] In any event, the final version of an international climate agreement is signed and ratified by both the EU and all the Member States. This, according to some, is also a reason why the climate change mandate should be supported by consensus. However, in trade negotiations conducted within the WTO, voting is used for the adoption of the EU's negotiating mandate and here, the final agreement also is signed by both the EU and the Member States.[37]

All issues coming up in the climate negotiations have to be discussed in EU coordination, and any Member State can block progress. This limits the EU's ability to react swiftly in the negotiations. According to Denmark's Climate and Energy Minister Connie Hedegaard there have been several cases where the EU's reaction time has been too slow.[38]

---

35. Oberthür and Ott 1999, 66.
36. For instance the emissions trading Directives 2003/87/EC and 2009/29/EC were adopted on the basis of Article 175(1) of the EC Treaty, which implies adoption by qualified majority voting in the Council is possible. Renewable Energy Directive 2009/28/EC was adopted on the basis of Article 175(1) and Article 95 of the EC Treaty. The latter also implies adoption by qualified majority voting in the Council.
37. Kerremans 2004; Meunier and Nicolaïdis 2006.
38. Hedegaard 2009.

3.2 Preference congruency

Despite the consensus required, Member States have stood remarkably united. Apparently, they all have come to consider climate change a priority issue for the EU. There are a number of reasons for this.[39]

First of all, European politicians, or at least a considerable number of them, appear to be truly concerned about the threats to humankind posed by climate change. They are firm believers of the scientific evidence presented by climate scientists gathered within the Intergovernmental Panel on Climate Change (IPCC). EU citizens also consistently rank climate change among the issues of high concern to them.[40] The attention given to Al Gore's movie "An inconvenient truth", the Stern report on the economic impacts of climate change, and the fourth assessment report of the IPCC, all contributed to a growing concern among European populations. Even those EU politicians who are not fully convinced have to admit that by following the precautionary principle, the EU has agreed to undertake action when, according to a scientific consensus, environmental damage is likely to occur.

Secondly, the Kyoto Protocol embodies almost everything the EU believes in, most importantly that it is possible to address a problem of the commons by means of inter-state cooperation. The EU's international climate agenda links with the EU's ambition for effective multilateralism and sustainable development.[41] At the same time, backing the Kyoto Protocol so strongly proved an opportunity to demonstrate Europe's preference for a course different to the unilateral one advocated by the Bush government of the US.[42] Moreover, climate policy proved to be one of the few success stories of EU foreign policy. Together with the EU support for the International Criminal Court, support for the Kyoto Protocol demonstrates that the EU can act with a single voice in international affairs.[43] Thus, the opposition to the US made the EU realise the importance it attached to the Kyoto Protocol, and thereby indirectly enabled it to become an emblem of EU foreign policy.

Thirdly, climate change increasingly has been used as a vehicle to address energy security concerns. Reducing GHG emissions is intimately linked to reducing the use of fossil fuels. The EU is, and increasingly will be, an

39.   Van Schaik and Van Hecke 2008.
40.   Commission 2008a.
41.   Cf. Commission 2003.
42.   Bretherton and Vogler 2006; Schreurs and Tiberghien 2007.
43.   Groenleer and van Schaik 2007.

importer of fossil fuels. These fossil fuels, for the most part, come from countries with which the EU has an uneasy relationship. When Putin's Russia closed gas pipelines to neighbouring countries in 2006, many people feared Russia would increasingly use energy as a political weapon.[44] The EU's security of supply by then had already become a key issue. Rising oil prices fuelled the fear that the end of oil and gas reservoirs was near. As a consequence, while EU Member States have always been reluctant to hand over policy-making authority on the choice of energy sources, it makes absolute sense to them to reduce their dependency on imported fossil fuels by increasing energy efficiency and shifting to renewable energy. At the same time, these policy options can be presented to the public and other countries as climate policies.

Fourthly, climate change became a saviour issue for the EU itself. In 2005, the EU was in desperate need for an appealing issue to demonstrate its added value to European citizens. The European integration project had come under serious pressure, evidenced particularly by the negative votes on the European Constitution in two EU-founding states, France and the Netherlands. Politically, it became almost impossible to continue discussions on institutional reform. Instead, it was considered more appropriate to focus on concrete projects where "Brussels" could show its ability to solve pressing cross-border policy problems. Climate change clearly fitted the profile and became a priority policy item.

The above-mentioned reasons not only explain why the EU can act as an international leader on climate change, but also why it can put forward ambitious internal climate policies. It is important to realise that some of the factors are rather unique to the EU. Although climate change has gained in importance in other parts of the world, it is nowhere so politically important as in the EU.

The importance attached to international climate policy by the EU Member States and the European Commission has resulted in the EU's negotiating strategy stretching beyond the negotiations conducted within the context of the UNFCCC. Climate change has been included in a wide range of bilateral meetings and has featured on the agenda of many international organisations and bodies (e.g. World Bank, UN General Assembly, UN Security Council, UN Development Programme, G8, World Health Organization, etc). Climate change and (renewable) energy have become more important topics within the EU's development cooperation activities, European Neighbourhood Policy and bilateral agreements. Thereby, it

---

44. See the chapter by Douma et al. in this volume.

seems that climate change has increasingly been included in the overall framework of EU external relations, where it is almost as important as trade and security relations. This is reinforced and stimulated by the Green Diplomacy Network that consists of diplomats working at the foreign ministries of Member States.[45]

However, support for an ambitious climate policy and the continued world leadership of the EU on this issue should not be taken for granted. With more stringent GHG emission reduction targets and a growing realisation that new and additional financial resources will be needed to compensate developing countries, Member States seem to have already lost some of their enthusiasm. During the consideration of the climate and energy package at the end of 2008, the new EU Member States (led by Poland), Italy and, to a lesser extent, Germany were critical and demanded increased protection for targeted industry sectors.[46] Subsequently, reaching agreement on financial support for developing countries has proved difficult, making it less certain that the expectations raised at the Bali conference in 2007 can be met. Increased pressure can also be expected because, in order to achieve GHG emission reductions and mobilise financial resources, Environment Ministers increasingly have to rely on their colleagues for support. In previous years they have received relatively strong backing at the highest political level, but this may decline when other issues, such as the economic crisis, attract the attention of Presidents and Prime Ministers. The potential for clashes of interests with the EU's trade, development cooperation, agriculture, and foreign politics agendas has risen. In general the economic crisis is expected to put pressure on an ambitious internal and external climate policy.

Despite the overall unity in the climate negotiations, EU Member States also have had diverging national preferences. Consider for instance the treatment of nuclear energy, where France, as a producer of nuclear electricity, has a very different position than Germany, which has decided to phase out nuclear energy. Another issue has been the extent to which offset projects in third countries should be allowed to help reach the target. Internal division has proven problematic for the acceptance of the external representation. In 2000, the UK bypassed the French Presidency at the Hague conference, because it felt the need to build a bridge to the US position.[47] This was not appreciated by France and other Member States

---

45. Oberthür 2009.
46. Bulletin Quotidien Europe No. 9803, 13 December 2008.
47. Grubb and Yamin 2001; Ott 2001.

and resulted in negative media coverage for the EU. At New Delhi in 2002, the EU once more lacked negotiating flexibility because of internal division.[48] Hence, although overall EU unity has not been breached, differences of opinion on specific issues have certainly occurred. Since the EU has generally been the most ambitious in the negotiations, these differences thus far have not drawn a lot of attention. However, if negotiating partners were to come closer to the EU position, differences between EU Member States are likely to become more visible.

3.3 EU socialisation

The representatives of the EU Member States and the European Commission who deal with international climate negotiations spend many hours in EU coordination meetings during the international negotiations. They also meet about every other week in Brussels and at informal meetings, roundtable discussions, seminars and conferences. At the international negotiations, the EU coordination meetings take place on a daily basis lasting in total about two hours. Although EU coordination takes a considerable amount of time, it generally helps the EU to firmly unite around an issue. The internal discussions also tend to strengthen the EU's argumentative capacity. Perhaps most importantly, the EU coordination leads to a sense of "we-ness", a common European understanding on how to proceed in the negotiations. It thereby helps to understand why the EU nowadays is truly operating as a single block.

Whereas in the 1990s individual Member States at times took the floor and submitted their own proposals, undermining the single voice,[49] this has now become unacceptable. In informal contacts, Member States may still undermine the official EU efforts by disclosing internal EU divergences and EU tactics to negotiating partners, but in formal settings, breaking lines is "not done". Everywhere in the world, it is nowadays known that the EU is keen on promoting climate policy internationally and internal quarrelling would not help the EU's reputation in this regard.

Because climate change increasingly has become an emblem of EU foreign policy, EU foreign policy actors have also increasingly realised the need for the EU to sustain consensus on the issue of climate change. Their interest in the issue increased all the more because of a link to security highlighted *inter alia* in a study by former US generals.[50] In the EU, High Representative

48. Vogler 2005.
49. Oberthür 2009.
50. The CNA Corporation 2007.

Solana and the Commission also presented a paper on the issue.[51] This illustrates an increased interest, which could be interpreted as going beyond the relationship with security only. In 2008, Solana appointed a personal representative for energy security and climate change, Steven Everts. It seems EU foreign policy constituencies have realised the importance of climate change to the EU's image in the world.

This poses the question whether environmental experts need to be in the lead in order to keep the EU's ranks closed in international climate negotiations. On the one hand, the involvement of foreign policy actors contributes positively, because this makes it easier to link the climate agenda to other international agendas. On the other hand, it has increased tensions, since environment officials are not always convinced diplomats are sincerely concerned about climate change. These diplomats, moreover, pretend to be better skilled in international negotiations and claim credit for diplomatic successes, which the environment community has achieved. The environmental experts in the past operated as an epistemic community on the basis of a shared understanding of the problem and policy directions.[52] This reinforced the process of socialisation, and hence unity. The involvement of diplomats may jeopardise this, although to date this seems not to have occurred.

The common opposition towards the US withdrawal from the Kyoto Protocol is an important factor that has united EU Member States and the Commission in the international climate negotiations.[53] As a result of the US withdrawal, the international climate change agenda became largely a European agenda. This may change under the Obama administration, which envisages a much more ambitious US climate policy. Paradoxically, while the EU warmly welcomes the US reengagement, it may result in making it more difficult to keep ranks closed internally. The EU position may need to become more detailed and nuanced. The absence of a "common enemy" may moreover make it more difficult to sustain a united EU position and EU leadership.

A systemic factor that increases the sense of ownership of EU Member States in the international climate negotiations is the system of the rotating Presidency. Since all Member States take on this role at some point, they can more easily identify with it. Either they have been responsible for developing the EU position, or they will be in the future. Similarly, the system of lead negotiators and issues leaders enhances the sense of

51. Commission 2008b.
52. Haas 1992.
53. Vogler 2006; Groenleer and Van Schaik 2007.

ownership. Because they take responsibility for the EU position, lead negotiators and issue leaders ought to be truly committed to it. The system thereby leads to a considerable degree of "Europeanisation" of Member State representatives.

3.4 Inherent shortcomings in the EU's model for climate diplomacy

While the EU's model for climate diplomacy has thus been relatively successful in recent years, a number of inherent shortcomings of the model have become apparent. Two dominant issues are, firstly, the need for consensus, which leads to time-consuming coordination and a relatively inflexible mandate, and, secondly, the risks for continuity and performance of the rotating Presidency, which leads and coordinates the EU in the negotiations, without being chosen on its merits.

The need for consensus means that EU unity in the climate negotiations can never be taken for granted.[54] With GHG emission reduction targets becoming steeper and the need to pay for adaptation and technology transfer to developing countries becoming more obvious, the support of new EU Member States, in particular, may diminish. The "old EU-15" may also find it difficult to put their money where their mouth is, particularly in times of economic crisis. The need to agree by consensus can moreover lead to inflexible positions should other states, such as the US, come closer to the EU position or become even more ambitious than the EU.

An intensifying coordination and differentiation of internal coordination structures have accompanied increased unity in external representation.[55] Preoccupied with internal coordination, little time and resources are left for outreach to, and negotiations with, the partners (or opponents) in the negotiations. The increased delegation of work to the expert level has, moreover, reinforced a compartmentalisation of EU external climate policy-making and has increased the risk of inconsistencies between different expert groups.

Perhaps most importantly, the effectiveness of the EU's external representation is still highly dependent upon the effectiveness of the rotating Presidency. Although at lower levels lead negotiators from other Member States and the European Commission have been appointed to take care of the technicalities of the negotiations, the Presidency is formally responsible and its Environment Minister is the EU's main spokesperson

---

54. Lacasta et al. 2007; Oberthür and Roche Kelly 2008.
55. Oberthür 2009.

during high-level political negotiations. As a consequence, the EU's performance is closely related to the negotiating capacity and skills of the Environment Minister of the country holding the rotating Presidency and his or her advisors. He/she acts as spokesperson, main contact point, main negotiator and representative of the EU in the international negotiations and is responsible for the EU's internal management and coordination.[56] Continuity and visibility of this leadership is hampered by the six-monthly change. Whilst the involvement of the incoming Presidency and Commission in the troika supports consistency, the lead negotiator changing every six months continuously endangers the efficacy of EU climate diplomacy.

4. Alternative models for EU climate diplomacy

It remains to be seen whether Member States will continue to see international climate policy primarily as an environmental issue or as a foreign policy issue. This may have considerable implications for the current model of consensus decision-making and external representation by the EU Presidency. In particular, should the Copenhagen conference be less of a success than anticipated by the EU, the current model may come under pressure. Below, two alternative models are described and analysed.

4.1 Commission take-over

After the adoption of the climate and energy package in December 2008 (and particularly the more centralised emissions trading system), climate policy has become more of a common European policy than ever before.[57] As a result, the European Commission may claim the issues discussed in the international climate negotiations fall largely within the EU's competence. In line with earlier rulings of the European Court of Justice on the parallelism of internal and external EU competence, this would imply the Commission might successfully claim authority over external representation.[58] This would likely also entail that a negotiating mandate would be proposed by the Commission and adopted in the Council by qualified majority voting.

---

56. Oberthür 2009.
57. See also the chapter by Oberthür and Pallemaerts in this volume.
58. Hoffmeister 2007.

The model would hence look very similar to the way the EU is currently conducting its trade negotiations. A team of Commission negotiators under a Commissioner responsible for climate change would take over the negotiations and report regularly to a committee of the Member States. This committee would look similar to the current EU coordination meetings, but its focus would change from defining the common EU position to disposing and controlling what the Commission is doing in the negotiations. As is the case in the WTO, it is likely that the EU Member States would still become individual signatories to climate treaties giving them a kind of ultimate veto over the end result of the negotiations, but during an often multi-annual negotiating endeavour, their influence would be less than it is today.

Advantages of the "Commission take-over" model are that it would greatly increase the consistency of the EU and reduce the current coordination challenge of having a team of lead negotiators employed in different EU Member States and the Commission. In theory it would moreover make it easier to decide upon the EU position in the negotiations, leading to more flexibility for the negotiator. It could be questioned, though, whether the Member States would trust the Commission to a sufficient degree and whether the Commission would start to have its own agenda in the negotiations. This may make it more difficult for the EU to agree upon a mandate. In the WTO negotiations, Member States in the Article 133 Committee have been described as "mothers-in-law", watching closely what the Commission is doing in the negotiations.[59] The Commission is also accused of advocating too much of a liberal trade agenda in the negotiations, neglecting to look after other interests.[60] It could also diminish the degree of EU socialisation, which is clearly catalysed by the system of the rotating Presidency and the team spirit among the lead negotiators and issue leaders from the different Member States.

Birkel found through interviews that Member State representatives involved in the climate negotiations would not prefer the Commission to take over the negotiations, since it would damage their sovereignty in international affairs.[61] However, they are not opposed to the Commission's role as a strong partner in the troika and lead negotiator on specific issues.

59.   Delreux and Kerremans 2008.
60.   Kerremans 2004.
61.   Birkel forthcoming.

4.2 EU High Representative and External Action Service take-over

An alternative option would be to hand authority on external representation over to the EU foreign policy coordinator foreseen in the Lisbon Treaty. Officially this function is named High Representative of the Union for Foreign and Security Policy, but this is somewhat misleading, as its tasks are much more encompassing than the previous High Representative function. The High Representative is Vice-President of the European Commission, which has led to the common use of the acronym HR/VP. The person chairs the Foreign Affairs Council and takes care of its external representation. Within the Commission, the HR/VP is responsible for tasks incumbent on it in external relations and for coordinating other aspects of the Union's external action. The HR/VP is also responsible for the consistency of EU external action and has at its disposal a so-called European External Action Service (EEAS) composed of the staff of the previous HR, Commission civil servants working on external relations, and national diplomats.

The exact tasks, responsibilities and remit of the HR/VP and EEAS still have to be defined, and have already been subject to intense negotiations between the EU Member States. Key questions, such as whether trade and development should be included in new foreign policy institutions,[62] are still to be sorted out at the time of writing. Responsibility for external representation in international organisations, including environmental ones, is one of the sensitive questions. The reasoning behind the establishment of a foreign policy coordinator was to put an end to the system of the rotating Presidency in external representation of the EU, but it is unclear if this also applies to issues not previously belonging to the remit of Foreign Ministers. Former Belgian Prime Minister Dehaene, in his capacity as a Member of the European Parliament, in March 2009, for example, presented a draft report in which he argued in favour of making the HR/VP responsible for the external representation of the EU in all international organisations.[63]

The advantage of a take-over by the HR/VP and EEAS would, like in the Commission-take over model, be a more permanent structure for the coordination and external representation of the EU. It may also lead to the EU becoming a more diplomatic and strategic climate negotiator. On the

---

62. Van Schaik 2008.
63. Dehaene 2009. In this context, the extent to which the EU's position in the climate negotiations will be considered foreign policy becomes relevant. In this respect, it is interesting to note that climate change has been inserted into the Environment Chapter of the Lisbon Treaty.

negative side, the support by, and EU socialisation of, the Member States may diminish. In addition, the level of knowledge on the substance of the negotiations and the real commitment to tackling climate change may be less guaranteed than if Environment Ministers remain in the lead.[64]

Lastly, after the entry into force of the Lisbon Treaty the European Parliament may also become more involved. Its previous advisory role changes to that of giving assent to any international agreement decided upon. A future climate agreement would hence become subject to a possible veto by the Parliament. The European Parliament may use this veto position to demand a more prominent role in determining the EU's negotiating position and in the EU's external representation. However, it seems unlikely that the Parliament would vote down an international climate treaty, because it has always stressed the importance of obtaining such a treaty.

4.3   The influence of the Copenhagen conference

After the entry into force of the Lisbon Treaty, it will be interesting to note who will represent the EU at (high-level) UN climate conferences. Although this did not affect the EU's representation at the Copenhagen conference, the performance of the EU as a negotiator in Copenhagen is likely to have a great influence on how EU external representation will be organised afterwards. If the rotating Presidency system fails to function well, for instance when the EU is confronted with severe internal and/or external pressure, it is likely that either a Commission or HR/VP take-over will take place (or even a mixed model, e.g. a continuation of the lead-negotiators system in combination with coordination by the Commission or HR/VP). If the system functions well, it may be used to claim that external representation in the field of environmental policy should stay within the remit of the rotating Presidencies. It may even be claimed that the model used for the climate negotiations should be extended to other policy areas. Still, in this scenario, a chance exists that the Commission will bring a case before the European Court of Justice. When it comes to emissions trading, it seems as if a claim by the Commission could hardly be denied on the basis of judgements in earlier cases.[65]

---

64.   The option of the HR/VP taking over responsibility is hardly discussed among those currently involved in the negotiations, possibly because they have been preoccupied with the Copenhagen conference.
65.   Eeckhout 2004; Hoffmeister 2007.

5.   Conclusions

The current climate model has clear shortcomings, but has operated relatively well since the turn of the twenty-first century. The EU has stood at the forefront in the international fight against climate change and has managed to keep its ranks closed. In the future, EU unity may be threatened by more heterogeneous preferences of Member States, and a decreasing conviction of the need for a strongly united European position, resulting, *inter alia*, from the US comeback in the climate negotiations. Under such conditions, it could be argued that a more centralised system is needed in which the EU negotiating mandate can be agreed upon through voting and authority for external representation is attributed to a permanent negotiator.

The two alternative models that were discussed in this chapter – a take-over by the European Commission or by a EU foreign policy coordinator, as foreseen in the Lisbon Treaty – provide interesting options, but new shortcomings are likely to emerge. In terms of effectiveness, both models may strengthen the continuity of the EU in the negotiations, but it is not clear whether they will foster EU unity in external representation. If Member States are unwilling to cooperate because their preferences diverge or they do not see the need for a common European position, neither the European Commission nor the HR/VP is likely to improve the EU's performance in the international climate negotiations. The EU socialisation processes emerging from the rotating Presidency, combined with the lead negotiators and issue leaders from various EU Member States, are also likely to decline, if a more supranational model is used. This could threaten EU unity directly and indirectly, since it could jeopardise mutual understanding and, by extension, the homogeneity of preferences of the Member States.

Perhaps most surprisingly, the fact that climate change has become such a high profile issue has not drawn more attention to how EU climate diplomacy is organised. In discussions on the reform of EU foreign policy, there is hardly any mention of the rather specific model used in the climate negotiations, with a rotating Presidency supervising and coordinating a team of lead negotiators and issue leaders. At the same time, the EU Member States and the European Commission seem unaware of the possible effects following from creeping legal competences and the entry into force of the Lisbon Treaty.

The discussion on the most effective model for EU external representation is also relevant for other policy areas falling outside the scope of either the EU's Common Commercial Policy or the EU's Common Foreign and

Security Policy (CFSP). Agreements reached in international organisations such as the WHO (health), FAO (agriculture), ICAO (aviation) and IMF (monetary policy) have tremendous impact on EU legislation. However, models used for EU coordination and external representation within these organisations are hardly scrutinised or compared systematically. Reform of the system of the rotating Presidency in external representation was at the root of institutional innovations proposed in the Lisbon Treaty, but it is still unclear how it will evolve outside the traditional areas of foreign policy. The Copenhagen conference is likely to become the litmus test for the EU's current model used in the climate negotiations. If it fails, it could be argued that the system of the rotating Presidency should also be reconsidered for the EU's external representation in other international organisations. Conversely, if the system, including the functioning of the lead negotiators and issue leaders, functions effectively, its use may also be considered in other settings.

Another, more researched question is the extent to which the EU operates like a state in international negotiations. In the climate negotiations we see that national representation persists, but whether the delegates of the EU Member States involved in the negotiations still consider themselves national delegates can be questioned. A clear identification with the EU as the primary affiliation seems to have emerged. "Team Europe" may be rather preoccupied with internal coordination, but to outsiders it clearly acts as one. The model of the rotating Presidency, lead negotiators and issue leaders has made a large number of actors responsible for the development and delivery of the EU's position. In that respect the current model may be rather sustainable. It proves that understanding the EU in international affairs requires more than portraying it either as a state-like entity or a coalition of sovereign nation states.

References

Aggestam, Lisbeth, Francesco Anesi, Geoffrey Edwards, Christopher Hill and David Rijks. 2008. *Institutional Competences in the EU External Action: Actors and Boundaries in CFSP/ESDP*. Stockholm: Swedish Institute for European Policies Studies.

Avery, Graham, Jolyon Howorth, David Rijks, Simon Duke, Cornelius Adebahr, Julia Lieb, Antonio Missiroli, Anne-Marie Le Cloannec, Richard Whitman, Stephan Keukeleire, Giovanni Grevi and Andreas Mauer. 2007. The EU Foreign Service: How to Build a More Effective Common Policy. *EPC Working Paper No. 28*. Brussels: European Policy Centre.

Beyers, Jan and Jarle Trondal. 2004. How Nation States "Hit" Europe: Ambiguity and Representation in the European Union. *West European Politics* 27(5): 919-42.

Birkel, Kathrin. 2009. EU Member States, "the EU", and International Climate Change Negotiations. Unpublished article.

Bretherton, Charlotte and John Vogler. 2006. *The European Union as a Global Actor*. London: Routledge.

Buchner, Barbara. 2001. What Really Happened in The Hague. *Report on the COP 6*, Part I, 13–25 November 2000. The Hague, The Netherlands: Fondazione Eni Enrico Mattei. Available at: http://www.feem.it/Feem/Pub/Publications/WPapers/WP2001-038.htm. Accessed: 18 July 2009.

Cameron, Fraser. 2007. *An Introduction to European Foreign Policy*. New York: Routledge.

Commission (EC). 2003. *The European Union and the United Nations: The Choice of Multilateralism*. Communication from the Commission to the Council and the European Parliament. COM (2003) 526. Brussels: European Commission.

Commission (EC). 2008a. Europeans' Attitudes towards Climate Change. *Special Eurobarometer Report 300*. Brussels: European Commission.

Commission (EC). 2008b. *Climate Change and International Security*. Paper from the High Representative and the European Commission to the European Council.

Costa, Oriol. 2008. Is Climate Change Changing the EU? The Second Image Reversed in Climate Politics. *Cambridge Review of International Affairs* 21(4): 527-644.

Damro, Chad. 2006. EU-UN Environmental Relations: Shared Competence and Effective Multilateralism. In *The European Union at the United Nations – Intersecting Multilateralisms*, edited by Katie Verlin Laatikainen and Karen Smith. 175-192. Basingstoke: Palgrave MacMillan.

Dehaene, Jean-Luc. 2009. Report on the Impact of the Treaty of Lisbon on the Development of the Institutional Balance of the European Union, European Parliament Committee on Constitutional Affairs, European Parliament. 18 March 2009. Available at: http://www.europarl.europa.eu/sides/getDoc.do?type=REPORT&reference=A6-2009-0142&language=EN. Accessed: 18 July 2009.

Delreux, Tom. 2006. The European Union in International Environmental Negotiations: a Legal Perspective on the Internal Decision-Making Process. *International Environmental Agreements* 6(3): 231-248.

Delreux, Tom. 2008. The EU as a Negotiator in Multilateral Chemicals Negotiations: Multiple Principals, Different Agents. *Journal of European Public Policy* 15(7): 1069-1086.

Delreux, Tom and Bart Kerremans. 2008. How Agents Control Principals. *IIEB Working Paper 28*. Leuven: Institute for International and European Policy.

Duke, Simon. 2008. The Lisbon Treaty and External Relations, *EIPASCOPE* 2008/1. Maastricht: European Institute of Public Administration.

Eeckhout, Piet. 2004. *External Relations of the European Union – Legal and Constitutional Foundations*. Oxford: Oxford University Press.

Frieden, Jeffrey A. 2004. One Europe, One Voice? The Political Economy of European Union Representation in International Organizations. *European Union Politics* 5(2): 261-276.

Govaere, Inge, Jeroen Capiau and An Vermeersch. 2004. In-Between Seats: The Participation of the European Union in International Organizations. *European Foreign Affairs Review* 9(2): 155-187.

Groenleer, Martijn L.P. and Louise G. van Schaik. 2007. United We Stand? The European Union's International Actorness in the Case of the International Criminal Court and the Kyoto Protocol. *Journal of Common Market Studies* 45(5): 969-998.

Grubb, Michael and Farhana Yamin. 2001. Climate Collapse at The Hague: What Happened, Why, and Where Do We Go from Here? *International Affairs* 77(2): 261-276.

Gstöhl, Sieglinde. 2009. "Patchwork Power" Europe? The EU's Representation in International Institutions. *European Foreign Affairs Review* 14: 385-403.

Haas, Peter M. 1992. Introduction: Epistemic Communities and International Policy Coordination. *International Organization* 46(1): 178-224.

Hoffmeister, Frank. 2007. Outsider or Frontrunner? Recent Developments under International and European Law on the Status of the European Union in International Organizations and Treaty Bodies. *Common Market Law Review* 44: 41-68.

Jørgensen, Knud Erik, ed. 2009. *The European Union and International Organizations*. London and New York: Routledge.

Kerremans, Bart. 2004. What Went Wrong in Cancun? A Principal-Agent View on the EU's Rationale Towards the Doha Development Round. *European Foreign Affairs Review* 9(3): 363-393.

Keukeleire, Stephan and Jennifer MacNaughtan. 2008. *The Foreign Policy of the European Union*. Houndmills: Palgrave Macmillan.

Laatikainen, Katie V. and Karen E. Smith, eds. 2006. *The European Union at the United Nations – Intersecting Multilateralisms*. Houndmills: Palgrave Macmillan.

Lacasta, Nuno S., Suraje Dessai, Eva Kracht and Katharine Vincent. 2007. Articulating a Consensus: The EU's Position on Climate Change. In *Europe and Global Climate Change – Politics, Foreign Policy and Regional Cooperation*, edited by Paul G. Harris. 211-231. Cheltenham: Edward Elgar.

Meunier, Sophie. 2000. What Single Voice? European Institutions and EU-U.S. Trade Negotiations. *International Organization* 54(1): 103-135.

Meunier, Sophie and Kalypso Nicolaïdis. 2006. The European Union as a Conflicted Trade Power. *Journal of European Public Policy* 13(6): 906-925.

Oberthür, Sebastian and Hermann E. Ott. 1999. *The Kyoto Protocol: International Climate Policy for the 21st Century*. Berlin: Springer.

Oberthür, Sebastian and Claire Roche Kelly. 2008. EU Leadership in International Climate Policy: Achievements and Challenges. *The International Spectator* 43(3): 35-50.

Oberthür, Sebastian. 2009. The Performance of the EU in International Institutions: Negotiating on Climate Change. Paper presented at International Studies Association Annual Convention. New York, 15-18 February.

Ott, Hermann E. 2001. Climate Change: An Important Foreign Policy Issue. *International Affairs* 77(2): 277-296.

Rhinard, Mark and Michael Kaeding. 2006. The International Bargaining Power of the European Union in "Mixed" Competence Negotiations: The Case of the 2000 Cartagena Protocol on Biosafety. *Journal of Common Market Studies* 44(5): 1023-1050.

Sapir, André. 2007. Europe and the Global Economy. *Fragmented Power: Europe and the Global Economy*, edited by André Sapir. Brussels: Bruegel.

Schout, Adriaan and Louise G. van Schaik. 2008. Reforming the EU Presidency. *Zeitschrift für Staats- und Europawissenschaften/ Journal for Comparative Government and European Policy* 6(1): 36-56.

Schreurs, Miranda and Yves Tiberghien. 2007. Multi-Level Reinforcement: Explaining European Union Leadership in Climate Change Mitigation. *Global Environmental Politics* 7(4): 19-46.

Smith, Karen E. 2006. Speaking with One Voice? European Union Co-ordination on Human Rights Issues at the United Nations. *Journal of Common Market Studies* 44(1): 113-37.

The CNA Corporation. 2007. *National Security and the Threat of Climate Change*. Alexandria: The CNA Corporation.

Van Schaik, Louise G. and Christian Egenhofer. 2005. Improving the Climate – Will the New Constitution Strengthen the EU's Performance in International Climate Negotiations? *CEPS Policy Brief 63*. Brussels: Centre for European Policy Studies.

Van Schaik, Louise G. 2008. Recuperating the European Union's Foreign Policy Machinery: Beyond Institutional Fixes. *Challenges in a Changing World-Clingendael Views on Global and Regional Issues*, edited by Jaap de Zwaan, Erwin Bakker and Sico van der Meer. 117-130. Cambridge: Cambridge University Press.

Van Schaik, Louise G. and Karel Van Hecke. 2008. Skating on Thin Ice: Europe's Internal Climate Policy and its Position in the World. Working Paper Egmont Institute, December.

Vanhoonacker, Sophie. 2005. The Institutional Framework of EU External Relations. In *International Relations and the European Union*, edited by Christopher Hill and Michael Smith. 67-90. Oxford: Oxford University Press.

Vogler, John and Charlotte Bretherton. 2006. The European Union as a Protagonist to the United States on Climate Change. *International Studies Perspectives* 7(1): 1-22.

Vogler, John and Hannes R. Stephan. 2007. The European Union in Global Environmental Governance: Leadership in the Making? *International Environmental Agreements* 7: 389-413.

Woll, Cornelia. 2006. The Road to External Representation: The European Commission's Activism in International Air Transport. *Journal of European Public Policy* 13(1): 52-69.

Russia and the International Climate Change Regime

Wybe Th. Douma, Michael Kozeltsev and Julia Dobrolyubova

1. Introduction

Climate change has become the top priority issue on the international agenda, with ongoing efforts to find an effective global response to the challenge. The attention of the world community is focused on the international negotiations on a new climate regime to regulate global greenhouse gas (GHG) emissions for post-2012 (after the Kyoto Protocol commitment period). The Bali Action Plan, adopted by more than 190 countries in 2007, paved the way towards a new comprehensive agreement, which was to be agreed by the fifteenth Conference of the Parties to the UN Framework Convention on Climate Change (UNFCCC) in Copenhagen in December 2009.

Russia has always been one of the key players in the international negotiations on climate change. To a large extent, the fate of the Kyoto Protocol depended on Russia's decision to ratify the agreement. Persuading the Russian Federation to ratify the Protocol was not an easy task, in spite of the apparent benefits for the country. However, it will seem a simple procedure in hindsight compared to ensuring that Russia joins the post-2012 regime. Reaching a new international agreement without Russia is not an option. Russia is the world's third largest emitter of GHGs, after China and the USA, and still has a lot of potential to achieve more energy efficiency. While much attention has been paid to the involvement of the USA and emerging economies like China, India, Brazil and South Korea, the role of Russia in the creation of new international rules on climate change for the period after 2012 should not be underestimated.

This chapter investigates the prospects for keeping Russia on board and, more generally, for furthering cooperation with Russia on climate change issues. It will do so by, first, examining the climate change impacts that the country is experiencing (section 2). Then, attention will turn to Russia's activities in implementing the UNFCCC and the Kyoto Protocol, including Joint Implementation (JI) investment projects under Article 6 of the Kyoto Protocol that are under development. Particular attention will be paid to the fact that while more JI projects have been devised and submitted for approval than in any other country, by July 2009 not one of these was formally approved (section 3). An analysis of the key Russian stakeholders' positions, their capacities and needs, as well as barriers for successful development of climate policy will be presented next (section 4). Finally, the prospects for Russia accepting binding post-2012 targets in Copenhagen are examined, taking into consideration the lessons learnt from the rocky road to Russia's ratification of the Kyoto Protocol (section 5).

2.   Climate Change Impacts in Russia

Annual temperature rise in Russia is even more drastic than at the global level due to its location in the high latitudes of the Northern hemisphere.[1] While global surface air temperature increased by 0.74 degrees Celsius (°C) during the last century, in Russia, the temperature increase amounted to 1.29°C (Figure 1). According to different forecasts, this dramatic trend will increase further in the near future. By 2015 the average temperature in the country is expected to increase by another 0.6°C.[2]

Figure 1 – Mean abnormalities of annual air temperature in Russia, the Northern hemisphere and the World (1901-2004 in °C)

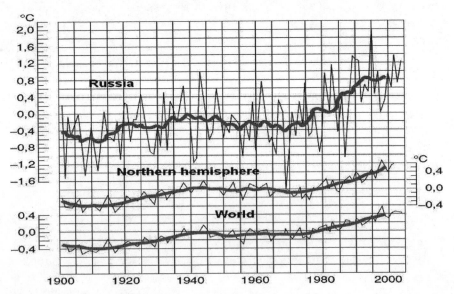

Source: Roshydromet 2006a, 6.

1.   In the Northern hemisphere, the percentage of land compared to water is higher than in the Southern hemisphere. As the land absorbs the heat better than the ocean, it is warming more quickly.
2.   Roshydromet 2008.

Due to its vast territory and variety of geographical conditions, there are considerable spatial and seasonal variations of climate impacts in Russia. According to meteorological data, average winter temperatures are increasing faster than the summer temperatures (Figure 2), even though temperature decrease in some of the regions (for instance in Eastern Siberia) was registered in the winter period.

It is expected that air temperature in winter will increase by 1°C by 2020 compared to 2007 with some variations in the different regions of the country. In summer, in general, the expected warming will not be as considerable as in winter (approximately 0.4°C on average).

A popular misconception among the Russian public is that since it is a northern country, Russia will only benefit from global warming. The benefits are primarily foreseen in a considerable drop in heating costs, an increase of crop yields and the development of the Northern Sea Route. Even former Russian President, Vladimir Putin, mentioned several times that climate change will mean that Russians will need fewer fur coats.

Figure 2 – Mean temperature abnormalities in Russia in winter (left) and in summer (right) in 2007, compared with 1976-2006 average (in °C)

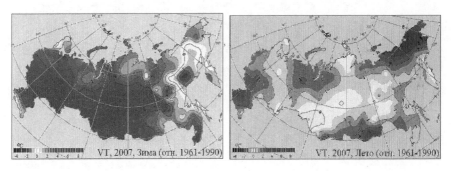

Source: Roshydromet 2007, 10.

This is only partly true, however. According to the "Assessment Report on Climate Change and its Consequences in the Russian Federation" presented in 2008 by the Federal Service for Hydrometeorology and Environmental Monitoring (Roshydromet), the heating season in Russia will be between three and five days shorter on average in 2015, compared to 2000. The most significant reductions – up to five days – will be observed in the far eastern regions. However, the same report also states that, due to an increase of the number of hot days in summer, air conditioning expenses for indoor cooling will increase, including for industrial buildings.

The high probability of warming-related droughts in the south of Russia will decrease crop yields by up to 22 per cent, compared to the 2005 levels for grain crops in Northern Caucasia, in the Volga and Ural regions. In the south of Western Siberia, crop yields will also decrease by 12-14 per cent compared to 2005, if no actions are taken to combat the predicted intensification of aridity.[3] Further decreases in rainfall in the southern regions of the country may not only lead to reduction in crop yields, but also to river-flow decreases and significant water shortages.

Furthermore, the increased annual and seasonal runoffs from rivers in other Russian regions, and the changes in their ice conditions predicted up to 2015, will significantly raise the pressure on submerged pipelines. By 2015, the probability of pipeline damage (due to rupture) will increase.[4] This might be accompanied by oil spills and gas leakages that cause severe environmental disasters and serious economic losses.

The examples mentioned above prove that Russia is not immune to the negative impacts of climate change, which are experienced in all regions of the country. Temperature increase, melting ice, sea-level rise and coastal erosion, thawing permafrost in the Arctic, and water shortages in the southern territories are already having a discernable impact on the industrial and public infrastructure in Russia.

Changes taking place in the cryosphere are the most vivid example of climate volatility in Russia. The cryosphere is the Earth's surface consisting of sea-ice, snow and glaciers, ice caps and ice-sheets, frozen ground (including permafrost) and other such elements. These elements are of principal importance for Russia, especially for the Arctic territories and, at the same time, are the most vulnerable to climate impacts.

Ice-cover of the Arctic seas in the summer period has decreased significantly (over 15-20 per cent) between 1979 and 2008. Data in Figure 3 show the continuous reduction of the ice surface by 2.7 per cent per decade on average, and by 7.4 per cent during the summer period. This trend may lead to total Arctic ice melting in summer by 2030.[5]

3.   Roshydromet 2006a.
4.   Roshydromet 2006a.
5.   Dobrolyubova et al. 2009.

Figure 3 – The Arctic ice analysis from satellite imagery in summer (September 1998 and 2007)

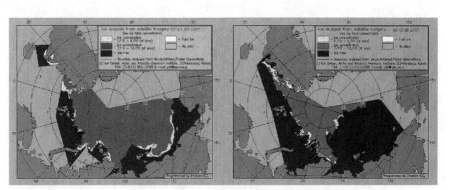

Source: Data from the website of the Arctic and Antarctic Research Institute: http://www.aari.nw.ru/clgmi/sea_charts/sea_charts.html.

In the second half of the twentieth century, the degradation of mountain glaciers in Russia also became evident. Such changes in mountain glaciers were observed in the Caucasus, in Ural, in Altai, in north-eastern Siberia and in the Kamchatka Peninsula. The total volume of mountain glaciers has decreased by ten per cent since 1952.[6] This tendency will accelerate in the twenty-first century under expected continuous warming.

In the twenty-first century, the southern permafrost boundary is expected to move northward in Western Siberia, by 30-80 km in the next 20-25 years and by 150-200 km by 2050.[7] Permafrost occupies more than 60 per cent of land in Russia. Changes in the frozen ground have a significant impact on the ecosystems of the permafrost regions. These changes lead to a decrease in the carrying capacity of the ground resulting in infrastructure damages, and they increase methane emissions from soil into the atmosphere (Figure 4). Methane is a much more potent GHG than carbon dioxide. Scientists are warning against the vicious cycle of feedback where global warming causes the release of GHGs from permafrost, which, in turn, causes more warming and, hence, more release from permafrost.

A rapid growth in the number and severity of extreme weather events in Russia is another example of adverse climate change effects. Between 1991 and 2007 the average number of such events more than doubled. According to the World Bank, the annual losses caused by such extreme events amount to 1-2 billion Euro.[8]

6.   Dobrolyubova et al. 2009.
7.   Roshydromet 2008.
8.   Roshydromet 2008.

A warmer climate also deteriorates the health situation in Russian regions, with increased incidents of infectious diseases and sickness caused by enhanced weather volatility.

Figure 4 – Risks related to permafrost thawing in Russia

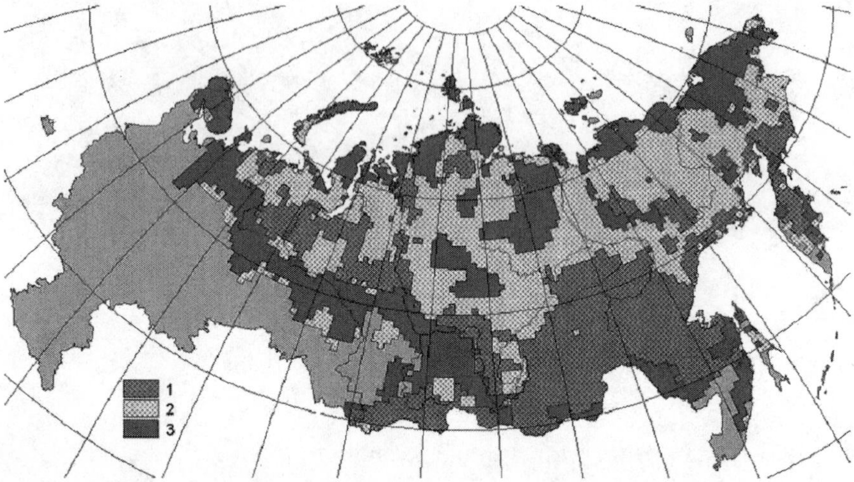

Note: 1 = low; 2 = average; 3 = high.
Source: Anisimov and Reneva 2006.

In conclusion, climate change in Russia will have both positive and negative impacts on the environment and the sustainable socio-economic development of the country. Unfortunately, there are still no economic assessments of the potential benefits or damages and the cost of mitigation measures in Russia (e.g. similar to the "Stern Review" in the UK). Therefore, the need for quick response measures by the government and businesses is unclear, and thus the development of efficient adaptation strategies is greatly hindered.

3. Implementation of the UNFCCC and the Kyoto Protocol in Russia

3.1 Research

An assessment of on-going and predicted climate changes and their impacts is an important component of an information system for the development of climate policy at national and international levels. Research in this field in

Russia is carried out by Roshydromet – mainly because coordination of implementation of the UNFCCC and the Kyoto Protocol in Russia has historically been the responsibility of this national hydrometeorological service. Roshydromet has 17 prominent scientific and research institutes under its jurisdiction, which have different profiles for research, including monitoring of climate, climate change impacts assessment, applied climatology, GHG observation, climate of the Arctic and Antarctic regions, climate of oceans and water basins of rivers and lakes, climate extremes assessment, etc. There are also a lot of scientific institutes under the Russian Academy of Science that have specialised departments dealing with climate change and its impacts on various environmental components or economic and social aspects in almost all regions of Russia.

Russian scientists always contribute to the Intergovernmental Panel on Climate Change (IPCC) reports and technical papers. More than 15 Russian experts from Roshydromet and the Russian Academy of Science institutes were among the authors of the IPCC Fourth Assessment Report (2007). Yu. Izrael, director of the Institute of Global Climate and the Environment was vice-president of the IPCC from 2002 to 2008. In 2008, the deputy director of the same institute, S. Semenov, was elected as vice-chair of the IPCC Working Group II on climate change impacts, adaptation and vulnerability.

In addition, Russian researchers carry out assessments at national level employing comprehensive data sets collected by national hydrometeorological services. They thoroughly use results of national research and take into account inherent regional features and social conditions. Each year, Roshydromet prepares a national report on climate characteristics containing climate change observation data and results of modelling.

In 2006, the "Strategic Prediction for the Period of up to 2010-2015 of Climate Change Expected in Russia and Its Impact on Sectors of the Russian Economy" was presented. This research contains results of the assessment of the most probable climatic conditions on the territory of the Russian Federation and its regions in a 5-10 year period and general recommendations on primary adaptation measures for five sectors of the national economy (the energy sector, agriculture, water management, construction, human health). However, the "Strategic Prediction" did not cover several important sectors, such as transport, forest management and tourism, which are extremely vulnerable to climate change and play an important role in the Russian economy.

In 2009, Roshydromet presented the first "Assessment Report on Climate Change and Its Consequences in the Russian Federation" – a national analogue to the IPCC reports. It is the most comprehensive and up-to-date assessment of past, present and future climate change. The report synthesises information on climate conditions in the country and considers the following topics: observed and expected climate change, consequences of climate change for environmental and economic systems, human health, and possible adaptation measures, as well as further research needs.

The report was prepared, primarily, for federal and regional executive authorities and other organizations responsible for the planning and implementation of specific tasks relevant to various sectors of the economy and programmes on sustainable development. It also targeted research and educational institutions, and public organisations concerned with issues of climate change in the Russian Federation.[9] Along with the report itself, general and technical summaries in both Russian and English were prepared.

Even though many of the impacts of global warming are still regarded as positive for Russia, the conclusion of the authors is to call for the Russian government to develop a serious set of domestic mitigation policies and engage in international cooperation. The report also urges the Russian government to come up with an adaptation plan to prepare society and the economy for the impacts of climate change, both positive and negative.

This study is, undoubtedly, an important step towards a more profound understanding of climate change impacts by Russian stakeholders and further incorporation of climate change factors into the decision-making process. Despite the comprehensive nature of the study, it does not, however, contain a cost-benefit analysis of the proposed adaptation strategies and measures. It provides only general recommendations for different regions, even though the elaboration of adaptation policies and measures requires an individual regional approach with due respect to the concrete geographical and socio-economic circumstances of a certain territory. The main obstacles to conducting such an assessment by Roshydromet, or any other Russian federal agency, are the limited authority of the body, insufficient interagency co-operation on climate change, and, in general, a lack of targeted funding for research.

9.   Official press release of the "Assessment report" published on Roshydromet web-site www.meteorf.ru.

3.2   Policies and measures

The Russian Federation is an Annex B country, or in other words, is a developed country with an economy in transition, for which the Kyoto Protocol imposes legally binding GHG-emission limits. Since the USA chose not to ratify the Kyoto Protocol, Russia is the country with the highest emissions among the states bound by the Protocol. Like New Zealand and the Ukraine, the country is under an obligation to keep its emissions at the 1990 levels for the period 2008-2012.[10]

However, because of the economic crisis that hit Russia after the fall of the Soviet Union in the 1990s, this obligation poses no challenge. In 2006, Russia's emissions were 2.19 billion tonnes CO_2 equivalent, 34 per cent below 1990 levels. A slight increase in emissions (about 1-1.5 per cent per year) was observed between 1999 and 2006 (Figure 5). Nevertheless, it is relatively low compared to the high rate of growth in the Russian economy (5-7 per cent increase of GDP annually).[11] This is due, first of all, to the modernisation of industrial equipment and, secondly, to the promotion of more energy-efficient technologies. If economic growth had continued with the same high pre-crisis rate, Russia would not have reached 1990 emissions levels until 2018, at the earliest.

Figure 5 – Quantitative commitments and the emissions profile of Russia (1990-2006)

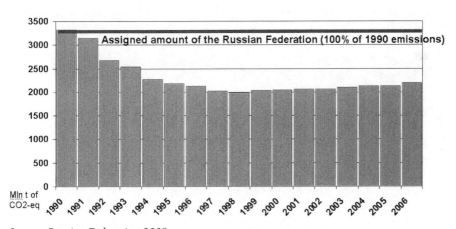

Source: Russian Federation 2008.

10.   Initially, Russia's 1990 emissions were calculated to amount to 3.22 billion tonnes. In 2007, a review calculated Russia's 1990 emissions at 3.32 billion tonnes, allowing the country to emit an additional 535 million tonnes from 2008-2012, under the Kyoto Protocol.

11.   Roshydromet 2006b.

The expected matter-of-course fulfilment of the Kyoto quantitative commitments by Russia has long discouraged the Russian government from adopting concrete targeted emission reduction policies or programmes. Things are changing slowly however, and low-carbon principles are being incorporated into the decision-making process due to a number of reasons, including:

- the high energy-saving potential in Russia, especially in the energy, housing and municipal sectors;
- the need for the technological modernisation of industrial facilities;
- the political will to enhance energy efficiency;
- the high business interest in emissions trading; and
- the enhanced prestige of the country and the desire to remain an active player in the international climate process.

A vast potential for energy efficiency and GHG emission reductions exists in the Russian Federation, in particular with regards to energy generation and industrial energy use. Although Russia's carbon intensity (the level of GHG emissions per unit of GDP) decreased significantly between 1999 and 2003,[12] it is still four times higher than in the EU-15 countries, 2.4 times as much as in the USA, and twice as much as in Canada.[13] Investing in energy efficiency would enhance the competitive strength of Russia's industry, and – combined with measures stimulating energy efficiency with regards to commercial, residential and public buildings that at present consume more than 50 per cent of the country's total energy usage[14] – would enable Russia to meet the foreign demand for its oil and gas reserves more easily.

Energy efficiency is moving up the national agenda. Through Decree No. 889 "On some measures to promote energy and environmental efficiency of the national economy" of 4 June 2008, the Russian government ordered the creation of energy-efficient technologies and announced a goal of slashing Russia's energy wastefulness by 40 per cent by 2020.[15] The Decree envisages:

- introducing efficiency standards in energy-intensive sectors;
- introducing strict restrictions on the further use of obsolete technologies;
- promoting the leading role of public sector;

12. Perelet et al. 2007.
13. Yulkin 2009. These numbers are based on UNFCCC data regarding GHG emissions, and World Bank data regarding PPP GDP; data for Russia refer to 1999, for EU-15 to 2002.
14. Izeman and Pike-Biegunska 2009.
15. According to data from the Ministry of Energy of Russia, this 40 per cent energy efficiency improvement means the realisation of almost 100 per cent of current energy-saving potential.

- labelling power-intensive goods;
- creating incentives for businesses to make efficiency improvements;
- underlining public support for research and development in the area of energy-saving technologies.

The programme to improve energy efficiency also encompasses an increase in the share of renewable energy from less than one per cent of the total energy generation and use by Russia in 2009 to 4.5 per cent by 2020. Further legislative acts, including a Federal Law on energy efficiency, are in development.

Significant GHG emission reductions could be achieved in Russia by curbing gas flaring. Flaring and venting of associated gas contribute significantly to global GHG emissions, as well as wasting a valuable resource that could be used productively. Russia has been flaring by far the greatest amount globally.[16] Rostehnadzor, a government environmental, industrial and nuclear supervision service, has introduced legislation to increase fines for associated flaring above 15 per cent of the total associated gas output from January 2009. Russia's current limit for gas flaring is 25 per cent of the total gas output, and penalties are small.

A large potential for GHG emission reduction exists in Russian regions and Russian enterprises. For instance, the Republic of Buryatia developed a comprehensive Kyoto Protocol implementation plan. An interdepartmental commission on Kyoto Protocol implementation was set up in the Kemerovo region. A set of measures to reduce GHG emissions are implemented in the Kursk region under the programme "Energy Conservation in Kursk region in 2006-2010". The programme aims to reduce GHG emissions by two per cent. GHG emission stocktaking was performed in some Russian regions (Arkhangelsk, Chelyabinsk, Novgorod, Sverdlovsk etc.) following the methodology adopted by the Intergovernmental Panel on Climate Change. Projects to reduce GHG emissions in various sectors have been developed in many regions.

Russia also needs to develop proposals for additional regulation of GHG emissions based on energy-efficiency norms. Such schemes can be implemented in line with the Energy Strategy to 2030 and other legal documents, which were under revision in 2009.

The global economic crisis of 2008/2009 encouraged the Russian government to take more ambitious actions in the field of energy efficiency. Improving energy efficiency was identified as a top-priority issue in the national policy

---

16. US National Oceanic and Atmospheric Administration 2006.

agenda by the President of the Russian Federation Dmitry Medvedev in 2009. Even the "2009 Anti-crisis Action Plan of the Russian Government" stipulated the implementation of energy-saving policies and measures.

Climate change adaptation is also gaining more government attention. The elaboration of an adaptation policy is not only an environmental task, but also an economic and social one. By implementing an efficient adaptation strategy it is possible to reduce any negative climate impacts on the economy and on society, as well as profit from any possible positive effects of climate change, which is especially true for Russia. Roshydromet has prepared a Climate Change Doctrine. This document represents an important step in forming national climate policy. The document contains important provisions on the objectives, goals and tasks of the Russian policy on climate change, as well as recommendations on priority measures for different stakeholders. The Climate Doctrine was approved by the Russian government in April 2009 and was then forwarded to the President of the Russian Federation for official adoption.

The document contains recommendations on priority adaptation measures. The first actions are already being taken at the sectoral or regional level. For instance, the perspectives for the Northern Sea Route development are being assessed. The non-governmental Russian Regional Environmental Centre and UNDP-Russia are currently implementing a pilot regional adaptation study project in the Murmansk oblast in the north of European Russia.

The elaboration of effective adaptation and mitigation policies and measures in Russia is complex and requires coordinated action at various administrative levels, as well as the maximum involvement of all stakeholders, including decision-makers, representatives of business, and the general public. It is also important to study and to apply the best international experience and to enhance international co-operation in this field.

3.3 Kyoto mechanisms[17]

As already mentioned, Russia is expected to easily meet its GHG emission limits set under the Kyoto Protocol. It will thus have a huge surplus in the period until 2012. This surplus could be put to good use, notably in the area of energy efficiency. The Kyoto Protocol mechanisms, primarily Joint Implementation (JI), can help the Russian Federation achieve the goal of increased energy efficiency and could bring additional foreign investments.

17. Douma and Ratsiborinskaya 2007, 135-145.

Under JI, foreign enterprises can invest in Russia to realise emission reductions and acquire emission credits. They are interested in JI projects in Russia because of comparatively low abatement costs. Russian enterprises have more possibilities than western ones to enhance energy efficiency, and consequently for emission reductions, due to deteriorating equipment. The energy-saving potential of Russia is estimated as 39-47 per cent of its current energy consumption, with the fuel and energy sector and energy-intensive industries accounting for two-thirds, and housing and public utilities for one quarter.[18]

Being aware of all the advantages that JI projects may bring to the Russian economy, the Russian government took the necessary steps in order to promote JI projects. Under the Kyoto Protocol and its implementing rules, all industrialised Parties with an emission target wishing to participate in JI projects should satisfy so-called eligibility requirements, including:

- the ratification of the Kyoto Protocol *(Done according to the Federal Law No. 128-FZ dated 4 November 2004)*;
- the definition of the assigned amount of the country for the first commitment period *(16.1 billion tonnes of CO_2 equivalent for a five-year period, presented in the Russian Initial Report on the Assigned Amount, which was submitted to the UNFCCC Secretariat on 20 February 2007)*;
- the existence of a national registry *(its establishment is regulated by the Government Decree No. 215-p dated 20 February 2006. According to the Government Decree No. 1741-p of 15 December 2006, the Federal Centre for Geo-information Systems (FCGS) "Ecology" is designated as National Registry Administrator;[19]*
- the elaboration of a national GHG inventory system *(assigned to Roshydromet under Government Decree No. 278-p of 1 March 2006. Roshydromet established this system under its Order No. 141 of 30 June 2006)*;
- the presentation of the annual GHG emissions inventories *(the data is presented annually in the National Inventory Reports, submitted to the UNFCCC Secretariat)*; and
- the presentation of supplementary information in annual reports to the Secretariat *(regularly submitted to the UNFCCC Secretariat)*.

On 28 May 2007, the long awaited Decree No. 332 "On the procedure of approval and verification of the realisation of projects carried out under Article 6 of the Kyoto Protocol to the UN Framework Convention on

18. Ministry of Energy of the Russian Federation 2008.
19. Further information on the registry can be found at the FCGS "Ecology" website http://www.ecoinfo.ru/default_e.htm (Accessed: 11 August 2009).

Climate Change" in Russia was adopted. According to this Decree, the Ministry of Economic Development and Trade of the Russian Federation (MEDT)[20] is designated as the national body responsible for the adoption of JI projects under Article 6 of the Protocol, aimed at GHG emission reduction by sources and/or their removals by sinks "to economically and technologically feasible and environmentally appropriate levels". Other concerned federal agencies review project documentation and assess the realisation of projects within their competence.

The list of projects chosen by the Ministry is sent to the government where it receives final approval in consultation with the federal executive bodies. The Russian government can dismiss approved projects for various reasons, such as exceeding deadlines in reporting to the MEDT, which acts as coordinating centre, and a discontinuation of the activities of a private entrepreneur.

In pursuance of the Decree, the Rules on approval and assessment of JI project realisation were adopted. These include the following provisions.

- The project proponent submits a project concept, project documenta-tion and project passport to the coordinating centre; the documents shall be prepared according to the templates available on the website of the coordinating centre and signed by the proponent.
- The concept is approved by the commission set up by the coordinating centre, which also chooses independent expert organisations using the criteria given in Article 6 of the Kyoto Protocol. The final list of expert organisations shall be available on the website of the coordinating centre.
- Foreign proponents shall deposit the documents in the language of the respective country, with a notarised translation in Russian.
- It is possible to conclude an international agreement on JI project implementation with a foreign counterpart.
- Projects' realisation shall not take place before 1 January 2008 or after 31 December 2012.
- It takes ten working days for the coordination centre to register the project concept deposition, 30 days for the respective federal body to deal with the concept and to provide a positive or negative conclusion thereon, and ten working days for the government to give its final approval to the list of JI projects.

20. Since 12 May 2008, the Ministry of Economic Development (MED).

- The JI projects' realisation is assessed by a designated body (that differs according to the project's implementation sector), which on certain grounds (an incorrect project implementation) can come up with suggestions to the coordination centre for the project's termination.
- The reporting period on the project is one calendar year.
- Any disputes related to project realisation are settled by means of negotiations within six months; otherwise the parties can resort to the courts or to national court of arbitration in accordance with the legislation and the international obligations of the Russian Federation.

At the end of 2007 and in 2008, MEDT issued a number of additional orders, thereby completing the legal framework necessary for the consideration and approval of JI projects in Russia, including:

- Order of 30 November 2007 No. 424 "On the Commission on consideration of applications for approval of projects carried out under the Article 6 of the Kyoto Protocol to the UN Framework Convention on Climate Change";
- Order of 30 November 2007 No. 422 "On approval of limits for greenhouse gas emission reductions";
- Order of 20 December 2007 No. 444 "On approval of methodological instructions on consideration of the project documentation";
- Order of 1 February 2008 No. 21 (amended as of 10 November 2008) "On approval of structure of the Commission on consideration of applications for approval of projects carried out under the Article 6 of the Kyoto Protocol to the UN Framework Convention on Climate Change";
- Order of 22 February 2008 No. 52 "On approval of the passport form of the project carried out under the Article 6 of the Kyoto Protocol to the UN Framework Convention on Climate Change";
- Order of 3 March 2008 No. 79 "On approval of the list of independent expert entities";
- Order of 15 August 2008 No. 248 "On approval of the typical targeted efficiency criteria of projects and their limits".

The Russian Federation established a limit for GHG emission reductions and/or GHG removals that can be realised through JI projects in 2008-2012 (300 million tonnes of CO_2 equivalent), and also its sectoral distribution:

- Energy sector – 205 million tonnes;
- Industrial processes – 25 million tonnes;
- Use of solvents and other products – 5 million tonnes;
- Agriculture – 30 million tonnes;

- Waste management – 15 million tonnes;
- Land-use, land-use change and forestry – 20 million tonnes.[21]

Priority is given to the energy sector, since projects in the field of energy efficiency and energy saving are the most attractive and have the highest potential for Russia. About 70 per cent of total GHG emission reductions will result from projects in the energy sector between 2008 and 2012. Nevertheless, there exists a possibility to redistribute the limits between sectors in case there is a lack of applications or an insufficient amount of reductions under projects in one or several sectors.

At the beginning of 2008, a commission was created under the chairmanship of the MEDT to consider JI project applications. The composition of the commission was set by the Order No. 21 of 1 February 2008 and restructured in November 2008 due to personnel reshuffles within the relevant ministries. According to the Order, the representatives of various interested federal ministries and agencies, including the Ministry of Energy, the Ministry of Natural Resources and the Environment, the Ministry of Regional Development and the Ministry of Industry and Trade were included in the list of its members.

The Commission's responsibilities include:

- the consideration of project applications;
- the selection of independent expert organisations;
- the preparation of proposals for appointments to the relevant authorised body for monitoring the project realisation;
- the consideration of the sectoral redistribution of limits;
- the confirmation of target indicators for project efficiency.

The first session of the Commission took place on 21 February 2008. At this meeting, proposals on the list of independent expert organisations were prepared, requirements for expert conclusions were defined, and the issue of target indicators for project efficiency was considered. Consequently, MEDT began to accept applications on the Russian JI projects on 10 March 2008. The list of accredited expert organisations was approved by the JI Commission and introduced by MEDT through the Order No. 70 of 14 March 2008.

By the end of January 2009, 156 potential JI projects had been registered internationally according to information available from the JI website of the UNFCCC. 90 of these projects (about 58 per cent achieving emission reductions of approximately 200 million tonnes of CO_2 equivalent) are

---

21. Ministry of Economic Development of the Russian Federation 2007.

hosted by Russia (Figure 6). Most of them are implemented in the energy sector and include the prevention of methane emissions in gas-distributing networks as a result of the replacement of outdated pressurising materials with more modern ones, the transition to more environmentally-friendly fuel, energy-saving measures, etc.

The projects to replace "dirty" coal and boiler oil fuel with carbon-neutral biofuel are probably of most interest for the Russian enterprises, in particular, for the housing and public utilities sectors. For example, Russia has enormous timber resources. Thus, the use of wood-processing waste as the fuel for the energy needs of the wood-processing factory or of a town located near it is a logical option. In addition to emission reductions achieved from the replacement of "dirty" fuel, such projects would also result in reductions of methane emissions from the decomposition of wood waste on dumps.

Figure 6 – JI projects by host country (as of January 2009)

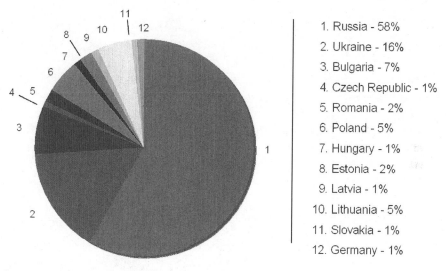

1. Russia - 58%
2. Ukraine - 16%
3. Bulgaria - 7%
4. Czech Republic - 1%
5. Romania - 2%
6. Poland - 5%
7. Hungary - 1%
8. Estonia - 2%
9. Latvia - 1%
10. Lithuania - 5%
11. Slovakia - 1%
12. Germany - 1%

Source: www.pointcarbon.com

By mid-2009, the Ministry of Economic Development had presented information on 31 projects submitted for consideration by the Russian government. In total, they envisage emission reductions of 84.5 million tonnes of CO_2 equivalent, covering various sectors.

Earlier, the main obstacle to the promotion of JI projects in Russia had been the lack of a national procedure and appropriate documents to concretise it. The governmental staff shifts that occurred after the

Presidential elections in 2008, and after the global financial crisis, have considerably slowed down the consideration of projects. Another barrier is the lack of certainty on the post-2012 international regime. However, in spite of all these obstacles the interest of Russian business in JI projects remains very high.

4. Existing barriers for further actions in Russia

There exist a number of barriers that hinder the effective participation of the Russian Federation in the global efforts to tackle climate change, in general, and in negotiations on a post-2012 regime, in particular.

4.1 Domestic barriers

The principal barrier to Russia's effective participation is that there is little concern for climate change domestically. Russian stakeholders, including business, municipal authorities and the general public, still have a low awareness of climate change, the urgent need for countermeasures, the existing capacity for mitigation and adaptation options, development of sustainable energy solutions and relevant international activities. Many Russians do not regard climate change as a serious problem. There are still many sceptics (even among famous Russian scientists) who suppose that either Russia will only benefit from global warming, or, even worse, deny the existence of a climate change problem at all or its anthropogenic origin.

One of the reasons for such an attitude is the lack of a professional or accurate portrayal of such issues in the Russian mass media. Inaccurate reporting, lack of interest and poor analysis of policy debates on climate change result in poor coverage of the topic by Russian journalists. Another reason for such a public attitude is the insufficient popularisation of the recent scientific findings on climate change. In spite of the numerous studies and research being done by Russian academics, the results of their work are rarely officially presented or disseminated. This situation is changing slowly, however.

Furthermore, climate change is not among the top priorities of the federal government or of the regions. Compared to other concerns in other policy areas, such as economic development, the financial crisis recovery plan and more urgent environmental priorities including local air pollution, poor waste management and deforestation, climate policy development fades into the background.

A cumbersome decision-making process also hampers the development of climate policies. In fact, climate change and energy efficiency issues are split up between at least ten different governmental bodies:

- **Roshydromet** – a national coordinator for the UNFCCC and Kyoto Protocol implementation;
- **Ministry of Natural Resources and Ecology** – supervises Roshydromet and is in charge of the Russian registry system of carbon units;
- **Ministry of Foreign Affairs** – in charge of international negotiations, elaboration of post-2012 position (jointly with Roshydromet);
- **Ministry of Economic Development** – Designated National Authority for Kyoto mechanisms;
- **Ministry of Energy** – in charge of national policy in the energy sector that is responsible for more than 80 per cent of GHG emissions;
- **Ministry of Regional Development** – responsible for housing and municipal sector policy;
- **Ministry of Industry** – responsible for policies in the industry sector;
- **Rosleshos** – the Federal Forestry Agency, responsible for forest programmes and policies;
- **Ministry of Emergencies** – natural disaster risks prevention and recovery measures;
- **Ministry of Transport** – emissions from aviation, maritime transport, etc.

In 2003, an Interagency Commission to enhance inter-ministerial co-operation was created. In 2004, it adopted an action plan on the implementation of the Kyoto Protocol, containing provisions on the development of sectoral policies and measures, the regulatory framework for Kyoto mechanisms, the formulation of a negotiation position, and capacity-building, awareness-rising and other such activities. The implementation of the action plan and other activities of the Interagency Commission was curbed after the resignation of its chairman, Mr. Sharonov, from the post of Deputy Minister of Economic Development and Trade. In 2009 the Commission, *de facto,* no longer existed and the action plan has never been implemented. On 16 February 2009 in commemoration of the Kyoto Protocol entry into force, 37 Russian environmental organisations published an open letter calling on the government to establish a new governmental commission on climate change including not only representatives of various ministries and agencies, but also business, academia and non-governmental sectors.

Russia holds the world's largest natural gas reserves and the eighth largest oil reserves, being the world's largest exporter of natural gas, and the second largest oil exporter. Russia's economy is heavily dependent on oil and natural gas exports. Its enormous oil and gas resources slow down the shift to low-carbon and renewable sources of energy because it is not economically feasible.

Other barriers include:

- low level of social and environmental responsibility of business;
- low level of awareness on climate change and clean energy opportunities in regions;
- low potential for broad promotion of renewable energy;
- bureaucratic barriers for active involvement of Russian business in emissions trading;
- poor co-operation between stakeholders – policy-makers, business, academia, mass media, general public – on the issue;
- growing energy consumption due to economic development.

Moreover, government and business, being somewhat obsessed with the potential advantages of JI, should not forget that it is only a supplementary instrument. It is more important to take measures aimed to reduce GHG emissions through the enhancement of energy efficiency, the promotion of renewables, energy-saving programmes, etc.

All the abovementioned barriers are serious but can be overcome. The role of non-governmental organisations here can hardly be overstated. They are the most active players in the field of climate change and clean energy in Russia. Some of them, like the Russian Regional Environmental Centre, Centre for Energy Efficiency (CENEF), Centre for Sustainable Energy Development (CSED), WWF-Russia and Greenpeace-Russia have an extensive project profile and have strong international relationships that enable them to share best experiences and innovative ideas and approaches.

The role of NGOs in promoting climate change countermeasures and sustainable energy principles in Russia lies in:

- the development of an environmentally-aware general public and business in Russia;
- building capacity among Russian stakeholders (business, mass media, local government and the general public) to answer climate and energy challenges and promote inter-sectoral co-operation;

- popularising scientific information and promoting its dissemination;
- encouraging the Russian government, local administration, and business to do more;
- promoting the best low-carbon approaches in Russia, sharing the best international experience and assisting in the development of international co-operation on climate change.

4.2   The bumpy road to ratification of the Kyoto Protocol

The story of the ratification of the Kyoto Protocol by Russia illustrates the barriers climate policy can face in Russia. The entry into force of the Kyoto Protocol depended on the Russian Federation. The reason for this was that Article 25 of the Protocol made its entry into force dependent on ratification by not less than 55 Parties to the UNFCCC, incorporating Annex I Parties accounting for at least 55 per cent of the total carbon dioxide emissions for 1990 of these Annex I Parties. As the USA decided not to ratify, reaching this threshold depended on Russia.

At first, this did not seem to be a problem. In 2001, Russia announced that it would work together with the EU with a view to ensuring an early ratification and entry into force of the Kyoto Protocol.[22] At the Johannesburg World Summit on Sustainable Development in September 2002, Russia's Prime Minister Kasyanov stated that "ratification will occur in the very near future". However, at the same forum, Deputy Minister of Economic Development and Trade, Muhammed Tsikanov, indicated that there was a risk that Russia would not ratify because "we don't have the economic stimulus, the economic interest in the Kyoto Protocol". He did add that, for the moment, the plan in Moscow was still to ratify.[23]

In the autumn of 2003, the World Conference on Climate Change took place in Moscow and examined the issue of climate change and a very wide range of problems linked to it. However, consensus on the benefits to Russia as a result of the ratification of the Kyoto Protocol was not reached. President Putin's opening speech made it clear that Russian ratification was

22. Brussels EU-Russia Summit of 3 October 2001, Joint Statement, http://www.delrus.ec.europa.eu/en/p_238.htm (Accessed: 22 August 2009).
23. Independent news from RussiaJournal.com 31 August 2002, Russia may not ratify Kyoto Protocol, http://content.mail.ru/arch/1139/166572.html&clean=1&print=1 (Accessed: 10 October 2009).

still not imminent.[24] The opponents of Kyoto advanced fierce arguments. Andrei Illarionov, an economic adviser to President Putin, warned, for instance, that "the Kyoto Protocol will stymie economic growth; it will doom Russia to poverty, weakness and backwardness", claiming (incorrectly) that each percentage point of GDP growth is accompanied by a two per cent growth in CO_2 emissions.[25] He also claimed that EU legislation would stand in the way of EU entities buying any emission credits from Russia.[26] Later on, Illarionov even went as far as to compare the Kyoto Protocol regime to Auschwitz.[27]

In all likelihood, the extremely negative stance towards the Kyoto Protocol was part of a strategy to gain concessions from the EU in negotiations on Russia's World Trade Organisation (WTO) accession, as European Commissioner Verheugen explained in a hearing in the German Parliament.[28] At the EU-Russia summit on 21 May 2004, President Putin announced that "[t]he European Union has made some concessions on some points during the negotiations on the WTO. This will inevitably have an impact on our positive attitude to the Kyoto process. We will speed up Russia's movement towards ratifying the Kyoto Protocol". Indeed, President Putin decided in favour of the Protocol in September 2004, along with the Russian cabinet. Subsequently, ratification by the State Duma and Federation Council (lower and upper house of parliament) did not

24. "Russia is being actively called on to ratify the Kyoto Protocol as soon as possible. (...) I want to say that the Government of the Russian Federation is carefully examining and studying this issue. A decision will be made after this work is finished. And, of course, it will be made in accordance with the national interests of the Russian Federation". Opening Address at the International Conference on Climate Change, 29 September 2003, President of Russia, Official web portal, http://eng.kremlin.ru/text/speeches/2003/09/29/0001_type82912type84779_53028.shtml (Accessed: 10 October 2009).

25. See http://www.rusnet.nl/news/2003/10/07/print/commentary_01_5423.shtml.

26. Ebell 2004.

27. "The Kyoto Protocol is a death pact (...) because its main aim is to strangle economic growth and economic activity in countries that accept the protocol's requirements. At first we wanted to call this agreement a kind of international Gosplan, but then we realized Gosplan was much more humane and so we ought to call the Kyoto Protocol an international gulag. In the gulag, though, you got the same ration daily and it didn't get smaller day by day. In the end we had to call the Kyoto Protocol an international Auschwitz." The Moscow Times 2004.

28. Deutscher Bundestag, Protokoll der 40. Sitzung des Ausschusses für die Angelegenheiten der Europäischen Union, 28 January 2004. Verheugen explained: "Indeed there are signs that Russia would like to create a political link between the conclusion of the WTO-accession negotiations and the ratification of the Kyoto Protocol. Russia regards this not so much as a formal, legal link but rather as a political package. It seems to be striving for a lowering of the conditions to a Russian WTO accession by ratification of the Kyoto Protocol."

encounter any obstacles.[29] On 4 November 2004, the Protocol was approved by President Putin, and Russia officially notified the UN of its ratification on 18 November 2004. In Russia itself, the ratification of the Kyoto Protocol was described as a necessity in exchange for the EU's support for Russia's accession to the WTO.[30] 90 days after Russia's ratification, the Kyoto Protocol entered into force on 16 February 2005.

5. Negotiating position of the Russian Federation on a post-2012 regime

Russia recognises that the basis of the future climate regime should be the Bali Action Plan (decision 1/CP.13) and shares a vision of 50 per cent emission reductions of global GHG emissions by 2050 as a goal. Russia has expressed its readiness to consider this goal under the UNFCCC negotiations, recognising that this global challenge can only be met by global efforts, and in particular, by contributions from all major economies, consistent with the principle of common but differentiated responsibilities and respective capabilities. In December 2008, the Head of the Russian delegation, deputy Minister of Natural Resources and the Ecology Stanislav Ananiev, underlined that the specified long-term goal should be aspirational and should not be a starting point for a "top-down" approach in the distribution of GHG emission reduction commitments among countries.

Russia stresses the importance of taking national circumstances into account when considering future emission reduction targets. It usually points to its severe climate conditions, the vastness of its territory, its rapid economic development, and the dependence of the economy on income generated from the production, processing, export and consumption of fossil fuels and associated energy intensive products. The Russian economy is still at a stage of transition and is developing rapidly. Lots of effort, resources and energy are needed to keep the pace. The growing needs are satisfied mainly by renovating old equipment and promoting energy-efficiency, rather than by expanding industrial capacities. However, since the generation capacity is fully utilised, increased demand will be met by

---

29. The Duma voted by 334 in favour of ratification, with 73 against and two abstentions.
30. "Russia forced to ratify Kyoto Protocol to become WTO member", Pravda, 2004-10-26. Retrieved on 2006-11-03. It is misleading to say that "Moscow offered prompt and unambiguous support to the relevant European policies, easily ratifying the Kyoto Protocol" RIA Novosti 2007.

increased coal consumption (30-62 per cent compared to 2008 level) accompanied by investments in nuclear power stations by 2020.[31] This strategy will lead to a further increase in GHG emissions. This could have serious implications on Russia's level of ambition for the post-2012 period and change the role of the country from a seller to a buyer of carbon credits soon after the end of the first commitment period, if the positive trend of economic development continues. However, the data presented above were assessed before the beginning of the global financial crisis in 2008, which most likely will mitigate such high growth rate figures.

A further key point of the Russian position is a request to reconsider the outdated grouping of countries as "Annex I Parties" and "non-Annex I Parties" in the UNFCCC. Parameters, such as GDP per capita and other standard criteria for social and economic differences between countries, should be elaborated for a new regrouping of Parties. Authoritative organisations such as the UN Statistical Commission, the World Bank, etc., could be involved in the development of such criteria. In this context, Russia emphasises the urgency of developing measures to broaden the participation of the developing countries in climate change mitigation. Without their participation and contribution to global climate change mitigation efforts, the post-2012 regime will not be comprehensive and would be ineffective.

Russia puts forward a principle that mid-term Kyoto-style targets should be based on the national initiatives and measures in the sectors, using a bottom-up approach. It considers setting a collective range for the reduction of emissions for a country group as unreasonable, whether they are Annex I Parties or those who are referred to as developed countries.

Russia also believes that a new climate regime should provide for continuity of the efforts of the world community – it is necessary to preserve the 1990 base year for setting the commitments and to assess the implementation of the commitments under the Convention and Kyoto Protocol.

Russia furthermore considers that JI and other flexibility mechanisms are effective means to reduce the costs of mitigation actions, and should continue to be available for countries, but that they are not a panacea for tackling climate change. For instance, the 2008/2009 economic and financial crises show that the global market is not yet a reliable mechanism for addressing the global challenges of mankind.

---

31. Federal Programme 2008.

At the end of June 2009, the President of the Russian Federation Dmitry Medvedev announced the long-awaited national mid-term quantified emission reduction objectives. He declared that Russia pledged to decrease its national GHG emissions by 10-15 per cent by 2020 "based on the current situation". He added that compared with 1990 levels, that means an overall 30 billion tonnes in emission reductions in 30 years. The President explained that "in this way, we would not deprive ourselves of development opportunities, while at the same time making our contribution to the international efforts to fight climate change".[32] The Kremlin's chief economic adviser, Arkady Dvorkovich, clarified later that the reduction target would actually be from 1990 levels, while stressing the need to find "the right balance" between addressing climate change and reaching Russia's goals for economic growth.

This commitment is not as high as the international community has expected of Russia. Indeed, considering that by 2006, Russia was some 34 per cent below the 1990 levels (see section 3.2 above), a 10-15 per cent reduction by 2020 compared to 1990 would actually mean that Russian emissions could rise considerably – by some 0.8 billion tonnes. This increase would be much more than economic growth could account for. In other words, Russia's economy could grow and become less energy efficient.

On the positive side, President Medvedev's declaration was a step forward compared to earlier statements by Russian officials insisting that they would not take on any post-2012 mandatory emission cuts for fear of hindering the country's economic development. Moreover, the negotiations leading to Copenhagen in December 2009 may encourage Russia to take more ambitious targets depending on other countries' decisions.

Russia supported the G8 leaders declaration on the 80 per cent GHG emission reduction target by 2050 for the developed nations (L'Aquila, Italy, July 2009) and stressed its readiness to contribute to achieving this goal by halving its national emissions by mid-century.

In conclusion, Russia's position in the post-2012 negotiations might significantly depend on the eagerness of other major emitters to take comparable efforts, the broader participation of countries, including the US and key developing economies, the carbon-market demand-supply situation, the prospects for economic development in Russia and the establishment of a new comprehensive agreement based on the proposed

---

32. See http://www.kremlin.ru/eng/text/speeches/2009/06/18/1241_type82916_218210 .shtml (Accessed: 11 August 2009).

new differentiation of countries. Although the recent Russian concerns are better founded than some of those brought forward when the ratification of the Kyoto Protocol was debated, meeting them will certainly not be easy. In the absence of leverage such as WTO accession, or of a well-informed Russian public, ensuring that Russia joins in a new global climate change agreement remains a major challenge.

References

Anisimov, Oleg and Svetlana Reneva. 2006. Permafrost and Changing Climate: The Russian Perspective. *Ambio* 35(4): 169-175.

Chiavari, Joana and Marc Pallemaerts. 2008. European Parliament Note. *Energy and Climate Change in Russia 2008*. 3-7. Brussels: DG Internal Policies.

Dobrolyubova, Julia and B. Zhukov. 2008. *Ten Popular Misconceptions about Climate Change and the Kyoto Protocol*. Moscow: Russian Regional Environmental Centre.

Dobrolyubova, Julia et al. 2009. Melting Beauty. *Impacts of Climate Change*. Moscow: Russian Regional Environmental Centre.

Douma, Wybe Th. and Daria Ratsiborinskaya. 2007. The Russian Federation and the Kyoto Protocol. In *The Kyoto Protocol and Beyond. Legal and Policy Challenges of Climate Change*, edited by Wybe Th. Douma, Leonardo Massai and Massimiliano Montini, 135-145. The Hague: T.M.C. Asser Press.

Ebell, Myron. 2004. Illarionov Explains Russian Position on Kyoto Protocol in Washington. Competitive Enterprise Institute. http://cei.org/gencon/014,03867.cfm. Accessed: 12 August 2009.

Federal Programme. 2008. Federal Programme of Socio-economic Development of Russia by 2020. Adopted by the Russian Government in October 2008.

Götz, Roland. 2007. Russia and Global Warming – Implications for the Energy Industry. *Russian Analytical Digest* 23(7): 11-13.

Izeman Mark and Edith Pike-Biegunska. 2009. Time to Get Serious About Saving Energy. *The Moscow Times*. 17 February 2009. http://www.themoscowtimes.com/article/1020/42/374611.htm. Accessed: 12 August 2009.

Ketting, Jeroen. 2008. Focus on Russia. Moscow Turns a Cold Shoulder to Kyoto. *European Energy Review* January/February 2008: 108-111.

Kokorin, Alexey O. and Inna G. Gritsevich. 2007. The Danger of Climate Change for Russia – Expected Losses and Recommendations. *Russian Analytical Digest* 23(7): 2-4.

Korpoo, Anna and Arild Moe. 2007. Russian Climate Politics: Light at the End of the Tunnel. Climate Strategies, briefing paper, April 2007.

Kaspar, Oldag. 2008. Russia Dragging Its Feet on Kyoto. *The Moscow Times.* 26 November 2008.

Ministry of Economic Development of the Russian Federation. 2007. Order of 30 November 2007 No. 422 "On Approval of Limits for Greenhouse Gas Emission Reductions".

Ministry of Energy of the Russian Federation. 2008. Presentation made at the "Business Forum on Energy Efficient Technologies". Rostov-on-Don. 15 February 2008.

Perelet, Renat, Serguey Pegov and Mikhail Yulkin. 2007. Climate Change: Russia Country Paper. UNDP Occasional Paper 2007/12. http://hdr.undp.org/en/reports/global/hdr2007-2008/papers/Perelet_Renat_Pegov_Yulkin.pdf. Accessed: 20 October 2009.

RIA Novosti. 2007. G8 Summit Promises Nothing Sensational. *RIA Novosti* 3 June 2007.

Roshydromet (Federal Service for Hydrometeorology and Environmental Monitoring). 2006a. *Strategic Prediction for the Period of up to 2010-2015 of Climate Change Expected in Russia and its Impact on Sectors of the Russian Economy.* Moscow: Roshydromet.

Roshydromet (Federal Service for Hydrometeorology and Environmental Monitoring). 2006b. *Fourth National Report of the Russian Federation on the Implementation of the UNFCCC and the Kyoto Protocol.* Moscow: Roshydromet.

Roshydromet (Federal Service for Hydrometeorology and Environmental Monitoring). 2007. *Report on Climate Characteristics in Russia in 2006.* Moscow: Roshydromet.

Roshydromet (Federal Service for Hydrometeorology and Environmental Monitoring). 2008. *Assessment Report on Climate Change and Its Consequences in the Russian Federation.* Moscow: Roshydromet.

Russian Federation. 2008. National Inventory Report of Russia 1990-2006, Moscow. http://unfccc.int/national_reports/initial_reports_under_the_kyoto_protocol/items/3765.php. Accessed: 3 September 2009.

Statement of S. Ananiev (Deputy Minister of Natural Resources and Ecology of Russia, Head of the Russian Delegation) at COP-14 High-level Segment. 2008. Poznan: COP-14.

Tushinskaya, G. and Julia Dobrolyubova. 2008. *Guidelines on the Implementation of Business-Projects in the Field of Energy Efficiency through Kyoto Mechanisms.* Moscow: Russian Regional Environmental Centre.

The Moscow Times. 2004. Illarionov Likens Kyoto to Auschwitz. The Moscow Times, 15 April 2004. http://www.moscowtimes.ru/article/852/49/231596.htm. Accessed: 12 August 2009.

US National Oceanic and Atmospheric Administration. 2006. National Geophysical Data Center (NGDC) Provides Global Estimate of 2004 Gas Flaring Volume, December 2006 News. http://www.ngdc.noaa.gov/nndc/struts/results?eq_0=2006/12&op_3=eq&v_3=N&t=102750&s=3&d=10,6,11. Accessed: 19 October 2009.

Yulkin, Mikhail. 2009. Involving Russian Business in Kyoto. In *Environmentally and Socially Responsible Investment in Russia*, edited by Fiona Mucklow and Wybe Th. Douma. The Hague, 2009 (forthcoming).

Public Perceptions of Climate Change and Energy Issues in the EU and the United States

Camilla Adelle and Sirini Withana[1]

1. Introduction

Government responses to climate change on both sides of the Atlantic have been very different. The European Union (EU) and its Member States have been strong political supporters and promoters of the Kyoto Protocol and the EU is keen to depict itself as the world's leader in climate policy. On the other hand, the United States (US) is historically the world's largest emitter of greenhouse gases (GHG). While the Obama administration appears to be taking US climate policy in a more positive direction, the previous Bush administration did not submit the Kyoto Protocol to the Senate for ratification, a necessary step for the Protocol to be legally binding in the US. "Differences in public opinion are often used to explain, if not justify, differences at the governmental level"[2] and public policy decisions that do not take into account public opinions will inevitably prove problematic. Climate policies require a certain degree of "buy-in" or public acceptance in order to be successfully implemented and should be in line with public perceptions of the risk of climate change in order to be supported by the electorate.[3]

Consequently, public perceptions of environmental issues in general and climate change in particular have long been of interest to researchers and policy makers. In the EU, for example, Eurobarometer (a regular public opinion survey conducted across the EU on behalf of the European Commission) has published a number of surveys of citizens' views in this area since 1992. These include several surveys covering EU perceptions of environmental issues in general as well as more recent surveys of perceptions of climate change in particular. In the US, several

---

1. This chapter builds on research undertaken in the context of a project co-funded by the European Commission (Directorate General for External Relations) through the European Community's 2006 budget line 19.050200 "Transatlantic Dialogue at Non-Governmental Level".
2. Reiner et al. 2006, 2093.
3. Lorenzoni and Pidgeon 2006.

polls, amongst which the Gallup Poll, Harris Poll, and Pew Surveys, include questions related to the environment and global warming. In addition, numerous academic studies, public consultations and consultants' reports on both sides of the Atlantic have explored public perceptions of specific climate change mitigation technologies, such as bioenergy and carbon capture and storage (CCS),[4] and compared changes in public opinion over time. It is therefore possible, and potentially illuminating, to consider whether the different approaches being taken by the US and EU in their climate and energy policies reflect a broader difference in public perceptions of climate change and energy issues.

This chapter examines the perceptions of the EU and US public towards climate change and explores how they vary across time and space within each of these jurisdictions. First, the public perceptions of citizens across the EU Member States and in the US will be explored, respectively. In both cases, the levels of concern about and understanding of climate change will be examined, followed by consideration of public opinions on climate technologies, and where available on policy options for tackling climate change. In Section 4, the implications of these perceptions in the EU and US for climate policy will be discussed in general and in light of the different policy approaches taken in these two jurisdictions. The chapter ends with a brief conclusion.

Before proceeding, however, it is important to note the limitations of survey data and the difficulty in directly comparing different surveys, given their varying approaches to questioning, articulation of questions, timeframes and geographic scope. In addition linking public opinion and perceptions with specific policy developments is fraught with difficulty. Despite these limitations, the analysis of a number of different public surveys allows us to identify certain trends in public perceptions over time and make some tentative conclusions and comparisons.

2. EU public perceptions

In recent years climate change has received increased media coverage and risen dramatically up the political agenda in Europe. This has been reflected in both an increasing concern for climate change in public attitudes as well as the adoption of new climate policies – most notably

---

4. See the chapter by Chiavari in this volume.

the climate and energy package agreed in December 2008.[5] The EU now has a series of tough climate and energy targets to meet by 2020, which will involve a number of implementing measures in all 27 Member States.

2.1 Public concern for climate change

Climate change is a major concern for EU citizens. In a Eurobarometer survey conducted at the end of 2007 on perceptions of environmental issues in general, climate change was the top environmental concern of European citizens.[6] Of the top three environmental issues Europeans were most concerned about, climate change was identified by 57 per cent of respondents, water pollution by 42 per cent and air pollution by 40 per cent. In a similar survey in 2004 climate change was identified by only 45 per cent of the respondents as a top environmental issue and of less concern than water pollution and man-made disasters.[7] In particular, the survey showed that the level of concern about climate change is highest in the southern Member States with people in Spain, Cyprus, Malta and Greece the most worried.[8]

In contrast, concern for climate change in relation to other social and economic issues appears to have decreased recently. In a Eurobarometer survey conducted in the spring of 2009 which focused entirely on perceptions of climate change issues, 50 per cent of the respondents said that climate change was a major challenge, down from 62 per cent one year before. The survey suggests that this sharp decline is comparable to the sharp rise recorded – from 24 per cent to 52 per cent – in concern for the global economic recession. Furthermore, concern for climate change in both the 2008 and 2009 surveys came below that for world poverty (Figure 1).

5. See the other relevant contributions to this volume.
6. Commission 2008.
7. Commission 2004.
8. A more recent survey showed that people in Sweden also demonstrate a high level of concern about climate change (Commission 2009).

Figure 1 – EU public perceptions of serious problems facing the world in 2009

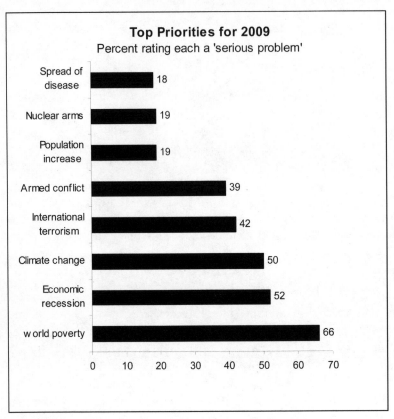

Note: Responses to the question "What, in your opinion, are the most serious problems facing the world today?"

Source: Commission 2009.

2.2 Public understanding of climate change

The 2009 Eurobarometer survey indicated that more than half of European citizens feel very well or fairly well informed about different aspects of climate change. 56 per cent of respondents confirmed that they were well informed about both the causes and consequences of climate change, whereas slightly less (52 per cent) reported that they felt very well or fairly well informed about the ways of fighting it.[9] However, for all three aspects of climate change (i.e. the causes, consequences and ways of fighting

9.   Commission 2009.

climate change), more than a third of respondents did not feel well informed or felt not at all informed. Just less than one in ten respondents confirmed that they are not at all informed. Citizens in Bulgaria, Romania, and Portugal felt the least well informed about the causes, consequences and ways of fighting climate change. In addition, 62 per cent of respondents claimed that they understood that there were economic benefits to be derived from combating climate change.

When this level of understanding of climate change was tested more explicitly, the majority of Europeans (58 per cent) linked the impact of CO_2 emissions and climate change. However 30 per cent of those surveyed thought that CO_2 emissions only have a marginal impact on climate change and 12 per cent confirmed they did not know what the link was.[10] Similarly, another Eurobarometer survey, published in 2007, focused on investigating attitudes to nuclear energy, found that "not all Europeans are well-aware of the low level of greenhouse gas emissions of nuclear energy compared to many other energy sources, such as oil and coal".[11]

2.3   Public opinions of climate technologies

Understanding and knowledge of energy technologies appears to be less developed and widespread. For example, a Eurobarometer survey published in 2007 focusing on energy technologies found that, while at first glance Europeans appeared to be quite familiar with new energy technologies such as nuclear energy, clean coal and hydrogen energy, one fifth of EU citizens (19 per cent) admitted that they had not heard of any of these technologies. Only 21 per cent of respondents had heard of carbon capture and storage (CCS). Citizens in northern Europe tended to be more familiar with these technologies than their fellow citizens in southern Europe and in the new Member States.[12]

Awareness of bioenergy has been found to be very low at, for example, two per cent in Ireland and eight per cent in the Netherlands.[13] In this context, a general lack of understanding of renewable energy technologies correlates to a low level of acceptance of some of these technologies. A study in the UK found that, while 85 per cent of respondents wanted to increase renewables, only 16 per cent supported biomass, nearly five per cent opposed the use of biomass, and the vast majority of respondents did

10.   Commission 2009.
11.   Commission 2007b, 5.
12.   Commission 2007a.
13.   Thornely and Prins 2008.

not know about it. Therefore, while the public accepts the need for renewables, they often do not accept the need to build the necessary facilities locally. However, the situation in some Member States is more encouraging. Bioenergy (mainly from biomass) is well established in Sweden where negative public perception is not an issue due to the longstanding use of waste from the paper and pulp industry to produce energy. In addition, biofuels, rather than biomass, may be gaining in popularity and awareness among the public. The 2009 Eurobarometer survey found that acceptance of biofuels has increased since the last survey in 2008 with 75 per cent of Europeans considering that the use of alternative fuels, such as biofuels, should be harnessed to reduce GHG emissions.[14] This result may reflect the considerable attention devoted to biofuels in the media throughout 2008-2009. However the debate about sustainability criteria across the EU may begin to temper this enthusiasm.

The relatively limited knowledge among the EU public of CCS (as discussed above) is reported to be associated with a somewhat sceptical opinion of the technology.[15] However, it appears that once (even limited) information is provided on the role of CCS in reducing CO_2 emissions, opinion tends to shift towards slight support for the concept. This is particularly true if CCS is seen as part of a wider CO_2 emission reduction strategy or as fulfilling a temporary/bridging role until long-term alternatives are developed. As a stand-alone option, there is evidence that the public feels that CCS might delay more far-reaching and necessary long-term changes in society's use of energy.[16]

While some renewable technologies are supported in abstract terms, their deployment at the local level can still be rejected. A majority of 71 per cent were in favour of wind technology in the Eurobarometer survey of energy technologies in 2007, including 63 per cent of UK respondents.[17] However, a study for the UK Government found that about one fifth of the British public was against wind farms in its local area, mainly on aesthetic grounds, while only 28 per cent strongly approved it.[18] This opposition has in general led to problems with local planning procedures in the UK and to the government considering expensive plans to site large-scale wind farms offshore. This negative perception of wind turbines is not, however, the case in all Member States. For instance, Germany and Portugal have

14. Commission 2009.
15. Shackley et al. 2004.
16. Shackley et al. 2004; ICF International 2007.
17. Commission 2007a.
18. TNS Plc. 2003.

numerous wind turbines situated on land and even close to recognised areas of natural beauty. There is some evidence in the UK that wind farms can receive a more positive consideration in remote areas where they offer direct local benefits such as jobs, and also after respondents have actually seen a wind farm.[19]

By comparison to other low-carbon technologies, the levels of support for nuclear power have been relatively low in many Member States such as Germany and the UK, which have been phasing out nuclear power stations or at least have not built new ones for some years. An opinion poll in the UK conducted by Ipsos MORI, however, shows a significant increase in support for nuclear power stations in the UK in recent years. In 2001, only 20 per cent of the UK population supported the building of new nuclear power stations to replace those being phased out compared to around 60 per cent who were opposed to it; by mid 2007 this had changed to 35 per cent in support and 29 per cent in opposition.[20] The apparent redemption of nuclear power in the minds of some UK citizens may be due to links being made between nuclear energy and climate change mitigation in recent UK political discussions and media coverage. A study by Poortinga et al. demonstrates that people interpret nuclear energy in a rather more ambivalent or even positive way when it is positioned alongside climate change. However, few of their participants actively and wholeheartedly supported climate change mitigation through building new nuclear power plants as an acceptable policy position.[21]

In contrast, a more positive attitude towards nuclear power is apparent in France where its use is more widespread. A 2001 Ipsos poll found that 70 per cent of the French population had a "good opinion" of nuclear energy in France and 63 per cent wanted their country to remain a nuclear leader.[22] In general, however, EU attitudes to nuclear power are still fairly negative. Eurobarometer found in 2007 that only 20 per cent of the public were supportive of nuclear power compared to 37 per cent that opposed it.[23]

19. TNS Plc. 2003.
20. Ipsos MORI 2007. However, McGowan and Sauter (2005) indicate in their review of public opinion surveys in the UK that opinion on future nuclear construction varied considerably according to different polls and surveys.
21. Poortinga et al. 2006.
22. Embassy of France in the US 2001.
23. Commission 2007b.

2.4 Public opinions of climate policy

The European public is highly supportive of EU leadership to help tackle environmental issues but the picture is more ambiguous in terms of their own individual role. The Eurobarometer survey published in 2008 focusing on environmental perceptions in general showed that while 86 per cent of EU citizens saw themselves as having a role to play in protecting the environment as individuals, their green attitudes did not always translate into concrete actions.[24] On average the survey revealed that a European citizen had done only 2.6 things for environmental reasons in the past month. A large number (59 per cent) had separated their waste, followed by nearly half (47 per cent) who indicated that they had cut down their energy consumption and over a third (37 per cent) who had cut down their water consumption. The 2009 Eurobarometer survey focusing on perceptions of climate change issues indicated similar figures with 59 per cent of respondents stating that they had taken some kind of action on climate change. However, 34 per cent of respondents stated that they had not.[25]

In addition, it should be noted that all of the positive environmental choices described in the 2008 survey discussed above were considered to be linked to the citizens' everyday life and somewhat "passive".[26] More "active" choices directly linked to environmental concerns were more unusual. For example, while 75 per cent of respondents said that they were ready to buy environmentally friendly products even if they were more expensive, only 17 per cent had actively done so in the last month.

The 2008 Eurobarometer survey revealed that EU citizens felt that the best way to tackle climate change and energy-related issues was at the EU level.[27] Two-thirds (67 per cent) of European citizens preferred environmental decisions to be jointly made within the EU. Environmental policy actions at the EU level were widely encouraged in every country, 82 per cent of respondents agreed that European environmental legislation was necessary and 80 per cent believed that the EU should assist non-EU countries to improve their environmental standards.

Furthermore, the European Commission claimed that the survey also showed that Europeans do not see environmental legislation as a threat to the EU's competitiveness. Nearly two thirds of Europeans surveyed felt that protecting the environment was more of an incentive to

24. Commission 2008.
25. Commission 2009.
26. Commission 2008.
27. Commission 2008.

innovate (63 per cent) than an obstacle to economic performance (16 per cent). In addition, two thirds (64 per cent) of respondents felt that protecting the environment should be given priority over economic competitiveness. Indeed, 78 per cent of respondents would have accepted increased EU funding for environmental protection even if it came at the expense of other areas. However, *which* other policy areas should be subordinate to environmental protection was not specified.[28] Other studies have found that the importance of climate change was in fact secondary in relation to other personal and social issues such as health, family, safety and finances.[29] Therefore, it is possible that the responses to Eurobarometer's question would have been different if the question had been phrased differently or if concrete choices had had to be made by individuals.

3. US public perceptions

The American public has become increasingly aware of the threat of global warming as a consequence of extreme weather patterns experienced in the 2000s as well as more frequent media coverage. Despite some scepticism, most Americans now believe that global warming is a serious problem. However, it continues to rank low on the public's list of policy priorities, with other issues such as the economy, jobs and terrorism perceived to be of relatively higher national importance. Under the Bush administration, action at the federal level lagged behind and frustrated international efforts to tackle climate change and there appears to have been general public dissatisfaction with the government's approach at the time. Environmental issues were afforded significant attention during the 2008 presidential campaign and raised high public expectations that President Obama would do a good job in protecting the environment.

3.1 Public concern for climate change

There has been a significant increase in public concern about global warming in the US in the 2000s. A comparison of the results of two surveys, carried out in 2003 and 2006, indicated that the percentage of the American public that ranked global warming as the top environmental priority tripled between 2003 and 2006.[30] A New York Times/CBS News

---

28. Commission 2008.
29. Lorenzoni and Pidgeon 2006.
30. MIT LFEE 2007.

Poll, conducted in April 2007, indicated that over 90 per cent of the 1052 people surveyed considered global warming to be a serious or very serious problem and 78 per cent maintained that action to counter the effects should be taken immediately.[31] These results were reflected in another poll undertaken in the same time period by the Washington Post, ABC News and Stanford University which revealed that of a nationwide sample of 1002 adults, 33 per cent considered global warming/greenhouse effect/ climate change to be the single biggest environmental problem being faced by the world; this is double the number who ranked it as the top environmental problem in the same poll carried out in 2006.[32] However, concern for global warming appears to have decreased slightly in 2009, with results of the 2009 Gallup Environment Survey showing that of eight environmental issues, public concern for global warming ranked last and moreover has dropped in the past year.[33]

Despite growing recognition of the problem of global warming over the years, the US public does not consider it a major national priority. A 2006 survey sponsored by MIT indicated that the main concerns of the American public were the economy, terrorism, foreign policy and health care.[34] Comparing these results to a similar survey carried out in 2003 revealed that concern about the environment grew slightly but continued to rank in the middle range of all national issues listed.[35] In contrast to environmental issues, the US public tends to rank energy security as an issue of relatively high national importance. A survey by the Pew Research Centre in February 2008 indicated that the majority (54 per cent) of those surveyed considered developing new sources of energy to be a more important priority for the country than protecting the environment.[36]

In 2008/2009, there was an overwhelming focus on domestic policy issues, in particular on strengthening the economy and improving the job situation. The 2009 Gallup poll showed that for the first time in 25 years, Americans put economic growth ahead of environmental protection. A Pew survey of top priorities for 2009 revealed that support for protecting the environment fell significantly during the economic crisis with just 41 per cent rating it as

31. New York Times 2007.
32. Washington Post 2007.
33. The seven environmental issues that the public expressed more concern for were: pollution of drinking water, water pollution, toxic contamination of soil/water, supply of fresh water for households, air pollution, loss of rain forests, and the extinction of plants and animals. Gallup 2009b.
34. MIT LFEE 2007.
35. MIT LFEE 2007.
36. Pew Research Centre 2008.

a top priority, down from 56 per cent a year ago; global warming fell to the bottom of the list of 20 policy priorities for 2009. Furthermore, it is interesting to note that the American public's concern for issues related to energy security has remained relatively high with 60 per cent of those surveyed highlighting energy problems as a priority for 2009 (see Figure 2).

Figure 2 – Ranking by US public of top priorities for the President and Congress in 2009

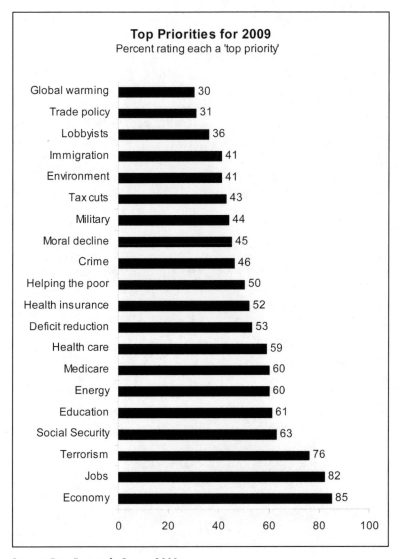

Source: Pew Research Centre 2009a.

3.2   Public understanding of climate change

The American public is often perceived to be relatively sceptical of the science behind climate change. A 2007 Washington Post poll revealed that 56 per cent of the sample believed that there is still a lot of disagreement among scientists on the issue of whether or not global warming is happening. This public doubt over the scientific consensus behind global warming, which in general terms has been declining, is contrasted by growing evidence of the effects of climate change.[37] A 2007 New York Times poll found that 75 per cent of those surveyed recognised that weather patterns over the past few years have been "stranger than usual". Of this group 43 per cent recognised that this peculiarity was due to global warming, with only 11 per cent saying it was part of the natural cycle. Furthermore, 41 per cent of those surveyed felt that the rise in world temperatures is being caused "mostly by things people do". Regarding their knowledge of global warming, 51 per cent of the sample felt they knew a "moderate" amount about the issue, with 37 per cent admitting they knew little/nothing about it.[38] A 2009 Gallup poll indicated that 44 per cent of those surveyed believed that the seriousness of global warming was exaggerated in the news; this is the highest degree of public scepticism of mainstream reporting on global warming in more than 10 years of Gallup surveys on this issue.[39]

A 2007 New York Times poll found that 89 per cent of the sample had heard or read of the term global warming (42 per cent had heard a lot and 47 per cent had heard something about it). 21 per cent of the sample agreed that GHG emissions are the most important factor causing global warming, while 62 per cent thought GHG emissions were one among many factors.[40] In analysing public understanding and knowledge of CO_2 sources and sinks, two MIT surveys provided a list of technologies and natural resources and asked about the CO_2 emissions/reductions of each. In both 2003 and 2006, the public seemed to understand that automobiles, coal burning power plants and factories were significant sources of CO_2, while they were unsure of the impacts of nuclear power plants and oceans.[41] Thus, while the problem of global warming is increasingly recognised, understanding of the underlying carbon cycle and detailed knowledge of global warming appear to be limited.

37. Washington Post 2007.
38. New York Times 2007.
39. Gallup 2009a.
40. New York Times 2007.
41. MIT LFEE 2007.

3.3   Public opinions of climate technologies

Two MIT surveys attempted to analyse changes in the public's awareness of the technologies available to address global warming from 2003 to 2006 and included questions on whether or not participants had heard or read about certain environmental and energy technologies. The majority of those surveyed in both 2003 and 2006 had at least heard of hybrid/efficient cars, renewable energy technologies and more efficient appliances. However, hardly any had heard of CCS or carbon sequestration, and very few had heard of bioenergy/biomass. The results of the survey also indicated that respondents were unclear of the environmental problem CCS aimed to address.[42] These perceptions may have changed in recent years following increased media coverage and political attention to CCS and bioenergy.

A 2007 New York Times poll revealed that 48 per cent of those surveyed considered using coal to generate electricity "mostly a bad idea" compared to 43 per cent that considered it to be "mostly a good idea". 87 per cent of the sample considered using renewable energy sources to generate electricity "mostly a good idea" while only 9 per cent agreed with the statement that renewable energy sources are costly and unreliable and considered their use to be "mostly a bad idea". 70 per cent supported the use of ethanol as a substitute for foreign oil and 58 per cent of the sample thought the use of nuclear power to generate electricity was a "bad idea" given the associated risk and the issue of waste disposal.[43] The survey also revealed that the American public remains divided over the issue of nuclear power, with 44 per cent favouring government policies that supported nuclear power and 48 per cent against it. 57 per cent of those surveyed also supported increased federal funding for ethanol research, a fall of 10 per cent from 2006. The 2008 Pew survey indicated that when asked about energy policy priorities, 55 per cent of those surveyed favoured more conservation and regulation of energy, compared to 35 per cent that supported expanded energy exploration.[44]

3.4   Public opinions of climate policy

US public support for action to address climate change has increased, as revealed by the 2006 MIT survey in which the majority of those surveyed

---

42.   MIT LFEE 2007.
43.   New York Times 2007.
44.   Pew Research Centre 2008.

felt that the scientific evidence available warrants action, representing a significant increase in support since 2003.[45] The 2007 New York Times poll revealed that 63 per cent of those polled agreed with the statement that "protecting the environment is so important that requirements and standards cannot be too high and continuing environmental improvements must be made regardless of costs". However, only 6 per cent of the sample had purchased a hybrid/fuel-efficient car, 18 per cent had purchased environmentally friendly household products, and 45 per cent had done nothing. While the vast majority (92 per cent) supported requirements for car manufacturers to produce more energy efficient cars; 58 per cent were opposed to the introduction of a federal tax on gasoline to reduce energy consumption. Interestingly, 64 per cent supported a federal tax on gasoline for the purposes of reducing US dependence on foreign oil. A 2009 Pew survey revealed that 59 per cent of the public favoured setting limits on CO_2 emissions and making companies pay for their emissions even if this would result in higher energy prices,[46] while a 2009 Washington Post/ABC News poll revealed that three quarters of those surveyed supported government regulation of GHG emissions with 52 per cent supporting a cap and trade approach and 42 per cent opposed to such an approach.[47] These results are interesting in light of the American Clean Energy and Security Act 2009 (also known as the Waxman-Markey bill), under consideration by the US Congress (at the time of writing), the centrepiece of which is the establishment of a national cap and trade system. The results of these surveys indicate an increasing willingness among the American public to make lifestyle changes in certain areas, i.e. reducing energy/water consumption, while there is greater reluctance to take on "costly" measures in other areas, such as reducing personal car use.

The US public showed significant dissatisfaction with the way the last Bush administration handled the issue of climate change. According to an analysis of over forty public opinion surveys from 1989-2002, the majority of the US public supported the participation of the US in the Kyoto Protocol and disapproved of the administration's withdrawal from the process in 2001. Comparing US public perceptions with the opinions of US leaders, it also indicated that, while almost half of the public surveyed considered global warming to be a significant threat to the interests of the US in the next ten years, less than a third of US leaders surveyed felt the same way.[48] This significant gap between perceptions of US leaders and the

---

45.   MIT LFEE 2007.
46.   Pew Research Centre 2009b.
47.   Washington Post 2009.
48.   Brewer 2003.

public is evident in the public's dissatisfaction with the approach of the Bush administration. In contrast, a 2009 Gallup poll revealed that the public has high expectations of the Obama administration with 79 per cent of those surveyed believing that President Obama will do a good job in protecting the nation's environment.[49]

The divergence in opinion between the American public and its perceptions of the risk of global warming and the perceptions and actions (or lack thereof) of US leaders appears to be narrowing under the new administration. The American public has very high expectations of the Obama administration, including its ability to address environmental concerns. However, President Obama's ability to meet these expectations could be hampered by a shift in the attitude of Americans away from the environment and towards the economy given the current economic context. The government may, however, still feel encouraged to show leadership for steering society towards long-term solutions to environmental problems. In a 2009 Washington Post-ABC News poll, 59 per cent of those surveyed thought the US should take action on global warming regardless of whether other industrial countries, such as China and India, take similar steps,[50] thus providing positive impetus for US efforts in ongoing international climate change negotiations.

4.   Discussion

The previous sections presented the results of several surveys of EU and US public perceptions on climate change. In this section we attempt to identify possible policy implications of these perceptions.

4.1   Relating public perceptions to policy development

The public's perception of climate change can have two implications for policy: first, it can determine whether the public alters their own lifestyle to reduce their individual contribution to GHG emissions; second, it can affect whether the public supports government initiatives to mitigate and adapt to climate change.[51]

---

49. Gallup 2009a.
50. Washington Post 2009.
51. Bord et al. 1998.

There have been numerous studies loosely focusing on the first point exploring public perceptions in relation to personal behaviour.[52] Understanding the links between public attitudes and public behaviour is not only important for achieving significant cuts in GHG emissions directly, but also indirectly for the success, or otherwise, of government initiatives intended to alter individual behaviour through "soft" policy instruments such as information campaigns etc. (in contrast to "harder" policy instruments such as legislation or taxes).[53] Whitmarsh, for example, showed that there is a clear divergence between actions prescribed by policy makers (e.g. energy conservation) and those taken by the public to mitigate climate change. She also found that those people that do take action (e.g. to conserve energy) do so for reasons unconnected to the environment (e.g. to save money).[54] Many of these types of studies focus on why concerns about climate change and the environment as well as good environmental intentions do not necessarily result in improved environmental behaviour. This behaviour is evident in the results of the surveys analysed in this chapter. For example, the results of Eurobarometer surveys show that while the majority of EU citizens saw themselves as having a role to play in protecting the environment, their green attitudes did not always translate into concrete actions. Similarly results of surveys in the US reveal reluctance among the public to make "costly" changes to their personal lifestyles despite an increased recognition of the problem of climate change.

In this section, however, we will focus on the second point relating to public opinion and support, or otherwise, for policy solutions at a government level. According to Bord et al. "policy makers need to know what the public wants, in order to design policies that will be supported or at least tolerated".[55] In addition, policy makers need to know to what extent these opinions vary across regions.[56] What then are the possible policy implications of the perceptions of the EU and US citizens presented in this chapter?

Before addressing this question, it is first worth discussing some possible limitations to this approach. Leiserowitz points out that very little data has been collected on global public support or opposition to local, national or international policies to mitigate climate change.[57] This is despite the fact

---

52. See e.g. Whitmarsh 2008; Norton and Leaman 2004; Poortinga and Pidgeon 2003; Lorenzoni et al. 2007.
53. Nilsson et al. 2004.
54. Whitmarsh 2008.
55. Bord et al. 1998, 75.
56. Bord et al. 1998.
57. Leiserowitz 2007.

that these policies will have a profound impact on the level of GHGs in the atmosphere and the extent of climate change, and they will also have significant economic and social impacts. Perhaps this lack of research on public opinion on policy responses is not unsurprising since the science of climate change is complex and the range of policy instruments and the pros and cons of their application are not particularly transparent. However, it is possible to gain insights into the opinions of the public on some general policy options through questions on: willingness to pay for renewable energy, fuel efficient cars etc.; opinions on renewable energy options; attitudes to increasing taxes on fuel, and so on. Many of the studies reported in this chapter have at least touched on some policy-relevant areas of questioning. In addition, understanding of and concern for climate change issues are by themselves illuminating as they are a prerequisite to supporting climate policy, especially if it is costly to individuals and society.

Linking attitudes to specific policy choices, however, is tricky and we are not aware of specific research that has traced the extent of the influence of public support on eventual choices of particular items of climate policy – although such research has been suggested.[58] There is, however, evidence from other public policy fields that public perceptions can influence policy developments. For example, in the field of immigration policy, Facchini and Mayda argue that strict immigration policies, which restrict the flow of labour around the world despite the recent increase of flows of trade and capital globally, reflect the high level of public opposition to immigration in destination countries. They also argue that policy would be even more restrictive if it were not for the action of organised interest groups.[59] However, other authors warn that politicians have to be politically savvy when considering public opinion because when confronted with economic or social costs, the public may lose interest and cease pressuring the government to make policy reforms.[60] Taylor-Gooby et al. argue that politicians at times do not believe that the public will always put "their vote where their mouth is" when there is a significant cost involved in their professed policy preferences. It is therefore not always easy to design a system that politicians regard as electorally feasible and radical enough to also address the policy issue at hand.[61]

58. See Lorenzoni and Pidgeon 2006.
59. Facchini and Mayda 2008.
60. Hunt 2006.
61. Taylor-Gooby et al. 2003.

Another limitation of attempting to link public opinions to policy solutions is that surveys often overstate the levels of concern from respondents.[62] This is a perpetual problem when interpreting surveys on certain topics such as the environment, which can lead to "socially desirable" responses.[63] Few people, in the EU or US, are likely to admit a lack of concern for environmental degradation, because this is "akin to being ignorant and uncaring".[64] In addition, the structure of most environmental surveys reinforces the perception that the environment is a serious issue and demands concern from any respectable citizen. For example, surveys seldom put environmental concerns in the comparative context of other social and personal problems. When they do, for example the recent Eurobarometer survey on EU perceptions of climate change and the Pew survey on top US priorities in 2009,[65] environmental issues that are professed to be of significant concern slip below many other socially and economically salient issues.

Finally, while comparing the public perceptions of environmental issues and climate change on either side of the Atlantic is tempting, it is also fraught with difficulties. Not only do the survey approaches, articulation of questions and time frames vary between studies, but there are also significant differences in geographical scope. Although perceptions vary across the States in the US, studies discussed in this chapter mainly refer to the US population as a whole. In contrast, only Eurobarometer studies conducted on behalf of the European Commission have so far given a picture of public perceptions across all EU Member States. From these studies, it is clear that public opinion and understanding of environmental issues varies significantly between different EU Member States. Many of the other studies conducted in the EU focus on only one Member State. It is therefore difficult, though not impossible, to make generalisations on an EU public position with which to contrast that of the US. While these shortcomings should be borne in mind when interpreting survey results, they do not preclude their usefulness entirely. Therefore, despite these difficulties, a few obvious points of comparison do appear from the surveys discussed in this paper.

62. Sterngold et al. 1994 in Bord et al. 1998.
63. Kidder and Campbell 1970 in Bord et al. 1998.
64. Bord et al. 1998, 76.
65. Commission 2009; Pew Research Centre 2009a.

4.2 Relating differences of EU and US public opinion and climate policy

The overall impression from the survey results of EU and US citizens presented in this chapter is that there are more similarities between public perceptions of climate change than one might expect considering the difference in government responses. This finding supports that of Reiner et al. who also found that despite sharp differences in government policy, the views of the US public on energy and climate change are "remarkably similar" to those in Japan, the UK and, perhaps more surprisingly considering its traditionally strict environmental policies, Sweden.[66] The analysis of EU and US public opinion surveys in this chapter reveals that:

- While concern about climate change has increased in both the EU and US over the last decade, it appears to have declined to some extent in light of the recent economic crisis.
- There is also an apparent discrepancy in both the US and EU between the high level of importance placed on climate change, including the apparent willingness to pay for this choice at a policy level, and individual behaviour.
- There is, in general, support for renewable energies and mixed attitudes towards nuclear power.
- The understanding of the underlying causes of climate change and the technologies available to address it remains limited among both the EU and US public.
- Support for action to protect the environment and to tackle climate change at the federal level in the US and at the EU level in Europe is high.

It therefore appears that both EU and US citizens are concerned about climate change and are looking to their governments to respond to this perceived threat. As pointed out by Bord et al.,[67] an understanding and acceptance of the importance of climate change may not necessarily lead the public to support climate policy, but they will at least indicate a likely absence of opposition to such policies. However, the lack of personal action taken by respondents to change their own behaviour appears to confirm the conclusions in other policy areas,[68] other reviews of climate change opinion surveys,[69] as well as in general studies on individual

---

66. Reiner et al. 2006, 2093.
67. Bord et al. 1998.
68. E.g. Hunt 2006.
69. E.g. Bord et al. 1998; Reiner et al. 2006; Patchen 2006.

environmental behaviour,[70] which found that such behaviour usually focuses on actions which require little effort or sacrifice. For governments faced with tough policy choices, the public's reluctance to accept costly policy choices could limit the use and range of policy solutions in the transition to a low-carbon economy.

Issues of trust in governmental institutions may also play a role. Lorenzoni and Pidgeon suggest that personal action can be seen as useless in isolation and that people expect the government to take action.[71] Without adequate governmental action and sufficient trust in the government and relevant institutions, frustration and disempowerment may contribute to a lack of personal action and little willingness to accept tough policy choices. Therefore, strong government action may be both the driver for and the response to "improved" public attitudes and behaviour towards climate change, revealing the two-way relationship between public policy and public perceptions.

While public opinion and government action are inter-related, public support for a policy direction chosen by government can be out of synch. One of the most worrying examples of this, highlighted in this chapter, is the potential lack of support for certain "clean" energy technologies. While support for renewables in general is high, a lack of understanding appears to be related to a low level of support for specific renewable technologies such as on-shore wind turbines and for CCS in some countries. This level of support may however have increased in the last year or so due to increased political and media attention to these technologies. Public acceptance is recognised as an important issue shaping the widespread implementation of renewable energy technologies and the achievement of energy policy targets.[72] It is commonly assumed that public attitudes need to change to make more radical scenarios of implementing renewable energy technologies feasible. Thus, the limited understanding of certain renewable technologies in the EU could have serious policy implications as this could limit options available to Member States for increasing the share of renewables in the energy supply as required under the 2009 Renewable Energy Directive.[73] In the UK, for example, which needs to increase the share of renewables in its total energy supply from 1.5 per cent in 2006 to 15 per cent by 2020, the government is struggling to find publicly

70. Whitmarsh 2008.
71. Lorenzoni and Pidgeon 2006.
72. Devine-Wright 2007.
73. See the chapter by Howes in this volume.

acceptable ways to meet this target given the apparent low tolerance for on-shore wind turbines and local biomass plants.

In addition to the above-mentioned similarities, there are also differences between public perceptions in the US and EU. Although, in general, levels of understanding of and concern about climate change are high in both jurisdictions, a significant degree of scepticism of the science of climate change continues to exist in the US. Reiner et al. warn against resorting too easily to European stereotypes of Americans,[74] and it should be noted that there is no directly comparable question in the EU surveys with which to compare this result. However, it could reflect one side of the multi-faceted reasons for differences between EU and US policy approaches to climate change in the recent past. It is also apparent in the survey results presented in this chapter that energy security is considered a much more important factor in the US than in the EU and is given greater priority than environmental protection by a significant number of Americans. This attitude is also reflected in the high degree of support that is still found in the US for electricity generated by coal-fired power stations.

5.   Conclusions

In general, public perceptions of climate change and energy issues in the US and the EU have much in common and do not mirror the large differences seen between the policy approaches that have historically been taken in these two jurisdictions. In certain respects, this is not surprising given that public attitude is one of many factors that shape public policy. Other factors include cultural values, historical precedence and political expedience. Placing emphasis on the importance of public attitudes also assumes that we operate in a pluralist society. However, in practice, specific interest groups have a significant influence on government policy. This is especially true in policy areas and political jurisdictions where the interests of well-organised and strong industries, such as the car and petroleum industries, are well represented.

It is also possible that the last Bush administration significantly under-estimated the degree of public concern for climate change in the US. The decision by the Bush administration not to join the Kyoto Protocol was, in fact, against public opinion at the time, which supported participation in the Kyoto Protocol and disapproved of the administration's withdrawal from the process in 2001. Growing public awareness of climate change,

---

74.   Reiner et al. 2006.

and dissatisfaction with the way the Bush administration handled the issue, might have been a driver of the numerous and ambitious climate change initiatives developed at the local and regional level in the early 2000s such as the Regional Greenhouse Gas Initiative among ten North-eastern and Mid-Atlantic States. Rising public concern may have also been a factor behind the more prominent role given to environmental issues during the 2008 Presidential campaign and the positive public response to the Obama administration, which seeks to take climate change more seriously than the previous administration.

Recent public support for government regulation of GHG emissions and US action on global warming, regardless of efforts by other industrial countries, is particularly encouraging. The divergence between the American public's perceptions of climate change and the perceptions and actions of US leaders appears to be narrowing under the Obama administration. However, President Obama's ability to meet the public's high expectations could be hampered by a shift in the attitude of Americans away from the environment and towards the economy in the context of economic crisis. In light of the American public's prioritisation of domestic economic issues and the economic context in which policies to address climate change will be rolled out, the Obama administration will likely need to stress the positive impacts on growth and jobs of any proposed climate policy measures in order to secure adequate public support for them.

In the EU, in contrast, policy-making on climate change may even lead public opinion on the issue. This may, in part, be explained by political expedience, as pursuing climate change policy both within the EU and on a global stage has provided the EU institutions with a powerful "raison d'être" at a time of constitutional crisis. Therefore the Eurobarometer surveys reported in this chapter showing public support for action on climate change may have served as a way of legitimising not just EU action in this area but also potentially the EU project as a whole. As McGowan and Sauter warn us:

"It is not unreasonable to assume that many of these polls are commissioned as much to shape the public agenda as they are to gather information on public attitude. Most of the organisations involved in polling have specific causes or interests, which they are seeking to promote or defend."[75]

75.   McGowan and Sauter 2005, 28.

An EU-level solution to the climate problem has served as a convincing narrative to persuade EU citizens that there is a need to continue the process of European integration.[76] This proved particularly useful in the period following the rejection of the Constitutional Treaty in 2005 when the EU's role in the global struggle against climate change was frequently put forward by EU leaders and institutions as an example of how a united Europe can make a difference. For example, the EU's role in climate change was emphasised in the Berlin Declaration issued by EU leaders on the occasion of the 50th anniversary of the signing of the Treaties of Rome. This renewed political interest in climate (and energy) policy culminated with the agreement of the 20-20-20 climate targets at the 2007 Spring European Council. This agreement was among the factors that helped to create a favourable political climate for EU leaders to agree on a mandate for a new Intergovernmental Conference to prepare what eventually became the Lisbon Treaty.

While public perspectives and attitudes are important in shaping public policy, the relationship between policy-making and public attitudes is often subtle and complex. Public attitudes are one of the many factors that shape public policy and can play a limited role in supporting and persuading governments to take specific policy action. A certain degree of buy-in or public acceptance of policies is also necessary for successful implementation of specific policies. At the same time, public attitudes can hold back governments from making certain policy choices, for example when trying to deploy unknown and mistrusted technologies. Governments can also use public perceptions and attitudes to encourage wider public acceptance of certain actions, legitimise its preferred policy approach, and influence the public agenda.

References

Adelle, Camilla, Marc Pallemaerts and Joana Chiavari. 2009. *Climate Change and Energy Security in Europe: Policy Integration and its Limits.* Stockholm: SIEPS.

Bord, Richard J., Ann Fisher and Robert E. O'Connor. 1998. Public Perceptions of Global Warming: United States and International Perspectives. *Climate Research* 11: 75-84.

---

76. Adelle et al. 2009.

Brewer, Thomas L. 2003. U.S. Public Opinion on Climate Change Issues: Evidence for 1989 – 2002. Paper Presented at the Conference on Climate Change Issues at the Georgetown University McDonough School of Business, Washington D.C., 18 June 2003.

Commission (EC). 2004. Attitudes of European Citizens Towards the Environment. *Eurobarometer Special Report 271/Wave 62.1 Opinion and Social.* Brussels: European Commission.

Commission (EC). 2007a. Energy Technologies: Knowledge, Perceptions, Measures. *Special Eurobarometer 262/Wave 65.3.* Brussels: European Commission.

Commission (EC). 2007b. Europeans and Nuclear Safety. *Special Eurobarometer 271/Wave 66.2.* Brussels: European Commission.

Commission (EC). 2008. Attitudes of European Citizens Towards the Environment. *Eurobarometer Special Report 295/Wave 68.2. Opinion and Social.* Brussels: European Commission.

Commission (EC). 2009. European Attitudes Towards Climate Change. *Special Eurobarometer 313/Wave 71.1.* Brussels: European Commission.

Devine-Wright, Patrick. 2007. *Reconsidering Public Attitudes and Public Acceptance of Renewable Energy Technologies: a Critical Review.* Published by the School of Environment and Development, University of Manchester, Oxford Road, Manchester M13 9PL, UK. http://www.sed.manchester.ac.uk/research/beyond_nimbyism/. Accessed: 26 October 2009.

Embassy of France in the US. 2001. Nuclear Notes from France: Summer 2001. http://www.ambafrance-us.org/intheus/nuclear/n2f2/summer2001.asp. Accessed: 15 April 2008.

Facchini, Giovanni and Anna M. Mayda. 2008. From Attitudes towards Immigration to Immigration Policy Outcomes: Does Public Opinion Rule? http://www.voxeu.org/index.php?q=node/1247. Accessed: 26 October 2009.

Gallup. 2009a. Gallup Poll – Environment. 5-8 March 2009, http://www.gallup.com/poll/116962/Americans-Economy-Takes-Precedence-Environment.aspx. Accessed: 26 October 2009.

Gallup. 2009b. Gallup Poll – High Expectations for Obama on the Environment. March 2009, http://www.gallup.com/poll/117775/High-Expectations-Obama-Environment.aspx. Accessed: 26 October 2009.

Hunt, Valerie F. 2006. Political Implications of U.S. Public Attitudes Toward Immigration on the Immigration Policymaking Process. *Proceedings*. 2006: 121-37. http://econpapers.repec.org/article/fipfeddpr/ y_3a2006_3ap_3a121-137.htm. Accessed: 27 October 2009.

ICF International. 2007. Analysis and Interpretation of Responses from the Carbon Capture and Storage Internet Consultation. Brussels: European Commission.

Ipsos MORI. 2007. The Role of Public Perception in Creating a Nuclear Future. Presentation by Robert Knight.

Leiserowitz, Anthony. 2007. Public Perception, Opinion and Understanding of Climate Change – Current Patterns, Trends and Limitations. *Human Development Report Office Occasional Paper*. 2007/31. http://hdr.undp.org/en/reports/global/hdr2007-2008/papers/ leiserowitz_anthony.pdf. Accessed: 26 October 2009.

Lorenzoni, Irene and Nick Pidgeon. 2006. Public Views on Climate Change: European and USA Perspectives. *Climate Change* 77(1): 73-95.

Lorenzoni, Irene, Sophie Nicholson-Cole and Lorraine Whitmarsh. 2007. Barriers Perceived to Engaging with Climate Change Among the UK Public and Their Policy Implications. *Global Environmental Change* 17(3–4): 445-59.

McGowan, Francis and Raphael Sauter. 2005. Public Opinion on Energy Research: A Desk Study for Research Councils. Brighton: Sussex Energy Group, SPRU.

MIT LFEE. 2007. A Survey of Public Attitudes Towards Climate Change and Climate Change Mitigation Technologies in the United States: Analyses of 2006 Results. *MIT LFEE 2008-01 WP*. Cambridge: Massachusetts Institute of Technology, Laboratory for Energy and the Environment.

New York Times. 2007. New York Times/CBS News Poll, April 20-27 2007. http://graphics8.nytimes.com/packages/pdf/national/20070424_poll.pdf. Accessed: 27 October 2009.

Nilsson, Andreas, Chris von Borgstede and Anders Biel. 2004. Willingness to Accept Climate Change Strategies: The Effect of Values and Norms. *Journal of Environmental Psychology* 24(3): 267-77.

Norton, Andrew and John Leaman. 2004. The Day After Tomorrow: Public Opinion on Climate Change. London: MORI Social Research Institute.

Patchen, Martin. 2006. Public Attitudes and Behaviour About Climate Change: What Shapes Them and How to Influence Them. *PCCRC Outreach Publication 0601 October 2006.* West Lafayette: Purdue University.

Pew Research Centre. 2008. Public Sends Mixed Signals on Energy Policy: Ethanol Research Loses Ground, Continued Division on ANWR. Washington D.C.: The Pew Research Centre for the People and the Press. http://people-press.org/reports/display.php3?ReportID=400.pdf. Accessed: 27 October 2009.

Pew Research Centre. 2009a. On Obama's Desk: Economy, Jobs Trump All Other Policy Priorities. Washington D.C.: The Pew Research Centre for the People and the Press. http://pewresearch.org/pubs/1087/economy-jobs-top-public-priorities-2009. Accessed: 27 October 2009.

Pew Research Centre. 2009b. Americans Favour Carbon Cap, Gays in the Military and Renewing U.S.-Cuba Ties. *Policy Update.* Washington D.C.: The Pew Research Centre for the People and the Press. http://people-press.org/reports/pdf/501.pdf. Accessed: 27 October 2009.

Poortinga, Wouter and Nick F. Pidgeon. 2003. Public Perceptions of Risk, Science and Governance. Norwich: UEA/MORI.

Poortinga, Wouter, Nick F. Pidgeon and Irene Lorenzoni. 2006. Public Perceptions of Nuclear Power, Climate Change and Energy Options in Britain: Summary Findings of a Survey Conducted during October and November 2005. *Understanding Risk Working Paper 06-02.* Norwich: Centre for Environmental Risk, University of East Anglia.

Reiner, David M., Thomas E. Curry, Mark A. De Figueiredo, Howard J. Herzog, Stephen D. Ansolabehere, Kenshi Itaoka, Filip Johnsson and Mikael Odenberger. 2006. American Exceptionalism? Similarities and Differences in National Attitudes Toward Energy Policy and Global Warming. *Environment Science and Technology* 40(7): 2093-98.

Shackley, Simon, Carly McLachlan and Clair Gough. 2004. The Public Perceptions of Carbon Capture and Storage. *Working Paper 44.* Norwich: Tyndall Centre for Climate Change Research.

Taylor-Gooby, Peter, Charlotte Hastie and Catherine Bromley. 2003. Querulous Citizens: Welfare Knowledge and the Limits to Welfare Reform. *Social Policy and Administration* 37(1): 1-20.

Thornely, Patricia and Wolter Prins. 2008. Public Perceptions and Bioenergy: Some Remarks in Preparation of the Workshop Scheduled for the

Themalnet Meeting in Vicenza, October 2008. http://www.thermalnet.co.uk/docs/Barriers%20Precisfinal.pdf. Accessed: 27 October 2009.

TNS Plc. 2003. Attitudes and Knowledge of Renewable Energy amongst the General Public. *Report of Findings.* Prepared for Central Office of Information on behalf of: Department of Trade and Industry, Scottish Executive, National Assembly for Wales, Department of Enterprise, Trade and Investment, JN9419 and JN9385. London: Taylor Nelson.

Washington Post. 2007. Washington Post–ABC News–Stanford University Poll: Environment Trends. 20 April 2007. http://www.washingtonpost.com/wp-srv/nation/polls/postpoll_environment_042007.html. Accessed: 27 October 2009.

Washington Post. 2009. Washington Post – ABC News: Most Back Moves on Climate Change, but with Cost as a Consideration. 25 June 2009. http://abcnews.go.com/images/PollingUnit/1091a3GlobalWarming.pdf. Accessed: 27 October 2009.

Whitmarsh, Lorraine. 2008. Behavioural Responses to Climate Change: Asymmetry of Intentions and Impacts. *Journal of Environmental Psychology* 29(1): 13-23.

List of Contributors

Camilla Adelle is a Policy Analyst at the Institute for European Environmental Policy (IEEP), London. She conducts research on EU environmental governance, impact assessment, environmental policy integration, and the EU's role in global sustainable development.
cadelle@ieep.eu

Jessica Ayers is a PhD researcher at the Development Studies Institute (DESTIN), London School of Economics and Political Science, where she works on climate policy and community-based adaptation in Bangladesh and Nepal.
j.m.ayers@lse.ac.uk

Pedro Barata is Senior Economic and Policy Advisor at Portugal's Climate Change Department (CECAC) and alternate member of the Clean Development Mechanism's Executive Board.
pedro.barata@sg.maotdr.gov.pt

Achala Chandani is a PhD researcher at Kent Law School, University of Kent, where she is working on a thesis entitled "Towards an equitable and acceptable climate agreement". She is also a Robert S. McNamara Research Fellow at the Institute for Environmental Studies (IVM), Vrije Universiteit Amsterdam.
achala.kent@yahoo.co.uk

Joana Chiavari works on sustainable energy policy and technology issues, including carbon capture and storage, at the International Energy Agency. She also previously worked at the Institute for European Environmental Policy (IEEP) from 2007 to 2009.
joana.chiavari@iea.org

Julia Dobrolyubova is an expert on climate change and the Kyoto Protocol at the Russian Regional Environmental Centre (RREC), Moscow.
dobrolubova@rusrec.ru

Wybe Douma is a Senior Researcher at the T.M.C. Asser Instituut in the Netherlands. He works at the research department on topics related to European Union law, International Trade Law and in consultancy projects.
w.t.douma@gmail.com

Christian Hey is Secretary General of the German Advisory Council on the Environment (Sachverständigenrat für Umweltfragen), Berlin, and chair of

the Energy Working Group of the Network of European Environment and Sustainable Development Advisory Councils (EEAC).
christian.hey@uba.de

Tom Howes works as a policy officer at the European Commission Directorate General for Energy and Transport (DG TREN).
tom.howes@ec.europa.eu

Saleemul Huq is the Head of the Climate Change Group at the International Institute for Environment and Development, London. His work focuses on climate change adaptation.
saleemul.huq@iied.org

Michael Kozeltsev is Executive Director of the Russian Regional Environmental Centre (RREC), Moscow.
kozeltsev@rusrec.ru

Nuno Lacasta is Director of the Portuguese Climate Change Commission and Manager of the Portuguese Carbon Fund. He is also Assistant Professor of Environmental Law and Policy at the New University of Lisbon's Faculty of Science and Technology, and Visiting Lecturer on EU Climate Change Law and Policy at the American University's Washington College of Law.
nuno.lacasta@maotdr.gov.pt

Sebastian Oberthür is Academic Director of the Institute for European Studies (IES) at the Vrije Universiteit Brussels (VUB). He is a renowned expert in international and European environmental and climate policy and law.
sebastian.oberthuer@vub.ac.be

Marc Pallemaerts is Senior Fellow and head of the Environmental Governance Research Team at the Institute for European Environmental Policy (IEEP), Brussels. He is also a Professor of European environmental law at the University of Amsterdam and teaches international environmental law at the Université Libre de Bruxelles.
mpallemaerts@ieep.eu

Claire Roche Kelly is a Research Fellow at the Institute for European Studies (IES) at the Vrije Universiteit Brussels (VUB). Her research focuses on EU climate policies.
claire.roche.kelly@vub.ac.be

Eduardo Santos is Senior Project Manager at Portugal's Climate Change Department (CECAC) in charge of international and EU negotiations.
eduardo.santos@sg.maotdr.gov.pt

Louise van Schaik is a Research Fellow at the Netherlands Institute for International Relations 'Clingendael', The Hague, and Associate Fellow at the Centre for European Policy Studies, Brussels.
lschaik@clingendael.nl

Jon Birger Skjærseth is Senior Research Fellow at the Fridtjof Nansen Institute, Oslo. His research focuses on international and regional environmental cooperation, marine pollution and climate change.
jon.b.skjaerseth@fni.no

Patrick ten Brink is Senior Fellow and Head of the Brussels Office of the Institute for European Environmental Policy (IEEP). He conducts research in topics of environmental taxes and charges, voluntary agreements, climate change and industrial pollution.
ptenbrink@ieep.eu

Jørgen Wettestad is Senior Research Fellow at the Fridtjof Nansen Institute, Oslo. His work focuses on EU climate politics and international environmental regimes.
Jorgen.Wettestad@fni.no

Sirini Withana is Policy Analyst of EU developments and environmental governance at the Institute for European Environmental Policy (IEEP), London.
swithana@ieep.eu

Other titles available in the IES Publication Series

RETHINKING EUROPEAN MEDIA AND COMMUNICATIONS POLICY

Caroline Pauwels, Harri Kalimo, Karen Donders and Ben Van Rompuy (eds.)

978 90 5487 603 8 – 370 pp. – € 42,00

This book is a collection of expert insights on EU media and communications policies in the era of convergence. The media and ICT (Information and Communications Technology) sectors are at the heart of a competitive and inclusive European knowledge society. Since the late 1980s, the boundaries between these sectors have been blurring. It appears therefore necessary to fundamentally reconsider the existing legal and policy frameworks. Have they become completely outdated? What are the main problems, and how should they be addressed? These are the very questions that top experts address in this book.

THE EUROPEAN COMMISSION AND INTEREST GROUPS
Towards a Deliberative Interpretation of Stakeholder Involvement in EU Policy-Making
Irina Tanasescu

978 90 5487 546 8 – 286 pp. – € 36,00

The analysis and understanding of the particular nature of the interactions between organized interests and the European Union institutions has had a prominent place on the research agenda of the past decade. This volume seeks to contribute to the debate by providing an in-depth assessment of European Commission consultation exercises from a novel perspective, namely a set of criteria inspired from deliberative democracy theories. While previous studies have explained how interest groups are organized at the EU level, which strategies they use and what the different access points to the EU institutions are, this book analyzes what happens in concrete instances of consultation.

Institute for European Studies
Vrije Universiteit Brussel

IES Publication Series

JUSTICE, LIBERTY, SECURITY
New Challenges for EU External Relations
Bernd Martenczuk and Servaas van Thiel (eds.)

978 90 5487 472 0 – 524 pp. – € 48,00

The European Union is rapidly creating a European space in which citizens can live in Justice, Liberty and Security. This bold push forward in the European integration process touches on three highly sensitive societal subjects: immigration and asylum, civil law, and criminal law. This book gives an excellent overview over the many current topics in these sensitive areas. Justice, Liberty, Security is structured in a user-friendly way and should be easily accessible to a broad audience of students, teachers, practitioners and the interested public. It is warmly recommended to anybody who wants to broaden his or her understanding of the increasing importance of the external side of European policies on Justice, Liberty and Security.

POLITICS BEYOND THE STATE
Actors and Policies in Complex Institutional Settings
Kris Deschouwer and M. Theo Jans (eds.)

978 90 5487 436 2 – 295 pp. – € 36,00

Politics Beyond the State seeks to capture the changing nature of politics both within and beyond the state. Its analysis clarifies that the central state continues to guide our understanding of politics but that it needs to be complemented with ample attention to both the sub- and the supranational tiers of government.

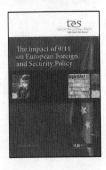

THE IMPACT OF 9/11 ON EUROPEAN FOREIGN AND SECURITY POLICY
Giovanna Bono (ed.)

978 90 5487 409 6 – 295 pp. – € 35,87

The contributors to this book argue that the events of 9/11 and the 'war on terror' are having a significant transformative impact on European Foreign and Security Policy. This is demonstrated through an analysis of changes in the attitudes of EU officials and politicians towards the laws and norms governing the use of force and through an analysis of changes in strategies towards the Balkans, sub-Saharan Africa, the Middle East and the United States.

MULTICULTURALISM OBSERVED
Exploring Identity
Richard Lewis (ed.)

978 90 5487 330 3 – 156 pp. – € 28,00

This book offers a timely and unique perspective on a phenomenon which is highly divisive and splits academic and public opinion alike. In the wake of the terrorist attacks in New York, Madrid and London, the question how western society integrates its minorities has become one of the most crucial issues facing government today and excites media attention and frequent public controversy. This volume presents a number of points of view both from Europe and North America by academic, religious and political authors from a variety of cultures, all with a very different perspective on whether multiculturalism is a valid answer to ensuring harmony in our societies.

THE EUROPEAN UNION AND SUSTAINABLE DEVELOPMENT
Internal and External Dimensions
Marc Pallemaerts and Albena Azmanova (eds.)

978 90 5487 247 4 – 342 pp. – € 40,00

Since the Treaty of Amsterdam, sustainable development is legally enshrined among the fundamental objectives of European integration. But how has the European Union addressed this issue? Is sustainable development a truly innovative policy paradigm which will revolutionize the way Europe approaches economic, social and environmental issues, or is it little more than a fashionable but vacuous political buzzword? These are some of the questions addressed by the contributors to this volume, who bring a diversity of perspectives to bear on both the internal and external dimensions of the EU's ambiguous relationship with sustainable development.

SANCTIONING ECONOMIC CRIME
An Integrated Policy
Dirk Merckx

978 90 5487 360 0 – 445 pp. – € 44,00

The sanctioning of economic crime has traditionally been a part of general criminal law. However, an economic criminal law appears to have been developed in modern economic systems as well. Administrative penal law and punitive civil law are also becoming increasingly important. The key question in this study concerns the use of sanctioning systems in combating economic crime. To this end, four central themes have been studied: the social definition of the issue of fraud, the legal techniques for sanctioning, the characterisation of the notion of sanction and the concrete implementation of sanctions as far as modalities and severity are concerned.

REGIONAL SECURITY AND GLOBAL GOVERNANCE

A Study of Interaction between Regional Agencies and the UN Security
Council with a Proposal for a Regional-Global Security Mechanism
Kennedy Graham and Tânia Felício

978 90 5487 404 1 – 362 pp. – € 42,00

This ground-breaking book explores, for policy-makers worldwide, how
peace and security might best be attained in the 21st century. Its central
message is the importance of realizing UN Secretary-General Kofi Annan's
vision of a "regional-global security mechanism" within the next decade. The
book reviews the historical tussle between universalism and regionalism as
the cornerstone of international security over the past century, culminating in
the "new regionalism" that has characterized international relations in recent
decades.

EU AND WTO LAW

How Tight is the Legal Straitjacket for Environmental Product Regulation?
Marc Pallemaerts (ed.)

978 90 5487 403 4 – 327 pp. – € 40,00

Do free trade rules impose a legal straitjacket on product-oriented
environmental measures? While environmental law increasingly relies on
product regulations as an important policy instrument, supranational
economic law, as laid down within the framework of the EU and the WTO,
tends to view such regulations as trade barriers which are to be removed as far
as possible. This book aims to help clarify the legal boundaries of the policy
space that remains open to public authorities at the national and
supranational level to regulate trade in products in pursuit of legitimate
objectives of environmental protection and sustainable development.

UNDERSTANDING THE EUROPEAN CONSTITUTIONAL TREATY

Why a NO Vote Means Less Democracy, Human Rights and Security
Servaas van Thiel, Richard Lewis and Karel De Gucht (eds.)

978 90 5487 390 7 – 316 pp. – € 40,00

In this book, a selection of well placed authors, who as political and judicial
leaders (Belgian Prime Minister Verhofstadt and Foreign Affairs Minister De
Gucht, former Commissioner Vitorino, European Court Judge Lenaerts),
Union officials (Devuyst, van Thiel, Martenczuk, Lewis) and academics (De
Schouwer, De Hert, Biscop, Gerard), know Europe from the inside, analyse
and explain how the Constitution would contribute to a more efficient and
democratic Europe that would be better equipped to face the challenges of a
globalising world.

Institute for European Studies
Vrije Universiteit Brussel

ABOUT GLOBALISATION
Views on the Trajectory of Mondialisation
Bart De Schutter and Johan Pas (eds.)

978 90 5487 360 0 – 344 pp. – € 40,00

Globalisation is probably one of the most controversial issues of the last decade, but too often it has been looked at from within one discipline only. The present book particularly wishes to point out to the reader that, due to its different aspects, globalisation can only be grasped from within a multi-disciplinary approach. Therefore the different authors look at the issue from a politics, law, philosophy ... point of view.

The book also sheds a light on various contested topics relating to globalisation, such as information and communication technology, intellectual property rights and currency transaction taxation.

BOOKS IN DUTCH

DE NIEUWE EUROPESE UNIE
Een heldere gids door de Europese doolhof
Youri Devuyst

978 90 5487 370 9 – 296 pp. – € 36,00

Voor de gewone burger is de Europese Unie bijzonder ondoorzichtig. Ons dagelijks leven wordt nochtans voortdurend door de EU beïnvloed. Het nodige inzicht in de besluitvorming en het beleid van de EU is daarom van belang. Enkel diegenen die op de hoogte zijn kunnen immers de werking van de EU bijsturen. Wie bijvoorbeeld naar sociale vooruitgang streeft, kan vandaag niet anders dan strijd voeren op Europees niveau. Maar dit vergt de nodige kennis van de Europese besluitvorming. Vanuit dit perspectief tracht dit boek een heldere gids te zijn die belangstellenden op een eenvoudige wijze doorheen de Europese doolhof loodst. Het bevat daarbij de meest recente informatie over de ontwikkeling van de Europese Unie.

GLOBALISERING: INTERDISCIPLINAIR BEKEKEN
Jacobus Delwaide and Gustaaf Geeraerts (eds.)

978 90 5487 490 4 – 336 pp. – € 40,00

De globalisering raakt aan alle aspecten van ons dagelijks leven. Ze is meer dan alleen maar een economisch fenomeen. Daarom moet ze vanuit verschillende disciplines worden belicht. Deze bundel brengt vijftien auteurs samen die vanuit vijf disciplines - communicatiewetenschap, economie, geschiedenis, politieke wetenschap en rechten - de oorsprongen, vormen en gevolgen van de globalisering analyseren.